Unsportsmanlike Conduct

A history of the development and financial growth
of intercollegiate athletics with recommendations
for restoration of basic freedoms for players and
equitable treatment for competing teams

Unsportsmanlike Conduct

Exploiting College Athletes

Walter Byers

with Charles Hammer

Ann Arbor

THE UNIVERSITY OF MICHIGAN PRESS

Copyright © by Walter Byers 1995
All rights reserved
Published in the United States of America by
The University of Michigan Press
Manufactured in the United States of America
⊖ Printed on acid-free paper

1998   1997   1996   1995   4   3   2   1

A CIP catalog record for this book is available from the British Library.

Library of Congress Cataloging-in-Publication Data

Byers, Walter, 1922–
    Unsportsmanlike conduct : exploiting college athletes / Walter
Byers with Charles Hammer.
        p.   cm.
    Includes bibliographical references.
    ISBN 0-472-10666-X (alk. paper)
    1. National Collegiate Athletic Association–History. 2. College
sports–United States–Moral and ethical aspects.   I. Hammer,
Charles H.   II. Title.
GV351.B94   1995
796.04′3–dc20   95-16973
                                                          CIP

To the free competitive spirit of this
nation's young men and women

Contents

Introduction

The longest, most raucous, and most expensive infractions case in the history of intercollegiate athletics was the National Collegiate Athletic Association versus the University of Nevada at Las Vegas and Coach Jerry Tarkanian (case number 123[47]). An *infractions case* is college sports terminology for what, in the larger social order, would be a civil or criminal indictment and trial. This NCAA case had a life of 21 years.

The professional ethics, personal morality, and NCAA violations involved were not much different than many other major college crime cases. The UNLV engagement, which began in 1971, reached full flower in the 1980s, however, and with multimedia outlets available, Coach Tarkanian brought his run-and-gun offense to bear upon the NCAA's deliberate, step-at-a-time approach to justice. A man who never seemed to turn down an interview, Coach Tarkanian took control of the matchup for almost the entire time. He still looks like the winner to me; UNLV clearly was the loser.

The NCAA, primarily because of the integrity of its enforcement staff and, particularly, its chief, Dave Berst, came out of the shoot out in better shape than expected. Thereafter, a psychology of complacency seemed to permeate the minds of the policy groups that set the NCAA agenda. In disposing of the Tarkanian matter, good had conquered bad; the NCAA had been proven right; on with business as usual.

So instead of adapting to the changed conditions of the times, the national governing body entered the decade of the 1990s by

> **reemphasizing** that players must be "amateurs" to qualify for any of the varsity teams at some 900 four-year colleges;
> **adopting** more rules, instead of fewer restrictions;

> expanding its compliance inspection service, essentially an exercise in self-emolument designed to soft pedal rules violations;
>
> establishing a centralized bureaucracy to clear the eligibility of players in the belief that the national government can do a better job than the local people; and
>
> funding a beefed-up public relations program to emphasize college athletics' virtues and the fact that college presidents are in charge.

The UNLV case, in a sense, was historic. It served as a catharsis for past violators and the current closet sinners of college athletics. They could seek higher ground by pointing with scorn at the outrageous conduct of an upstart university operating in the shadows cast by the neon lights of casinos dedicated to all-night gambling. Greased admissions, suspect grades, under-the-table payments—this one had it all.

In fairness, however, it was not strikingly different than the Kentucky case of the 1950s, UCLA in the 1960s, Michigan State in the 1970s, Southern Methodist University in the 1980s, and Florida State or other cases yet to surface in the 1990s. The ambitious have-nots of yesteryear enjoy the moneyed good times of today. They are clustered together with other rich schools in major athletics conferences and look with scorn at the new breed of opportunist colleges that use shenanigans similar to those that made today's nouveau riche well-to-do in the first place. The UNLV-Tarkanian matter ex post facto also became a part of the argument against changing the way the colleges do their business. A liberalizing of NCAA recruiting and financial aid rules, it is said, would only elevate the cheating to higher financial levels. Look at UNLV.

The current, 10-year-old presidential reform movement, originally dedicated to change, now has endorsed the status quo. It started out with a show of force under the leadership of John Ryan, then the president of Indiana University, who successfully managed the NCAA's special Integrity Convention of 1985. Today, the NCAA Presidents Commission is preoccupied with tightening a few loose bolts in a worn machine, firmly committed to the neoplantation belief that the enormous proceeds from college games belong to the overseers (the administrators) and supervisors (coaches). The plantation workers performing in the arena may receive only those benefits authorized by the overseers. This system is so biased against human nature and simple fairness in light of today's high-dollar, commercialized college marketplace that the ever increasing number of primary and secondary NCAA infractions cases of the 1990s emerge in the current environment as mostly an indictment of the system itself.

Chapter 1   **The Business of Our Business**

We Were the Police

In the late 1940s, I was one of a small group that patched together the diverse interests of college athletics into a body politic, the modern National Collegiate Athletic Association. I then became the NCAA's first full-time executive director and, until my retirement in 1987, its only one.

I was charged with the dual mission of keeping intercollegiate sports clean while generating millions of dollars each year as income for the colleges. These were compelling and competing tasks, and, in my enthusiasm for sports, I believed it possible to achieve both.

We proved barely adequate in the first instance, but enormously successful in our second mission. Persistent efforts to contain college sports' explosive growth and enforce the rules to which the colleges annually pledge their allegiance brought no reduction in intercollegiate crime through the years. As the rewards for winning multiplied, so did breaking the rules and cheating.

I was 30 years old when the NCAA handed me the job of organizing the first nationwide enforcement program for college athletics. To say we were the police is a large exaggeration. Our task more closely resembled that of study hall monitors maintaining some semblance of order within a rambunctious college family. For most of the 36 years I served in the hot seat of the NCAA executive director's office, I passionately believed NCAA rules could preserve the amateur collegiate spirit I so much loved as a youth and admired as a young sports reporter.

On a hot August day in 1977, in the Hyatt Hotel in Knoxville,

Tennessee, I found myself, at the age of 55, angrily defending the NCAA enforcement staff's integrity. The NCAA Infractions Committee had cited Coach Jerry Tarkanian and the University of Nevada, Las Vegas, for rule violations typical of hustling collegiate programs—mainly gifts of money and merchandise to players plus questionable academic standards.

The Knoxville hearing was not Coach Tarkanian's first battle with NCAA enforcement. His earlier performance at California State University, Long Beach, had been cited in a major case. For that reason, in this second round, the Infractions Committee demanded that UNLV suspend Tarkanian from coaching for two years. Jerry Tarkanian, praised for his attack-oriented coaching philosophy, followed that instinct in a high-pressure, full-court attack as he appealed to the NCAA Council in Knoxville. The 18-member council was the NCAA's adjudicating body in these matters.

UNLV's lawyers criticized the NCAA enforcement staff, implying that S. David Berst had conspired with his investigators to concoct phony evidence. The suggested scenario was that six different investigators had interviewed different witnesses and then, ignoring what was said, made up detailed sets of facts, names, and dates, carefully constructing imaginary events to railroad the UNLV coach.

Listening to those distortions, I felt my anger heading out of control. I had hired David as an investigator when he was a young man. At this writing, he is the NCAA enforcement chief, a man more responsible than anyone else for the enforcement department's reputation for integrity.

Disgusted by the UNLV tirade, I protested.

"I know these investigators as decent human beings," I told the council. "This attack on their character is an obvious effort to divert discussion from the violations to personalities. It's not a personality issue."

When the meeting ended, I walked out of the room and met Berst in the hall. We walked a few steps into the elevator. Though I had never personally met Jerry Tarkanian, he stepped into the elevator right behind us.

In public Tark the Shark had blamed a supposed vendetta by David Berst for most of his problems. I was surprised that in private they seemed to get along with ease, somewhat like business associates who have been through a lot together. David introduced us. We all agreed that it had been a long day. Then Jerry turned to me with the air of a sophisticated wheeler-dealer.

"Say, isn't there some way we can work this out?" he asked, in the manner of a friend wanting to do me a favor. His attack squad had just spent hours before the council unjustly condemning the enforcement staff, and now he was ready to make a deal.

"Come on, coach," I said, "after all *that?*"

Tarkanian's desire to work things out was an early hint of what became the UNLV position: the school itself would accept severe penalties if we would remove the suspension of Tarkanian. The NCAA Council refused.

Technically, we won this battle in 1988 through a Supreme Court decision. But Jerry Tarkanian never stopped coaching until he left UNLV in 1992, after legally whipsawing the NCAA and forcing it to pay about $1 million in legal fees. The clock is still running since he and his wife, Lois, have a pending lawsuit against the NCAA and three current and former employees.

As for Tarkanian's financial fortunes, let's forget about his hefty income from salary, endorsements, and basketball camps. I estimate that solely for his teams' appearances at the NCAA basketball tournament and 1990 Final Four victory, his employment contract with built-in bonuses enabled him to take home more than $500,000 from the NCAA's *own* coffers.[1]

During the next few moments of that 1977 elevator ride in Knoxville, Coach Tarkanian just stared at me, his face impassive. Not another word was spoken.

The Business of Our Business

In 1982, I was sitting within the bare, painted walls of an Oklahoma City federal courtroom observing the trial of an antitrust lawsuit against the NCAA's football television plan.

The lead witness against us was University of Georgia President Fred Davison, also head of the College Football Association (CFA). He and others alleged that the NCAA was a cartel, unjustly limiting the profits of the biggest big-time teams. The plaintiffs wanted to sell their own games to television, cutting smaller NCAA teams out of the deal.

Davison was a big man, ponderous in thought. He seemed comfortable sitting amid the Puritan plainness of that courtroom. He testified he operated a football business that generated more than $5 million a year for a university athletics corporation that carried a $12 million debt. He said he did not want "other people imposing themselves on my business. . . . My general feeling is that our people would be better able, taking everything into account, to run our business than would be the NCAA—the business of our business. . . .

"I'm not discrediting the democratic [NCAA] processes. I'm discrediting a process, indeed, that allows a tyranny of the majority to impose itself on the commercial enterprise of a minority group."[2]

Here was a businessman arguing about the corporate balance sheet and the unfairness of government (NCAA) regulations. University of Oklahoma President Bill Banowsky told the federal judge more of the same.

"It is virtually impossible to overstate the degree of our resentment of the controls of the NCAA," Banowsky declared. He asked that OU be free to make its own "market and business judgments."[3]

During a recess moments later, Bill Banowsky walked past me in the courtroom, then swung around and grinned.

"Walter," he said, "I've been reading a book about J. Edgar Hoover. You remind me of him."

I had to laugh. I asked him to send the book to me. He walked away nodding his head and chuckling to himself.

Then I seriously considered the testimony I had heard. It may seem naive, but I was shocked that presidents of two major universities were testifying under oath that "amateur" collegiate sports were dead.

Throughout my career I had fought for the amateur ideal against such big-time coaches as Barry Switzer, Joe Paterno, and

Jerry Tarkanian. I supported any rule that sought to keep college athletics more a student activity than a profession. Although we lost one engagement after another, I hoped we could recapture some philosophy of yesteryear. It finally became clear that the new generation of coaches and staff didn't know and didn't care to learn about old ideals.

At the same time, I had joined college leaders in fighting to prevent college sports from paying the taxes levied against entertainment businesses—ticket taxes, sales taxes, and corporate income taxes. To accomplish that, I had testified before Congressional committees that college sports was essentially amateur, oriented to education and not to profit.

Meanwhile, down the years I had negotiated nearly 50 sports television contracts that piled multimillion-dollar deals one on top of another—money that funneled directly to the colleges. The new money was to pay for more sports, more championships, and better support services for athletes. As the rewards multiplied, unanswered contradictions quickly followed.

In 1975, his last year at UCLA, Coach John Wooden's salary was $32,500, the compensation of a coaching legend who took 16 of his teams to the NCAA tournament and won 10 national championships. John signed none of the athletics shoe deals, wherein players are required to wear a certain brand so the coach can collect big bucks for the advertising endorsement.

"I got one shoe contract offer worth somewhat more than my salary," John told me. "I didn't sign because I didn't think that money belonged to me."

John Wooden got no big-money TV contracts. He did receive $50 per home game for radio broadcast commentary.[4]

Compare John with Jim Valvano of North Carolina State in the Atlantic Coast Conference some 10 years later. He took seven of his teams to the NCAA tournament and won a single championship. Valvano resigned with North Carolina State involved in multiple NCAA violations.

Valvano reportedly was grossing $850,000 a year from his combined business enterprises (shoe contract included). He left North Carolina State, before making a deal with ABC-TV, on the

John Wooden, head basketball coach of UCLA (1949–75) with Sidney Wicks, 1971 All-American. Wooden coached 10 NCAA championship teams. Wicks was a key player in keeping the UCLA dynasty going between the end of the Alcindor era (1969) and the beginning of the Walton era in 1972.

condition that he would still receive $212,000 (two years' salary) and $250,000 of a $375,000 deal he had with the Wolfpack booster group.[5]

In a decade, the top basketball coaches' earnings jumped more than twentyfold. Today, the financial package for Lute Olson at Arizona nets out at more than a million a year. It reached that level when Arizona persuaded the coach to withdraw from consideration for the Kentucky job at the time the university at Lexington hired Rick Pitino. Coach Mike Krzyzewski at Duke is in the million per year class with $375,000 from a shoe contract reportedly on top of that.[6]

Players' earnings, however, haven't changed appreciably above the terms set 39 years ago (1956) for the athletics scholarship— tuition, books, room and board, and incidentals.

In the name of amateurism, the NCAA has been stingy with the size of the company logo on a player's uniform, although the player receives no money for it. So Rumeal Robinson would have been ruled ineligible if he had worn a manufacturer's label larger than 1-1/2 inches by 1-1/2 inches on his Michigan jersey.

Yet as Rumeal stepped up to the free throw line in Seattle in 1989 to win the national championship for the Wolverines, he repeatedly twirled the NCAA Rawlings basketball, the trademark and NCAA endorsement clearly visible to the 47 million people who watched the CBS telecast. The size of the label on the NCAA "official basketball" appeared twice, each imprint measuring nine inches wide and two inches high.

In 1990, the three-year Rawlings basketball deal was worth more than $1.1 million to the NCAA, of which 60 percent was allocated to the NCAA men's and women's basketball tournaments. The NCAA organization's own share was 40 percent. The players' share was zero.

Not that all big-time universities make a profit from collegiate sports. Far from it. Most of the Division I NCAA members run consistent sports deficits, which must be paid off by subsidies from state legislatures, booster donations, or fees levied on all their students. But along the way these colleges continue to pay excellent salaries to various university officials, coaches, and athletics department staff. The upper elite, the richest of Division I, generate big money and pay their managers even more handsomely than the rest.

A highly commercialized outside world thoroughly commercialized college sports—big business at work, as sworn to by Messrs. Davison and Banowsky.

In 1984, obviously out of step with the times and heading for retirement, I estimated during an Associated Press interview that as many as 30 percent of major sports schools were cheating on the rules—15 percent simply to win, another 15 percent because they felt they must fight fire with fire. Jack McCallum of *Sports Illustrated* noticed the AP story and interviewed me for an *SI* "Scorecard" feature.

"We're in a situation where we, the colleges, say it's improper for athletes to get, for example, a new car," I told Jack. "Well, is that morally wrong? Or is it wrong because we say it's wrong....

"An alumnus can't send a kid to school to play athletics. But is it wrong for the donor to give the boy the money? It's only the colleges with the rules that say it's wrong....The public doesn't think it's so wrong."[7]

McCallum fairly reported what I said and then was asked whether this "radical stuff" had been proposed by a "raving anarchist." "No," he said, "these were the words of Walter Byers, the NCAA's powerful and ordinarily reticent long time executive director and the leading architect of the big time intercollegiate athletics he's now openly criticizing."

"Byers is essentially right in what he says," McCallum concluded.

Those were among the few words of praise for the position I'd taken. Such old friends as Bill Flynn of Boston College, Don Canham of Michigan, and Fred Jacoby of the Southwest Conference thought my advocacy of money to the players surely was a sign of early senility.

I was called on the carpet for my comments at an NCAA Council meeting closed to the media. Between annual conventions, the expanded Council is the chief NCAA legislative and appeals body. The 40-plus members were sitting in a tiered arrangement of three rows. On this occasion, I was seated with two other officers at ground level, looking up at the elected assemblage.

To the displeasure of some council members, I had previously commented that the colleges were confiscating part of the student-athletes' Pell grants (a federal subsidy for economically deprived students) to underwrite collegiate athletics costs. I said the situation could become explosive. I still believe that practice is wrong.

Now the NCAA Council also had my *SI* interview to consider. Gene Corrigan, then athletics director of Notre Dame, was a College Football Association supporter and yet a friend of 20 years. He was seated in the third and highest row. He inquired about my demand for freer compensation of players.

"Walter, when you gave that interview to *Sports Illustrated,* did you mean to infer that..." He paused for a moment. Then he said,

"Well, Walter, why don't you just tell us exactly what you had in mind when you said that?"

I looked at the collection of stern faces staring down at me—not a smile in the crowd. An execution was sure to follow. I suddenly empathized with the college sinners who come before the council to answer for athletics crimes.

"I believe it's time to change what we're doing," I said, trying to fill that solemn silence. "My comments here as well as to *SI* are destined to begin the process."

My words evoked a negative reaction throughout the power structure of the NCAA. It happened again when I raised questions in March 1985 with the leadership of the NCAA Council and Executive Committee.

I suggested allowing student-athletes to endorse products, with the income going first into a trust fund, then to players when they graduate or completed eligibility. In an unpublicized written memo to the top NCAA management group, I said full-need student-athletes should be given additional financial assistance over the permitted grant-in-aid. The memo said: "I earnestly hope that the membership does not take a righteous stand in favor of old-time amateur principles for the athlete, but modern-day commercial involvement for coaches and institutions, and somehow expect a relatively small NCAA enforcement crew to keep the situation clean."[8] I did not say at the time that student-athletes necessarily deserved higher college pay. I argued that since the colleges were exploiting their talent, the athletes deserved the same access to the free market as the coaches enjoyed.

All I accomplished with those efforts was a hardening of the NCAA position on "amateurism." Players must be shielded from exploitation and the taint of commercial gold, the NCAA officially reiterated in the early 1990s, and it then confirmed that the gold belonged to the coaches and the colleges.

What Footprint?

A third development midway through the 1980s underscored the colleges' growing resentment toward enforcement. Efforts to cripple

NCAA enforcement seem irrational as possibly the worst case of corruption in the history of intercollegiate sports was unfolding.

At the 1985 "Integrity Convention," a group of seven universities, four from Texas, introduced the "Texas resolution," which would have required NCAA investigators to alert college officials in advance about possible investigations. Hearing this on the convention floor, I imagined what would happen if the police—before they secured the evidence—had to tell a suspected burglar they had seen a footprint in the mud outside the ransacked premises.

"Footprint?" the burglar says. "What footprint?" Sure enough, when the officers return to make a plaster cast, there is no footprint. Luckily, members of the Infractions Committee and others diverted the Texas resolution before it became NCAA law.[9]

Then a prominent NCAA officer, Wilford S. Bailey, escalated the struggle over enforcement. A consistent supporter of the College Football Association and long-time Auburn University faculty representative, Bailey is the sort of man casual acquaintances would call a "real gentleman." He didn't strike me that way when we finally confronted each other in San Diego's Town and Country Hotel during the 1987 NCAA Convention.

He was then secretary-treasurer, soon to be national president of the NCAA, but he bore the emotional scars of an earlier NCAA rules-breaking case against his beloved Auburn. In the months before the 1987 convention, and without prior notice, Wil Bailey had tried to restrict interviews of college transfer students by our investigators.[10]

Student-athletes will seldom talk about illegal activities at the college where they play. Having moved to another college, where they usually cannot be intimidated by coaches or fellow players, they often tell the truth about their former school.

This is one of the frail reeds NCAA investigators cling to, which may not seem important until you consider some history. Down the years the colleges bound up collegiate sports in a straitjacket of NCAA rules, heaping paragraph on paragraph in a futile effort to maintain long-lost amateur principles and playing field equality. The colleges then challenged the NCAA to enforce the rules with rigidly rationed tools of the trade.

I never wanted the kind of wiretapping and "bugging" authority available to law enforcement agencies. But NCAA investigators wrestle for truth while wearing procedural handcuffs that journalists and particularly policemen—despite their worries about Miranda warnings—would find laughable. Even private citizens have more means to investigate sports corruption than the NCAA.

Private citizens in most states can legally question anyone they wish, tape-record conversations to which they are a party, attend meetings using an alias, eavesdrop on conversations that occur within their hearing, or secretly film clandestine meetings. None of those techniques is freely available to NCAA investigators.

The NCAA enforcement staff and Infractions Committee, to date, will accept conversations recorded by a parent or an athlete without the NCAA's knowledge. But the NCAA enforcement staff may not be a partner, even in absentia, to *arranging* a secret although completely legal taping session. And NCAA investigators may not ask a parent, for example, to tape a forthcoming conversation. Paying a booster's expenses in gathering information about secret money raising is forbidden. The NCAA may not provide the funds for the booster to make a contribution to the booster clubs. These restrictions stem from the long-nurtured belief that it wouldn't be dignified for NCAA employees to engage in such nefarious undertakings against their campus-based superiors. Gentlemen don't read each other's mail!

So when Wil Bailey set out at the 1987 San Diego convention to win formal support for his attack on transfer student interviews, I became upset. As one meeting broke up, I moved to intercept him as he crossed the floor. When he stopped to look at me, I told him: "Wil, if you're going to bring up here the issue of interviewing transfer students, I want to let you know ahead of time that I'll strongly oppose you."

He threw his head back. A tall man, he was so wrought up he quivered as he stared down at me.

"It was in this same town almost 10 years ago that they put Auburn on probation," he said. "We have risen from that so far that I've become secretary-treasurer of the NCAA. I'm proud of that! This isn't right, what you're doing!"

He flipped open the NCAA manual in his hand, pointing to a marked paragraph. He said our investigators were violating the paragraph by interviewing transfer students without advance permission. I told him once again that I disagreed with his interpretation. I wasn't yielding on the point, and I didn't give a damn whether he liked it or not.

"I'm not going to stand idly by while you attempt to undermine NCAA enforcement," I told him.

I walked away, and Wil Bailey did not succeed in blocking our interviews with transfer students. But even as we argued, a fourth event unfolding in Texas provided new reason for dismay.

It was the case I mentioned above, probably the worst case of institutional connivance in the history of NCAA sports.

Notes

1. The amount cited here is based on the bonuses called for in Tarkanian's February 1983 contract with UNLV; see chap. 12.
2. Fred Davison, Deposition, February 1982.
3. William S. Banowsky, Deposition, December 1981.
4. John Wooden, interview with the author, February 20, 1991.
5. Mark Bradley, *Atlanta Constitution*, February 2, 1988.
6. Frederick C. Klein, *Wall Street Journal*, November 25, 1994.
7. Jack McCallum, *Sports Illustrated*, September 17, 1984.
8. Walter Byers, memorandum no. 5 to NCAA president, secretary-treasurer, and division vice-presidents, March 22, 1985.
9. Resolution No. 3-3, NCAA Special Convention, New Orleans, Louisiana, June 20–21, 1985.
10. Steven R. Morgan, memorandum to Walter Byers, May 20, 1986; Walter Byers, letter to Wilford S. Bailey, September 29, 1987.

Chapter 2　　## The Governor and the "Death Penalty"

Clandestine Crime

My first NCAA enforcement case was decided in 1952 after a point-shaving scandal engulfed the University of Kentucky's Fabulous Five basketball team, the great machine that won back-to-back NCAA championships in 1948 and 1949. The starting five was a core unit of the U.S. Olympic team that won the gold medal in London in 1948.

Illegal payments and point manipulation were the heart of that case. In a life-or-death test of the fledgling NCAA's police powers, the Southeastern Conference and the NCAA combined to eliminate Kentucky from competition for an entire basketball season.

For 33 years afterward, faintness of heart prevented imposition of such a heavy punishment on any big-name Division I-A university. The penalty was reinvented in 1985 at the NCAA Integrity Convention, labeled by the media the "death penalty," and used in 1987 after a series of hand-in-glove violations involving top management, coaches, and players engulfed a respected school, Southern Methodist University of Dallas.

The two death penalty cases—one at the beginning, the other near the end of my career—symbolize the change in the athletic environment: from simple rules and personally responsible officials to convoluted, cyclopedic regulations with high-priced legal firms defending college violators against a limited NCAA enforcement system. This current system contributed to making the Southern Methodist University case worse than it should have been.

Replete with subterfuge and clandestine agreements, the case should have unmade a governor of Texas; yet, because of his determination and dominance, it critically wounded a proud university instead.

It was not as if that university hadn't been warned. Long before its death penalty case, SMU had achieved dubious distinction as the most penalized institution in the history of the NCAA: 1958, 1974, 1976, 1981, and 1985.

Through much of that history the gossip mill of college athletics had it right. Old friends Frank Broyles at Arkansas and Darrell Royal of Texas warned me that Southwest Conference recruiting was a cesspool. They flew to meet me at the Kansas City airport to tell me face-to-face how bad things were. As to the Mustangs of SMU, violations seemed to flourish in the Southfork atmosphere reminiscent of the Ewings' dealings in the "Dallas" television series. Money paves the road to victory!

Rule breaking had been raised to a new level during the tenure of Head Coach Ron Meyer. Meyer was hired in 1976 by James H. Zumberge, then president of SMU. Meyer was attractive, smooth talking, and a natty dresser. He and SMU Athletics Director Russ Potts were first considered a double dose of the medicine necessary to cure the Mustangs' football ills. Potts saw himself as a genius promoter and Meyer was considered a genius recruiter.

Unfortunately, Potts's ticket promotions, including supermarket giveaways, frequently resulted in a "papered" stadium. The announced attendance looked good, but the game settlement accounting revealed that many spectators were admitted with tickets worth little or nothing. Potts's legacy was the Southwest Conference rule that home teams must settle with visiting teams at a minimum of $5.00 per ticket for nonstudent admissions. The Potts-inspired promotions resulted in SMU sending its own money to competitors to keep them happy.

"My calling card"

Coach Ron Meyer went about his business more efficiently. One of his recruiting techniques was to visit a prospect's high school and ask to confer in a private room with the player. Meyer would sit down and the youngster would sit down. Meyer would then pull out a plump money clip and peel off a hundred-dollar bill. He would get up, walk to a nearby bulletin board, pin up the C-note, and announce: "Young man, this is my calling card."

When their conversation was over, Meyer would put the bill back in his wallet. No NCAA violation there. The player understood that he would be contacted again in the near future.[1]

Meyer did not negotiate the money deals; SMU boosters did that work, promising jobs, hidden money accounts, or regular cash payments. It was not uncommon during that era in the Southwest Conference for certain boosters to be assigned to certain players. The trick of the boosters was to "nickel and dime" the prospect with small favors until he signed and arrived on campus, then deliver big. This was a hard system for NCAA enforcement to crack, since neither the booster nor the player was likely to talk.

We turned up enough evidence to penalize SMU with two years' probation in 1981, but we could never link Meyer directly to the payments. I personally believe that the restrictions placed on NCAA investigators were a factor in our failure to make a major case against SMU before and during the Ron Meyer era. Had we nailed down the case in 1980, we might have prevented the far worse infractions that were yet to come.

Coach Meyer brought together one of the best freshman football classes in Southwest Conference history in 1979. Eric Dickerson, an all-time great, came from a run-down, one-bedroom house in Sealy, Texas, 60 miles west of Houston. Awed neighbors watched as reporters, recruiters, an NCAA investigator, and an SMU booster (who arrived in a Mercedes) approached the front porch of the little house for Dickerson's historic signing of the letter-of-intent that committed him to SMU.

Bob Minnix, our tireless Southwest area investigator, had first met Dickerson through the high school "intercept program." In this effort, NCAA investigators contacted prominent high school prospects to acquaint them with the pitfalls of high-society college recruiting. As a result of that first contact, Bob told me he knew Eric was one player who wanted more than after-enrollment promises.

Minnix was one of our first black investigators and one of our best. Dickerson had arrived for that earlier meeting with Minnix in a new Trans Am sports car. He told Minnix it had been purchased for him by his grandmother, with whom he lived in Sealy next door to his mother and stepfather.[2]

After Dickerson finished college ball, he disclosed that the $15,000 Trans Am was purchased by Texas A&M boosters who tried to recruit him but had failed. In any event, Dickerson decided to keep the Trans Am, drive it to Mockingbird Lane in Dallas, and enroll in SMU. As to the little house where the media event occurred and Dickerson signed with SMU: He later built a fine new house for his grandmother on the same site.[3]

Among Coach Ron Meyer's other great recruits that year were Craig James and Michael Carter. A repeat all-pro with the San Francisco 49ers, Carter is as good a nose tackle as ever played the game. Lance McIlhenny joined the team a year later, his father having previously played at SMU. Dickerson, James, and McIlhenny were among eight SMU players on the 1982 All–Southwest Conference team; Dickerson was a consensus All-American in 1982. He was a unanimous pick that year along with John Elway of Stanford and Herschel Walker of Georgia.

Our 1981 penalty kept the Mustangs out of the 1982 Cotton Bowl, but they made the bowl a year later. Pregame predictions indicated a high-scoring affair, since Dan Marino was the Pittsburgh quarterback and Dickerson was carrying the ball for the Mustangs. Competing in the sleet and rain that New Year's Day in Dallas were two of the all-time greats. SMU won it by a niggling 7-3. It was the brilliant McIlhenny who threw the touchdown pass.

Russ Potts had drilled nothing but dry holes with his promotions until Meyer began to win. SMU football soon generated profits. With the help of money-saving efforts, the SMU deficit for all sports was cut to $500,000 for the year, a remarkable turnaround.[4] From 1981 through 1983 the Mustangs' record was 31-3-1 (or .900). Breaking NCAA rules does have an up side.

Key SMU officials, however, seemed to sense that the good times were about to end. Jim Zumberge resigned so abruptly in 1980 that the irritated SMU trustees told him to leave the presi-

Eric Dickerson in the 1983 Cotton Bowl in which Southern Methodist University beat the University of Pittsburgh 7 to 3.

dent's office immediately. He then became president of the University of Southern California.

Meyer cut his college ties cleanly in 1982 and went to the pros, first to Baltimore and then Indianapolis. Meyer, as head coach of the Indianapolis Colts, hired Dickerson away from the Los Angeles Rams in 1987. Meanwhile, Athletics Director Russ Potts had also resigned.

Thus the SMU president, the head coach and the athletics director escaped the deluge. Their successors—soon to be burdened with it all—were L. Donald Shields in the president's spot, Bobby Collins as new head coach, and Robert Hitch as athletics director.

I knew Bob Hitch from casual meetings before he bought into trouble at the Dallas school. He's a former football player, a big man, ruggedly good looking. Since the 1987 shakeout, we've talked over the disaster. He sees himself as a man who bore a blame that should have been more widely shared.

Coaches and athletics directors in big time sports observe a sort of fraternal honor code in which, to some degree, they privately come clean with each other. It broke down here, Hitch told me. He said Meyer alerted neither him nor Collins to what had been going on under the table.[5]

Soon after he took office, Bob Hitch found signs of trouble. A full-page ad in the 1981 football program had listed some 110 people that Ron Meyer thanked for "tremendous support in the form of materials, services, time and effort" given to SMU football. But athletics department books revealed no record of *official* contributions from over half the people on the list.[6]

Not long after, Collins told Hitch he had received a call from a relative of Dickerson's, who wanted to know when the monthly check would arrive. Thus the situation became known to Collins and Hitch. It was then that university management decided to honor the money promises of the previous era but make no new commitments. Hitch later told me unequivocally that they went three years without promising money to any *new* recruits.[7] Other insiders attest to that. But the two had set themselves up for a fall by agreeing to honor the Meyer-era payroll plan.

Tragedian of the Plot

Looking back on it, I can see the SMU case contained elements of an old-time melodrama with the soul of a university at issue. The tragedian in the plot was President Don Shields. Just as Julius Caesar was warned of approaching trouble by a soothsayer, Shields had been warned even before taking office by SMU's NCAA faculty representative, Mike Harvey, that boosters were making improper payments.[8]

Shields did not respond. Harvey resigned the faculty rep post.

Hitch told me he also alerted Shields to the problem. Still, Shields had convinced himself that NCAA investigations of his program amounted to "selective enforcement."

I suppose NCAA investigators did function as good highway patrolmen. There are not enough patrol cars to catch all the speeders, but the faster the driver, the greater the risk. In that era of college athletics, SMU was the fastest driver on the highway—but admittedly not far ahead of some competitors.

President Shields was incensed that reports of violations had come from athletes recruited by SMU who eventually enrolled in other schools. In December 1983, Shields decided to hit back, giving the NCAA some of its own medicine. He ordered attorney John McElhaney (no relation to player McIlhenny) to question SMU athletes about offers they might have received from other schools.

Shields's suspicions about other Southwest Conference schools were well founded. Indeed, from 1985 to 1988 we hit seven of the nine schools in the Southwest Conference for major NCAA violations. Questioned by Lawyer McElhaney, several SMU athletes reported receiving cash offers from other colleges. Shields had found what he was looking for, but, alas, his SMU players did not confine their remarks to problems at other schools.

Two SMU football players told McElhaney they were receiving monthly cash payments, as were many other players. They told of promises made, of cars provided, of coaches who delivered cash, and the boosters who funded it all. Finally Shields was convinced.

Disturbed, he carried the "news" to a November 1983 breakfast meeting with William P. Clements, chairman of the SMU Board of Governors, and a former Republican governor of Texas. The question before the house was whether Clements, Shields, and Hitch were going to stop the payments. They apparently felt one SMU booster, Sherwood Blount, would not stop his payments, regardless of their decision.

Clements told Shields he must have been naive not to have known anything about the payments.[9] He asked Shields whether he thought nationally recruited high school players had found their way to SMU by accident or because they liked the school's red and blue colors. Clements suggested the president could better spend his time running the university.

The following fall, a Pennsylvania football player named Sean Stopperich surfaced with a story of being recruited by an SMU coach and Blount. Stopperich said he received a $5,000 cash payment to come to SMU. Boosters had arranged for his family to move to Dallas and found his father a job.

The SMU melodrama leading up to the death penalty unfolded in two phases. It was principally the Stopperich findings that formed phase one, Case no. 915 which was presented to the NCAA Council August 14, 1985. There were also indications of cash payments and gifts of cars to other players.

"Never give an inch"

SMU's response was to appeal the 38 charges listed by the NCAA Infractions Committee to the 1985 council meeting in the America South room of the Westin Hotel in Boston. Outside, the day was sunny. Inside there was an aura of gloom. I, along with the council members, hoped we would witness a confession without confrontation.

That was not to be. Notably absent from the hearing was Clements, who by this time was committed to regaining the Texas governor's chair. But among those there to tell the SMU story were President Don Shields and attorney John McElhaney.

The SMU lawyer showed again that he was a true-blue defense attorney like many who defend today's colleges against athletics prosecutions. He appealed nine findings in the case and all sections of the penalty. He had the advantage of interviewing all of our witnesses and making tape recordings, a simple procedure denied to NCAA field investigators.

What I heard that day from McElhaney sprang from deep wells of Mustang commitment. This was analyzed best in a report by a committee of United Methodist bishops who later studied the case. The bishops said: "SMU's consistent position with the NCAA was:

'You have made your allegations, now let's see you prove them.' SMU's attitude communicated to coaches, staff and players was: 'Never volunteer anything, never give an inch. You are on the SMU team, and the SMU team sticks together.'"[10]

Listening to the legal wrangling, I felt disengaged, as if part of a surrealist painting. What connection was there between all this and the fun of campus sports, the welfare of 18-year-old athletes?

The SMU delegation left the room, and the council then privately debated the merits of their appeal. An oversized jury, the council was composed of 5 college presidents, 10 faculty athletics representatives, 14 athletics directors, 13 women athletics administrators, and 3 conference commissioners. They were obviously ill at ease.

When the Kentucky case developed in 1952, the NCAA's final adjudicating body was composed of nine members. Since then it has grown fivefold in a determined effort to give representation to all factions. Many council positions are more honorary than functional, and I had felt for some time that the highly political mix of people diluted responsibility and encouraged expediency in such matters. But the council was in Boston for a major decision.

I wondered whether I should stay for the debate. Southwest Conference members had been brainwashed to believe that Walter Byers directed all enforcement actions. The word was that I had my "hit list" of victim schools, that I told the council what penalties to impose.

In truth, I wasn't sure I could restrain myself from speaking out against the ugly SMU record. If I now told the council my opinions, the SMU crowd would have grist for their mill, pointing the finger at Byers instead of themselves. I got up and walked out of the room.

Although eight of its members voted against the majority, the NCAA Council agreed that SMU be deprived of football television appearances and all its football scholarships for new players for one year, plus other restrictions. It was arguably the most serious sentence imposed to that time on an NCAA football program, although it fell far short of the 1952 Kentucky basketball boycott. I didn't think the penalty was severe enough.

There have been many cases in which NCAA investigators have felt they missed the main course. I knew in my heart that Case no. 915 had not plumbed the depths of the SMU scandal.

The Bishops Play Hardball

A unique characteristic of the SMU drama was the involvement of a committee of United Methodist bishops, who studied that situation to a depth that the NCAA itself seldom achieves. The NCAA usually goes deep enough only to make the case. But the United Methodist bishops' committee and the law firm it employed questioned widely, made tape recordings, and took voluntary sworn testimony from every member of the SMU Board of Governors and most other material witnesses.

When I was writing this book, I asked key SMU officials about the veracity of the report. They said the bishops had a motive beyond cleaning up athletics, namely using the scandal to reassert control over SMU, which key trustees, particularly Robert H. Stewart III, Edwin L. Cox, and Bill Clements, had dominated for many years.

"Exaggeration and distortion" are embedded in the *Bishops' Report,* one key loyalist told me resentfully. No one, however, seriously questioned the bishops' fact finding. Certainly, the United Methodist Church's South Central Jurisdiction College of Bishops had a legitimate interest. It owns SMU's capital assets, including the campus.

The bishops began their investigation after the NCAA had wrapped up its inquiry. The point here, however, is that while some self-righteous college leaders hide facts and impede NCAA investigations, these bishops played hardball enforcement with the best of them.

I applaud them for taking a gloves-off, "grand jury" approach that would have warmed the heart of any good district attorney. They revealed previously secret events from the era of Coach Ron Meyer. They also documented details of the second and far worse phase of the SMU scandal.

A Horror Story

The payments to SMU players had stopped with the end of the school term in May 1985—well before the council finally imposed the SMU penalties that August in Boston. On April 27, 1985, Clements told NCAA officials at a meeting in Kansas City that he was going to clean things up, though he never admitted the widespread payments that in fact had been taking place. Clements acknowledged that booster Sherwood Blount may have gotten carried away in the Stopperich case, but Clements insisted the NCAA could count on him to prevent wider violations. Since Clements was in charge, there would be no more payments, period. NCAA listeners were impressed by the man's commanding presence, his aura of authority.

The players had not received money during the summer of 1985, but with fall approaching, 13 players recruited during the Meyer coaching era would be back on campus looking for the money they had been promised—monthly payments ranging from $85 to $750. A crisis was in the making.

The first ripple involved Assistant Coach Bootsie Larsen, who since 1982 had distributed the monthly cash payments to players and was already on probation with the university. The entire coaching staff had been warned by the university to have no further contacts with nine boosters who had been disassociated from SMU by action of the university in April 1985. In August Shields learned Larsen had spent a summer vacation at the Wisconsin lake home of John Appleton, one of the nine.

For that sin Shields fired Larsen without continuing compensation. Meanwhile, others in the leadership were planning far worse violations.

In late August 1985, after the Boston council meeting, Clements met in Perkins Hall at SMU with Shields, Board of Governors member Cox, and Athletics Director Hitch. Clements made it clear he wanted the payments continued, saying if they were stopped, the players would go to other schools and reveal the full story.

Less than a month before, Clements had announced he would run for a new term as governor of Texas. With the election little more than a year away, this was the worst possible moment for washing dirty linen.

Shields and Cox pointed out that the NCAA had enacted the new death penalty legislation in June 1985. The rule was effective against violations occurring after September 1, 1985. Clements nevertheless told the group it was worth the risk of future exposure to go forward. As the bishops reported, "He reminded the group that if the payments stopped, it would all blow up right there and then, and that was a certainty. By continuing the payments, there was a chance they might get by."[11]

Shields and Cox wanted the payments halted. Clements and Hitch were on the other side. No formal decision was made, but when Clements and Hitch walked to the parking lot, the two agreed the existing payments would continue and no new deals would be made. Clements in effect told Hitch, "You take care of it, and if the worst comes to light, I'll take care of you."[12]

Texas Christian University had been a major bidder against SMU in the escalating Southwest Conference war for talent. The SMU-TCU football rivalry reflected a half-century of Dallas–Fort Worth business competition, and Dallas's commanding success is resented by many Fort Worth old-timers. A TCU booster had been told by an SMU friend that during Hayden Fry's time (1962–72) as SMU head football coach, twenty key supporters were organized to contribute $20,000 each annually and "with that kind of budget" SMU was expected to compete successfully with the University of Texas, and surely overwhelm TCU.

By 1980, TCU had had enough. F. A. Dry had been hired from the University of Tulsa by TCU Athletics Director Frank Windegger. At a dinner meeting of coaches and boosters, it was agreed TCU should meet the competition. Eventually, as many as 60 people may have been involved with contributions apparently ranging from $1,000 to $25,000. Players' compensation ranged from free airline tickets home for Christmas to annual stipends approaching $30,000.

In the middle of all this was an ex-TCU player (1948–50) from the Dutch Meyer era. Dick Lowe, a geologist turned oil exploration executive, was increasingly uncomfortable with the escalating payoffs. To Lowe's surprise, SMU booster Sherwood Blount came to see him one day. Blount told Lowe that the pay scale "really is getting out of hand." Lowe told Blount that he (Lowe) was no longer contributing. He was out of it.[13] At least the TCU crowd had made those Mustang boosters raise the white flag.

In September 1985, the football coach who replaced Dry at TCU, Jim Wacker, did take steps to get TCU out of the mess by dismissing seven football players who admitted taking payments. One casualty was Ron Zell Brewer, a tight end from Dallas who reported receiving from $200 a month to $1,500 a semester. Was Brewer sorry or bitter?

"Heck no," Brewer told reporters, "I enjoyed myself while it was happening."[14]

When the players started talking, a furor swept the Texas sports scene. TCU was headed for major NCAA penalties that would not be announced until May 1986. But thanks to the parking lot agreement, the SMU campus was quiet at this time. Clements's political campaign was not endangered.

That fall a telephone rang in the Mission, Kansas, office of David Berst, a 14-year NCAA veteran and the enforcement officer overseeing the SMU case. This time it was a strange, wild-card call from Athletics Director Hitch at SMU. Hitch told David he had learned of new problems on campus but did not know all of the details. David replied that Hitch should investigate the trouble, and he urged Hitch to lay out the facts for the NCAA. "If you work within the system," Berst said, "it will be to your advantage—the fact that you discovered it."

After his call to Berst, Hitch never called back. Bob apparently decided to stay on the Clements team.

The corrosive atmosphere at SMU did not go unnoticed by the athletes. Some time before, the coaches and administrators up through the university president had signed the annual NCAA certification, in which they confirmed they were not committing violations. The players had signed an eligibility form attesting to their NCAA amateur standing. The university had thus involved both its own officials and those of its students who were getting payments in an intramural cover-up.

Even the innocent students were influenced by administrators who saw the school's NCAA penalties as the product of "selective enforcement" and persecution. SMU player David Richards, who as a high school senior was designated top football recruit in the nation by *Parade* magazine, repeated that notion to the *Fort Worth Star-Telegram* in 1985.

"It's the feeling of the coaches and players that all this was instigated by other schools which have more clout with the NCAA than SMU does. They went after us. Okay, so other schools head hunted on us. Now, we'll return the favor. We may go down, but we'll take the whole ship with us."

As for Sean Stopperich, who had told his story to the NCAA, Richards commented, "I could cuss that guy. . . . I gave him a lot of hospitality. Everyone treated him well. And then he goes home and does that to us. I'll say this—he'd better not ever come to Texas again."[15]

An SMU assistant coach later reported that when position coaches began handling payments it led to demands by the players for more money, an internal game of extortion. At one point a star player's demand for cash escalated to the extent that the booster originally assigned to him could no longer afford his payments. He was switched to another booster.

Cash awaiting surreptitious distribution was kept in individual envelopes locked in the desk of an assistant coach, Henry Lee Parker. As the affair lurched toward a climax in 1986, two football players broke into the desk and stole the entire month's secret payroll. Confronted later by their coaches, the two players refused to return the money, which was replaced by the booster who had supplied it.

"The players realized that they were above discipline," the *Bishops' Report* reads. "And in fact they were not disciplined."

Later, I learned of these events with a growing sense of sickness. These coaches and university administrators were teaching their students lessons that could not be undone in classroom courses on the Old Testament.

An athletics department employee who had been dismissed threatened a lawsuit, alleging among other things that she knew of payments and rent-free apartments for players. Lawyer McElhaney negotiated a $17,500 settlement, reminded the employee that she had signed annual statements that she was not aware of NCAA violations, then tape recorded her declaration that she had no knowledge of violations.

Even the resolve not to start "new" payments to players cracked near the end of the 1986 football season when an athletics department member learned that money going to a senior leaving school would be passed on to a younger player of demonstrated promise.[16] Hitch again is adamant that this was done by a booster without his or Coach Collins's knowledge.

Now I wonder, as it all unfolded, why so many bright people concluded they could keep such widespread corruption secret. Even after the 1985 season, the cover-up would have to be maintained. Of the 13 paid performers, 5 players were expected back in the fall of 1986. Puzzled about that madcap scene, I telephoned a friend who was in the middle and asked: "Why didn't the money people make a lump-sum settlement with the players before September 1, 1985, effective date of the death penalty?"

"You underestimate the avarice of the athletes," he answered. "They would have spent the lump-sum payment, then held the Clements-Hitch group hostage for yet more money."

One stone of the cover-up left unturned involved a former SMU linebacker, David Stanley of Angleton, Texas, who had left the team after receiving treatment at university expense for drug abuse. Stanley wanted to return to SMU in the fall of 1986. Collins said "no." The coach had made a courageous if dangerous decision. Since the linebacker knew the closets where the skeletons were hidden, he became a threat.

The facade began to crack in October 1986. Butch Worley of the NCAA enforcement staff interviewed David Stanley, who reported he had been paid $25,000 to sign with SMU, then got cash payments of $750 a month through December 1985. Stanley said other players were still receiving payments. Giving the information to Worley in confidence, Stanley said Worley could not use it without his permission.

About that time, Stanley started talking to Dallas Channel 8 television. TV reporters came to the campus October 27, with the gubernatorial election still eight days away, ostensibly to interview Collins and Hitch about SMU's further appeal to the NCAA.

They unexpectedly confronted the unprepared SMU officials with an envelope supposedly addressed by Coach Parker to Stanley for purposes of transmitting a cash payment. The station delayed broadcast of the interview, however, reportedly because they felt they had to give Stanley a lie detector test and check the handwriting on the envelope.[17]

Keeping the Governor's Secret

The entire scandal, as well as Clements's personal involvement, was still a secret on November 4, 1986, when William Clements was elected governor of Texas. But on November 12, Channel 8 broke the Stanley story to the public.

Already Clements and other Board of Governors members had decided to force President Shields to resign, but they never had to carry out their plans. He announced his retirement for medical reasons on November 22.

"Classic Clements," wrote *Dallas Times-Herald* columnist Molly Ivins after the affair surfaced. "They bullied the poor man until his health broke."[18]

Still the Board of Governors inner circle, including Clements, was struggling to limit the story. The employment contracts of Athletics Director Hitch, Head Football Coach Collins, and Assistant Coach Parker included clauses obligating them to comply with regulations of the NCAA, the Southwest Conference, and SMU.

Yet, arguing that he had been following orders from Clements, Hitch told the inner circle he would cooperate and resign only if his contract were fully honored. In the end he had to yield his Cadillac. He received $246,442 in termination payments, Coach Collins, $556,272, and Parker, $60,299—a total of $863,013 to three employees.

The payments would have bankrupted the SMU athletics program. Certain board of governors members and other supporters, however, raised the necessary money, set up an account separate from the university, and made payments on schedule, according to one source.

With revelations becoming more unpleasant, SMU Board of Governors members flew to Kansas City to meet with NCAA enforcement officials, including David Berst. Hoping to avoid being dragged through the mud, they suggested that the SMU case be closed with a negotiated penalty but without a complete investigation. Edwin Cox did the talking.

"If you want us to terminate football," he said, "we'll stop playing the game tomorrow."

They were prepared to accept a *two*-year suspension—a two-year death penalty—one year more than the school eventually received. Berst, however, turned down their offer, saying that without an investigation, the full facts could not be determined and changes made to prevent future problems.

Berst is a former college basketball player, six feet four inches tall, carrying his 230 pounds lightly through his favorite sport, tennis. I enjoy watching the man play. With racket in hand, his full wingspread is almost nine feet. He plays tennis much as he plays the game of enforcement. He's steady, he comes to the net and presses; he stands there with his long arms spread and, in effect, says: "Try to get one by me."

Though he has dealt with athletics crime for many years, he still has some idealism left as he struggles to keep the game behind the games under control.

The final acts of the SMU drama featured Lonnie Kliever, the bearded theology professor who had been appointed in the fall of 1984 as SMU's faculty representative to the NCAA. Lonnie grew up in a depression-poor Oklahoma family and was trained to believe in the innate goodness of man. He accepted the word of Governor-elect Clements, Shields, and Hitch when they assured the NCAA in April 1985 that payments had been stopped. After all, Hitch was his good friend.

Inner-circle members used this highly regarded professor in a press conference early in 1987, when he told the media that no one on the board or in the top administration, including Clements, was aware of the ongoing payments. Lonnie believed that at the time, and I believe him.

Finally Kliever was put in charge of the university's own investigation and eventually uncovered many of the facts that were the basis of the NCAA prosecution.[19] It took him months to overcome the personal hurt inflicted by the treachery of presumed friends.[20]

At this stage of the drama, many had sacrificed varying degrees of honor to keep the governor's involvement secret. But after continued probing by the *Dallas Morning News,* Governor Clements apparently decided to take control of a deteriorating situation. He gave the *News* an interview and the next day, on March 3, 1987, called a press conference at which he said the NCAA had approved continuing the post–August 1985 player payments to honor the old obligations.

My first word of that came when Berst walked into my office. I knew he was upset.

"This is really outrageous, Walter," David told me. "The governor is saying we authorized illegal payments. I think you should say something."

"Why so?" I asked. "You're the man. You tell the people what the truth is."

"This is important enough to have the head guy come forward with an independent viewpoint," he responded.

I studied a transcript of the NCAA meeting with Clements and concluded the governor was not telling the truth. I immediately issued a statement challenging Clements to back up his false claims. Nothing more came from him, and the media's attention moved on to other events.

The "Slimeball NCAA"

Dismayed by the SMU case, I thought it surprising that so little indignation was expressed within the wider collegiate community. This was deliberate corruption at the highest level. Few except the Methodist bishops and some media people seemed shocked by SMU's corruption. The resentment the death penalty aroused was directed elsewhere—not anger at the men who made the fateful decision in the Perkins Hall parking lot, but at the NCAA.

Dan Jenkins, sports columnist for the *Dallas Times-Herald,* wrote in his usual forceful manner: "I'll never cease to be amazed at the astounding number of presumably capable college presidents who continue to let Walter and his gang of hypocrites tell them what to think and do."[21]

Sherwood Blount mailed that column to the NCAA office. He sent a string of abrasive communications to Dave Berst, addressing him as "Big Time."

"See you at the courthouse, Big Time," he wrote.

For another column Jenkins invoked a fictional character named Ed Bookman, who denounced the "slimeball NCAA."

"It's the unfair and ignorant rules that cause all the problems in the first place," Jenkins quoted Bookman as saying. "The NCAA don't want to catch nobody big. In fact, the pipsqueak little snoopers ain't gonna catch nobody who don't panic and cooperate with 'em.

"And now everybody's shocked and dismayed at how Governor Bill Clements wanted the Mustangs to be able to compete with the big boys. Hell, it's the best damn thing I've ever heard about him."[22]

Coming near the end of my decades as executive director, the SMU case confirmed my growing conviction that the colleges could not get the job done under the old structure; that, indeed, I was an anachronism, my philosophy rendered obsolete by a new generation with millions of new dollars to spend and a desperate desire to win.

What I have described here is far from the romance of sports that I believed existed when I was young. In the early years, many college officials were willing to lay their integrity on the line and strive to correct abuses. In management terms, the NCAA was then a direct-line organization with responsibilities fixed at the athletics conference and campus levels.

Today the NCAA's structure with layer upon layer of administrators and managers is designed to obscure responsibility. It is difficult even to identify the wily saboteurs who work from inside to subvert real reform. Their determined efforts are facilitated by the very organization of the NCAA–diffused responsibilities, a complicated governance process that lends itself to manipulation, and rules upon rules based on abandoned principles.

Notes

1. Information for this account was drawn from conversations with Robert J. Minnix, NCAA Enforcement Department, including Robert J. Minnix, interviews with author, February 12 and March 3, 1990.
2. Ibid.
3. Ibid.
4. Information for this account was drawn from conversations with Lonnie D. Kliever, professor of religious studies, Southern Methodist University, including Lonnie D. Kliever, interviews with the author, March 5 and September 14, 1990.
5. Robert L. Hitch, interviews with the author, March 1, 1990, and January 10, 1991.
6. Ibid.
7. Ibid.
8. *The Bishops' Committee Report on SMU–Report to the Board of Trustees of Southern Methodist University from the Special Committee of Bishops of the South Central Jurisdiction of the United Methodist Church*, June 19, 1987 (hereafter referred to as *Bishops' Report*).
9. Ibid.
10. Ibid.
11. Ibid.
12. Hitch, interviews.
13. Dick Lowe, interview with the author, December 20, 1990.
14. David Leon Moore, *USA Today*, September 20, 1985.
15. Whit Canning, *Fort Worth Star-Telegram*, August 19, 1985.
16. *Bishops' Report*.
17. Information for this account was drawn from *Bishops' Report*; newspaper articles; Kliever, interviews; Hitch, interviews; S. David Berst, interview with the author, March 16, 1990.
18. Molly Ivins, *Dallas Times-Herald*, June 25, 1987.
19. Southern Methodist University Infractions Report by the NCAA, February 25, 1987.
20. Lonnie D. Kliever, interview with the author, September 14, 1990.
21. Dan Jenkins, *Dallas Times-Herald*, October 12, 1986.
22. Dan Jenkins, *Dallas Times-Herald*, March 8, 1987.

Chapter 3   The Birth of Big Time

Steamrolling the President

Coach Fielding Yost vs. President James Burrill Angell of the University of Michigan: In a drama to be reenacted many times in college athletics, a football coach defeats the president through a vote of university trustees. I believe this showdown was more significant in charting the course of college athletics than the founding of the NCAA that same year.

The contest started in 1906 when the high-minded Angell talked his fellow Big Ten presidents into adopting rules to keep football within reasonable bounds. On March 9 of that year, they limited the season to five games, restricted eligibility to three years with graduate students banned, and capped student ticket prices at 50 cents. The training table and training quarters were prohibited.

There was an added condition: The coach must be a full-time employee of the university.[1] Yost had substantial outside business interests. Faced with these new Big Ten limits, the founding father of today's Michigan football tradition rebelled.

Though he supposedly was responsible to President Angell, Fielding Yost took his complaint to the university's board of regents. The Big Ten presidents on November 30, 1907, attempted to mollify Yost and raised the number of football games to seven. No deal. On January 14, 1908, the Michigan regents voted to withdraw their university from the Big Ten so that Coach Yost and Wolverine football could forge ahead unimpeded.

Angell could move a whole conference, but where football was concerned, he could not convince his own coach and his own board. Michigan did not rejoin the Big Ten until November 1917. This act of a coach steamrolling his college president had historic significance although the lesson had to be relearned time and again by succeeding generations of college chief executives. One of the more recent was the president of nearby Michigan State University.

During the winter of 1989–90, the popular John A. DiBiaggio tried to prevent his football coach from also becoming athletics director. John, a gregarious man, well met, felt sure he could win this one. The trustees overruled their president and supported the coach. Thus, George Perles kicked off the 1990 football season, his eighth at Michigan State, with the title of athletics director. Angell couldn't win the big one, and 82 years later DiBiaggio couldn't win a little one.[2]

Play Is Not Business

It was rough going in those early days when Yost was at Michigan, Pop Warner at Cornell, and John Heisman at Akron and Oberlin. Some schools would bring in burly, anonymous ringers to substitute for authentic students. Teams used the bone-breaking wedge and gang tackling to mow down opposition. The hurdle play was introduced, whereby one of the smaller players jumped into the arms of two teammates and was literally thrown feet first over the massed defensive line.

By the end of the 19th century, football had gained the admiration of the East's sports-minded public. The Thanksgiving Day Game, usually matching Yale and Princeton, became a major event. It was moved to New York City's Polo Grounds where as many as 40,000 spectators attended in the 1890s.[3] That was the premier event but many prestigious, smaller liberal arts colleges—including Amherst, Hamilton, and Williams—were intensely competitive.

A reported 18 boys were killed and 149 seriously hurt during the 1905 football season, but by then President Theodore Roosevelt had declared things had gone far enough. In October 1905, he summoned officials from Harvard, Yale, and Princeton to the White

The above team inaugurated intercollegiate football competition at Hamilton College in 1890.

House to urge their leadership toward restoring ethical conduct and eliminating the brutality. In 1906, Roosevelt's admonition motivated the colleges to found the organization that became today's NCAA.[4]

Roosevelt spoke for many who believed athletics were good, "especially in their rougher forms, because they tend to develop courage." But, as he told Harvard students in 1907: "I trust I need not add that in defending athletics, I would not for one moment be understood as excusing that perversion of athletics which would make it the end of life instead of merely a means of life.

"It is first-class, healthful play, and is useful as such. But play is not business, and it is a very poor business indeed for a college man to learn nothing but sport."[5]

Roosevelt's attitude was enshrined at the birth of the NCAA, when it adopted the basic principle that "No student shall represent a college or university in any intercollegiate game or contest...who has at any time received, either directly or indirectly, money, or any other consideration." The NCAA's first president, Capt. Palmer Pierce of the U.S. Military Academy, said "Amen!" in a 1907 speech. He declared: "This organization wages no war against the professional athlete, but it does object to such a one posing and playing as an amateur. It smiles on the square, manly, skillful contestant, imbued with love of the contest he wages; it frowns on the more skillful professional who, parading under college colors, is receiving pay in some form or other for his athletic prowess."[6]

Thanks to Teddy Roosevelt and the fledgling NCAA, death among football players became rare, and academic cheating and pay-for-play were kept sufficiently under control for the games to go on. As the enormous financial rewards for winning expanded during the 1960s and multiplied in the 1970s and 1980s, NCAA enforcement never kept pace and the effectiveness of conference commissioners as regulators and enforcers became virtually nonexistent.

Periodic countertrends through the years have caused endless debates, noteworthy for maximum verbiage and minimum results. Only occasionally has the lifeblood of college sports programs been placed at risk.

One such rare episode during the 1940s involved a maverick Big Ten president. I remember reading with shock the heretical remarks of the renowned liberal educator Robert Maynard Hutchins, president of the University of Chicago. Hutchins ridiculed the essence of athletics. "Whenever I feel a desire to exercise," the university president said, "I lie down until it goes away."

Hot as I was with my youthful belief in sports, I thought his bias arose from a 1939 Chicago-Michigan football game in which his team lost 85 to 0. That would be enough to unbalance anyone's equilibrium.

Hutchins fought for elimination of football at his school, and his board of trustees agreed Chicago should leave the Big Ten

Conference effective June 30, 1946. The official reason provided by the then "big nine" conference was Chicago's "inability to provide reasonable equality of competition."[7]

Hutchins, rejecting the sports rationale of his former presidential associates, explained it this way. "Education is primarily concerned with the training of the mind, and athletics and social life, though they may contribute to it, are not the heart of it and cannot be permitted to interfere with it. . . .

"An educational institution can make one unique contribution, one denied to a fraternal order or a bodybuilding institute: It can educate. It is by its success in making this unique contribution that it must be judged."[8]

Hutchins foresaw far better than I did the antiacademic pressures of big time athletics. But I suspect today's generation of college CEOs would prefer a more positive statement than Hutchins's about the place of college athletics—something like the 1986 judgment by columnist George Will: "Sport is a realm of discipline, skill and excellence, and hence has a legitimate role on campuses."[9]

Indeed, aside from the fact that much of the activity is *off* campus, the trick has always been to determine what constitutes a legitimate role. That was the issue separating Hutchins from John Hannah, who in 1941 became president of Michigan State at East Lansing. Hannah's "cow college," with an enrollment of 6,000 and a yearly budget of $4 million, was determined to scratch its way up the pecking order of American universities.

Athletics Bootstraps

Hannah intended to use athletics for his school's hoped-for climb from the status of instructional school for tradesmen and farmers to that of a nationally respected university. Athletics bootstraps are the most convenient ones available in an academic world that has no clear-cut academic standards.

The athletics-academic balance at Michigan State had been skewed before Hannah arrived. By 1933 it had tilted so far that the

North Central Association of Colleges and Schools decried the overemphasis on athletics there, citing high grades that were being given away to athletes.[10] Michigan State paid no attention to its regional academic accrediting agency. Not long afterward, the nation's regional accrediting agencies abandoned the cauldron of athletics inspection and have done little to show much gumption in their roles as academic inspectors (see chap. 17).

If the balance had been skewed in 1933, Hannah set about making it more so. His eye was fixed on the vacancy that the defection of Chicago left in the now Big Nine Conference. At a luncheon pause during the 1949 NCAA boxing tournament in East Lansing, almost as if he were responding to President Hutchins, Hannah consecrated athletics as an essential element of American culture, folkways, and education. "This may all sound superficial or apologetic to the serious-minded who tend to dislike games because they dislike seeing people enjoy themselves," he said. "I believe that somehow athletics are tied up with that fiercely burning spirit of competition which has been the trademark of America since the day it was discovered."[11]

Sounded good—almost like Theodore Roosevelt. I believed it. I wanted the NCAA to do what it could to keep the competitive spirit pure.

In practice, however, Hannah was turning Teddy's theory that "play is not business" upside down.

Sleepy Jim Crowley, one of Notre Dame's legendary Four Horsemen, was Michigan State football coach. Fred Jenison, a local insurance executive, willed a half-million dollars to the university, and Hannah put the money into *athletic scholarships,* a term that in that day was thought to be an oxymoron. It still abuses the English language, but the contradiction now is ingrained in the American idiom.[12]

Determined to overtake the University of Michigan and operating at first outside the rules of the major conferences, Hannah freely encouraged the award of full-ride grants. Ostensibly, each recipient had to maintain a C average. While he encourage maximum development of Michigan State's sports prowess, Hannah used his formidable political skills to maneuver his institution into the "big nine" over the objections of other member schools, which didn't like his free-wheeling administration of the Jenison Scholarships and the loose money in the Spartan Foundation, a depository for donations by sports supporters.

Coach Crisler Spills His Scotch

I saw dramatic evidence of that opposition during an evening with Kenneth L. (Tug) Wilson, the conference commissioner, in Tug's beautiful home in Wilmette, Ill., a few houses away from Lake Michigan. I was Tug's young assistant then. Several of us were enjoying conversation and a drink with the nationally respected University of Michigan football coach, H. O. "Fritz" Crisler. Fritz detested Michigan State.

We stood around the bar in Tug's basement rec room. We were having a great time until the athletics director of the University of Minnesota, Frank McCormick, a good friend of Fritz's, dropped a verbal bomb. "You know, Fritz," Frank said, "We just scheduled a regular home-and-home football series with Michigan State."

Fritz stared at him. The Minnesota-Michigan game for the "Little Brown Jug" was an annual classic. It was unthinkable that Michigan's respected opponent, Minnesota, would schedule a series with its hated rival, Michigan State.

"What? What did you say?"

Fritz was stunned. Pouring some of Tug's good Scotch into his highball glass, the shaken coach knocked the glass off the bar. When Frank repeated the bad news, Fritz shook his head.

"I can't believe it," he muttered.

Believe it or not, the Minnesota series was a major breakthrough for Michigan State. Not long after that, John Hannah himself walked into the conference office in Chicago. He was a big, loose-bodied man with Ralph Bellamy mannerisms. Deliberate in speech, Hannah would deflect or simply not acknowledge arguments that ran counter to his mission. Persistence and calm persuasion were his sales tools.

By then Tug and I were aware of the situation Hannah had

created. Whether or not Crisler and other Michigan officials de-tested Michigan State, they dared not openly oppose its entry into the "big nine." The state legislature sat in Lansing, almost within sight of the Michigan State campus. Michigan could oppose Han-nah only at peril of jeopardizing its own state appropriations.

Tug and I realized the new conference entry could not be the University of Pittsburgh, known to covet conference membership. Ohio State didn't want Pittsburgh as a rival in the conference, principally because of the recruiting advantages Ohio State be-lieved conference membership gave it in talent-laden Pennsylva-nia. It surely could not be Penn State, located in the inaccessible hill country of that state. Just as Hannah was carefully neutralizing the University of Michigan back home, he had come to our office in Chicago to neutralize any potential opposition by the conference commissioner.

"The point is," he told Tug, "we're the logical new member. Detroit is only 65 miles away. We're in a growing population center. We're located in the middle of the conference, so travel will be easy for the teams. I just want you to consider these things."

That was when I knew Hannah's arguments would prove irre-sistible. In May 1949, his school replaced the University of Chicago to restore the Big Ten Conference in both name and membership.

Yet what a contrast between the university that the Big Ten had lost and the one it gained! Chicago's undergraduate enrollment stood at 3,200 when Hutchins took it out of the Big Ten; by 1969 its enrollment was 2,600. Yet when John Hannah retired in 1969, his cow college with 6,000 students had become a mega-university of 40,000 students (including 32,300 undergraduates), a yearly budget of $100 million, 15 colleges, and 250 academic programs. He had the advantage of direct tax support (not available to the private University of Chicago) plus the advantage of big-time ath-letics.

When the University of Chicago withdrew from the Big Ten, other Big Ten presidents defended their athletics programs in a *Chicago Tribune* series. They implied they could, without difficulty, link big-time athletics with education. Asked why these presidents did not follow his lead, Robert Hutchins of Chicago responded: "They could not stand the pressure."[13]

Given the outcome, it's easy to see why. Michigan State got the growth, the money, and the students. Chicago maintained a renowned academic reputation.

Michigan State was plagued by NCAA penalties starting in 1953, coming back for major encores in 1964 and again in 1976. Its athletics operation also spun off coaches whose later programs reflected the original Michigan State concept and the consequent NCAA penalties—Sonny Grandelius at Colorado, Bill Yeoman at Houston, and Frank Kush at Arizona State.

For most of my career, I have felt uncomfortable with the extremes dramatized by the rampaging athletics opportunism of Michigan State and by the loss of collegiate morale in Chicago's farewell to the memories of Amos Alonzo Stagg and Jay Berwanger. I would prefer some decent synthesis, but if one has to choose, I go with Stagg and Berwanger in a serious academic environment.

Incidentally, Chicago did return to intercollegiate football in 1969 (NCAA Division III). The team won two games that year and netted $62.50. Walter Haas, athletics director, told me the net would have been larger except for an unexpected development. "The students tore down the goal posts," Haas explained, "and the university charged the football budget to replace them."

The "victory" of Michigan State and the "defeat" of the University of Chicago is only one of the historical factors that have made today's collegiate policies weigh heavily in favor of athletics readiness over academic preparedness. In 1966 Ray T. Ellickson, NCAA faculty representative at the University of Oregon, meditated on the Michigan State experience. In a talk obviously meant to push athletics on his own campus, he said: "I am convinced that if a state institution wants equal treatment with another institution in that state, it must present an image of equal stature and, perhaps unfortunately, that image is most easily presented in athletics.

"There is little doubt in my mind that President Hannah made a wise decision when he decided that, if he was to get for his institution equal treatment at the hands of the Michigan legislature, he would have to compete effectively with Michigan on the athletic field."[14]

Michigan State thus became the inspiration of other growth schools. I have watched this drama, in one form or another, enacted and reenacted repeatedly, whether it be UCLA, UNLV, or Florida State.

The University of Houston, founded in 1927 as a junior college, became a four-year college in 1934, pressured its way into the Southwest Conference in the mid-1970s, and competed in four Cotton Bowl games from 1977 through 1985. It also ran big athletics deficits—$3.4 million in 1982—resulting in fee increases for all students. Students protested that subsidies to athletics were curtailing health services. It did, in other words, enjoy the typical big-time athletics experience.

Florida State at Tallahassee, a former women's college, replicated the Michigan State–Michigan struggle. Like Michigan State, Florida State is located in the state capital. The Seminoles took dead aim at the University of Florida at Gainesville, achieving national rankings in multiple sports and an average home football attendance of around 56,000. After six consecutive bowl game victories (1985–90 seasons), Florida State moved into the Atlantic Coast Conference while Florida was on NCAA probation.

Similarly, the University of California, Los Angeles marched to the fore with the all-out support of chancellors Ray B. Allen in the 1950s and Charles E. (Chuck) Young, the current president who took office in September 1968. Chuck has never lost his love for big-time athletics with all its showbiz trappings, including a seat with the players on the sidelines. Being where the action is can be intoxicating.

Chuck Young knows you can't hold an alumni rally around a Bunsen burner, but you sure can raise a lot of money after beating USC before 100,000 fans in the L.A. Coliseum. A former faculty athletics representative at UCLA, Chuck stood aside as the strong-willed J. D. Morgan ran a net-profit program as athletics director. After J. D. left the scene and his able aide Bob Fisher departed,

Chuck has supervised athletics from the chancellor's office and incurred deficits in the process.

In the old days it seemed a certain truth that big-time sports could turn a profit and make a university grow. But as more and more schools crowded into an already crowded NCAA Division I, competing for audience and television time, that precept began to fade. Slicing the pie into more pieces reduced the individual servings.

Yet most big-time university presidents firmly believe major league sports, national publicity, enlarged financial support, and more students go hand in hand. Respect for academic quality is seldom the governing criterion for university undergraduate decision making. More than ever, money and numbers of students are the test, and these facts of financial life merely intensify the pressures on the coach to win.

As academic leaders, college presidents have an inherent urge to engage in public relations exercises. In one speech they "view with alarm" the athletics orgy while in another speech "point with pride" at the growth of big-time sports on their own campuses.

John Hannah was one of those. On his way to becoming administrator of the U.S. Office for International Development, the Michigan State president headed up a national committee—dubbed the Hannah Commission—that was to recommend a program to make certain that college athletics would function as a legitimate educational activity. Hannah thus set out to reform athletics.

Each time a new commission is created to clean up college sports, I can't help but recall the words of Claude Rains, playing the French police inspector in *Casablanca*. Faced with a political murder, he orders his men to "round up the usual suspects."

A more recent athletics cleanup was mounted by the Knight Foundation Commission, created in 1989 with a two-year, $2 million grant. One of its co-chairs was Bill Friday, who presided over the North Carolina university system while Jim Valvano ran wild at North Carolina State. Another commission member was Clifton Wharton, who was president at Michigan State during a major athletics scandal in 1975.

In more ways than one, the John Hannah I knew mapped the route for the modern college president. He proved on one hand that big-time sports jump-start the engine that makes universities grow. On the other, he proved the public relations value of bemoaning the lack of support from fellow college presidents in achieving real reform.

Hannah's big time also fueled a new era of cheating, which soon brought the colleges to a crisis comparable to the one that drove Teddy Roosevelt to act.

Battling the Gamblers

During the birth of big time, I learned big money attracts all kinds of people and problems, including sports gamblers and game fixers. At the age of 27, as a part-time employee of both the NCAA and the Big Ten Conference, I took on a point-shaving investigation into what could pass for a Damon Runyon story plot.

It started for me at Gibbey's cafe, which was across the alley from the Big Ten headquarters in the Sherman Hotel on Clark Street in Chicago. Gibbey himself (I've forgotten the man's first name) came over to my table with a nice-looking fellow, introducing him as C. K. McNeil.

"Mac's a professional gambler," Gibbey told me. "He has something he wants to tell you."

I later concluded the restaurant owner had offered to serve as the bridge, because Mac never pushed himself on anyone. He was a quiet guy, just old enough to be showing some gray at his temples. He sat down to have a drink with me. When I asked what he had on his mind, Mac replied: "I've been watching the betting odds before some of these Big Ten basketball games, some of the other Midwest games, too. The shift in the point spreads don't make sense. Something funny's going on."

First off I had to decide whether McNeil was legitimate. He could have been a disgruntled gambler trying to get even. I learned he was reputable gambler with no ax to grind, except that he wanted to bet on honest games. A University of Chicago product, he was making $30,000 to $50,000 a year from sports betting in the late 1940s. He had his own handicap system.

When the bookmakers posted their basketball point spreads and there was sufficient discrepancy between Mac's handicap and the betting line, he would back his judgment by betting large sums. It was Mac who introduced me to the subculture of sports betting, which basically operated then much as it does today.

There are honest gamblers. There are dishonest ones. The honest professional gamblers do not like the dishonest ones. The crooked gambler who wants to fix a collegiate contest must get to a vital participant—a player, an official, or a coach. Their goal usually is not to achieve a "dump," which means the deliberate throwing of a game. Normally the fixer wants only a shaving of the points.

A common strategy was to let the favored team win, but not by as many points as expected. The gambler would take the underdog team plus five points. The gambler or his straw man would arrange with a player, for example, for the favorite to win by less than five points. Everybody wins: the player's team, the player who receives an agreed-upon cash stipend, and the fixer. "Nobody gets hurt," the fixer tells the player.

It's a beguiling story, particularly for a youngster who knows the gross value of a full house of spectators and a national TV contract compared to the dollars in his own grant-in-aid. Also, point shaving is almost impossible to detect.

Sometimes unexpectedly heavy betting on a team can be explained by injuries to or ineligibility of opposing players or intense college rivalries. But when it happens several times to the same team with no obvious explanation, the red flags go up. C. K. McNeil knew the symptoms.

He had been tracking the unusual movements and had concluded the only common thread was a particular official, who apparently was making strategic floor calls to protect the point spreads of his gambling friends. In a typical college game then, 150 points might be scored by both teams, and a difference of 1 point could decide the bet.

National handicappers set point spreads and game odds on

nationally prominent contests for bookies who use their service. The bookmaker's aim is to balance as closely as possible his money bets on a game, so he can collect his vigorish (his handling fee), and walk away with a profit no matter what the outcome.

To illustrate: Villanova is posted by a Philadelphia bookmaker as a 3-1/2-point favorite in a game against Kentucky. A Villanova supporter bets $1,000 on Villanova minus 3-1/2 points. Two days later, with Villanova plus 4-1/2 points he bets another $1,000 on Villanova. He will win both bets if Villanova beats Kentucky by 5 points or more.

Simultaneously, comparable bookie postings and wagering are going on in Lexington, Louisville, Chicago, and New York. With the movement of the handicap to 4-1/2 points, a gambler in Chicago meanwhile has bet Kentucky two different times in the days before the game: $5,000 each with bookmakers in Chicago and Louisville (for Kentucky not to lose the game by more than 4-1/2 points). The betting is closed at 5 P.M. of game night.

The Chicago gambler, who has backed Kentucky at plus 4-1/2, wants to make certain that Villanova does not win by 5 points or more. He turns out to be a fixer and has a collaborator. One late, timely call by a game official can get the job done. A fumbled pass or strategic foul by a Villanova player could bring about the same result.

Unexpectedly heavy wagering by bettors like the Chicago gambler might throw individual bookmakers' accounts out of balance between pro-Kentucky and pro-Villanova bettors. Then the bookies will try to "lay off" their unbalanced bets with one another so their money is equalized. If simple, book-to-book trading isn't enough, they might go to a central clearinghouse, which at one time was in Cincinnati.

After getting the critical tip from C. K. McNeil, we took the unusual step of asking the official to undergo a polygraph test. The first test proved inconclusive, and we asked for a second. As the official waited alone in a room for the new test, Big Ten Commissioner Tug Wilson and I moved into an adjoining room to watch through a one-way window. Tug and I stared through the glass, fascinated at the scene.

"Look at that," Tug whispered.

The man was stepping up onto a wooden chair and then down, up and down, up and down, repeating the motion in quick time. I saw his chest move with his panting. The official was pumping up his blood pressure to confound the polygraph.

Apparently realizing he might be watched, the man suddenly stepped down and turned to the mirrored glass through which we were peering. My face was inches from his. Instinctively, we drew back. Then he pulled away.

He did beat the machine, because the operator called all the results inconclusive. Suspecting the high-profit days were over, he nevertheless gave up his post as an official. I'm convinced Mac was right about the official. He also read correctly the many other signs of increased gambling and its threat to college sports.

Point shaving and fixing are threats to which the colleges are most vulnerable and to which they give occasional attention. This is not due to lack of concern but a sense of helplessness about how to deal with the problem successfully.

Notes

1. Official Big Ten Conference Historical Chronology, Commissioner's Office, Schaumburg, Illinois; David M. Nelson, "College Football Problems Same as Century Ago," University of Delaware, NCAA football rules historian, conversations with the author in October 1980, and interview with author, October 11, 1988.
2. William F. Reed, *Sports Illustrated*, February 5, 1990; Mitch Albom, *Detroit Free Press*, January 24, 1990.
3. Ronald A. Smith, *Sports and Freedom* (New York: Oxford University Press, 1988), 79.
4. Jack Falla, *NCAA: The Voice of College Sports* (Mission, Kans.: National Collegiate Athletic Association, 1981), 13; Smith, *Sports and Freedom*, 193–94.
5. Extracts from Theodore Roosevelt's speech, February 23, 1907, as reported by the *New York Sun,* and reproduced by the Helms Athletic Foundation, Los Angeles, California, in a Special Release, October 23, 1951.
6. Palmer Pierce, speech at the 1907 convention of the Intercollegiate Athletic Association of the United States, quoted in Falla, *NCAA*, 32–33.
7. Big Ten Chronology.
8. Robert M. Hutchins, "Football and College Life," a speech delivered Janu-

ary 12, 1940, quoted in Hal A. Lawson and Alan G. Ingham, "Conflicting Idologies Concerning the University and Intercollegiate Athletics: Harper and Hutchins at Chicago, 1892–1940," *Journal of Sport History* 7, no. 3 (Winter 1980): 37–67.

9. George F. Will, *Newsweek,* September 15, 1986.

10. Beth J. Shapiro, "John Hannah and the Growth of Big-Time Intercollegiate Athletics at Michigan State University," *Journal of Sport History* 10, no. 3 (Winter 1983): 26–40.

11. John A. Hannah speech to officials and participants, NCAA Boxing Tournament, East Lansing, Michigan, April 9, 1949.

12. The word *athletic* is an adjective whose first meaning is "muscular, robust, or vigorous." *Athletics* is a noun referring to sports and games. The colleges recruit athletic young men and women for their teams, but they employ athletics directors, run athletics departments, and engage in college athletics.

13. Lawson and Ingham, "Harper and Hutchins at Chicago, 1892–1940," 37–67.

14. Ray Ellickson, address to the Oregon Assembly, Eugene, Oregon, February 25, 1966.

Chapter 4   # A New NCAA: Enforcement Begins

The Sanity Code

I was riding on a train one January day through snow and cold from New York to Chicago. The year was 1950. I had just attended the annual NCAA Convention in New York City, where the group had failed to enforce the Sanity Code, a national academic and financial aid rule it had adopted only two years before to clean up college sports.

Commissioner Tug Wilson, of the Big Ten, Hugh Willett, the new NCAA president, and I were seated together in the lounge car of the New York Central's 20th Century Limited. At first there was little talk. We were depressed over the loss of the Sanity Code.

This was a time when the regional sports scene in the United States—governed reasonably well by the area athletics conference—was giving way to nationwide recruiting and scheduling. We needed national rules, and the 1948 Sanity Code had been our first attempt. It touched on most of the areas covered by present-day rules—recruiting, the amateur status of athletes, scholarships, and specific academic requirements. The Sanity Code was designed to rein in the growing "full-ride" practice of awarding grants-in-aid based on how well the player played the game.

The key problems were the emotional opposition voiced principally by southern universities and an ineffective enforcement mechanism based on self-disclosure.

Up for punishment at the convention held at the Commodore Hotel in New York that January had been schools dubbed by the press as the "Seven Sinners": University of Maryland, The Citadel, Virginia Military Institute, Virginia Polytechnic Institute, Villanova, University of Virginia, and Boston College. All seven had voluntarily revealed their violations. Otherwise they probably would have gone undetected.

The University of Virginia led the fight against the Sanity Code, contending that full expense "scholarships" for football athletes were essential. That is why the school had helped players outside the rules. Virginia president Colgate W. Darden's position was that athletes were given no special academic treatment, but a student who had to work on a job and play football could not at the same time maintain acceptable academic standards. The university explained that 24 members of the football team received financial help from an alumni association covering all or part of their educational expense.[1]

The question before the convention was whether to drop from membership—*banish from the NCAA*—the seven colleges that had confessed to rules violations. Never since then has anyone proposed expelling even one college, although violations have increased tenfold in grossness and number. The convention voted 111 to 93, a 54 percent majority, to expel the Seven Sinners, but a two-thirds majority was required.

Too many voters couldn't bear punishing those who confessed while letting the silent violators go free by default. They refused to enforce the Sanity Code. I still remember the gloom of that ride in the lounge car homeward toward Big Ten headquarters in Chicago. By then I was working half time for the Big Ten Conference and half time as the executive assistant for the NCAA.

Tug was sipping bourbon and branchwater, NCAA President Willett unadulterated branchwater. He seldom imbibed. A kindly but determined man, Willett was faculty representative at the University of Southern California, a distinguished educator prominent in the management of the Los Angeles school system.

I had the list from the convention showing how each college voted. As we rode through the darkening countryside, I read parts of it aloud, calling off the yeas and nays.

"It wasn't just the southern colleges that did it to us," Hugh Willett remarked. "Look at all the northern votes."

It was a discouraging realization, pressing home the point that we might never find a consensus among the colleges on how to enforce the rules. Arriving at the station the next morning, I bought a *Chicago Tribune* and read a blaring, eight-column headline that proclaimed the death of the NCAA.

I took a taxi with Tug and Hugh to a somber meeting in the combined Big Ten-NCAA office, which amounted to three remodeled adjoining bedrooms on the second floor at the Sherman Hotel. My small office was on the left, the secretaries in the middle, and Tug's large office on the right. One full-time secretary and Walter Byers at half time made up the entire paid staff of that era's NCAA. We sat down in the large office and started talking again.

Willett said the code itself actually had not been voted down. The problem was the lack of a mechanism for uniform implementation and enforcement.

"I can see we're going to need a central organization to handle this," Hugh said.

The $11,000 Test

Out of that little gathering grew a new kind of NCAA with specific enforcement powers. Mostly I listened as they sketched out the tentative blueprint. Over the next year that blueprint was expanded and, when the time came, I applied for the job of first full-time executive director of the new kind of NCAA.

Asa S. Bushnell, head of the dominant Eastern College Athletic Conference, was a member of the hiring committee. He counseled me that if I asked for too much salary, the money might attract applications from more qualified people, including Athletics Director Robert J. Kane of Cornell University, a mutual friend. I was already earning $10,000 a year from two part-time jobs. I said an extra $1,000 would be fine and I got the job.[2]

I had been NCAA executive director only 19 days when the

harbinger of the first case arrived. I immediately was going to be given a chance to prove whether I was worth $11,000.

When I took office in 1951, Tug Wilson warned me that the job was high risk. On his advice and without legal counsel, I wrote myself an "evergreen contract."

Under it I was hired for five years at a stretch, the contract renewing automatically if no one challenged it. To fire me, the powers-that-be would have to provide notice eighteen months before the given five years expired. From the date of the first signing forward, no one ever so much as inquired about the terms of my contract until I announced my intention to retire.

Anyway, now I had the job. The question was whether I could do it.

On the night of October 20, 1951, the University of Kentucky's great Alex Groza and teammate Ralph Beard were picked up in Chicago by representatives of the New York district attorney's office.[3]

They had been the heroes of the Kentucky basketball team that had won two NCAA championships and an Olympic gold medal. Almost simultaneously, Dale Barnstable was taken into custody at his home in Louisville. All were wanted for questioning in connection with point-fixing scandals.

Judge Saul S. Streit of the General Sessions Court, County of New York, heard the allegations of outright law breaking.[4] His interrogation of the players and Coach Adolph Rupp went far beyond gambling. He probed into the financial arrangements in Lexington for the Kentucky basketball team. When it was all over, the scorecard read:

> Five key basketball players were convicted of fixing points on basketball games over a three-year period; three were sentenced by Judge Streit.
>
> Adolph Rupp was condemned by Judge Streit for "consorting with bookmaker Ed Kurd." One player testified that before a game in Cincinnati, Rupp came into the hotel and told the team, "I just called Kurd to get the points. Now these guys will be tough tonight so I want you to pour it on." Judge

Streit blasted the school's athletics policy as "the acme of commercialism and overemphasis."

The Southeastern Conference and the NCAA later found that players had received illegal cash payments, some of which were made with the knowledge of Coach Rupp.

In another development, Coach Rupp of Kentucky had been fighting Indiana University over the Hoosiers' attempted recruitment of the top Kentucky high school basketball star, Cliff Hagan. Kentucky and Indiana were bitter rivals. Indiana had won the NCAA title in 1940 (second year of the tournament) and Kentucky won its first one eight years later. Rupp sanctimoniously charged Indiana Coach Branch McCracken with improper inducements and told McCracken to leave Hagan alone. McCracken replied: "I don't run away from good players like Hagan."

The highly prized recruit nevertheless chose Kentucky and became a minor part of Case no. 1, the maiden effort of the newly created NCAA Subcommittee on Infractions. I filed Case Report no. 1 September 20–21, 1952.[5]

Ten players were named as having received illegal outside aid. The report also indicated Hagan "probably was ineligible in 1951–52" because of a $125 gift certificate he had received, but no specific finding was made regarding him. He was not involved in the gambling.

With the report finished, I felt heartbroken over the Kentucky scandal. As a good high school athlete and a mediocre college athlete, then as a sports reporter on my college newspaper and later for United Press in Chicago and New York, I loved college sports. I could scarcely believe that members of this great basketball team—still regarded as one of the most skilled of all time—had shaved points and played into the hands of gamblers. In that era, I do not believe there was the hardened expectation and cynical acceptance of misbehavior that permeates today's society.

I still see the 1950s and 1960s as a romantic era—at least in the minds of a public that was deeply shocked when coaches and young heroes it admired went wrong. Those ideals lived also in the minds of faculty and athletics officials who wanted to keep college

Indiana University 1940 basketball team, coached by Branch McCracken, defeated the University of Kansas Jayhawks to win the second National Collegiate basketball championship, the first under NCAA administration.

sports the kind of campus and student activity they nostalgically remembered from their own younger days.

What was I to do about all of this? Luckily, Bernie H. Moore, the Southeastern Conference commissioner, was my great friend and strong supporter. He had served on the committee that hired me. We talked over the Kentucky case regularly as it developed.

At this time Bernie was playing a major role in NCAA policy. He had been head football and track coach at Louisiana State during the Huey Long years. He had dealt with the Kingfish not just in the governor's mansion but with Governor Long sitting beside him on the team bench at Tiger Stadium in Baton Rouge on Saturday afternoons. Bernie was not one to be surprised by unexplainable quirks of human nature or political manipulation.

Neither of us were disturbed by the agonized editorials we read in the *Lexington Herald,* which condemned the SEC and NCAA investigations by recalling a biblical statement of Jesus. "The stone has been cast," the writer lamented, "and Kentucky was the target. Now it becomes the obligation of those who cast it to prove that they are without sin."[6]

I've heard that justification many times during the ensuing years of NCAA enforcement. Another persistent excuse is that a successful team, charged with violations, was turned in by its humiliated opponents to be stopped by unjust penalties. "If you can't beat 'em, suspend 'em," wrote sports columnist Ed Ashford of the *Herald*. "That evidently is the theory of the Southeastern Conference."[7]

Nonetheless, Bernie took a courageous stand against Kentucky's violations by suspending the team from conference basketball for one year. That didn't close them out, however, because they could build a full schedule with teams outside the conference. I was chairman of the NCAA Subcommittee on Infractions, which was willing to back Bernie's stand. But how? There had never been a vote by the NCAA Convention to impose a complete one-year boycott. Ashford sensed our weakness. In his column he crowed that we couldn't terminate Kentucky's NCAA membership for at least two years because the notice date required by the NCAA constitution had passed. "So Kentucky basketball fans now can quit worrying about the possibility of any immediate punitive action of the NCAA," Ashford wrote.[8]

Bernie and I concluded, however, that terminating Kentucky's NCAA membership was not necessary. Our enforcement committee cobbled together a custom-made boycott, based on a constitutional provision that members had agreed to play games only with colleges that abide by NCAA rules.

Bowing to the Truth

We planned to enforce our 1952 death penalty by asking NCAA members to cancel games with Kentucky. That proved unnecessary because of developments that today I remember as courageous acts seldom repeated by later generations of university officials. It happened in a drab meeting room in Chicago's Sherman Hotel, where the NCAA Membership Committee, then the organization's judicial body, met to decide the Kentucky case. The unexpected happened.

Kentucky's representatives, A. D. (Ab) Kirwan and Leo Chamberlain, did not cover up. They didn't need high-powered attorneys to speak for them. Unlike SMU officials three decades years later, they didn't attack the "system" or the NCAA. They stood before the committee and the NCAA Council telling the truth as they knew it.[9]

Ab Kirwan later became my good friend and an outstanding chairman of the NCAA Infractions Committee. He served the University of Kentucky at various times as a history professor, head football coach, and acting president. To me he represented the best attitudes of chivalry and intellectual pursuit.

I telephoned Ab and Leo Chamberlain in their hotel room to tell them first of our admiration for their openness and integrity, then of the committee's verdict: cancellation of all intercollegiate basketball at Kentucky for an entire year.

Ab later told me how he and Chamberlain packed their suitcases in stunned silence and entered a taxi for the ride to the train station. Shocked and struggling to recover his humor, Chamberlain turned to his companion and said: "If we hadn't been so forthright and made such a good impression, Ab, I wonder what the penalty would have been?"

Despite the openness of the Kentucky representatives, we girded ourselves for battle over the shaky death penalty we had carpentered together. NCAA President Willett sent letters to all member institutions urging them to cancel games with Kentucky, explaining that a resolution to make the action mandatory would be voted upon at the January 1953 convention. We expected a fight there.[10]

Meanwhile, Ab and Leo Chamberlain had talked it over on their train ride from Chicago. There was no question the violations had been real. The penalty did seem unduly harsh, but they would recommend that the university accept it. Because of them, the University of Kentucky bowed to the truth.

Had they fought us on the technical, legal grounds so many university-hired lawyers used in later years, Kentucky probably would have carried the day at the convention in January 1953. Instead, their decision to accept the penalty erased the haunting failure of the Sanity Code. It gave a new and needed legitimacy to the NCAA's fledgling effort to police big-time college sports.

Certainly, it did not spell an end to college sports crime—nor an end to it at the University of Kentucky. It did show that people of good will could at least begin the work of keeping the system clean. Central to that victory was the direct line of campus responsibility that the early NCAA made possible.

The NCAA had survived as a vehicle for national order, resolving doubts about whether the colleges themselves were capable of policing intercollegiate athletics. But that first Kentucky case and others like it led certain coaches to demand that we find a permanent way to end all this buying of players—"all this cheating."

To cure the problem, prominent coaches of that day had in mind the full-ride grant-in-aid, John Hannah's "athletic scholarship," magnified and made legal for all NCAA institutions. The recruiting wars and operating costs were about to escalate.

Bucks on the Table

The 1950s basketball scandal is the best-known segment of the University of Kentucky case, but that wasn't its only legacy.

While public attention had fastened on the Wildcat basketball scandal, Paul (Bear) Bryant, as head football coach at Kentucky, had set out to disprove conventional wisdom that a strong football program could not survive on the same campus with strong basketball.

While at Kentucky, Bryant roiled athletics sensibilities by prospecting for players far across state lines and conference boundaries, demonstrating how truly national recruiting had become. Ohio, Pennsylvania, and the Chicago area were clearly marked on Bear's recruiting map.

There was evidence of NCAA violations by Bryant simultaneous with those of Coach Rupp. One of our investigators recorded complaints by Ohio State coaches, particularly Ernie Godfrey, that Bryant's representatives were trying to buy one of the state's best high school prospects who lived in Conneaut, Ohio. The report said the Kentucky recruiters left $1,000 in $20 bills at the prospect's home, where he lived with his widowed mother.

However much his infractions may have matched some of Rupp's, Bear Bryant left Kentucky relatively unscathed because of the public's and our own preoccupation with the basketball problems. He took a new coaching job at Texas A&M, where he would soon become involved in new NCAA rules violations.

History does repeat itself. Basketball star Cliff Hagan, who was an All-American in 1952, became Kentucky's athletics director in 1975. In 1989, exactly 359 NCAA infractions cases after the 1952 Kentucky boycott decision, the Kentucky program was hit with major infractions charges.[11] The new case had similar ingredients, including an undercover payment of $1,000 in cash to one recruit via overnight delivery service.

The *Lexington Herald Leader* exposed the 1980s problems in a hard-hitting series. Consistent with the NCAA's philosophy of the times, the NCAA Committee on Infractions asked the university to investigate.

University officials telephoned some witnesses quoted in the newspaper articles. Others who could not be contacted by phone were sent a letter—written by a top university official—containing the following peculiar statement: "In order for us to complete our investigation, it is necessary for us to interview you regarding the article, or obtain your refusal to be interviewed. In an effort to assist you in making this determination, I am enclosing a list of questions we would like to ask you."[12]

What did the University of Kentucky really want—the interview itself or the written refusal to be interviewed? Even though vital witnesses had apparently talked to the newspaper reporters, they did not talk to the university. They did not talk to NCAA investigators.

Still, there was enough evidence of problems to convince the Committee on Infractions to impose a public reprimand as punishment in March 1988. Cliff Hagan was relieved of his duties as

Kentucky athletics director in November. The *Lexington Herald Leader* was deluged with protests by Wildcat fans, many of whom canceled subscriptions.

Notes

1. NCAA, Proceedings of the 44th Annual NCAA Convention, New York City, January 14, 1950.
2. Walter Byers, Letter of Contract, September 19, 1951.
3. NCAA Subcommittee on Infractions, Report to the NCAA Membership Committee, September 20–21, 1952; NCAA Membership Committee, meeting minutes, January 6, 1953.
4. Ibid.
5. Ibid.
6. Editorial, *Lexington Herald*, August 13, 1952.
7. Ed Ashford, *Lexington Herald*, August 12, 1952.
8. Ed Ashford, *Lexington Herald*, September 16, 1952.
9. NCAA Council, meeting minutes, October 14–16, 1952.
10. Hugh C. Willett and Earl S. Fullbrook, circular letter, October 31, 1952; NCAA, Resolution no. 1, 47th NCAA Convention, January 8–10, 1953.
11. NCAA, Enforcement Summary (concerning public disciplinary actions from October 16, 1952, to February 1, 1993).
12. NCAA, University of Kentucky Infractions Report, March 3, 1988.

Chapter 5

Full Rides in the Name of Amateurism

Small Hands, Small Feet

During the 1930s and early 1940s, it was not uncommon for an alumnus to adopt a local high school athlete and "put him through college." The alumnus, proud of his own school, came to know a gifted high school prospect, established a friendship with the young man's parents, and helped the youngster attend the sponsor's alma mater. It was considered a decent thing to do.

That's how many of the earliest and best players attended college, including the renowned All-American Tom Harmon, who went from the Chicago area to the University of Michigan.[1]

The colleges then banned this practice, claiming it was "pay for play" and inconsistent with the amateurism espoused by Teddy Roosevelt and Captain Pierce. The athletics world of the 1940s and 1950s was populated with college people who believed that patriots out-fought mercenaries in the real world. I was one of them. For years I argued college teams should be made up of patriots, not mercenaries. I believed college students playing solely for the honor and joy of it would be good for the country's future.

Nevertheless, in 1956 the colleges, acting through the NCAA in the name of "amateurism," installed their own pay system called the athletics grant-in-aid or athletics "scholarship." This originally was designed to eliminate the need for booster payments. In the end it proved far more professional than anything the players of the 1940s experienced. For all its noble purpose, the grant-in-aid system didn't stop the surreptitious, private payments that today still cause the knottiest enforcement problems for collegiate sports.

I was in the middle of all this as college leaders fought it out—beginning with my own experience as an athlete. I had played football at Kansas City's Westport High School, with little size, average talent, but lots of spirit. Despite a serious ankle injury in my junior year, I was named All-City center in 1938, my senior year.

In those days, most college grants for run-of-the-mill talent amounted to college-paid tuition and fees with a job to cover room and board. I received such an offer from the celebrated Don Faurot, the University of Missouri's head football coach, but I decided on Rice University in Houston because of my father's belief that Texas and Houston would be the business world's new frontier.

In 1938 Coach Jimmy Kitts had taken the Rice team to the Cotton Bowl, where the Owls beat the University of Colorado and its great All-American halfback, Byron (Whizzer) White, by a score of 28-14. The nation's leading college running back and scorer in 1937, an All-Pro performer, and a Rhodes scholar, Byron White went on to be appointed to the Supreme Court by John Kennedy in 1962.

On the Rice campus in the summer of 1939, I took my press clippings and went to see Coach Kitts in his sparsely furnished, cinder-block office, hoping I could talk him into providing that day's version of an athletics scholarship. Jimmy Kitts liked big football players, big linemen in particular. He sat behind his battered wooden desk, surveying me critically.

"Let me look at your hands," he said.

I held out my hands.

"Take off your shoes and socks," he told me.

I complied.

"Put your feet up here."

I placed them on the desk top. The sight of the bare feet troubled him.

"You know, young man," he said, "you're never going to get any bigger than you are right now."

The technique was that of an order buyer at a cattle sale appraising the growth potential of a feeder steer. Sadly, I hadn't measured up. The coach told me he wouldn't provide the scholarship starting that fall, but he wanted me to try out with the fresh-man team.

"If you make it, you'll get the scholarship," he said.

After three weeks on the Rice football field, I reinjured my ankle, ending my prospects of becoming the smallest lineman on the Rice varsity. That was the athletics scholarship system as I saw it at the time of my near miss in 1939.

Birth of the "Student–Athlete"

In the wider world a few years later, offers were skyrocketing for the best athletes as they were released from the services after World War II. Many of them were older and more experienced, having played on military-sponsored teams. Free-wheeling recruiting was at its zenith. Air travel was turning regional recruiting and sched-uling into national enterprises, beyond the enforcement reach of the respective regional conferences.

The NCAA's 1948 Sanity Code included a uniform, national financial aid rule.[2] Under the Sanity Code, a student-athlete could receive tuition and fees if he showed financial need and met the school's ordinary entrance requirements; this amounted to a merit award for athletic ability.

He could receive a scholarship exceeding tuition and fees *re-gardless* of need if he ranked in the upper 25 percent of his high school graduating class or maintained a B average in college. In either case the money could not be withdrawn if the student de-cided not to play. Athletes frequently worked on campus or at local jobs in town to pay for their room and board.

Enforcement of the Sanity Code had failed in January 1950, however, when supporting member colleges failed to obtain the necessary two-thirds majority to expel seven admitted violators. This left the NCAA with an unenforceable rule and no effective influence on the colleges' compensation practices.

Led by southern institutions, many NCAA colleges continued to denounce the Sanity Code concept. They believed the well-endowed and better-known schools of the Ivy League and Big Ten already had an advantage and would circumvent the restrictive measures of such a code through secret gifts from their richer alumni. The Ivy League, supported by the Big Ten, opposed the Southern, Southeastern, and Southwest conferences in their efforts to bury permanently the Sanity Code and establish a full-ride grant-in-aid system. It was an emotional fight, a sort of reverse rerun of the Civil War.

Great black athletes—including those from the South who played at northern colleges—were earning All-America honors, yet most southern universities found them unacceptable as varsity players or even as students. The South wanted to use the grant-in-aid to plunder the rich resources of white athletes in other parts of the country.

So the battle was joined between those who believed athletes should meet scholarship standards similar to those of other students, and those who believed athletes should get their education free, including room and board and incidental expenses (a full ride), regardless of their academic skills or financial need.

Bill Alexander of Georgia Tech, who had been college football's coach of the year in 1942, bitterly opposed the academically oriented Sanity Code. He importuned his northern colleagues to adopt the grant-in-aid system. He told all those who would listen that a grant-in-aid system providing an athlete with a free education would eliminate the need for booster payments to athletes. "We'll get rid of all this cheating and outside payments," he predicted.[3] The South, with support from many colleges north of the Mason-Dixon line, was headed for a win in what I now consider one of the three or four most important decisions in the history of intercollegiate sports. The Sanity Code was officially buried in 1951. There was no meaningful national regulation on the books.

The major conferences, with similar rules but multifaceted interpretations, tried unsuccessfully to keep the peace for a few years, but soon a majority of college leaders was ready for new national controls.

In the five years of fiery debate after 1951, former Sanity Code supporters labeled the emerging grant-in-aid system "pay for play." These arguments became muted, however, as more and more colleges went to grant-in-aid funding to meet the competition. It was then that they came face to face with a serious, external threat that prompted most of the colleges to unite and insist with one voice that, grant-in-aid or not, college sports still were only for "amateurs."

That threat was the dreaded notion that NCAA athletes could be identified as *employees* by state industrial commissions and the courts.

We crafted the term *student-athlete,* and soon it was embedded in all NCAA rules and interpretations as a mandated substitute for such words as players and athletes. We told college publicists to speak of "college teams," not football or basketball "clubs," a word common to the pros.

I suppose none of us wanted to accept what was really happening. That was apparent in behind-the-scenes agonizing over the issue of workmen's compensation for players. I had reluctantly accepted the professed purpose of the full-ride grant-in-aid as a device to clean up sports. I was shocked that outsiders could believe that young men on grants-in-aid playing college sports should be classified as workers.

The argument, however, was compelling. In a nutshell: the performance of football and basketball players frequently paid the salaries and workmen's compensation expenses of stadium employees, field house ticket takers, and restroom attendants, but the players themselves were not covered. Even today, the university's player insurance covers medical expenses for athletes, but its workmen's compensation plan provides no coverage for disabling injuries they may suffer. There is limited disability insurance available through the NCAA.

With grants-in-aid increasingly in vogue in the 1950s, college officials found that the term *employee* was being interpreted by state officials applying state laws in the interests of the people, not college faculty representatives and athletics directors interpreting college rules in the interests of the college. One typical state law of that era provided that an employee is "any person who engages to furnish his services for a remuneration, subject to the direction and control of an employer."[4] Two Colorado cases demonstrated the schizophrenia of the courts over this question.

The Meal Ticket

A 1953 case was filed by a player named Nemeth, who was injured during spring football practice at the University of Denver. Nemeth had not been awarded a football grant-in-aid but, after proving himself on the field, was given free housing for taking care of the furnace and cleaning the sidewalks. He got free meals in the cafeteria in exchange for keeping gravel and litter off the campus tennis courts. The appeal reached the Colorado Supreme Court, which pointed out that one witness had testified: "If you worked hard [in football], you got a meal ticket." Another testified that "the man who produced in football would get the meals and a job." The football coach stated that meals and the job ceased when the student was cut from the football squad.

The court ruled that the state Industrial Commission's award to Nemeth was correct, since "Nemeth was an employee of the university and sustained an accidental injury arising out of and in the course of his employment."[5]

Not long after, a Colorado case with similar elements hatched a diametrically opposite result. A widow applied for workmen's compensation death benefits after her husband, Ray H. Dennison, died of a head injury while playing football on the Fort Lewis A&M team.

Dennison had received a tuition waiver or "scholarship" for playing football and was paid for "work" on the college farm. The Colorado Supreme Court stated that the only evidence he was an employee was testimony by the player's coach: "Ray wanted to play football, and he had a job in town at a filling station that would require more time. I asked him if he could get a job that would make him as much as he made at the filling station ... would he play football, and he said yes."

Ray Dennison won from Fort Lewis the same deal I had sought

nearly twenty years earlier from Jimmy Kitts at Rice—tuition and fees for playing football, plus a "work job" for room and board.

Still, the Supreme Court reversed the Industrial Commission's award of death benefits to the widow because, it said, there was no evidence of a contract for hire or that his employment by the university would have changed had he quit football. Particularly significant was the court's argument that the college received no benefit from Dennison's activities, "since the college was not in the football business and received no benefit from this field of recreation."

"In fact," the court decision continued, "the state-conducted institution, supported by taxpayers, could not as a matter of business enter into the maintenance of a football team for the purpose of making a profit directly or indirectly out of the taxpayers' money."[6]

A lawyer in the NCAA's Kansas City law firm reviewed the two Colorado court decisions and said to me at the time: "A cynic might opine that football is a business at the University of Denver but only an extracurricular activity at Fort Lewis A&M."

I wonder what that same court's decision would have been if Ray Dennison, receiving a Big Eight Conference full ride, had died in the 1990 Orange Bowl, as Colorado lost to Notre Dame in a game sponsored by Federal Express for a rights payment of $2,035,411, televised by NBC for $6,150,000, watched by 74,705 spectators who paid $2,140,870 for tickets. The gross take split among the not-for-profit colleges and Orange Bowl committee was $10,765,859.[7]

Nonetheless, in the 1950s even with the workmen's compensation struggle still in doubt, advocates of the full ride eagerly pushed ahead to have the practice sanctified by the NCAA as a replacement for the Sanity Code.

As the debate peaked in the mid-1950s, the NCAA president, Clarence T. (Pop) Houston of Tufts University, did not believe in the full-ride concept. He was a lawyer by training and a quick-witted man. His skeptical view at the 1956 NCAA Convention was that if the big colleges thought nationally certified grants for athletes would cure under-the-table alumni subsidies, so be it.

His running mate, NCAA Secretary-Treasurer Ralph W. Aigler, a University of Michigan law faculty member, also did not like the full-ride grant. But he too was willing to go along as an elected official of all NCAA colleges.

We may have taken refuge in Ralph Waldo Emerson's thought that since all life is an experiment, "the more experiments you make, the better." Eventually, Pop Houston, Ralph Aigler, and I came to believe that the full-ride grant was a worthwhile experiment. I think it reflected the best intentions of college leaders dissatisfied with the conditions of the day.

More suspicious (and probably wiser) was a law professor from the University of Minnesota, Henry Rottschaefer. Smoking his meerschaum pipe in scholarly contemplation, he dueled jocularly with Ralph Aigler and said: "We both know this is a mistake. It would be much better for us to live with the evils we know instead of creating a host of new problems, the evils of which we know not."

Despite Henry's argument, the 1956 NCAA Convention took the final step, officially changing the organization's constitution to permit schools to pay to both the rich and the poor—regardless of need, regardless of academic potential or lack thereof—all "commonly accepted educational expenses" for the undergraduate athlete.

The following year those expenses were defined as tuition, fees, room and board, books, and $15 per month for nine months for laundry money. This compensation package represented an arbitrary but uniquely lucrative allowance at the time, all dedicated to amateurism. The rationale was that if a player received only expenses, even though it was more than other students received, he was not being paid to perform. An abrupt about-face thus had been accomplished from the 1948 Sanity Code to the 1956 full ride, and proponents swore it had been done to clean up college sports and establish true amateurism.

All sorts of safety proscriptions were added to the rule. Grants-in-aid could be awarded for up to four years; grants could not be withdrawn if the recipient chose not to play. Recruiting coaches could not *promise* a high school prospect financial assistance (they could only recommend the recruit to the university scholarship committee). The regular scholarship committee, which awarded aid to all students, must fix the amount and approve the application for each athletics grant. And so on.

In 1956 few college officials grasped the full implications of the grant-in-aid as it was enacted. Coach Fritz Crisler of Michigan was one of the few. He immediately recognized truths I didn't see. Fritz warned at the time that his Wolverines could play the money game with anybody in the country, "but a lot of good programs are going to mortgage their integrity by raising money from alumni" to pay for grants-in-aid, not only in football but also the other sports.

Twenty-six years later, Bob Hitch testified to the Crisler prophecy. As Southern Methodist University's athletics director, Hitch explained that it was impossible to run a spotless athletics program. "There are too many people outside the university [who help]," he said. "We need their help. We'll accept $1.5 million of boosters' money this year at SMU." He added that the donors wanted to tell him how to run the athletics department.[8] Even as he said it, the SMU football program was out of control, marching toward an NCAA death penalty.

Indeed, the full-ride grant did not achieve its announced purpose to stop "all this cheating and outside payments," as Bill Alexander had promised. It only intensified that problem. The NCAA, in effect, had put in place a nationwide money-laundering scheme. Alumni and boosters could give their money to the colleges for transmission to the players, but they no longer could give their money directly to the athletes or their parents.

Fritz Crisler's consistent criticism was dismissed, I suppose, because Michigan was winning—doing well without grants-in-aid. Opponents believed they could overtake Michigan under a uniform full-ride system and that Fritz was merely trying to protect Michigan's advantage. That turned out not to be so. Coach Crisler retired after the Wolverines' 1948 Rose Bowl victory and 18 years as a head coach with a .768 record, including a .806 average at Michigan for 10 years. Two decades later, Bo Schembechler, under the grant-in-aid system, coached 27 years and closed out with a .796 winning percentage after 21 years at Michigan (1969–89).

So much for the cynics of that day. I believe Fritz was sincere because he saw the new grant-in-aid policy as threatening for a far more important reason. We were forswearing old amateur principles without admitting it. "We're saying that these youngsters are amateurs," he argued to many of us, "and nobody should be permitted to professionalize them except the colleges. The *colleges* can pay them to play."

The president of a sister Big Ten university agreed with Crisler on the pay issue but echoed the Bill Alexander argument about cleaning up college sports. Writing to all Big Ten presidents and the conference commissioner, Virgil M. Hancher of the University of Iowa in the winter of 1957 said the full-ride grant "will make the rules so fair and equitable, so clear and understandable that an unintentional violation of them is almost impossible." As to paying students for talent, he cited the colleges' recruiting and compensation packages for research and graduate assistants, and then reported that the editor of the student newspaper was paid $720 per year.[9]

A California lawsuit in 1963 exposed the vulnerability of the colleges' pay-for-play rationale. A California State Polytechnic college football player, Edward Gary Van Horn, had been killed in a 1960 plane crash near Toledo, Ohio, during a team trip. The state Industrial Accident Commission ruled he was not a university employee, despite evidence to the contrary. The case was appealed.

His father had testified that his married son quit football because he needed to work for money to support his family, then took the game up again, as the boy himself said, when he got "a pretty good deal to play football."

Van Horn had reported to his wife the coach's promise that if he would resume playing football, he would receive $50 at the beginning of each school quarter and $75 rent money during the season. In ruling on the appeal, the California Second District Court of Appeals pointed out that only those who played on the team received athletics scholarships.

"The coach, with whom it was shown that decedent made the alleged contract, testified at length," the court stated, "yet nowhere in his testimony is there a denial by him that he made a contract with decedent. ...

"The only inference to be drawn from the evidence is that decedent received the 'scholarship' because of his athletic prowess and participation. The form of remuneration is immaterial."[10] The appeals court sent the case back to the Industrial Accident Commission for action on behalf of the widow.[11]

The California case "deeply concerned" the colleges, as Robert F. Ray of the University of Iowa, NCAA president at the time, and Everett D. (Eppy) Barnes of Colgate University, secretary-treasurer, said in a report to NCAA members in December 1964.

Bob Ray, Eppy, and I had pondered the issue at length. We agreed the NCAA's major athletics universities must change their course in handling financial assistance for athletes or serious problems lay ahead.

Bob and Eppy advised the colleges that, in order to avoid inclusion of athletes under workmen's compensation, the college should make certain "that no employment relationship was created between the institution and the student-athlete involving a duty to participate in athletics."

Some colleges were offering only one-year grants to recruits, who were being wooed away by colleges offering "no-cut" four-year grants. To offset the potential talent drain, many schools making one-year grant offerings stated that the grants would be renewed so long as the student continued in intercollegiate athletics. These oral and written commitments were perilously close to employment contracts. Bob and Eppy suggested such language be avoided and the following text be used.

"This award is made in accordance with the provisions of the Constitution of the [NCAA] pertaining to the *principles of amateurism* [emphasis added], sound academic standards, and financial aid to student athletes. ... Your acceptance of the award means that you agree with these principles and are bound by them."[12]

That approach may have enabled the colleges to hold off demands by injured athletes for workmen's compensation at the time, but the NCAA approach didn't help the one-year recruiters, who believed the four-year scholarship colleges had too big an advantage. The greatest hostility existed along the Oklahoma-Texas state line, with the Sooners from Norman bound by a Big Eight Conference rule limiting awards to one year, while the Texas Longhorns offered four-year grants.

Such hostility was one motivation for a not-so-subtle campaign among big-time coaches and athletics directors to place control of athletes' grants in the hands of coaches instead of scholarship committees. The well-intentioned restraints put in place when the full ride was accepted by NCAA colleges soon would be swept aside in the 1970s by permissive NCAA legislation and by coaches wheeling and dealing in the real world of recruiting. The law of survival quickly dictated that the colleges' money for full rides should go only to players who help the team.

Contributing to all this during the 1960s and 1970s were the escalating rewards received by the colleges for winning. An ever-rising flood of television money began pouring into collegiate sports. New money came in such proportions that the colleges abandoned one restraint after another, coveting the millions of new dollars and excited at being a part of big-time entertainment.

Notes

1. Information for this account was drawn from conversations with H. O. Crisler, University of Michigan; Commissioner Kenneth L. Wilson, Big Ten Conference; and Donald B. Canham, University of Michigan.
2. NCAA, Official NCAA Handbook on the Interpretation and Administration of Article III of the NCAA Constitution and Executive Regulation IV "pertaining to the 'Sanity Code.'"
3. Confirmed in conversations with David M. Nelson, University of Delaware, NCAA football rules historian; David M. Nelson, interviews with the author, October 11 and November 21, 1988.
4. C. H. Blumenfeld, letter citing the Oregon law to Glenn W. Holcomb, Oregon State University, January 29, 1965.
5. Marcus L. Plant, NCAA Appendix AA—Per Minute No. 7, Application of Workmen's Compensation Laws to Student Athletes Receiving Financial Assistance in College, July 1964.
6. Ibid.

7. Orange Bowl Management Committee, report to the NCAA on 1990 Orange Bowl game, April 9, 1990.
8. Robert L. Hitch, *NCAA News,* February 28, 1982.
9. Virgil M. Hancher, letter to President John A. Hannah, Michigan State University, February 11, 1957.
10. Annulment by Second District Appellate Court, State of California, of Decision by the State Industrial Accident Commission That the Award of a College Scholarship for Reasons of Athletic Ability Did Not Constitute Employment, August 21, 1963.
11. Plant, Appendix AA.
12. Robert L. Ray and Everett D. Barnes, memorandum to NCAA membership, December 21, 1964.

Chapter 6 — The Explosion of Growth

The jet airplane and coast-to-coast television took college sports from the campus into the biggest arenas and coliseums in the country, turning an extracurricular student activity into big business. While the airplane shrank the recruiting map, television brought fame and fortune in such proportions that the colleges simply were not able to handle the good times.

I was privileged to work with the first great impresario of sports television, Tom Gallery, a big, jolly Irishman. Representing NBC, he offered the first NCAA football television contract in 1952 for a dozen "Game of the Week" shows at a total rights fee of $1,144,000. We gladly accepted. Some 30 years later, I was also there for the last one—a multiyear, multinetwork deal for $281,196,000. Through the years virtually all of the escalating TV payments went to the colleges.

What a Job!

The television experience began for me in 1949 as I drove each Sunday to a westside Chicago film laboratory to prepare highlight movies of Big Ten Conference football games for midwest distribution. At the time, I was working for both Commissioner Tug Wilson of the Big Ten Conference and the NCAA.

During Sunday evenings, I ran through countless yards of 16-mm black-and-white film from Saturday's games to select the best plays. Then the lab editor made a work copy of the edited version, which I viewed for purposes of writing the script. The announcer would then put a voice on the master print, the lab would hurriedly print the 26-1/2-minute Big Ten highlight film, and copies would be dispatched to subscribing stations in the seven-state Big Ten territory. We used everything—buses, trains, cars, and planes—to deliver the prints.

This was syndication at its beginning and in its smallest form, moving Saturday's best plays to midwestern television screens for showing the following Wednesday or Thursday.

To me, it was a blast. So I worked on weekends—what else were weekends for? In those days I never thought about where I was headed or what I wanted to become. I was happy to have a job. And what a job! But bigger things were happening just out of my view.

Tom Gallery, a free-wheeling promoter in the style of P. T. Barnum, had begun making deals. Earlier Tom had been an actor, once portraying the pilot of a crashed aircraft in a Rin Tin Tin film for RKO. The super canine was supposed to grab a special harness Tom wore and drag him from the burning plane. The dog, presumably by mistake, bit his ear. That convinced Tom he should leave acting. So he turned to assorted promotions—boxing, football, golf, and baseball.

In the late 1940s sponsors and ad agencies usually bought the rights to sports events and then purchased time on television to show them. Working for Dumont Television in 1950, Gallery contracted for the entire Notre Dame football schedule, hired Mel Allen to handle play-by-play, and sold the package to Chevrolet. Later, as an employee of Dan Topping's New York Yankees, he sold Yankee television rights to Ballantine beer. Meanwhile, Dumont had acquired the rights to University of Pennsylvania football.

It was NBC, however, that was destined to be the early network sports leader and Gallery became their main man. Gen. Robert C. Sarnoff hired Tom from the New York Yankees, and he became director of sports for NBC radio and television in 1952.[1] Tom's efforts at televising professional sports flustered no one; the pro owners loved it.

But I heard numerous complaints from college athletics directors across the country about the television involvement of Penn and Notre Dame. Athletics administrators instinctively feared televised college football. They contended it would reduce attendance, and the more powerful teams' telecasts would diminish the programs of the less successful teams.

Ralph Furey of Columbia University, Tom J. Hamilton at the University of Pittsburgh, and Willis O. Hunter of USC urged the NCAA to declare a moratorium on television-rights contracting until a national study was completed and controls instituted.

The NCAA membership approved their suggestions, 161 to 7, in January 1951. After some experimentation, the NCAA "Game of the Week" plan featuring a dozen nationally televised games was developed—with Penn and Notre Dame strongly objecting. The idea was that the NCAA would put college football on television in limited quantities, while we tried to understand this phenomenal combination of video/audio presentation. The vote to proceed was 163 to 8 in favor at the January 1952 NCAA Convention.

We also wanted to give the lesser athletics programs an occasional chance on the new medium. That notion came out of a hotel room in Chicago, where we all gathered convivially one evening in early 1952 after a daylong meeting of the NCAA TV Committee.

Among those present were Coach Fritz Crisler of Michigan and E. L. (Dick) Romney, who had coached football at Utah State for 29 years before becoming commissioner of the Mountain States Conference (predecessor to today's Western Athletic Conference). Naturally, Fritz's great Michigan program had no need to share television coverage with more obscure teams, particularly in the sparsely populated Rocky Mountain area. Still, Dick tried the idea on him.

"Why couldn't each of the eight NCAA districts be accorded a minimum of one football game on the national program?" Dick asked.

Fritz nursed his Scotch highball and stared at Dick. It seemed long minutes until he answered, though the pause surely didn't last 15 seconds. "That's all right with me," Fritz said. "Our great game should be preserved as a national game."

Crisler, a product of Amos Alonzo Stagg and the University of

Chicago, believed with religious fervor in the importance of college football and the need to preserve it in a pristine form for future generations. Michigan's position was critical, and Crisler's word swayed the committee. A principle was put in place that served as the basic foundation for more than 30 years of NCAA television controls: limiting the number of televised games for the strongest and distributing the TV opportunities so all sections of the country were represented.

In stark contrast to Crisler's philosophy and Michigan's announced stand, Notre Dame fought the television agreement from day one. Before television Notre Dame had broadcast its games on its own radio network. Why should it now surrender dreams of its own national TV network? Especially since Notre Dame's overall university budget relied on profits from its athletics department.

In the early 1950s the Notre Dame president, the Rev. John J. Cavanaugh, manned the fortress to battle NCAA control of sports television. Serving beside him as Notre Dame faculty representative was the Rev. Theodore Hesburgh, who became president in 1952. In that post he used his considerable influence over 34 years to obtain maximum TV revenue for Notre Dame. (In 1991, when he was 74 years old, Father Hesburgh was appointed as board member of the Knight Foundation to help launch a new reform movement for college sports.)

I remember a Chicago meeting in the early 1950s arranged to placate Notre Dame. We had hired Joseph L. Rauh, Jr., an eastern lawyer who later achieved national prominence in Democratic Party circles, to help us with our TV affairs. He listened to the Notre Dame arguments and finally said: "If President Cavanaugh doesn't believe we even have the right to administer the television plan, why debate the merits of the plan itself?"

Rauh's statement was a harbinger of events more than 30 years later when Notre Dame was the behind-the-scenes player that held the College Football Association together. CFA members, all big-time football institutions, arranged an antitrust lawsuit that won a 7-2 decision before the Supreme Court in 1984 declaring our plan an illegal cartel and dismantling NCAA controls.

Notre Dame's Golden Halo

After my unsuccessful engagement with Father Cavanaugh, I quickly found myself at odds with his successor, Father Hesburgh, and Notre Dame's executive vice president, the Reverend Edmund P. "Ned" Joyce—not only about television but other matters as well. Father Joyce sincerely and forcefully advocated honor and integrity in athletics. Still, I wondered whether his negative attitude toward the NCAA arose, in part, from minor penalties we had levied against Notre Dame.[2]

The NCAA Council voted in 1953 to reprimand and censure Notre Dame for trying out athletes, which Notre Dame vigorously denied. As he left the NCAA Council hearing room, Father Joyce appeared upset by some of the skeptical questions asked of him by council members. Then I noticed a smile on the face of the Reverend Wilfred H. Crowley, faculty representative of the University of Santa Clara, who was sitting near me. "Well," Father Crowley said, "he certainly tried to enshrine the Notre Dame helmet with a golden halo."

Notre Dame disputed the NCAA's decision to control football television with even greater vigor. If consistency is a virtue, Notre Dame was singularly virtuous on that count.

We finally overcame the opposition of the University of Pennsylvania and Notre Dame, and the NCAA Convention approved the controlled program that led to the NBC contract in 1952. We worked out the details for the NCAA "Game of the Week" featuring a dozen nationally televised games. The Romney-Crisler allocation of one game to each of the NCAA's eight districts was included. But how would television executives respond to the plan?

"It's gotta work"

One of them could not have been more enthusiastic. That was NBC's Tom Gallery, in those days a round-faced, good-natured man with light Irish skin and a ready laugh. Asa S. Bushnell and I met him in Chicago's Palmer House to tell him about the game-of-the-week concept. Asa was commissioner of the Eastern College Athletic Conference and our New York contact with the TV industry. Gallery bubbled with enthusiasm. "Oh my gawd, it'll be wonderful," he said. "We'll make it work. It's gotta work!"

The first NBC television contract for 1952 was the result. We sealed the $1,144,000 deal with a brief letter and a handshake. So Tom was with us, but would the network higher-ups go along? In past ventures he had suffered much trouble from heel-dragging NBC bosses. Convinced that the potential audience base was too small, they couldn't get excited about his TV sports. Later, Tom told me: "The head of sales came into my office after I was only there a day or two and said, 'I want to straighten you out. We don't want any gawd damn baseball or football on this network. We don't have any clients that would buy it. And don't you be bringing it in.'"

Tom ignored the order. Working out of his hip pocket, recording deals on the back of envelopes, he signed up advertisers and events, arranged for the necessary telephone transmission lines, and dropped the deals on the network czars with a laconic: "Now what are you gonna do about this?" That was the kind of moxie that made it possible for Tom to sell NBC on our football Game of the Week.

After the original NBC-NCAA contract in 1952, we spent two years worrying about declining football attendance. Then it slowly began rising—from 17.3 million at 621 four-year colleges in 1955 to 20.4 million in 1960 and then 29.5 million in 1970.[3] Television seemed to create *more* interest in the stadium sport.

Those of us who worked hard to make football TV controls successful were exuberant about the result. We had chaperoned a match made in heaven: the best of college football on television in limited servings, with more people buying game tickets. This was good for everyone.

Tom had always envisioned the Rose Bowl on television, and he brought his vision to life in a deal with Lathrop K. Leishman, for more than 45 years the benevolent Godfather of the Pasadena classic.

"My gawd, it just had to work," Tom told me of what he considered his happiest deal. "I didn't know how we were going to handle it all, but I knew that the blue sky with white clouds and beautiful flowers, with beautiful girls on the floats, simply had to look wonderful on television. There would even be a great football game. I told Lay [Leishman] it will be one of the great all-time events on television."

Meeting in Los Angeles, Leishman and Gallery struck a deal for $200,000 for the first television and continued radio rights to the Rose Bowl.[4] Almost single-handedly, Tom made NBC the dominant sports network for nearly 15 years. Yet he was never a darling of the corporate executives.

"I really never felt comfortable sitting around places like the 21 Club with them," Tom said. "I knew sports. I adored the people who made it all happen."

Toots Shor's in New York was the place for Tom. That's where you could always find sports writers, pro athletes, fight managers. In my early days as a United Press sportswriter in New York, I went there to listen and learn. Toots, a man of girth, liked to insult his regular customers by calling them "crumb bums." For the jock crowd, including Tom Gallery, it was the place to be.

The House That Arledge Built

NBC's sports dominance lasted well into the 1960s. By that time Tom Gallery was being reined in by corporate executives. Back-of-the-envelope deals, confirmed by three-paragraph letters, were out.

We were entering a paper world controlled by lawyers and their 40-page contracts. They debated and argued, wrote and rewrote the contracts. Sometimes this went on for as long as two years after the principals had reached basic agreements. Perhaps just because of those corporate reins, Tom found himself less and less able to counter the competition.

In the winter of 1959–60, a supercharged salesman named Edgar J. Scherick plotted to grab the NCAA football television contract away from Tom Gallery. Scherick owned an independent sports TV agency. He had done business with Tom Moore, head of the ABC television network, which then had a sports radio department but was a nonentity in sports TV. Scherick, a nearly irresistible force, convinced Moore that he could snare NCAA football from NBC. Moore hired him for the job.

We scheduled a session at a midtown New York hotel to take contract bids for the 1960 and 1961 football seasons. Tom Gallery's approach was to have his bid letter typed in the office but leave the dollar amount blank, to be filled in later by hand. All bidding parties were to be in the hotel room at the same time and hand the bids to the NCAA TV Committee. They would later be informed of our decision.

Gallery arrived, looked around, and saw none of his familiar competitors. Secure in the belief that he was the only bidder, Gallery filled in a modest NBC offer, signed the letter, and handed it to the committee.

But the canny Scherick had arranged for an unknown from the ABC business department to present the ABC bid. The straw man, Stan Frankel, carried with him a high-bid letter and a low-bid letter.[5] After Tom handed in his letter, the man walked up to the table and presented the ABC high bid. ABC bought the rights for $3.1 million a year for two years. I hated to see Tom lose, but I liked the money.

Scherick, now in high favor at ABC, hired Jim Spence in August 1960. He lured Roone Arledge from NBC, where Roone was producing a puppet show called "Hi Mom." Chuck Howard and Chet Simmons were brought on board. ABC started college football telecasting that fall.

Moore wanted a sports program to follow football. Scherick told Arledge to put together a continuing sports series featuring championship sports events from around the world. Arledge returned with the "Wide World of Sports" concept, which began broadcasting in April 1961. Moore told Scherick: "We need 40 percent advertising support to air the show."

"Easy," Scherick replied.

So he sold TV options for the 1961 NCAA football TV series, a red-hot item at the time, on the basis that the advertisers would buy commercials the previous spring in "Wide World." ABC Sports was off and galloping, and "Wide World of Sports" was destined to become television's most successful sports anthology. Scherick moved on to new challenges. Arledge became close to Tom Moore, who in 1968 picked Roone over Chet Simmons to head up ABC Sports.

Arledge quickly learned that catching up to Gallery and NBC wasn't all that easy. Entering the decade of the 1960s, eight of TV's most-watched sports programs were on NBC; CBS had two, ABC none. By 1972 the scorecard for the top 10 attractions was: NBC, five; CBS, three; ABC, two.

As dominant sports television executives, Roone and Tom Gallery were much alike in those early years. Both were enthusiasts. Both grew impatient with the big egos and procrastinations of corporate insiders. They bemoaned the political maneuvering for network power that drained energy better used for planning television's seemingly unlimited future.

Both understood that the American people were fascinated by power struggles. Sports showcased the competitive urge, with a definite winner, a definite loser, and an allegiance of fans to their teams that surpasses most human loyalties.

In his approach to sports, Roone maintained a sense of conscience that kept him from totally accepting Howard Beale's view of the TV world. Beale, you may recall, was the anchorman in the film *Network,* who claimed, "We're in the boredom-killing business." Beale said television was "...an amusement park, a circus, a carnival, a traveling troop of acrobats."

Arledge believed it was ABC's job to never let the sports viewer be bored, even in lopsided games. Sheer technical mastery helped with that. ABC introduced to sports the instant replay, split-screen coverage, the zoom lens, and hand-held cameras.

The network began producing games with more and more cameras—several on top of the press box, others along the sidelines, in the end zone, suspended from a 150-foot crane overlooking the field. If two cameras were good in the old days, eight had to be better. A man of indefatigable energy, Arledge loved nothing better than to sit at the control panel in the ABC truck at the game site

Curt Gowdy with Roone Arledge, head of ABC Sports. Gowdy (*left*), a noted professional baseball announcer, handled college football play-by-play in the early days for ABC. As a collegiate broadcaster, Gowdy was best known for his announcing of NCAA basketball tournament games and the Rose Bowl, both for NBC.

pushing the buttons and dictating orders through the intercom. Watching him in the ABC truck, I saw a good-humored, hyped-up genius at work—stimulating everybody else by his enthusiasm.

His steady right hand, and a production superstar himself, Chuck Howard worked with Roone and ABC for 26 years. A Duke University alumnus, Chuck was a primary contact for us at ABC. We liked him. He patiently listened to all our complaints, yet had an inner fire that prompted him to tell us straight up when he thought we were wrong.

At the 1976 Olympic Games in Montreal, Roone, then 44 years old, went for a new record, covering the action with 25 ABC-operated cameras. ABC also could tap into the Olympic organization's pool coverage, which provided almost 120 additional cameras covering the expansive scene.[6] Roone's Olympics was a smashing production success.

As the Olympics and television embraced each other, television brought glamour and recognition to many relatively obscure sports. Millions of Americans, including a vast new audience of women, learned that there was more to athletics than the American male's addiction to football, basketball and baseball—gymnastics, to name just one.

I particularly remember Roone as a tough competitor for the U.S. champion night owl award. I did some prowling with him then, but I was out of my class. The night before a telecast, Roone would assemble some ABC compadres and college athletics friends and roam the town, striking up lively conversations. He thought touring the French Quarter in New Orleans with Phil Harris was all the fun anybody needed.

Roone's friends began thinking of excuses to avoid these nocturnal outings. Chuck Howard and certain color announcers like Bud Wilkinson discovered that after a night with Roone, they worked in pain the next day. Whereas Roone—after a few hours of sleep—would bound out of bed fresh as the morning flowers, ready to work a 12-hour day.

And, yes, we drank some whisky in that time. I'm not talking about knocking over bar stools on the way to the men's room, but rather enjoying the fun times when people forget their business demeanor, loosen their ties, and don't record the dialogue.

If in the view of today's pretentious social and political arbiters a couple of drinks and occasional silliness renders you forever ineligible to make sensible judgments, then it disqualifies many of the people I admire—including those who engineered the phenomenal growth of college sports and television.

It was a grand moment when Frank Kriedel, the madcap Manhattan Hotel executive, and Fritz Crisler, then a debonair Princeton football coach, rode a fire truck down Broadway in New York City during the early morning hours. That excursion became part of the folklore of sports. I never understood how Fritz, after a few hours of sleep, could wake up and promptly begin shaving with a straight razor, while I could hardly find the bathroom.

A major sportswriter of the day was the bulky Wilfrid Smith, *Chicago Tribune* sports editor. Wilfrid and I might meet at the

Horseshoe Bar near the Tribune building below Michigan avenue, sitting companionably on our stools like Mutt and Jeff. While Wilfrid drank boilermakers, whisky shots with beer chasers, I worked on my Scotch and water.

Wilfrid supported the good things in sports, suggesting ways I could emphasize the positive and eliminate the negative. Neither of us then took ourselves as seriously as later generations seem to. Today I see much highly advertised self-righteousness but little evidence that the worlds of sports or national policy are populated by leaders of higher standards or more honorable motivation.

The first NCAA headquarters office was established in Kansas City, Missouri, in 1952. We started in a building one block north of the prestigious Hotel Muehlebach and then moved to a building one block south of that landmark hotel. As the TV-fueled boom continued, the NCAA decided to move its offices from cramped, second-floor rooms in Kansas City's downtown Midland building. We acquired 3.4 acres of land in suburban Johnson County, Kansas, and constructed a handsome, 26,900-square-foot national headquarters building at a cost of $1.5 million. Senator James B. Pearson of Kansas, a rare, no-nonsense politician, turned the first shovel of dirt in February 1972, and Roone Arledge later arranged for ABC to televise the building's official opening on April 28, 1973.

The NCAA had always received a percentage of the football contracts we negotiated, ranging from a high of 12 percent the first year, down to 3 percent and then around 4 to 5 percent in most subsequent years. With most NCAA operating income originating from our annual men's basketball tournament, the football television assessment never loomed large in our financing–$6 million to $7 million by the 1980s in budgets of $60 million to $70 million.[7]

We did add a 1 percent extra assessment on football revenues to pay for the new building, unofficially dubbing the resplendent structure "the house that Arledge built."

Some 38 years after I first met Tom Gallery, I called him to say hello. The first thing he wanted to talk about was that NBC–the first and only network to televise his cherished Rose Bowl—had yielded the rights to ABC starting with the 1990 game. "I wake up in the middle of the night thinking about it," he said. "I simply can't believe it."

I reminded Tom that he was the matchmaker during television's whirlwind courtship of college sports in the 1950s. "What do you think about the way the love affair turned out," I asked him.

"Well," he groaned, "it kills me when you see some of the events they put on now, and the gawd-damn announcers don't shut up during baseball, football, and everything else. Three announcers! I could get a gun and go after them."

Despite the irritations he and many other viewers may share on that point, Tom was generally pleased with sports television's swashbuckling maturity. "I'm slow at a lot of things and my memory is left back," he told me. "But, my gawd, I just love to watch the different things now. And, I remember how we started and I'm very much interested in how they have progressed."[8]

Getting Smoked

Tom Gallery was replaced at NBC by Carl Lindemann, who moved from news to become the director of sports. Unlike Tom, Carl was not of the sports world. My first real contact with him was in 1963, when he invited me to join him at the Pump Room of the Ambassador East Hotel (on the near northside of Chicago) with some of his showbiz friends.

At the time I thought, this ain't bad—from Gibbey's restaurant on Clark street to the Pump Room in a little over 10 years. (Even so, I missed Gibbey's, where the sports gab had been as flavorful as the menu's specialty of steak tartare laced with onions.)

Carl ruled NBC Sports for 14 fourteen years (1963–77), a real survivor in a fickle business. He was a shrewd, quick-minded man who kept NBC at the top, fighting toe-to-toe with ABC. For all his initial lack of sports smarts, Carl Lindemann later skinned me in a round of negotiations. We were preparing to renegotiate TV rights for the NCAA basketball tournament in 1975.

Fundamental to any transaction is keeping quiet about what

you, the seller, are actually willing to sell for. If you reveal your asking price too early, you're negotiating only with yourself.

I was too relaxed the second day our group sat down at the table with Carl Lindemann and NBC's top management rep, Al Rush, in the O'Hare Hilton next to Chicago's O'Hare airport. I had worked hard to calculate the potential audience, ratings, commercial minutes available, and key sponsors' interest. After several hours of preliminary sparring, I laid it all out and, violating my own rule, gave them the figure we had to have.

Their faces might have been cast from concrete. Carl turned to Al. Then they both looked to me. Carl shook his head. "I don't know," he said gloomily. "We'll have go up to our room and call New York."

They left quietly, and I knew something was wrong. There hadn't been enough emotion. No arguments. After 30 minutes, they returned to the negotiating table.

"Well," sighed the long-faced Carl, "we had to talk awhile to New York, but they approved it."

The way he said it, I knew I'd been smoked. Nobody's fault but my own. It turned out that I hadn't correctly predicted the phenomenal audience growth for the tournament in the immediate years ahead. It became a profit center for NBC sports the next two years. Who knows how much was left on the table? Carl would never say. I'm not sure he and Al even called New York. Later, I asked Carl about it.

"What did you and Al do," I said, "play gin rummy up in your room?"

Smiling wryly, Carl replied, "And you went through all those rating figures . . . ha!"

All Things Bigger and Better

I tried to make up for my lapse next time around and, in successive negotiations, TV rights for the championship went from $4.0 million in 1977 to $36.6 million in 1987, when television revenues made up 74.6 percent of the tournament's gross.

The 1970s were high growth years. New dollars showed up as

a result of upbeat popularity and widely disbursed publicity exposure. In August 1975 we responded to Japan's growing fascination with the U.S. life style, particularly sports, by signing a licensing agreement with Descente Ltd., Osaka, for use of NCAA marks in Japan, mostly on apparel. The first royalty payment in 1976 was $47,121. (In 1994, the payment was $1.2 million.)

Also, in 1976, college football telecasts were reaching an average of 10 million homes each week. Meanwhile, college basketball in the 1970s emerged as a big-time athletics venture, all the more vivid for television. By 1976 the NCAA basketball tournament was televised for 20 hours, 50 minutes, and reached an estimated average of 7.5 million homes per telecast.[9]

It seemed to me all things were becoming bigger and better. The average weight of the All-America football team moved from 214.5 pounds in 1960 to 226.1 pounds in 1980. Interior All-America linemen ballooned from 227.4 pounds in 1960 to 253.8 in 1980. Points scored by both teams rose from an average of 31.1 per game in 1960 to 41.0 in 1980 while over the same period the collegian's passing completion percentage climbed from 45.4 to 50.0 percent.[10]

By 1974–75 the NCAA certified 11 postseason football bowl games, which generated gross income of $10.6 million and distributed $8.2 million to the participating colleges. By 1989–90 the 18 bowls we certified produced $75.0 million in gross income (the Rose Bowl alone grossing $16.3 million) and returned $58.4 million to the colleges.

Don't be misled. The audience for college sports was big before television. The Ohio State stadium was built in 1922 to hold more than 65,000 people. The Los Angeles Coliseum, built in 1923, held almost 105,000 spectators, and Soldier Field in Chicago held between 110,000 and 120,000 for Notre Dame-USC and Army-Navy games in the late 1920s.[11]

But television profoundly changed the magnitude of the affair. It was an elite, relatively localized phenomenon when 102,000 people cheered the Army-Navy game in Philadelphia on November 29, 1952, as Navy won. It was quite another when sets were switched on in 10 million homes so that perhaps 20 million additional people could cheer for one of the service academies in 1978.[12]

The NCAA's international marketing of its official seal and logo began in 1975 with Descente Ltd., Osaka, Japan. This negotiation involved the NCAA's Walter Byers (*second from right*) and Tom Jernstedt (*right*) and gave the Japanese firm the right to use the NCAA's and selected colleges' logos on various products, primarily wearing apparel.

Intellectuals stirred uneasily in college faculty clubs, exchanging critical comments about what came to be known as the boob tube. They decried overemphasis on sports as preoccupation with mundane matters. They said television would shut off a generation of youth from the process of thought. But for me and many others there was a positive dimension to sports. Certainly, there was joy in it for the players and the millions who watched.

From the 1950s onward, I felt we were on an express elevator ride up with no top floor. I traveled along so excited and enthusiastic I could barely contain myself. It was an explosion of popularity and growth American sports may never see again.

The new money promptly inspired big-time college advocates to new efforts. They wanted to spend the new money—not part of it, *all* of it, *more* than all of it. They wanted rules changes that soon would bring corporate planning and corporate budgets to college football, thus making obsolete all past concepts of how big the big time ought to be.

Notes

1. Tom Gallery, interview with the author, October 19, 1988.
2. Action taken by NCAA Council, August 17, 1953, related to Notre Dame University; identified as Case no. 6 in NCAA Enforcement Summary (concerning public disciplinary actions from October 16, 1952, to October 1, 1983).
3. NCAA, Official 1990 NCAA Football Records Book, August 1990.
4. Lathrop K. Leishman, interview with the author, January 2, 1991.
5. Information for this account and other TV material was drawn from my personal experiences and conversations at the time and subsequently with Roone Arledge, Chuck Howard, and Jim Spence; Chuck Howard, interview with the author, September 3, 1988; Jim Spence, interview with the author, March 4, 1991.
6. Announced ABC coverage of Olympic Games at Montreal, 1976.
7. NCAA, NCAA Television Program Financial Report, June 17, 1982.
8. Gallery, interview.
9. NCAA, Official NCAA Basketball Tournament Committee Records, July 1990.
10. James M. Van Valkenburg, Official NCAA Statistics and Records, July 1994.
11. NCAA, 1990 Football Records Book.
12. Nielsen Media Research, New York, June 13, 1991, confirmed there were 74.5 million television households and the 1978 Army-Navy game televised by ABC achieved a 14.6 Nielsen rating and a 35 percent share.

Chapter 7   The Tug of War

In the early years of this century, Fielding Yost, a role model for the power coaches of future generations, had demolished James B. Angell's idea of limiting the size of the Michigan football program. I doubt that Yost ever imagined how future rules changes would stimulate college football's uncontrollable growth. The NCAA, effective in eliminating the carnage on the playing field that marred the game's reputation in the early days, was unable to rein in the gridiron colossus in later years.

Having won on the issue of "athletic scholarships," the postwar generation of coaches hungered for a whole new menu of rules changes, the most important of which was unlimited or "free" substitution on the playing field.

The practice was first permitted during the college manpower shortages of World War II, presumably to make it possible to continue the game on many campuses. It quickly led to the two-platoon system, teams for offense, teams for defense, and the right to substitute at will. With fewer skilled players available, coaches were dealing with many volunteer players—later to be known as unrecruited "walk-ons"—and the modest-sized coaching staffs at that time found it simpler to organize one-way teams.

When the war ended, some of the veteran coaches—among them General Robert Reese Neyland of Tennessee, one of the great defensive coaches in the history of football—began fighting for a return to a game in which a given set of eleven players had to play both offense and defense.

Seeing it as a holy crusade, the senior coaches of that day thought of themselves as trustees of a sport that was important to the development of character and the future leadership of the country. Repeatedly, I heard them say that the game was for the players;

the coaches were the game's stewards, obligated to pass it on intact to their successors.

In the traditional one-platoon game, the player had to tackle as well as block. If the halfback lost the ball on offense, he had to stay in the game on defense and get it back. If he ran the ball on offense behind great blocking, he had to fight off the other team's blockers on defense and make the tackle. He had to practice against his weakness and prove his endurance.

The aggressive, ambitious younger coaches of the late 1950s thought two-platoon football, with its specialists in kicking, passing, and running, was more exciting and easier to coach. They knew that with persistence—the key word in any football coach's vocabulary—they would get their way on the issue. The choice was crucial for the long-term direction of college athletics—equal in importance to the grant-in-aid fight and as fateful as decisions yet to come concerning academics.

The two-platoon advocates lost in 1953, when a rules change limited players to one game entry per quarter. But the rule was liberalized every year thereafter.

College administrators then mounted a valiant effort to hold the line. The Rev. Wilfred H. Crowley, faculty representative of Santa Clara University and NCAA Executive Committee member, raised the platoon issue at the 1961 NCAA Convention. Santa Clara, once a great name in football, had beaten Louisiana State in back-to-back triumphs in the Sugar Bowl in 1937 and 1938, and then Kentucky in the Orange Bowl in 1950. But Santa Clara could no longer afford the escalating costs associated with larger squads.

Prominent football coaches were shocked that an academician like the articulate Father Crowley would tamper with *their* game. They openly criticized my position in support of the good Father.

In the hallways they grumbled that a faculty rep couldn't tell the difference between the Clark Shaughnessy T and the Notre Dame box formation. More diplomatic in the meeting itself, they argued the convention could express its viewpoint to the rules committee, but a room full of delegates should not try to write playing rules on the convention floor.

At Father Crowley's urging NCAA administrators endorsed

limited substitution, symbolic of smaller squads and fewer coaches. But the football coaches, with scarcely a tip of the helmet to college policy makers, continued their unrelenting campaign for two-platoon football.

The issue reached fever pitch at the 1961 meeting of the NCAA Football Rules Committee at the Monte Carlo Hotel in Miami Beach. David M. Nelson, athletics director and head football coach at the University of Delaware, was in the middle of it.

General Neyland presided as the insurgents argued passionately for free substitution. I had already advised the meeting once again that college administrators—speaking through the NCAA—supported General Neyland in his battle for traditional or two-way football. On the final day, in executive session, the general asked for a motion to adjourn.

Nelson recalls at that point Frank Howard, the coach who laid the foundation for Clemson's long-term football success, jumped up and accused General Neyland of not considering the issue most important to college football, free substitution. The general called for a straw vote to see if there was any sentiment for the concept.

"Eleven of the fourteen members put up their hands," Dave explained, "and when Neyland asked for all those opposed, he put up his hand, then grabbed mine and held it up." Nelson, as brilliant concerning offensive football strategies as Neyland was on defensive play, believed strongly in the one-platoon game anyway. The general got two votes for the price of one, but still far from the majority. Despite that, he announced: "There doesn't seem to be any sentiment for that chickenshit football! Meeting adjourned!"

Dave Nelson said the last he recalls of the session was Frank Howard chasing the general down the hall screaming, "Foul!"[1]

The coaches' persistence paid off; in 1965 they won the struggle. The two-platoon system overtook college football with a vengeance. It was corporate and bureaucratic America at work: a head coach, offensive and defensive coordinators, position coaches, special team coaches, and plenty of recruiting coaches. Sixteen to seventeen coaches with squads of 140 players were not unusual. Teams brought in 50 to 60 grant-in-aid freshmen for a one-year tryout, keeping the best 20 or 30.

While it had seemed merely a quarrel over subparagraphs in a musty rule book, the battle decided the question of how big college football would become. The answer: *Very* big. *Very* expensive.

Today the clock cannot be turned back on the issue of free substitution. The two-platoon system is imbedded in the game—high school, college, and professional. It conveniently spreads coaching responsibility. Head coaches can fire their offensive or defensive coordinators depending upon the perceived problem, thus saving their own jobs—at least for the time being.

The two-platoon system makes teaching simpler and playing the game less complicated. Many performers—for instance, interior defensive linemen—play only one position one way throughout their high school, college, and professional careers. It's a peculiar concept, like permitting one free throw artist to shoot all of the team's free throws, or having unlimited designated hitters in baseball but keeping the best defensive team on the field at all times.

Disturbing terminology also developed. No one seemed to mind. The interior linemen posts, by default, became known as nonskill positions, since coaches referred to positions such as quarterback or wide receiver as the skill positions.

At first glance, a simpler game with one-way players would seem to require fewer instructors. Expansionists had an answer for that: specialists need specialized instruction. This justifies the need for quarterback coaches, receiver coaches, and interior linemen coaches.

All of this means bigger support staffs, larger equipment and travel budgets, TV recorders at practice, VCRs for player film review—and more players! But *no* increased compensation for the players.

In a not-for-profit world where winning is the only barometer of success, cost accounting plays no part in a coach's game plan. There are no price/earnings ratios or per-unit-cost figures by which to evaluate management. No dividends are passed back to stockholders. It's a government-certified, not-for-profit activity. To hell with expenses. Winning the big ones and being ranked Number One is worth whatever it costs.

Even as the big-time advocates were winning the rules battles on grants-in-aid and free substitution, they opened the war on a third front—athletics dormitories. Many college people opposed the athletics dorm—initially dubbed "the zoo" on many campuses—because it further separated athletes from their fellow students. But recruiting coaches, charged with landing the targeted prospects, are always looking for a way to make a better offer.

College recruiters have no equivalent of the talent-balancing NFL draft system, in which great, new players are run through a winnowing system weighted in favor of last year's losing teams and end up in negotiations with one team. In college recruiting, the outstanding high school prospects have most of higher education at their feet. Many of these sought-after high school seniors will tell you that the educational offerings of all the pursuing institutions end up looking much the same. The decision comes down to recruiting salesmanship, the chemistry of the personalities, the success of the athletics program, and "the deal."

Athletics dorms became part of that deal. Texas A&M was among the earliest to escalate the dormitory armaments race during the 1950s when it built one that included television sets and a swimming pool. The Texas school had set a new standard for their recruiting competitors. Complaints from rival coaches proliferated.

In the late 1970s I received a call from Robert C. James, commissioner of the Atlantic Coast Conference. Bob was irate about the University of Kentucky's new basketball dorm. Kentucky had taken a local private mansion and remodeled and redecorated it into a lavish "rich man's club," in Bob's words. Because of its ski lodge motif, it became known locally as the Wildcat Lodge.[2]

We forced Kentucky to make the place less luxurious, arguing that these accommodations violated the "special benefit" rule that prohibited benefits that were not available to the student body generally. The negotiations reached ludicrous extremes: two players to a bedroom, no private bathrooms, no gold faucets—things like that. Fifteen years later, Otis Singletary, longtime president of Kentucky, still called the mansion negotiations "the pickiest thing" the NCAA ever did.

"Don't your investigators have anything better to do?" he asked me during a meeting of college presidents who were discussing, among other things, the escalating costs of big-time athletics.

On the other end of the spectrum, even cash-poor, debt-ridden Kansas State entered the dormitory sweepstakes. In 1969 it became the third Big Eight Conference member to build a special dorm: rooms for 200 players featuring better food, individual telephones, a special recreation area, swimming pool, sauna, weight room, and bigger and better beds.[3] In the 10 years after introducing this brave new recruiting tool, K-State had an overall .327 winning percentage, 97th among the 105 major football teams.

Still, the athletics dormitory—bigger and fancier as the years went by—won out. It's an accepted part of college athletics. Whereas speeches were made in 1990 reform meetings about abolishing them and going further to resurrect the idea of no training tables, coaches know that unity of purpose is at the heart of team success and rules will not stop the ingrained practice of common eating and sleeping facilities for team members.

While the tug-of-war over free substitution and athletics dormitories was being waged far above their heads, young college athletes increasingly were required to push themselves to their outer physical limits. The demand for more, whatever it might be, was rooted in the coaches' keep-up-with-the-Joneses syndrome, which remains omnipresent in college thinking today.

If USC's front four averages 265 pounds, then Oklahoma needs to add muscle and pounds to its linemen. If one coach orders new equipment, a more rigorous training regimen, higher bench-press weight minimums, or faster 40-yard dash times, then so must his rivals. Steroids frequently have been a part of the plan.

But the players are students first, according to the student-athlete terminology we crafted for NCAA rules. Many of us believed the players ought to get more out of college than athletics. Regional conferences and the NCAA over the years have tried to curtail the practice and playing seasons. At one time, rules stated the football season could not start until after the first day of classes, and freshmen were not eligible. Some conferences restricted to two hours per day the time a player could be required to practice, and only one training table meal was permissible: dinner during the season of the player's sport.

These old concepts were brushed aside in the 1970s as coaches began ordering their young charges to enroll in weight-training courses outside the permissible practice season. It was important to build upper body strength and achieve a 21-inch neck size.

First we ruled that mandatory attendance at weight classes constituted out-of-season practice. Innovative coaches simply posted the sessions as approved, not-for-credit courses, a part of the school's curriculum.

Then we tried to legitimize the weight programs by requiring that such classes not only had to be posted but open to all students, and that only a limited proportion of participants could to be varsity athletes. Mass circumvention brought about the demise of this modest effort at commonality.

In a short time, the coaches had what they wanted: a liberalized out-of-season training policy. Coaches now can prescribe training and practice regimens year round, but cannot require attendance or discipline absentees. Persuasion alone works well enough. The coach has only to ask the athlete, "Do you *really* want to play for us?" Both parties understand the grant-in-aid is given on a year-to-year basis, sometimes semester-to-semester, as permitted by NCAA rules. The coaches, in fact, control the renewals.

Although I believe the exploitation of college players is more economic than academic, there is genuine exploitation in the colleges' denying the serious students a real opportunity to apply themselves academically. If the player does not conform to the demanding college practice and game schedule, his or her grant-in-aid is not renewed and can be terminated for disciplinary reasons. Where else but in the present topsy-turvy state of athletics does the college officially require the student to skip classes for a college-scheduled function or risk loss of financial assistance?

There is nothing morally wrong with emphasizing athletic readiness over academic preparedness so long as the player who does want a quality education—as compared to a look-see, pass-through degree—is given a fair chance and enough free time at the school's expense to pursue it.

One long-ago evening I was sitting with Ab Kirwan and his wife, Betty, behind their home in Lexington. Ab was as much a part of the University of Kentucky as its bricks and mortar, and we were good friends. That evening he spoke of his son who was then playing football for Coach Blanton Collier at Kentucky.

Ab said his son was discouraged because, after practicing all afternoon, he had to return and watch game films at night. Despite the fact that he was a top-ranked sophomore player, running number two at his position, the boy wanted out of football—and he did get out. Today William E. (Brit) Kirwan is chancellor at the University of Maryland.

Brit visited me one morning and said that even worse for him than the hours spent watching game films was the lack of stimulation among companions whose only interest was football.[4] "Day and night we were talking about football," Brit recalled. "I simply didn't want to spend my years at Kentucky living and eating with students preoccupied with that one game."

"You know, of course," I remarked, "that compared to when you played for Blanton, it's twice as bad nowadays."

"Sure, I know it," he replied. "What can you do about it?"

If Chancellor Kirwan, reflecting on his own personal athletics experience, were to seek higher academics and less athletics for Maryland's young athletes, he would soon be looking for work. Unilateral disarmament would be suicidal for Maryland in the Atlantic Coast Conference, particularly with ACC members' accelerated efforts to meet the formidable football challenge of new member Florida State. In their first three years in the ACC, the Seminoles went undefeated in ACC play (24-0), and if the Maryland president backed real reform initiatives, he would be immediately smeared as anti-athletics by Maryland's Terrapin boosters. At least Maryland cast one of the two votes against Florida State's admission believing it would raise the stakes and demands for football supremacy within the ACC.

Do What It Takes

Not all coaches and not all colleges went along on the inexorable drive toward the big time. The Big Ten Conference, after supporting the Sanity Code, made a valiant, solo effort at reform for five recruiting seasons (1957–61) by becoming the only big-league sports conference to try (on its own) a financial aid rule based on the financial need of the recipient. Presidents at other major football colleges applauded the Big Ten's courage but deliberately took no action of their own. Competing coaches laughed at the Big Ten as they mined the lode of athletic talent in the Big Ten area.

After watching great midwestern athletes accept the unrestrained full-ride offer of schools in the Big Eight and Southeastern conferences, or wind up playing for neighboring Notre Dame and Penn State with all expenses paid, the Big Ten reluctantly reinstated its full-ride grant program.

In recent years, the Big Ten has been long in talking about financial aid restraints and higher academic standards but short on performance. If you want to be in the Top 20 nationally, win the Rose Bowl once in a while, place four teams in other bowl games, and have 6 or even 7 teams in the NCAA basketball tournament, you have to play the game the way the game is played.

Eastern institutions such as Rutgers, Syracuse, and Boston College, along with the Big Ten and Pac-10 institutions, occasionally pause to place flowers on the grave of the Sanity Code. They bemoan the unseemly financial pressure to win and urge less rowdyism at their basketball games. Meanwhile, they rush pell-mell to do whatever it takes to win at football and basketball, fill stadiums and field houses, and get themselves ranked in the *USA Today*/CNN and Associated Press polls. But the Big Ten's former allies, the Ivies, pursued a different course. They decided the price wasn't worth it.

A sports fan looking back from the present may find it hard to believe that, in 1947, Yale played the University of Wisconsin in the Yale Bowl before a sellout crowd of 65,000. The Elis were 6-3 that year. In 1952, with Notre Dame ranked 10th nationally and Penn listed 12th, their game ended 7-7, before a capacity 74,711 fans at Franklin Field in Philadelphia. The next year, with the Irish ranked first and Penn unranked, Notre Dame escaped with a 28-20 victory before another capacity crowd in Philadelphia.[5]

Eastern football was at its zenith in 1963. Coach John Michelosen's Pitt Panthers swept through a 10-game schedule, including 5 of the nation's Top 20 teams, and finished at 9-1 and in fourth place in the final Associated Press and United Press International polls. That year, eastern football featured Navy (9-1), Syracuse (8-2), and Penn State and Army (both 7-3).

Pitt did much to resurrect an all-but-forgotten argument: good football players do not have to be academic weaklings. Of the 71 players on the 1963 Pitt roster, 66 graduated. Some 50 percent of those went on to earn graduate or professional degrees. Ten years later among the alumni of that 1963 squad were 3 doctors, 15 dentists, 5 lawyers, 5 engineers, 7 educators, 2 ministers, a law enforcement official, and 28 others engaged in business or industry.

Nonetheless, the preeminence of eastern football was coming to an end as the grant-in-aid system fueled big-time football in other parts of the country. The presidents of Pitt, Syracuse, and Penn State choose to match the practices of the biggest big timers. The Ivy leadership, however, said no thanks: too much attention was being paid to game scores instead of academic results. The Ivies rejected the grant-in-aid.[6]

If they couldn't persuade their colleagues at other eastern colleges, they could at least conduct their own affairs in the manner they thought best. They eliminated spring football practice. They banned bowl game appearances. By the 1970s most of the Ivies concluded it was not feasible to compete successfully in big-time basketball because much of the talent pool was poorly prepared to do even medium-level college work. Schools such as Duke had too great a lead over Ivy institutions in the chase to get the basketball players with great athletic abilities and reasonable academic skills.

In a rare case, Bill Bradley of Crystal City, Missouri, son of well-to-do Susan and Warren Bradley, passed up the University of

Missouri's blandishments to go to Princeton, even though competing recruiters belittled the Ivies. Today Coach Pete Carril's coaching
genius does keep the candle burning in the Nassau Inn for those
Tiger alums who remember Senator Bradley's spectacular years at
Princeton and his team's appearance at the NCAA Final Four in
1965. Yet the thrill of being close at the finish is the best even
Princeton has done. That is because the big-time recruiters consistently spirit away most of those great players with good high
school grades and acceptable test scores.

Coach Al McGuire of Marquette, in recruiting the formidable
Butch Lee away from the University of Pennsylvania and other
Ivies in 1974, felt obligated to educate Lee about the facts of life.
"I told Butch he'd be playing in the Ivy League at 5:15 P.M. in a
third-floor walk-up gym against guys with a two-handed dribble
and their underwear hanging out," Al explained to the media. "I
told him come with me and it'll be SRO every night with balloons
and smoke rings, and the band will be playing and the cheerlead-
ers' skirts will be bouncing up and down."

Butch Lee was the 1977 NCAA tournament's most valuable
player and was vital in helping Marquette beat North Carolina for
the national title, 67-59.

Lew Alcindor of New York City, recruited by Princeton, went
to UCLA instead as an out-of-state "special admit" with a grant-in-
aid and a good-paying job.[7] History has recorded what Alcindor
meant to John Wooden, UCLA, and, eventually, the L.A. Lakers,
where he played as Kareem Abdul-Jabbar. For the Ivies, recruiting
losses like that meant obscurity in the big-money sports.

I was reared in the Midwest, where it was common to poke fun
at the intellectual elitism and athletics hypocrisy of the eight private Ivy institutions. But the Ivy Group (Ivy presidents don't like
the word *league* because of its professional sports connotation) has
done a far better job than any other major college community in
making their rules match their ideals.

They held their ground despite the high publicity payoff and
the enormous television revenues that went to other schools. The
Ivies literally paid an athletics price for their principles. Everybody
picked on them.

Joe Paterno complained to the media as late as the 1970s that big-time football schools spent too much time considering the Ivies' views on education and athletics. "They give athletic scholarships on need," he said, "unless you're at Yale, where a guy in town slips you a thousand dollars every week.... There are forty-some cases of illegal recruiting in the Ivy League that they know about right now. It will be interesting to see what the NCAA does about it."[8]

This was standard Paterno propaganda. An Ivy alumnus himself (Brown, class of 1950), Paterno had to justify the Penn State full-ride approach to college sports, emphasizing that he was right and those against him were wrong and dirty.

But for many years, Joe consistently refused my requests for information that might help the NCAA curtail the crime he bemoaned. He seemed to think it would be dishonorable to snitch on his brother coaches, but he had no qualms in damning the entire profession publicly, which he did frequently with generalized, highly publicized proclamations about the "cheating in college athletics." Strategically, the complaints probably served his purpose: protecting his rich Pennsylvania preserve of high school athletes from outside poachers. In the late 1970s, Joe did help the NCAA enforcement staff, according to enforcement chief Dave Berst.

Yet the Ivy experience, like the earlier University of Chicago saga, proves if nothing else that athletics gigantism was not inevitable. The individual schools have been free all along to make choices that would blaze their own paths to glory—whether via academics or athletics.

Stories about coaches who use raw power to get their way might suggest that college presidents, united, could outduel the coaches in a public shootout for sensible college sports policies. Today's highly publicized reform movement by the NCAA presidents commission has led to a nationally publicized contest between "the presidents" and "the coaches," as though they live in different worlds and are not doing daily business on the same campuses.

Playing out this charade to the media's delight, the presidents during the late 1980s excoriated the coaches and absolved themselves of blame. When no substantial reform took place, they condemned the NCAA establishment as being controlled by coaches and puppet athletics directors.

Nonsense. Presidents glory in all the good things about college athletics and blame others for the bad. They are more responsible than anybody else for the current hypocritical tone of college athletics.

While college presidents talked incessantly about their reform agenda during the early 1990s, they were facilitating the TV scheduling of CBS, NBC, ABC, ESPN, TBS, regional syndicators, and local TV stations. Their basketball teams make a live college game available for TV producers any day or night of the week. ESPN led the pack in 1990–91, for example, announcing an NCAA-endorsed 168-game college basketball TV schedule.

As for rules once limiting varsity practice and play to students who have earned at least 24 college hours of degree credit, practice to 2 hours a day, the football season to 9 games and basketball to 21 games—those rules are scarcely remembered. Today, football games such as the Kickoff Classic are played with "special admit" freshmen on the field before they take their first remedial fall course designed to correct their high school shortcomings.

Although an NCAA "reform convention" in 1991 reduced practice time, such prohibitions are largely unenforceable at the national level. In 1994, the NCAA enforcement department was relying on good faith efforts at the local level. The new rules will probably be as ephemeral as the attempt in 1990 to cut by three the number of basketball games—two of which were restored to the schedule the following year.

The fact is, from the college beer halls where enthusiastic students gather to the trustee level of university management, almost no one wants to change the structure or the rules of this successful entertainment enterprise. Today's enlarged NCAA rule book and the beleaguered NCAA enforcement program cannot produce the changes and restore the integrity many seek.

Notes

1. Information for this account was drawn from conversations with David M. Nelson at the time and subsequently; David M. Nelson, interview with the author, October 10, 1988.
2. Dave Kindred, *Washington Post,* April 21, 1978.
3. *Kansas City Star,* February 14, 1969.
4. William E. Kirwan, meeting with Walter Byers, February 1989.
5. James M. Van Valkenburg, Official NCAA Statistics and Records, July 1994.
6. Derek Bok, letter and statement in behalf of Ivy Group presidents, December 29, 1975, as to why the Ivies would not agree to grants-in-aid. "While agreeing with the need for reasonable limits on athletic expenditures and procedures, however, we believe that broad national legislation is sometimes unwise and inequitable as it applies to individual colleges or groups of colleges which may have widely differing philosophies concerning the role of athletics in college."
7. Robert A. Fischer, interview with the author, April 25, 1989.
8. Mark Hyman, *Philadelphia Bulletin,* August 16, 1981.

Chapter 8

Enforcement under Attack

Playing cops-and-robbers in the world of college athletics can be hazardous to your health. Too often the cops are blamed for the persistent crime rate. I learned and re-learned this lesson many times.

The first conference commissioner I came to know as a hard-nosed enforcer, Victor O. Schmidt, was removed in 1958 for being too competent in applying the rules his employers had adopted. One of the last conference commissioners to take on his members in the pursuit of honesty was R. Wayne Duke, who decided to take early retirement in 1989, discouraged by the attitude of modern-day college presidents.

Well into the 1950s many groups and individuals seemed determined to stop the unsavory practices besmirching the reputation of college sports. There were many committed coaches, athletics directors, and faculty representatives, as well as commissioners of the major athletics conferences, who sincerely believed the rules meant what they said and college employees had no business practicing chicanery.

As pressures mounted for winning teams, more and more crusaders found that their law-and-order campaigns attracted only a handful of campus supporters, while hero-worshipping legions rallied to the support of winning coaches. College presidents learned to read the tea leaves and they said go with the flow.

Universities began sending representatives to the meetings of athletics conferences who would pressure their commissioners to be more circumspect. The commissioners were looking across the table at the people who employed them. When some of their bosses said the charge of cheating was untrue, it took a person of courage to respond: "I don't believe you." As the years passed, fewer and fewer conference commissioners were willing to place their careers at risk.

The Sheriff as Scapegoat

Vic Schmidt, a lawyer, was hired as assistant commissioner in June 1940 by the Pacific Coast Conference, today's Pac-10. His duty was to assist Ed Atherton, a former FBI agent who had been hired in January 1940 to clean up collegiate sports within the conference. In 1944, weakened by cancer, Atherton died in office and Schmidt took his place.[1]

Vic was a tall, trim man with a quiet sense of humor, epitomized by his bemused response when a Nashville newspaperman asked why his conference habitually lost to the Big Ten in football. "If we were on the winning end," Vic told him, "I would try to find some generous excuse for the losers. But all I can say in the circumstances is that the better teams won whenever we have lost."[2]

Vic was among the first to set the early tone of integrity, not only for conference enforcement but for the NCAA as well, since he also served on the NCAA Council. His diagnosis of the ills of college sports, made some 40 years ago, is appropriate today.

"We cannot cure a disease by treating its symptoms.... We legislate against recruiting while allowing the pressures from winning teams to go on unabated. We know it takes winning material to win games. We know the fate of the coach who fails. We are all the guardians of a precarious balance between institutional idealism and practical college athletics.

"Ethically and idealistically, colleges and universities cannot accept the professional. Practically and realistically, they are unwilling or unable to govern the pressures for the highly organized, competitive and winning athletics program that their public, their alumni and, perhaps in lesser degree, their students demand."[3]

Vic Schmidt was an inspiration to me. I admired his courageous struggle to keep his conference straight. And I was tormented that two of my earliest supporters and best friends, Bill

Hunter and Wilbur Johns, the athletics directors of USC and UCLA, respectively, were among his harshest critics.

In the 1950s and early 1960s, UCLA was on the make. Raymond B. Allen had left the University of Washington in 1953 to head the lusty southern branch of the California university system. He hoped to use athletics to prove UCLA superior to the California mother ship at Berkeley. Under his brief stewardship, multiple rules violations surfaced.

Lynn (Pappy) Waldorf was then head football coach at Cal-Berkeley. After moving there from Northwestern University, Pappy had led the Golden Bears to three straight Rose Bowls from 1949 through 1951, losing to three different Big Ten teams by an average margin of less than six points.

A big man with plenty of belly, Waldorf was a friend of Tug Wilson's, who had hired him at Northwestern before Tug became commissioner of the Big Ten Conference. Pappy had been helpful to me during my United Press sports reporting days in Chicago during the 1940s.

But by the early 1950s, Waldorf was talking to me as an aggrieved football coach who wanted the NCAA to *do something.* He was bitter about the "spiraling bidding war for talent in southern California." He told Vic Schmidt the same thing.

A hoary platitude of the legal profession is "justice too long delayed is justice denied." Pappy felt that the promise of action by Vic Schmidt, and my assurances that we were investigating the matter, were too speculative for a realist whose livelihood depended on winning football games, so Cal-Berkeley entered the bidding war.

If only because of the huge Los Angeles population base, UCLA's triumph in the athletics battle with Berkeley may have been inevitable. But the contest became a four-way fight. The University of Southern California was an aggressive participant, and the University of Washington wasn't going to be outdone.

The Huskies got to where they are today (averaging more than 71,000 customers a game for football in 1993) by recruiting heavily in southern California and the Chicago area. In those early days, the Huskies used outside money, and their number one booster,

"Torchy" Torrance, had become so successful that even Big Ten coaches used his nickname when they complained about him to our office.

Washington took the first fall to Pacific Coast Conference penalties in 1956. The conference later that year charged multiple violations against UCLA, then against USC and Cal-Berkeley. Vic's office was in Los Angeles. Taking on faraway Washington was one thing, but challenging the three California powerhouses—primary pillars of the conference—was an entirely different game.

Orlando Hollis, dean of the University of Oregon law school, was the chief conference prosecutor in the three cases. Issues were clearly black or white in his view, and he was particularly disdainful of what he considered to be the corrupting climate of southern California. This attitude won no friends among the Los Angeles media.

Through his efforts and those of Vic Schmidt, the conference itself severely punished the violators, imposing the stiffest penalty in conference history on UCLA, three years of probation with accompanying sanctions. Wilbur Johns was outraged by the legalistic style of Hollis, the unrelenting attitude of Vic, and the negative conference vote of such schools as Idaho, Oregon State, and Oregon. Bill Hunter of USC spared little invective in telling me of his resentment.

When the NCAA Council met in Denver during August 1956, we were determined to support Vic and the conference. The council ratified the conference penalties and passed a resolution commending Vic's work, which said: "Its [the Pacific Coast Conference's] prompt and vigorous actions are more meaningful than any available to the Council."[4]

But Vic's troubles were multiplying. Angry members of the Trojans booster club at USC adopted a resolution demanding that USC President Fred D. Fagg, Jr., and the board of trustees withdraw the university from the conference.

In Berkeley, Pappy Waldorf claimed that his school's violations occurred only because money was given in "individual cases of genuine need."

"No promise of tuition help was ever made to an athlete as an inducement to enter Cal, nor was such aid ever given as a reward for athletic achievement," Pappy said. Pappy was seeking higher ground. Translated, I think his words meant that—in fighting fire with fire—he had helped poverty-stricken players but had not gone as far as the indiscriminate payoffs at USC and UCLA.

During an NCAA infractions hearing in Lexington, Kentucky, both UCLA President Allen and Wilbur Johns told me the NCAA at least treated them with respect, not as if they were rogues and renegades. "In the conference," Allen said, "they treat us as if our words cannot be believed. It's a vendetta."

Wilbur had hired Red Sanders from Vanderbilt and John Wooden from Indiana State to lead UCLA to football and basketball glory. My confidant and advisor on other matters, Wilbur would not deny to me that UCLA had violated the rules. The Bruin Bench and the Young Men's Club of Westwood were sources of the recruiting and financial aid that led to UCLA's troubles and probably its long-term success as well.

But someone had to answer for this highly publicized crime wave. The sheriff became the scapegoat. Thus began the calculated process of picking apart Commissioner Vic Schmidt.

At one meeting he was asked whether the rule against entertaining players off campus would preclude buying a cup of coffee for a student-athlete at a short-order place two blocks from the campus. In biblical times the Pharisees had used a similar approach, asking contrived questions to get Jesus into trouble. Indications are that Jesus may have answered more cleverly than Vic, who replied; "Yes, buying a cup of coffee would be a violation."

In fact, it was. But Bill Hunter, athletics director at USC, ridiculed him for being simpleminded and unrealistic.

Vic was asked by conference members to give up his NCAA Council and committee posts. The inference was that he was too busy with such outside matters to handle conference affairs properly. During the fall of 1957, athletics directors began seeking his resignation; they took their requests to the conference faculty group, which agreed. After being asked to resign, Vic did so effective June 30, 1958.[5]

At one NCAA meeting during this period I visited with Vic,

who seemed a little dazed with circumstances that had made him the cause of the problem and not the cure. "And they hired me to keep it clean," he sighed.

There was some residual guilt in the conference over his treatment. Nobel laureate Glenn Seaborg, celebrated Cal-Berkeley physicist, was the university's faculty representative for athletics at that time. Seaborg had been persuaded to represent the conference in press conferences during this stormy period, the thought being that his national reputation and attractive mien would put a better face on things.

He was not particularly comfortable with the assignment. When he was appointed to head the Atomic Energy Commission in Washington, D.C., he hired Vic as a lawyer for the commission. In preparing to leave for the East Coast, Vic wrote a memo to conference leaders about the task that would face any new commissioner they selected.

"Under the code," he wrote, "he [the commissioner] will have the rather unenviable position of sitting as judge of those who employ him.... He must preserve a judicial demeanor and temperament while those seeking his rulings, no matter how sincere they might be, are blinded by their own interests... his ruling in many cases disappoints the institution requesting his opinions.

"His decisions will prove too literal, too narrow, too technical, too liberal, or too broad. He will, moreover, require an objectivity and perspective which he cannot expect from those against whom he may rule. There is nothing abnormal or uncommon in this result; it is the thinking of all mankind. It is motivated by self-interest."[6]

This describes for me the original concept (and plight) of the conference commissioner. Vic's former employers were not about to give such authority to his successor.

Anger over the enforcement cases ran so deep that the Pacific Coast Conference broke up in 1959. A new group was formed, the nucleus being UCLA, USC, Cal-Berkeley, Washington, and Stanford. The continued resentment toward central authority was so great among these five prominent universities that they would not call themselves a conference, adopting instead the name Athletic

Association of Western Universities (AAWU). They also refused to call their new executive a commissioner, although they hired a prominent personality fully experienced in wielding authority.

The AAWU secured the services of the highly respected Tom J. Hamilton, a graduate of the Naval Academy, its former head football coach, and the executive officer of the USS *Enterprise* during World War II. Tom's love for all forms of college sports prompted him to take the job with a set of colleges that, through the years, had been in the front ranks of the NCAA membership in sponsoring a broad range of varsity sports.

Not wanting further enforcement action against their universities, the conference adopted a policy of institutional application of the rules, an honor system based on "mutual trust and confidence." Admiral Hamilton was told to leave enforcement alone. His job was to promote football and all other conference sports—not to stir up bad press by penalizing the members.

Wiles Hallock, who became the conference executive in 1971, told me later of the personal anguish Tom had felt. "He agonized over the fact that he would sometimes know about violations he couldn't report to anybody," Wiles explained. "I don't think he ever reported anything to the NCAA. The only thing he could do was to mediate a dispute between two institutions if such occurred."[7]

Within the new honor system, stimulated by "mutual trust and confidence," violations flourished on the West Coast. This insouciance would lead to a bigger scandal twenty years later.

Trouble in Texas

Meanwhile, a thousand miles to the southeast in Dallas, another conference commissioner was defending his integrity and fighting for his job.

Howard Grubbs, Southwest Conference commissioner, had grown up in Texas during the storied era of Dutch Meyer at TCU, Matty Bell of SMU, Jess Neely at Rice, and D. X. Bible of the University of Texas—all successful football coaches. Howard, a product of TCU, was taught that a man's word was his bond, and only a handshake was necessary to confirm a deal. He had succeeded his friend Jimmie Stewart in 1951, becoming the second chief operating officer in the history of the conference.

A plain-talking Texan who knew the intricacies of athletics as well as anyone in the country, Howard had been hired by a unanimous vote of Southwest Conference members even though, under existing rules, he only needed a simple majority.

Howard felt he was living among friends. He was completely unprepared for the pressures exerted by Texas A&M University because of a 1956 investigation into violations by Bear Bryant's A&M football program. Out of Aggieland came Chris H. Groneman, prominent in the engineering school at Texas A&M. With Bryant's violations under investigation, Groneman pushed a Texas A&M proposal to require that the commissioner could only be elected or reelected by a unanimous vote of conference members. Tension was high in the conference meeting room, but Howard's supporters blocked the maneuver. Nonetheless, the message was clear. Investigate a power conference team and you jeopardize your job.[8]

Howard was stunned. He was personally hurt, professionally concerned, and somewhat amused. "It's getting very rough down here," he told me by telephone. "You can't believe what the Texas A&M people are trying to do. Bryant has them charged up."

We of the NCAA vigorously pursued the Texas A&M investigation—first, because it was the right thing to do, and, second, because it would be in Howard Grubb's best interest to show his employers that the NCAA was on the case and that he in good conscience could not be part of any cover-up.

As to Howard's warning that things were getting rough, I saw signs of that in mail I received from south Texas, including one from a man who addressed NCAA investigators as "JERKS," calling us "the lowest bunch of scum in the country."

"Are you trying to be a BIG SHOT and take all the power away from the conferences?" he wrote. "It looks like you folks are trying to be dictators!"

What another A&M fan lacked in spelling acumen, he made up for in the vehemence of his rhetoric. "Just when the Texas

Aggies have a good team and are heading for the Cotton Bowl," the San Antonio man wrote, "you fools have to go rune them....Like I say, the *people* and *I* down here in the State of Texas are good and Dam mad, and if you don't do something very soon to take off the probation, then something is going to happen to you all....Oh boy, I pitty you."

I wondered at the time, however, whether a University of Texas at Austin booster had written the letter in order to do a public relations number on the Aggies. Disinformation was a recognized tool of the trade when it came to Aggie-Longhorn recruiting rivalries.

At the center of the storm was Aggie Coach Paul "Bear" Bryant. Few were more determined to climb to the top than Bryant, a coach cast in the relentless disciplinarian traditions of Bob Neyland at Tennessee, Bernie Bierman of Minnesota, and Jim Tatum of Maryland.

Bryant had suffered little damage from his brush with the NCAA at Kentucky, and, in his new post at Texas A&M, he again proved his coaching skill by establishing a 25-14-2 record from 1954 through 1957. He also got in trouble at Texas A&M when he used illegal inducements to acquire several players.

Jim Corbett, athletics director at Louisiana State University and a particularly good friend of mine, tipped us in 1954 that John David Crow of Springhill, Louisiana, who would soon be one of the great backs of the game, was driving a new Oldsmobile. Nine different colleges, including LSU, had tried to recruit the young man and lost to Bear Bryant. Jim was suspicious.

Gifts of new cars seem to be blatant transgressions, but they are not easy to prove. The difficulties were spelled out in a report by the Southwest Conference and Howard Grubbs in August 1954.[9] He said that on August 9 that year he had interviewed the football player, his wife of one month, and John David's mother and father at the parents' home in Springhill. He learned that Crow had been heavily recruited by SMU, Baylor, Rice, Texas, Arkansas, and TCU of the Southwest Conference, before he chose Texas A&M; that Crow's marriage had been performed at no cost by a local preacher on a Friday night; that the newlyweds had spent two nights honeymooning, one in Shreveport and one in Longview, Texas, before Crow returned to an oil field job Monday morning.

Crow's summer job, acquired from an A&M alumnus, paid $282 per month. Harry Crow, John David's father, whose annual income was reported as $7,000, said he bought the 1954 Olds 88 Holiday Coupe as a high school graduation present for his son. He said he paid $3,300, making a down payment of $950 and scheduling payments of $103 a month. His own bank did not handle the financing.

Howard went back to the Crow home the following day. He told Mrs. Crow he had heard of an earlier remark by her that both Texas A&M and Oklahoma had made generous offers, but the Texas school's offer was the best.

"She burst into tears," Howard reported, "and said that it was not true, and that she did not say that Texas A&M had made him a better offer, and that she felt she was being treated like a criminal."

Harry Crow then explained that his wife's statement about a better offer arose from a question he, Harry, had put to an A&M coach. He had asked what would happen if John David were injured playing football. The coach replied that the school would provide him with a paid four-year education anyway. The family regarded that as a better offer.

Howard followed the money trail from Springhill, Louisiana, to a bank in Magnolia, Arkansas, where the car loan originated. The family agreed to let the banker release the facts. After studying them, Howard had to conclude: "It has not been established that any rules of the Southwest Athletic Conference have been violated in the case of John David Crow."

Whatever the result, Howard had pushed hard for the facts in this case. Art Bergstrom, the first full-time NCAA enforcement officer, did his own investigation, going through many of the same procedures. He didn't understand why the Crow's car loan had not been handled by their hometown bank in Springhill, instead of an Magnolia, Arkansas, bank, 57 miles from Fordyce, Arkansas, Bear Bryant's hometown. Art found no evidence to contradict the Magnolia banker's statements. His investigation arrived at the same result: In regard to John David Crow, no findings.

There was strong evidence, however, that cash had been offered to other players to join the Bryant team. The program also was cited because the Athletic Council of Texas A&M, rather than the school's regular scholarship committee, was awarding grants to athletes. The Committee on Infractions believed the transgressions justified a major penalty. Bryant's surrogates at Texas A&M disagreed and were aggressively fighting the NCAA case against the coach.

One day in 1956, Paul surprised me by asking for an appointment with the Infractions Committee. I readily agreed. By that time Ab Kirwan had risen from the University of Kentucky disgrace to become one of our strongest leaders in enforcement and chairman of the committee.

Bryant walked into our second-floor Kansas City office during a meeting of the Infractions Committee. The office did not have air conditioning. It was warm. After discussing one or two of the disputed incidents with the committee, Bryant fell silent, looked at Ab Kirwan, squinting his eyes in a searching gaze, and said: "Ab, you mean to tell me that an alumnus can't give these kids money?"

"Of course he can't, Paul," Kirwan answered. "He can't do that."

"Well," the coach responded, "I guess I don't have anything to argue about."

He got up, put on his hat, and left. The rules had changed, but Paul hadn't.

To round off the story, Coach Jackie Sherrill at Texas A&M resigned after the 1988 season, following charges that he had paid money to hush up earlier illegal payments to a player. Who replaced Sherrill as athletics director? John David Crow, who was a unanimous 1957 All-American for the Aggies at six feet, two inches, 210 pounds.

Paul Bryant accepted the NCAA penalties, but, as far as he was concerned, the case was an insignificant interruption in his direct march toward Tuscaloosa and his alma mater, where he would lead

S. David Berst (*right*), former McMurray College basketball player and 23-year NCAA enforcement veteran, with John David Crow, Texas A&M All-American football player (1957) and operating head of his alma mater's athletic department (1983–93)

Alabama to preeminent football success and assure his standing as the winningest major football coach in history.

Soon after the episode, Howard Grubbs decided to get out of the line of fire and hired a private investigators' firm to handle the interviews and conduct investigations. Following his retirement in 1973, Southwest Conference enforcement became far less effective. This was one reason for the mass penalties visited on conference members in the 1980s, with SMU in first place.

One witness to the conference's decline was Charles Alan Wright, a law professor at the University of Texas at Austin, who was interviewed in 1981 about Southwest Conference affairs by Houston sports columnist Jack Gallagher. Jack wrote: "To the question of whether conferences police themselves, Wright's short answer told it all: 'I attended Southwest Conference meetings and it was a joke,' says the member of the Texas Athletic Council from 1966 to 1971. 'They'd say, let's keep Walter Byers from learning about this. We had cases proven beyond any doubt and nothing was done.'"[10]

When the published remark brought a protesting letter from another professor in the conference, Wright answered that he had been quoted correctly but not fully in the article.

"I did hear Howard Grubbs say more than once, 'Don't let Walter hear about this.'" Wright responded. But he added he did not mean Grubbs wanted a cover-up, only that Grubbs believed the conference itself should enforce the rules and could do the job as well as the NCAA.[11]

"That may have been true in the late 1960s," Wright recently explained. "I am certain it is not true today."[12]

The assaults on Vic Schmidt and Howard Grubbs were duly noted in the commissioners' offices of other major conferences. Self-preservation is indeed the first law of nature, a thought that Samuel Butler, the English poet and satirist, emphasized in the early 1600s.

Let the NCAA Do It

By the 1960s, most conference commissioners had decided to let the NCAA do it. One or two continued to believe their conference members wanted strong enforcement at the conference level. They decided to pursue separate and independent investigations of violations, regardless of what the NCAA decided to do.

By then we were walking a political tightrope, determined to maintain the integrity of NCAA enforcement. While we worked with *some* conference commissioners, it was necessary to avoid others—those who we believed would feed confidential information to their conference members in the hope of winning friends and thwarting the NCAA inquiry.

Observing the intramural conference attacks on commissioners, several NCAA Executive Committee members during the late 1950s told me I should personally distance myself from investigations—just as Howard Grubbs was doing—if I hoped to survive and be effective in other areas. The Subcommittee on Infractions, which

"I know it's a spontaneous reaction, and YOU know it's spontaneous, but try convincing Walter Byers and the NCAA."

Artist pokes fun at Southwest Conference's supposed efforts to keep evidence of rules violations from the NCAA and its executive director.

I once served as chair, had been replaced by a separate committee, and I ceased field investigations.

A new member of the staff, Wayne Duke, picked up the few actions under way until we hired Art Bergstrom, athletics director at Bradley University. He had suffered through the Bradley gambling scandal, which had been Case no. 2 of the fledgling NCAA enforcement program, just after the Kentucky case. Handicapped by a wishy-washy Bradley president, David B. Owens, Art had conducted himself so well during our point-shaving investigation that he caught my attention. As a former high school and college coach, he knew the system. I hired him during the 1956 NCAA Convention in Los Angeles.

As the stories about Eric Dickerson and John David Crow illustrate, college recruiters are unabashed believers in the American love affair with the automobile. For them, it provided an avenue for getting around NCAA financial aid rules, second only to the complimentary ticket scam.

Wilton (Wilt the Stilt) Chamberlain was in the vanguard of great athletes whose solicitation, we suspected, involved complimentary wheels. Coach Phog Allen recruited him out of Philadelphia for the University of Kansas in 1955.

Allen coached a record 48 college basketball seasons, including 37 consecutive years at Kansas, finishing with 746 victories and a .739 winning percentage. He was a premiere recruiter.

Prior to focusing on Wilt Chamberlain, Phog had recruited Clyde Lovellette away from the Big Ten and Indiana University to fashion a national championship team in 1952. Lovellette, a two-time All-American from Terre Haute, Indiana, was the NCAA tournament's leading scorer that year with 35.3 points per game. Coach Allen explained that the young man had come to Lawrence, Kansas, to alleviate his asthma problems, a promotional endorsement of the eastern Kansas environment that no one I know had used before or since. Incidently, a member of that 1952 team was Dean Smith, a native Kansan, who went on to surpass his mentor's coaching record. Following the 1994–95 season, Smith had coached 34 years at the University of North Carolina and his Tar Heel teams had won 830 games for a .779 victory percentage.

Phog Allen also made environment a critical issue in Wilt Chamberlain's recruitment. Phog said that he succeeded because he had convinced Mrs. Chamberlain that the small town environment of Lawrence was best for her son. Coach Allen told Art Bergstrom that he also had contacted Etta Moten, an opera singer, through her brother, Bennie Moten, a noted black Kansas City jazz musician. Etta had talked to Mrs. Chamberlain, convincing her that her son could avoid the bad influences of big cities like New York and Philadelphia by going to Kansas.

Wilt arrived in a 1950 Buick, but by May 1956 was driving a 1953 Oldsmobile that came from Greenlease-O'Neill, a prominent Oldsmobile dealership in Kansas City. Dick O'Neill, a major KU booster, told Art Bergstrom that Wilt was paying for the car at the rate of $25 dollars per month. He showed Art the ledger sheet on the transaction.

Dean Smith played for Kansas and coach Phog Allen in 1952 and 1953 and became head coach at North Carolina in 1962. Following the 1994–95 season, Smith had achieved 830 victories, the most of any active coach.

"Does he pay this by check?" Art asked the car dealer.

"No, Wilt comes in here with the cash."

"You mean that Wilt drives 45 miles from Lawrence to Kansas City every month on the same date to pay the $25?"

The dealer assured Art that Chamberlain came to town regularly to make the payments. Art went back to the NCAA office, got out the Kansas basketball schedule, and found that Chamberlain had been out of town on game trips when several payments were made. Still, we couldn't make the case.[13]

By 1957 Wilt was driving a 1956 Oldsmobile convertible, obtained from a Lawrence, Kansas, dealer. We had acquired good evidence uncovered by a part-time NCAA investigator, Charlie Gray, who was of great help during those early years. A former

Wilt Chamberlain (*left*), 1957 and 1958 All-American at Kansas, was selected the 1957 NCAA tournament's outstanding player although Kansas lost to North Carolina in the final game in triple overtime, 54 to 53. Clyde Lovellette (*above*), 1952 All-American, averaged 35.3 points per tournament game in leading the University of Kansas to the 1952 national title.

Arkansas athlete and coach, Charlie had shot pictures of the car parked in the Lawrence garage of Skipper Williams, a gung-ho Jayhawk booster and member of a family that had given much to University of Kansas educational activities.

Art and I interviewed Wilt about the cars in my office, the same one Bear Bryant had visited not long before. We noticed that, whereas the great player drove good autos and was known as a careful dresser, he submitted himself for questioning that day wearing scuffed shoes and a coat with worn sleeves.[14] He was not particularly articulate, but I saw intelligence and a quiet humor in his subdued manner.

We followed the trail of cars to its end, and the Infractions Committee did find a violation in the 1956 Oldsmobile transaction, concluding the wheels had been provided to Wilt without cost. Our investigation also found violations in KU's recruitment of a football player, Bert Cohen, and Kansas was placed on probation for two years beginning in October 1960.

By then, Wilt was gone. He had driven away in a 1958 two-tone Oldsmobile 98 convertible.

"Wilt paid for the car with a check he had received from *Collier's* magazine for his story," Dick O'Neill recalls. "The net cost was probably $2,800. He had added a special trunk assembly to the car, and it looked a block long as he drove out the drive."[15]

The seven-foot Chamberlain was a two-time All-American at Kansas, but the best the Jayhawks could do in the NCAA tournament was second place, losing the 1957 championship game to North Carolina by one point in a triple overtime thriller at the Municipal Auditorium in Kansas City.

Wilt left Kansas with one year to play and, since he was ineligible for the NBA draft, joined a touring black all-star team for a season before starting his NBA career.

The epilogue? In recent years, O'Neill Oldsmobile has been one of two dealers that have provided free Oldsmobiles for some 30 top-echelon NCAA staffers. An O'Neill promotional plate was prominently affixed to the front bumpers of many of the cars. In 1989–90, Steve Morgan and David Berst, the top NCAA enforcement officials at the time, were among those who rode comfortably in new Olds 98s furnished without charge by the automobile agency that took care of Wilt Chamberlain more than 30 years before.

No-cost autos still are unacceptable as perks for grant-in-aid athletes but they are regularly accepted for advertising or prime ticket trade-outs by today's college managers. Free cars are considered an extra employee benefit for coaches, athletics department employees, conference officials, and NCAA staffers. For example, the auditor's report to Chancellor Gene A. Budig for the fiscal year ended June 30, 1991, valued the Wheel Club donation of dealer cars for University of Kansas athletics department personnel at $175,100.[16]

As college sports moved in the 1960s, Art Bergstrom began assembling the key people responsible for the long-term integrity of NCAA enforcement. Art first recommended that we hire Warren Scott Brown, a Kansas State graduate who had been a key performer at guard for Tex Winter's good Wildcat basketball teams of 1960–62.

Warren came aboard in 1966 and, in turn, he recommended to Art that we hire David Berst, who became the number one man on the firing line for more years than anybody else. The enforcement team included Bill Hunt, Doug Dunlop, and Jim Delaney.

By then Art was occupied with other NCAA duties, and it was Warren who put together what we called the "Class of 1975," which ensured the long-term strength of the program. Included in that group were Ron Stratten, ex-Oregon football player who was head coach at Portland State; and Bob Minnix, former Notre Dame half-back and University of Washington law school graduate.

Stratten had become the first black head football coach at a large, predominantly white university when Portland State University hired him in 1972. An engaging, likeable man, Ron brought no hang-ups to the NCAA. He was as comfortable talking to a millionaire alumnus as to a confused eighteen-year-old football star.

In Minnix we acquired an energetic investigator who loved to be out on the street with the action. Today, he probably has three times the experience of any NCAA investigator.

For the most part our investigators were young, and member colleges had begun complaining that the NCAA's "Young Turks" were so eager to prove violations that they were manufacturing evidence to enhance their investigative reputations.

Warren and I knew such charges were grist for the universities' publicity mills in explaining away violations. But we did recognize that obtaining an experienced investigator would provide desirable leavening of the youth mix. Through Wiles Hallock, who was then commissioner of the Pac-10 Conference, we found what we needed in a retiring FBI agent.

Hale McMenamin had joined the FBI in 1950 and gone to

Quantico, Virginia, for the customary 12 weeks of intensive schooling. Considering retirement 25 years later, Hale was prompted to apply for an NCAA post by Hallock, a longtime friend. Hallock usually displayed unerring instincts about people and issues; he was on target in recommending Hale.

McMenamin brought a wealth of investigative experience to the Class of 1975. He also calmly accepted the fact that university people were little different from the human race at large in resenting the questions of investigators and, when cornered, attempting to intimidate them or undercut their reputations.

In the Class of 1975, Warren picked and I approved one sour choice, Brent Clark, a product of the University of Oklahoma law school. Brent, whose income from a family trust undoubtedly was larger than his NCAA salary, wanted to establish his own identity. He publicized a series of unsubstantiated and subsequently rejected allegations about NCAA enforcement that put him on the front pages of sports sections coast to coast and embellished a 1978 congressional investigation into our activities.[17] This inquiry had been started originally by Congressman Jim Santini of Nevada, on behalf of UNLV and Coach Jerry Tarkanian.

We withstood that high-profile onslaught from Capitol Hill just as we were able to endure other periodic attacks on the integrity of investigators and the NCAA program from penalized institutions, disgruntled alumni, and angry coaches.

When the NCAA started out with enforcement in 1952, I made a vow to myself that we would treat all institutions and all people the same, regardless of their success in sports or their lack of it, the pressure or lack of pressure from powerful alumni, state politicians, or university presidents, and irrespective of race. Bergstrom believed that, Warren Brown believed it, and they instilled it in the young people whom they hired: "Big or small, black or white—treat them the same."

It seemed that the more we followed that principle in our investigations, the more we were criticized by member colleges:

"Byers has his own hit list."

"The NCAA cops don't know what's going on in the real world."

"The Young Turks are out to get any and all."

Many of these aspersions came from the most powerful universities. Accustomed to getting their way in conference meetings, intimidating those who disagreed, the big hitters found out they could not intimidate the NCAA staff.

Working under such pressures, we decided the NCAA enforcement section should be insulated, as much as possible, from normal NCAA political channels and supervised independently by the Infractions Committee. I removed myself from approving the hiring of investigators and never attended meetings of the Committee on Infractions.

The experiences of my good friends among conference commissioners convinced me that only a national organization, insulated from local and regional power politics—the NCAA, to be precise—had even a faint hope of doing the enforcement job. I suppose that is why I earned a reputation as a puritanical dictator.

I required the NCAA staff to dress neatly. Coats and ties were necessary for men when they came to the office, though working in shirt sleeves with loosened ties was okay. Women could wear tailored slacks but no jeans. Offices and desks were to be regularly cleaned. Employees were expected to be courteous, keep accurate financial accounts, and take no coffee breaks. They could neither eat at their desks nor bring liquid refreshments there. I wanted no one standing in front of the elevator doors at 5:00 P.M. At that hour NCAA employees at their desks could begin putting away their papers. I intended for everyone to work a full day.

I established these policies because they made good sense; we had to earn the respect of our member colleges, and we could not afford to leave ourselves open to cheap shots. The NCAA boss or chief investigator would never be attacked for being a vigorous enforcer; more likely it would be for slovenly appearances, sloppy work habits, or questionable expense statements. I saw no reason to give the infidels an opening.

Historians regularly cite NCAA football television, the Final Four basketball tournament, and NCAA enforcement as the three pillars of the NCAA edifice. Indeed, all three were important. But NCAA football television lies buried in an Oklahoma graveyard under a headstone carved by the CFA. The basketball tournament finances the organization, but it would not be difficult to create a new Final Four outside the NCAA. Some 80 to 100 major basketball-playing institutions could do it easily.

I recall a morning in October 1984, when I was to meet with a large group of college presidents, including John Ryan, first chairman of the NCAA Presidents Commission. He had been caught in the crossfire between militant presidents who thought an entirely new group should be founded and those who felt the NCAA should continue but with changes.

"The NCAA has been here a long time," the Indiana University president said for openers as we had breakfast. "It certainly must have some redeeming value."

The redeeming value in the eyes of the colleges has been the NCAA's efforts to maintain order. For all the bitter criticism, only NCAA enforcement has enabled college athletics to move on from decade to decade with some semblance of decency. It's a job nobody else wants to do.

Whatever our problems in achieving an honorable workplace for college athletes, enforcement is the bedrock upon which the NCAA's edifice is based—from a cramped hotel room in Chicago with one part-time administrator and one full-time secretary to a multimillion-dollar profit distribution center with about 230 full-time employees authorized as of 1994–95.[18]

When others abandoned enforcement, the game changed and the players changed. The public didn't notice and probably didn't care until the only cop on the block—target of all the blame—was the NCAA.

The colleges and coaches never left us lacking for things to do. I wish I could say, in line with Bill Alexander's early prediction, that the grant-in-aid made "all of this cheating and outside payments" unnecessary. Or, it would be gratifying if the argument of Iowa's respected Virgil Hancher proved out; namely, that the grant-in-aid rules were so simple and explicit that there should be no good reason to violate them. Instead, the escalating struggle for money and fame made rule breaking too tempting for too many.

As Wilt headed for All-Pro stardom and Bear Bryant for all-time coaching success, the public's addiction to college sports was elevating winning coaches to near cult status. Not that coaches didn't have plenty of power in the days of black-and-white movies and the radio broadcasts of Bill Stern and Red Barber.

It was television, however, that converted winning college coaches into entertainment celebrities and conveyed their views to millions of homes week after week. As television broke into living color and reached full bloom, it enshrined the Power Coach and made him the controlling force in deciding the college's policies.

Notes

1. Wiles Hallock, Historical Manuscript of the Pac-10 Conference, 1990.
2. Victor O. Schmidt, letter to Fred Russell, June 16, 1954.
3. Hallock, Historical Manuscript.
4. NCAA, NCAA Council Resolution, August 21, 1956.
5. Hallock, Historical Manuscript.
6. Ibid.
7. Wiles Hallock, interview with the author, June 4, 1990.
8. Information for this account was drawn from conversations with Howard Grubbs at the time; Alan J. Chapman, telephone interview with the author, May 2, 1990.
9. Southwest Conference, Report of Inquiries Made in the Case of Mr. John David Crow, Springhill, Louisiana, from the Office of the Executive Secretary (Howard Grubbs), August 18, 1954.
10. Jack Gallagher, *Houston Post,* February 26, 1981.
11. Charles Alan Wright, letter to Professor Alan J. Chapman, March 5, 1981.
12. Charles Alan Wright, interview with Charles Hammer, April 8, 1989.
13. Information for this account was drawn from conversations with Arthur J. Bergstrom at the time and subsequently; Arthur J. Bergstrom, interview with the author, October 4, 1988.
14. Ibid.
15. Richard O'Neill, interview with the author, January 3, 1991.
16. Schehrer, Bennett and Lowenthal, CPA, memorandum to Dr. Gene A. Budig, as part of the 1990–91 audit of the University of Kansas Athletic Corporation statement of revenues and expenditures for the year ended June 30, 1991.
17. Record of hearings before the U.S. House of Representatives Subcommit-

tee on Oversight and Investigations, beginning February 27, 1978; Walter Byers, letter (with enclosures) to selected sports columnists and reporters, February 25, 1978.
18. NCAA, Records of the NCAA Business Department, November 1, 1994.

Chapter 9

Commercializing Christmas

Television was commercializing all of America's values. Everything had a Nielsen rating and advertising price—from God's messengers preaching from an electronic pulpit to beefy, 285-pound professional wrestlers performing in a roped-off square.

Is it any wonder that television, which hurled college athletics into big-time showbiz, permanently changed the complexion of football and basketball? I'm not sure any of us knew exactly what was happening as we inked contract after contract for more money and more appearances of college teams on the tube.

As the momentum grew, many considered the changes a crass betrayal of principle—something like the commercialization of Christmas. Critics charged the colleges' goal of providing more sports for more students had been abandoned in favor of generating more publicity and more dollars. The print media ridiculed the colleges for selling out to television. They cited the changes in the dates of games and hurried adjustments in starting times as a kind of prostitution to satisfy the networks and please the sponsors.

Then, writers and editors reluctantly accepted the new order of things. After all, a metropolitan newspaper with a circulation of 400,000 had a tough time arguing against a medium that brought the game live to millions of viewers.

Show Time

The need to compete with pro teams for the entertainment dollar became, ex post facto, a legitimate economic argument of the football coaches who had won rule changes allowing free substitution and the two-platoon system. With free substitution, fresh players were on the field and custom-trained specialists were at the skill positions. The successful crusade of the power football coaches for unlimited substitution had consumed some 12 years (1953–65) before they got their way. In the ensuing five years, major college scoring increased 43.5 percent.

During this period, searching for other ways to add excitement to the college game, the rules committee focused on the one-point conversion play. A group of coaches unexpectedly proposed in 1958 that an option be offered for scoring two points. The emotional battle in the January Football Rules Committee meeting involved many of the same contenders who, from time to time, had nearly come to blows over free substitution: Fritz Crisler, Dave Nelson, Ray Eliot, Bud Wilkinson, and Wallace Wade.

Wilkinson was for the two-point conversion. So was Dave Nelson, then head coach of the University of Delaware. The rules committee wanted a unanimous vote because they realized the surprise action would arouse violent opposition among many coaches.

It was Wallace Wade who finally sold Ray Eliot of Illinois on the idea at a social gathering the night before the crucial vote.[1]

Eliot had voted against the concept in previous sessions. Wade, a soft-spoken, taciturn man, was capable of scoring a lot of points while nursing a highball or two through a long evening. A Brown University grad who coached 24 years at Alabama and Duke (.765 winning average), Wade was respected throughout the coaching profession.

The next day Eliot said he would support the new rule if the ball was placed for kicking on the four yard line, from where a kick would be worth one point and a run or completed pass two points. It would be even better if the ball were placed on the five, Eliot argued, but definitely not the three yard line. A committee member asked Eliot why he opposed the three yard line. Eliot stealthily looked back over his shoulder and, sotto voce, replied: "Let me tell you, sir, in the Big Ten if you put the ball on the three-yard line for a two-point conversion, Woody Hayes [Ohio State coach] will score two points every time he shows up."[2]

Eliot finally gave in, and the committee met the wrath of the coaching fraternity, led by Bobby Dodd at Georgia Tech. Dodd blamed Dave Nelson for letting it happen.

The first season after the committee action, Lehigh successfully used the new two-point rule to win against Nelson's Delaware team. Soon after, Dave's team failed from the three yard line in trying to beat Lafayette. After the second loss, Nelson received a telegram addressed to:

DAVE NELSON, TWO-POINT CONVERSION ADVOCATE:
LEHIGH 8, DELAWARE 7. LAFAYETTE 7,
DELAWARE 6. YOU'RE SO DAMN SMART . . . COULD
NOT HAVE HAPPENED TO A MORE DESERVING
FELLOW.

BOBBY DODD

The heightened popularity of college football was gratifying to the coaches but aggravating to college presidents.

Harold L. Enarson came aboard as president of Ohio State University in 1972. He bemoaned the fact that the university president was not accorded public recognition and respect at least comparable to that of his head football coach, Wayne Woodrow (Woody) Hayes. Enarson complained to friends that his own presence at an alumni meeting might draw a hundred or so loyal ex-Buckeyes, but when Woody was scheduled to speak, the hall would overflow, five hundred or more.

The Woody Hayes I knew was an unpretentious man. He seldom participated in upscale society around Columbus. His best suits looked as if they came from a discount warehouse, and his ties seemed to be pure rayon. But more important, he was unparalleled at motivating and disciplining football players and gaining their respect. He did this for 28 years at Ohio State. Coach Hayes is still idolized today in Columbus, while Harold Enarson and his successors are accepted as necessary adjuncts to the educational

Wayne Woodrow (Woody) Hayes (1914–87) was head football coach at Ohio State University for 28 years with a winning record of 205-61-10 (.761).

system. It's hard on the ego of a president to be less admired than his football coach.

Reflecting the view of many people, then and today, during the 1970s Enarson became convinced the values of society were upside down, and it was time to do something about it. Television brought into focus this growing frustration, and Harold Enarson took aim at me, the NCAA, ABC, and Roone Arledge.

Harold stirred up other Big Ten presidents, including Robben W. Fleming of Michigan. Chancellor Herbert Schooling at the University of Missouri, Columbia, joined Enarson in his indignation. Marching in support was Jack Hubbard, then president of the University of Southern California.

The issue? In the taped show that preceded the 1976 Ohio State–UCLA football game, ABC had depicted Ohio State students drinking *beer*. ABC's Jim Lampley had interviewed the students in a bar. At the end of the feature, Bill Flemming, a color commentator, remarked, "Well, that's how some of the students spent their Thursday night prior to the big game in Columbus, Ohio. We hasten to add, however, that this is not how all of the students or even the majority of them spent their free hours this past week."[3]

I saw the pregame show and thought it was a fair representation of party time on most campuses. Many universities were selling beer in their student unions. Pregame tailgate parties by affluent season ticket holders who served mixed drinks in preferred parking slots abounded on campuses across the nation. In fact, maybe the students of that era were more circumspect. I recall my own student days at the University of Iowa in the early 1940s, where we transformed near-beer into a more potent brew by spiking it with ethyl alcohol. Fraternity brothers attending medical school were frequently called upon for supplies.

Harold Enarson, however, concluded that ABC had committed the ultimate outrage. In a letter to Elton Rule, ABC president, he accused the network of a "raucous, distorted, and, to some, thoroughly disgusting characterization of Ohio State students—all 55,000 of them—as football crazy beer drinkers. I protest in the strongest possible terms."[4]

He accused ABC of doing the same thing a year earlier at the University of Missouri, Columbia. He noted Chancellor Schooling was angry about that. Then he dragged in UCLA Chancellor Charles E. Young by saying that Chuck was "incensed" with a Jim Lampley feature from the previous year. According to Enarson, that TV scorcher portrayed UCLA as if it were "a farm club for centerfolds, a school with nothing more important to do than make certain attractive young ladies get a proper suntan."

This was no mole hill! This was a mountain! Playing second fiddle to football had gone on long enough for Harold Enarson. More correspondence flashed back and forth on this issue among college presidents, our office, and ABC than on such subjects as the low academic standards of undergraduate higher education or the increased number of athletes taking soft courses approved by university faculties.

The presidents insisted on reading the ABC-NCAA contract. They wanted to take TV football management out of the hands of the NCAA, which many viewed as a front for big-time athletics directors and coaches. They argued for control of adjunct ABC sports programming.

Roone Arledge wouldn't buy it. Unable to push him around, the presidents merely redirected their anger to the NCAA. As executive director, it was my fault that ABC hadn't shown the good side of higher education. The NCAA's inability to bring Rule and Arledge to their knees on this issue proved I had negotiated a bad contract by selling out to the network.

The NCAA was being given a new responsibility by presidential ad hoc decree: we should control all ABC shows related to college football and prevent viewers from learning that students drink beer and that good-looking girls sunbathe on sunny California beaches.

I suspect it was news to Chuck Young of UCLA that he was "incensed." A man who appreciates that extra glitz, Chuck no doubt thought those blonde, sun-tanned ladies who grace the UCLA campus could do nothing but make the university more attractive to future students.

There's no doubt, however, that where television is involved, football fever can impair one's eyesight and distort the power of reasoning. It happened to me in December 1977.

There were only a few "big" games each year: USC–Notre Dame, Texas–Arkansas, Ohio State–Michigan, or Alabama–Penn State. They were critical to the NCAA's Nielsen rating record. For ABC to take television time from one of them was unthinkable. Yet ABC had done just that in covering the visit to Israel by the Egyptian leader, Anwar Sadat. With blinders securely in place, I wrote to Roone Arledge on December 19, 1977.

"The NCAA feels that it has been seriously damaged by ABC's actions in preempting a substantial part of the Ohio State–Michigan telecast November 19. The preemption was made despite our vigorous protests that the landing of Mr. Sadat's plane in Tel Aviv could not reasonably be construed as [in our contract language] 'an event of overwhelming public importance.' We consider this a breach of our contract."[5]

Arledge wrote back that he was dismayed the NCAA would take so narrow a viewpoint. "The fact that Sadat set foot on Israeli soil," he said, "is itself of major historical importance. As important as the landing itself was the purpose of the landing, *viz.*, talks with Israeli officials on Middle Eastern peace after some 30 years of open and continuing conflict with ramifications which involved the entire world."[6]

Sadat is dead—assassinated by extremists among his own people—but the peace he initiated between Egypt and Israel still holds. It is difficult now to understand how presumably rational people can become so caught up in their immediate world. We were after exposure and Nielsen ratings for college football; I was as competitive and combative as a football coach.

The higher we pushed television contract money with the networks, the more they jazzed up coverage of the game to attract viewers and sell more commercials. Their cameras became ubiquitous, often obnoxious, poking into every corner.

Despite several pages of NCAA rules designed to keep television people out of restricted areas, ABC Cameraman Mike Freedman in November 1977 was shooting scenes from the 33-yard line, breaching the "neutral zone" in Ohio Stadium at Columbus. Coach Woody Hayes was already annoyed that, during a halftime interview, an ABC announcer focused on an incident involving Hayes and a fan rather than—as the coach suggested—concentrating "upon the great game at hand" between Ohio State and Michigan.

In the second half, Woody socked the cameraman for getting in his way—resulting in Big Ten probation for Hayes and a hurricane of paperwork for everybody else. There was a Big Ten memo expressing outrage at the cameraman, pages and pages of answers from the network, rebuttals by the Big Ten, and analyses by the NCAA's Tom Hansen, our man at the administrative controls through many years of NCAA TV football.[7]

It was Hansen who tried to unravel another tangle at Ohio State in 1980. UCLA team member Kenney Easley rolled out of bounds along with the Ohio State player he was covering, then rose and was thrust sideways by an Ohio State assistant coach. Easley turned and shoved back. Then he was taken in hand by his UCLA teammates, who pulled him out of one difficulty and into another.

As Easley backed toward an ABC cameraman, the cameraman used his forearm to strike the player in the back with sufficient force to change his direction. In his report of the incident, Tom Hansen wrote, "Easley, who at this point must have felt the entire sideline was after him, turned and identified the second person who had hit him. Despite the effort (of his teammates) to calm him, he takes a quick step toward the cameraman and with the flat of his hand strikes him on the upper part of the head, knocking him on his back."[8]

Meanwhile, Big Ten Commissioner Wayne Duke, who earlier had served on the NCAA Television Committee, accused his former colleagues of selling out: "It is my firm conviction...that the [NCAA TV] Committee has abdicated its role in protecting the interests of member universities in such presentations in the interest of 'showbiz.'"[9]

True. And the conferences and colleges loved the money television poured into their coffers. They wanted more of it. The networks usually had their way.

The thought of moving game starting times and dates to accommodate television had first been considered outrageous, but it wasn't long before games were scheduled according to network time availability.

Soon college managers were criticized for *not* moving games to facilitate television coverage. In 1982 Washington State was scheduled to play at Minnesota. Minnesota Athletics Director Paul Giel turned down an ABC television offer of $600,000 if he would reschedule the game from an afternoon to an early evening time slot.

Sam Jankovich, athletics director at Washington State, had quickly agreed to the evening slot. He told Paul Giel how shocked and upset he was that Paul wouldn't go along. He said Paul was unfeeling for not trying to help ABC, a good friend of college football.[10] A man with a sure eye for the dollar during his subsequent years at the University of Miami and with the NFL New England Patriots, Sam had motives, I suspect, that lay as much in helping Cougar finances as in building goodwill with ABC.

Paul didn't budge. He was the bad guy.

An Upward Spiral

During the growth years, we were novices trying to divine the wonders of the escalating sports television industry. We limited ourselves to two-year contracts, while the networks pushed us for longer deals so they could maximize profits in the later contract years from higher ad rates, based on inflation and the increase in the number of viewers.

By 1976, NCAA televised football games averaged a 14.1 Nielsen rating, reaching 10 million homes and garnering a 37 percent share of the sets turned on at the time. That was a 21 percent increase in the number of homes reached from six years earlier.[11]

Attendance at games had actually jumped over those six years from 29.5 million spectators to 32.0 million. We were on a heady upward spiral, intoxicating to all involved, and the expansion didn't come in football alone.

In 1977 NBC televised the NCAA basketball championship, reaching an average of 7.5 million homes for the 11 programs.[12] We had found a new basketball audience of 18.8 million people. Basketball, football's poor relation, was catching up.

For every commercial minute in the 1976 football broadcasts, ABC paid an average $42,857 in rights fees; that is, money to the college for a license to telecast the game.[13] The network, of course, would tack on production costs and profit dollars when it sold those minutes to sponsors.

During the same college season, NBC paid $25,974 in rights fees for each commercial minute of the 1977 NCAA basketball tournament. ABC was paying for football just over four-tenths of a cent for each commercial minute beamed into each home tuned to the telecast. For basketball, NBC paid slightly over three-tenths of a cent for each commercial minute in each home.

College basketball was emerging as a moneyed member of the college sports family, no longer to be treated as a needy stepchild.

We knew enough about this growing television audience to face 1977 rights negotiations confident that college football held a strong position in the marketplace. The difficult issue was whether there were enough good games to warrant creating two packages and dealing with two networks.

To do so would end the one-network exclusivity that so far had been crucial in the pricing of college football rights. You could see Walter Cronkite or "MASH" only on CBS, and the network viewer could watch college football only on ABC. How far would Arledge go to make sure that ABC was the only network with college football?

A two-network deal would increase the number of televised games by 50 percent, meaning more teams on the air and more total dollars. We decided to go for two networks unless ABC dramatically expanded the days and hours it would give to college football and also put a top-dollar evaluation on exclusivity.

It was a protracted negotiation. The leverage was on our side. Obviously, both NBC and CBS were potential partners. But Arledge had great support from ABC management during these years. When the top man, in this case Leonard Goldenson as chairman of the board of ABC, believes in you, it's a lot easier to do business.

ABC offered expanded coverage in a deal they ultimately announced as "the largest one-network sports agreement in the history of television."[14] This time we agreed to bend and write a four-year contract, but we demanded that a cost-of-living adjustment (COLA) be written into it. The rise in the consumer price index had been 11.0 percent in 1974 and 9.1 percent in 1975. We said that if the consumer price index reflected a cumulative 15 percent increase after the first two years, the rights fee would be increased accordingly. Roone fought this provision to the end. He argued that ABC management could not accept such a condition because of the horrendous precedent it would set for future labor contracts as well as other agreements. We were just as adamant.

Seaver Peters, athletics director of Dartmouth College, was chairman of our negotiating committee. A bright man, Peters paid attention to the details of bargaining and proved he knew how to say no when necessary.

Seaver delighted in poking fun at me. Dining at the best restaurants, he deplored my suggestion that we Dutch treat the bill. He would repeatedly accuse me of being chintzy, until I relented and paid. Laughing, he once told me: "Walter, you know, I think Roone brings out the best in you. You're probably afraid he might be your match, so you rise admirably to the occasion. It's a great thing to watch, but please don't use your negotiating tactics in dealing with me on these entertainment chits."

In the final half-hour of a long meeting on June 9, 1977, Arledge agreed to the money, $29 million for each of the first two years, $30 million for each of the second two.[15] The tension in the room seemed to evaporate. Everyone was about to push back their chairs preliminary to the ritual handshakes.

"And the cost-of-living clause?" I asked.

Roone paused, looked at me, and smiled. "Okay. And the inflation clause," he said. It proved to be worth $2 million.

The deal extended ABC's exclusive rights to the college game through the 1981 season. The rights for 1980 and 1981 came to $31 million for each year, up 72 percent from 1977, the last year of the old contract. The new four-year deal provided a 40 percent increase in opportunities for college teams to appear on the national program. That was made possible in part by ABC's agreement to present as many as six games on regional telecasts.

After acquiring the rights, ABC's announced price tag for advertising in college football shocked even the usually shockproof Paul John of the Campbell-Ewald advertising agency in Detroit, who was responsible for the Chevrolet account. Chevrolet had been a "franchise advertiser" in college football from the 1950s. It would be the first sponsor to step up and buy three minutes of the best commercial time for each game throughout the fall series at the asking prices and not haggle over discounts or free advertising in other network shows.

Paul called me, not really to complain but to tell me that pricing by ABC for one minute of commercial time the next two years was being set at $120,000, and this compared to $78,000 in 1977, an increase of almost 54 percent.[16] Based upon preliminary calculations, Paul thought the cost per thousand for reaching advertisers in college football entering the 1980s might be higher than ABC's charges for Monday night professional football. He clearly was leaning toward putting Chevrolet trucks into "Monday Night Football," probably thinking there might be some discounting for Chevrolet ads in college football as a result.

Here was one of our most loyal allies saying, "Ouch!" None of us, and that certainly includes me, foretold the time when the automotive accounts would forsake their longtime role as anchor advertisers of major sports events and beer manufacturers would replace them.

While Paul John was warning that prices were getting out of hand, we were being criticized from the college side for squandering the riches of the wealthy.

There was mounting resentment among some of the more powerful football universities—Oklahoma, Penn State, Alabama, and Notre Dame—against an NCAA structure that allowed Kent State, Long Beach State, Grambling, Furman, and similar institutions an equal vote on football issues. Included in the new ABC deal was the idea of using some of the TV money paid to the NCAA to subsidize a football playoff for these lesser-known schools if they would divide themselves into a separate division from the biggies.

The ABC contract specified that if the top division was divided between I-A (the most prominent football schools) and I-AA (less prominent schools), the national network would telecast a Division I-AA championship. In the overall deal, it was a small item.

Instead of complimenting the NCAA for at least trying to respond to the big timers' concerns, the anti-NCAA faction—which would become the cornerstone of the College Football Association—repeatedly protested that their football dollars were being used to set up a championship for lesser schools.

It was an ominous sign of developing trouble for the NCAA television plan and for intercollegiate sports. The TV plan had been good for college football. The experience of 30 years attested to that fact. Its very success in generating millions for the colleges, and in helping some less fortunate football schools along the way, would be its downfall.

Sadly, this was not the only portent of trouble in higher education. Even as the money flowed and the popularity of intercollegiate sports increased, destructive forces were subverting the academic standards and administrative integrity of colleges across the country.

Notes

1. Information for this account was drawn from conversations with David M. Nelson at the time and subsequently; David M. Nelson, interview with the author, October 10, 1988.
2. Ibid.
3. ABC, Audio Transcript of ABC Pregame Show, UCLA at Ohio State, October 2, 1976.
4. Harold Enarson, letter to Elton Rule, October 18, 1976.
5. Walter Byers, letter to Roone Arledge, December 19, 1977.
6. Roone Arledge, letter to Walter Byers, January 13, 1978.
7. Tom Hansen, letter to NCAA Television Committee, December 16, 1977; James R. Spence, Jr., letter to John O. Coppedge, March 17, 1978.
8. Tom Hansen, letter to Wiles Hallock, December 30, 1980.
9. Wayne Duke, memorandum, December 27, 1977.
10. Sam Jankovich, letter to Paul Giel, September 21, 1982.
11. NCAA, Official NCAA Football Television Committee records, 1976.
12. NCAA, NBC-NCAA Basketball Tournament records, 1976.
13. ABC, ABC-NCAA Football Television records, 1977.
14. ABC, ABC Press Release on 1977 NCAA Football Television Negotiations, June 11, 1977.
15. NCAA Television Committee, Minutes of Negotiating Subcommittee, June 9, 1977.
16. Walter Byers, telephone notes of conversation with Paul L. John, March 26, 1978.

Chapter 10   Riots of the Sixties

Higher education's critical shortcomings of today took root during the riots of the 1960s, when more than a few college presidents surrendered academic and campus social standards to the lowest common denominator among the faculties and students.

It was during and just after this period that many of the great collegiate sports dynasties were founded or reinforced. While academe faltered, tough-minded coaches and committed, highly disciplined athletes won the widest public support in the history of college athletics.

John Wooden at UCLA, Bear Bryant of Alabama, and Vince Lombardi of the Green Bay Packers were in the vanguard of coaches who demonstrated that determination, discipline, and motivation can move mountains. This generation of coaches believed the lessons taught them by their own college coaches.

Devoted to the traditional American work ethic, they won the admiration of a whole new generation of American fans. If soaring attendance at collegiate events is any indication, the love of college sports grew as never before. From 1965 to 1975, football attendance increased to 31.7 million annually at 634 four-year colleges, up 28.4 percent. By 1980, attendance climbed to 35.5 million, an overall increase of 44 percent.[1]

Meanwhile, something quite different was happening on the academic side of higher education. Campus riots broke out, with the apparent purpose of protesting a number of injustices including the Vietnam War and the draft. The campus rioters, including some outside agitators, staged a debilitating attack on the conduct of American higher education. In the forefront was the Students for a Democratic Society.

Part of the result was that standards of conduct and academic achievement were diluted and sometimes abandoned. "Peace in our time," was the motto of more than a few administrators.

At Cal-Berkeley, when radicals of the "free speech movement" fought to silence everyone else on campus, the university probably suffered more negative publicity than any institution in the nation. One of the America's most beautiful campuses began to resemble the streets of nearby Haight-Ashbury, situs of the area's drug colony. The drug culture was tolerated on many campuses.

Some Cal loyalists felt the West Coast media picked on them, and that just as much rebellion took place at nearby Stanford but was publicized less. Indeed, the picture at Palo Alto was not pretty.

Kenneth S. Pitzer, nationally renowned as a chemist, was inaugurated as Stanford president in June 1969. The speaker on that occasion was John W. Gardner, former Secretary of Health, Education, and Welfare, who said many fine university presidents had suffered destruction of their careers because of the campus conflict. "We have yet to prove that we can provide the kind of atmosphere in which a good man can survive," Gardner added.[2]

Not long afterward, the new Stanford president made concessions to radicals that only stimulated further violence. Police were called at least 13 times during the spring of 1970, making more than 40 arrests. Pitzer resigned on June 25, 1970, a year and 12 days after his inauguration.

The lack of support for Pitzer broadcast a negative message throughout higher education. You might assume the man was chased out of town because he favored the Vietnam War. On the contrary, he had labeled the war a monumental blunder and said: "We haven't the courage to admit it and get out."

Professor Philip B. Kurland, law professor at the University of Chicago, implored educational leaders not to give up academic standards as the price of peace. Kurland noted that radical students claimed higher morality but actually "typified all the zealots that have come before them."

"Theirs is the morality, for example, of the Spanish Inquisition," he said, "that sincerely sought to save the souls of men, even if it had to send them to Hell by fire."[3]

Although political change in the nation was the goal of many campus radicals, a frequent adjunct demand was lower academic standards, and far too many faculties agreed. By the 1970–71 academic year, about two-thirds of the nation's colleges were using some form of pass-fail grading; 85.3 percent gave a grade of "pass" for anything above a D. Whereas 92 percent entered failures on the students' records, only 43 percent included failures in figuring grade point averages, according to the *Chronicle of Higher Education*.[4]

Blame for the strife and damage caused by the campus riots was carefully dispersed. It was the fault of the Vietnam War. Revolutionaries had enrolled on the nation's campuses, and it wasn't the job of educators to deal with them. Too many students were in college with no interest in studies.

Higher education was careful to excuse itself, but, in fact, its leadership of the day should take a goodly share of responsibility for the damage done.

In 1967 the Military Selective Service Act came up for debate on a four-year renewal of its provisions. The law had previously authorized deferment for college students only until the end of the academic year in which a young man was inducted.[5]

The chief political force for higher education, the American Council on Education, campaigned for draft deferments for all undergraduate and graduate students who were successfully pursuing a degree. The ACE emphasized that the "students would be deferred in the national, not individual, interest." But the college would determine a student's satisfactory progress, and experience has shown that is a convenient standard indeed.

This proposal triggered an explosive debate, particularly about deferring students in time of war. There was bristling dissent from members of the House Armed Services Committee.

"We believe that in time of war student deferments are unconscionable," they wrote. "What we are in fact saying to this years' crop of high school graduates and to every graduating class for the next four years is, 'You may choose between going to war and going to college.' What we are saying to graduate students is, 'for the remainder of the time it takes you to get whatever degree you may be pursuing, you may continue to pursue your academic career and others will do the fighting for you."[6]

The language of the bill was carefully drawn to provide that a student would be deferred if he was "satisfactorily pursuing a full-time course of instruction at a college, university or similar institution of learning."

Dissenting members of Congress scored this distinction by pointing out that if a young man was "studying carpentry, or electronics, or auto mechanics at a trade school," he must go to war. Studying whatever the student might choose at a college or university would defer him.

Finally, the members of Congress took straight aim at the American Council on Education "national interest" argument when they noted that a "poor man helping to support his family by day and going to college part time by night would be sent to fight in Vietnam, while his wealthy fellow citizen going to college full time by day and to parties at night would be exempt."[7]

Nevertheless, the ACE position was accepted in the final version of the law that passed in June 1967. The colleges paid a heavy price when they had to deal with the resultant campus disorders, brought on in no small part by the many uninterested young people they enrolled as students, but colleges also reaped the anticipated dividend.

From 1965 to 1970, enrollment in all institutions of higher learning climbed from 5.9 million to 8.6 million, a 44.9 percent increase when the U.S. population between 18 and 21 years of age increased 15.5 percent.[8] In effect, it was open door admissions to be followed immediately by open door recruiting of athletes.

Racial Barriers Crumble

Modification of traditional academic standards in the 1970s also can be traced to other causes. Effective opposition to customary entrance requirements came from those who described themselves as advocates of black and underprivileged people. Most of that opposition was sincere but may well have been misdirected, with the ultimate results less than satisfactory.

My own perspective was that black athletes had been making brilliant but little noticed contributions long before academic requirements became a racial issue.

Paul Robeson, son of a former slave, became a two-time, All-America football star, a Phi Beta Kappa member, and class valedictorian. He graduated from Rutgers and then earned a law degree at Columbia University in 1923. With his magnificent singing voice and impressive physique, Robeson went on the concert stage.

He came to my hometown in 1942 to sing in Kansas City's Municipal Auditorium. He had been promised an integrated audience; instead, the blacks and whites he faced were seated in a checkerboard pattern. Robeson dropped the scheduled classics program and instead sang protest songs, including the fiery "Jim Crow."

I remember being devastated when I later learned this great college football player supported communism. It was reassuring when Jerome (Brud) Holland became an All-American at Cornell in 1938 and symbolized so many positive values. Brud, among his many accomplishments, later served as ambassador to Sweden. A man of fine humor with a terrific smile, he was a good friend of mine and contributed mightily in trying to make the NCAA a better organization.

Now I can see how both of these impressive men, traveling different routes, performed a lasting service by dramatizing what can be done and what needed to be done for blacks. Significantly, they competed equally and successfully with whites on the playing field and in the classroom. They needed no special academic exemptions.

The Sanity Code of 1948 had required that student-athletes meet ordinary entrance requirements of the college to receive tuition, books, and fees, while demanding that those who received the grant for room and board be in the upper 25 percent of their high school graduating classes. The Sanity Code was evidence of the early desire that all college athletes be genuine students, capable of profiting from higher education. Academic standards for athletes were not then—and are not now—a crafty way of limiting black athletes' access to college teams. Several black college presidents and others who have chanted this high-publicity refrain have done all sides a disservice.

The Sanity Code failed in 1950 for lack of enforcement, and the NCAA convention substituted a constitutional provision requiring that student-athletes make "normal progress" toward a degree. It was an elastic standard subject to local interpretation, to which all could subscribe.

During the 1950s, the northern teams that included black players in increasing numbers held the upper hand. As an example, in 1955 Coach Phil Woolpert's University of San Francisco Dons—with Bill Russell and K. C. Jones setting a new skill level—demolished the great Tom Gola and a fine LaSalle basketball team, 77-63, to win the NCAA basketball championship.

Still, most of the southern teams resisted the inevitable. In 1962, the University of Mississippi refused an invitation to the NCAA basketball tournament because they didn't want their players going up against blacks. The following year Mississippi State did play in the tournament and was defeated by Loyola of Chicago with its four black starters.

Gov. George Wallace might have looked impressive to voters when he blocked the front door to black students at the University of Alabama in Tuscaloosa, but the Crimson Tide football staff and their competitors in the Southeastern Conference were eager to open the back door to skilled black athletes.

The walls tumbled after 1966, when an underrated Texas Western basketball team took on the all-white, Number One–ranked University of Kentucky in the Final Four. Coach Don Haskin's five black starters toppled Kentucky in a 72-65 victory.

Major universities, regardless of location, leaped into the recruiting wars for black athletes. Violations increased, and the conclusion that I reached, along with members of the NCAA enforcement staff, was that many young black players from poverty-level homes were being influenced by extra benefits, usually cash in relatively modest amounts.

The head of NCAA enforcement at the time, Warren S. Brown,

believed that a white investigator talking to a black athlete or his parents would have little chance of finding out the facts.[9] It was essential that we have black investigators. Warren took time to impress on me that, whereas we were both aware of the impoverished circumstances of many black youths in the Kansas City area, he was encountering depressed living conditions beyond anything he had anticipated.

We soon hired several blacks. At the outset, the key man was Ron Stratten, who was one of the most respected investigators on the NCAA staff for a number of years.

The problems associated with the stepped-up college recruitment of black athletes was a sensitive issue that we preferred not to discuss in public. It took prominent black athletics leaders to tell that story. Eddie Robinson, having been head coach at Grambling for 32 years, said in 1975 his recruiting competition was no longer from similar, predominantly black schools but from major white universities with big money to spend. Speaking bluntly, Robinson said: "It would be real hard for me to tell a boy, living in a shotgun house with five sleeping in one room, to turn down a new house, a car, a better job for his daddy. I know it's wrong, but it's hard for a man to walk in another man's shoes."[10]

I had some sense of how it was. The NCAA basketball tournaments had reacquainted me with the discrimination against black athletes, as I tried during the 1950s to arrange integrated accommodations for the teams in my own segregated hometown, Kansas City, Missouri. One downtown Kansas City lunch counter served whites on china plates but blacks on paper plates that were thrown away—implying that black patrons left a residue that could not be washed off.

At the old M & O Bar near the *Kansas City Star,* white printers were welcomed to the booths, even though waitresses had to use paper towels to wipe away the ink residue their overalls left behind. It was a good workingman's bar for printers and journalists that—unlike some local cafes—did at least serve blacks. But until 1963 they were not permitted to sit down. They took their food from a window at the back and ate outside, leaning against the brick wall.

A similar contradiction in the 1960s had impressed Ron Strat-

Eddie Robinson, head coach at Grambling for 52 seasons, is second only to Amos Alonzo Stagg's 57 years in number of years as an active coach. Robinson's 397 coaching victories is an all-time record.

ten. A product of a San Francisco high school, he played center and linebacker for the University of Oregon—and competed for the first time against teams in the South. It was a scene he never forgot.

"How was it that you could take people who would not let blacks do anything," he asked me, "and then suddenly you have a team with star black athletes playing for them? You have them yelling, sixty or seventy thousand of them, yelling for their black stars. And you could only find a hundred blacks in the whole stadium audience."[11]

It was this incongruity that hastened integration. Intercollegiate athletics contributed as much as any segment of our society to dismantling racial barriers. I'm proud of the role the many NCAA volunteers and officials of my time played in shaping policy during the era when blacks became major contenders in college sports.

Bill Bell, a great black Ohio State lineman and All–Big Ten performer, graduated in 1931. He became nationally renowned as a coach and later served as athletics director at Fayetteville State University. He devoted many hours to NCAA affairs and, as a member of an NCAA basketball committee, he helped select two white and two black teams for a regional tournament in North Carolina in 1966. He told me of his satisfaction in arranging the first integrated basketball games played in the South. I was pleased that Bill commended me personally in an impromptu speech on the floor of the NCAA Convention in the 1970s, noting my 25th year as NCAA executive director. He went on to say: "As a result of the quite unpublicized work of the NCAA, thousands of black Americans are enjoying richer and better lives which have accrued from black participation in college athletics."

The decision of southern colleges to accept black athletes bolstered the sports quality of the predominantly white institutions but had an adverse effect on playing quality at predominantly black colleges.

Walter Payton, the all-time star halfback of the Chicago Bears, played at Jackson State as a senior in the 1974–75 college year. During that era, a dozen or more players were drafted each year by NFL teams from Grambling State University and Alcorn A&M alone. Following the 1986 season, however, only six were drafted from three of the strongest black institutions in the country, Jackson State, Southern, and Grambling.[12]

I do not believe now, anymore than I did then, that the renewed search in the 1960s for an academic standard was the work of white racists trying to lighten the color of their basketball teams, as some critics charged. We took up that academic pursuit again after the campus riots brought on a period of general chaos, undisciplined admissions, and capricious grading standards.

Exploitive recruiting coaches had rushed to take advantage of those facile conditions. Coaches did not establish the policies. They simply set out to reap the benefits of academic exceptions and special treatment. The principal NCAA academic requirement that athletes make "normal progress" toward graduation became a convenient phrase to be interpreted locally to the college's advantage. We tried to meet the burgeoning coast-to-coast recruiting crisis caused by unrestrained local option whereby many colleges chose to admit and keep eligible the athletes they needed to win.

One Six Hundred

In 1965 I worked with the NCAA committee that wrote the 1.600 rule (spoken of as the "one six-hundred rule"), meeting time and again with admissions officers, faculty, and Atlantic Coast Conference Commissioner James H. Weaver, chairman of the committee. I remain convinced it was the NCAA's soundest approach to a national academic standard.

It required that schools limit first-year athletics grants-in-aid and eligibility to those likely to achieve a freshman grade point average of at least 1.600 (or C-) on a 4.000 scale. Specifically, 1.599 was not good enough. The prediction was based on a formula that took into account not only the student's high school rank or grade point average but also scores on the ACT or SAT test. Whether a high school athlete was admitted to college was not at issue; the rule applied only to the eligibility of an athlete to receive a grant-in-aid and practice or play intercollegiate sports in his first year.

Testing, of course, is basic to all schooling, from kindergarten through graduate study. Passage from level to level throughout the educational system depends on testing. But when testing of athletes was suggested, the college antitest element said tests were biased and did not measure what they were supposed to measure. This charge was answered at the time by Ken Vickery, a nationally respected college admissions officer. "Yes, tests are biased," he said. "They're biased against ignorance."

The ACT-SAT test segment of the 1.600 rule provided an essential *national* comparative standard. In a letter to me discussing a later academic proposal, Boyd McWhorter, commissioner of the Southeastern Conference, underlined the value of testing as at least one of the criteria. "It is a common denominator which cuts across the differing academic quality of the nation's various high schools and, more important, it is less subject to manipulation than the other academic considerations."[13]

An athlete with a C average in a tough high school might get straight A's in an easy one. The B student in a weak school might barely hit D in a strong one. It is no secret that many times high school grades have been enhanced to help both athletes and nonathletes into college. Any standard based solely on high school ranking offers a huge advantage to athletes from inadequate schools, or from schools where admiration for the athlete is reflected in better grades. The 1.600 rule placed a check on that with its testing feature. At the same time, solid high school work could offset poor test results.

Confirmation of the rule's benefits was the fact that the college recruiter began visiting the academic office at the high school before calling on the prospect's coach. It was necessary to find out whether that great high school player had the grades and the test scores that would predict at least a 1.6 average in the freshman college year.

All of this sent a needed signal to high school coaches. They passed it on to their players—hit the books and take the test! "If you don't," they warned, "you won't get a full-ride scholarship."

Frank Howard, who in 1969 was athletics director and football coach at Clemson University in South Carolina, was a strong advocate of 1.600. Nevertheless, in February of that year, he was writhing under restraints in the Atlantic Coast Conference, which had developed standards higher than the NCAA's through use of a minimum SAT cutoff score, regardless of the NCAA prediction formula. He wanted the NCAA to toughen its 1.600 standard and force his bitter rivals in the Southeastern Conference to conform.

"Every year there are five or six football players in South Carolina who cannot predict a 1.6," he wrote to me then, "and they end up going to the University of Georgia, Auburn University, and the University of Alabama. They pretty consistently beat us. If I am not able to win from them in the next two or three years, my coaching days at Clemson will end!"[14]

By then, however, the 1.600 academic standard was coming

under increasing attack by those who wanted it abolished. Opponents protested the NCAA's intrusion into institutional autonomy. They complained of cheating on the tests; an old "ringer" concept from early-day football had been revived so that a bright student could take the test, signing the name of the less intelligent one.

But academicians and coaches who demanded that academic tests be eliminated because of cheating did not even mention elimination of the arbitrary financial ceiling of the NCAA grant-in-aid rule, where far more cheating took place every season of the year. Winning and the pursuit of income colored the academic debate. Scrap the academic standard, they argued, but don't increase the player's grant (thereby increasing the college's expenses) just because the alumni are paying him under the table.

The president of an Ivy Group college, Frank H. T. Rhodes of Cornell University, had announced he would not only recruit blacks as students but would find high-risk prospects in the inner city. Allan Bloom, author of the best-seller *The Closing of the American Mind,* was a professor at Cornell then. Bloom said Cornell silently and drastically altered admission standards and beginning the 1967 academic year "faced an inevitable choice: fail most of them or pass them without them having learned."[15] He said the faculty chose the latter.

Those who believed in motivation and discipline, the key ingredients for teamwork and sports success, marveled as some academic types preached nonsense. Dr. Dwight W. Allen of Stanford University urged the elimination of homework. Addressing a U.S. Office of Education conference, Allen said, "Homework is bad for several reasons. It gives children the maximum opportunity for learning the wrong things, and this mislearning takes 10 to 20 times as much effort to correct as teaching the right thing in the first place." He went on to condemn it for almost the opposite reason. "It discriminates. Chances are that the youngster who already is doing well in school has the best conditions at home under which to do his work, while the youngster who needs the most help has the poorest conditions for study."[16]

The year 1969 was critical. It was then that the National Association of College Admission Counselors adopted a resolution urging colleges to strive for a minimum 10 percent black student body, at least half at high risk.[17] These should be excepted from the 1.600 rule, we were told. Financial need would be the *only* factor in determining financial aid for minority students. Presumably, weak minority students—those who had scorned high school homework and classroom attendance—would receive scholarship help on an equal basis with strong minority students. No bonuses for the latter. The admission counselors simply wanted tests eliminated as a factor in the admission of minorities.

That fall at the annual business meeting of the College Entrance Examination Board, purveyor of the SAT test, certain advocates proposed the following motion.

"*Be it resolved* that the Scholastic Aptitude Test and Achievement Test be used by colleges and universities in the processing of minority/low-income students only *after* admissions decisions are made and then be used for research and diagnostic purposes only."

In a hot debate, Charles D. O'Connell, Jr., the University of Chicago's dean of students, relinquished the chair and took the floor with his substitute resolution.

"*Be it resolved* that the institutional members here present urge that colleges and universities in the selection of their minority/low-income students use the [tests] with sensitivity in the admissions process and that they also use them for diagnostic and placement purposes."[18]

He won the vote. But even today, the College Board tends to be ambivalent when the use and value of the scores are criticized publicly.

Sports Expediency

The 1960s ended, yet the full effect of the fallout did not register until two back-to-back NCAA conventions in 1972 and 1973. In 1972 the debate was over freshman eligibility to play. As an issue, it had been around for a long time.

Freshman ineligibility for varsity sports had been accepted as a benchmark of sound management for almost 50 years. The Big

Three of the Ivies—Harvard, Yale, and Princeton—had agreed not to play freshmen on varsity teams after the football crisis of 1905 that brought about formation of the NCAA. The policy became ingrained in subsequent NCAA eligibility standards.

Waived during manpower shortages of World War II and the Korean War, the one-year residence requirement that excluded freshmen was afterward reinstated by the colleges.

Keeping freshmen ineligible helped the marginal high school recruit adapt to college academic and social life before becoming preoccupied with big-time varsity sports. More important, it was a significant deterrent to quick-fix athletics recruiting, the unbridled desire of coaches to reach out indiscriminately for high school seniors to fill depleted varsity positions immediately.

A two-phase attack was mounted against this sound principle. The colleges in 1968 first voted 163-160 to make freshmen eligible for all sports except football and basketball. Proponents of the change argued it would be cheaper to operate one varsity squad for each sport. Knowing they could not win the vote if they included football and basketball, they contended it was proper to exclude those sports since their seasons started before the end of a freshman's first semester. In the spring sports, however, the freshmen would have a half year of academic performance behind them. Advocates also noted that participants in track, gymnastics, tennis, and baseball were generally better students than football and basketball players anyway.

Marcus L. Plant, a noted tort expert on the Michigan law faculty, was then president of the NCAA. He had an infallible instinct for fraud. After the vote, I asked him: "How long do you think it will take before football coaches point out that freshmen are playing on soccer teams in the fall?"

"Well, I suppose we could argue that foreign soccer players are better students than American football players," he said with a smile, "and don't need a year of residence."

It took four years. Major college delegates to the 1972 NCAA Convention at the swank Diplomat Hotel in Hollywood, Florida, voted to terminate some six decades of conventional wisdom that freshman ineligibility was sound policy. The football vote was 94-67. A show of hands accomplished the change in basketball.

But two more fateful decisions lay ahead. The debates got under way on January 13, 1973, at the 67th annual convention at Chicago's historic Palmer House. At that time many colleges still offered four-year grants-in-aid. Those that offered only one-year grants protested against the practice, saying it amounted to unfair competition, even though the complainers could guarantee four-year grants if they so desired.

They instead offered a constitutional amendment, Proposal no. 39, which decreed that any type of athletically related aid "shall not be awarded for a period in excess of one academic year." Careful subcommittee work and private discussions had taken place long before to ensure that Proposal 39 would be supported by the necessary two-thirds majority. Advocates said that academic scholarships for undergraduates were awarded only for one year and graduate students, presumably some of the best products of their undergraduate institutions, normally were assured of only one-year commitments as well.

Alan J. Chapman, a nationally respected engineering professor from Rice University who would be elected NCAA president at this convention, believed then—and believes now—that the argument was bogus.

"The contention that the one-year rule duplicated all other university practices was not true," Alan recalls. "Most awards then and now are for one year, but not all of them are. Some commitments were and are multiyear. As to graduate students, there always has been hot recruitment for the good ones, and there is no national agency enforcing a uniform ceiling on the academic offer."[19]

Support for Proposal 39 came from many major schools whose coaches believed it would be cost effective. Joining them were four-year scholarship coaches who complained that some athletes, once they had the four-year award in hand, decided not to play or at least not to give their best efforts. Such players were cheating the college, they pointed out, and young people should not be permitted to learn bad habits.

Proponents took elaborate precautions to make it acceptable

to doubters. They assured voters that if a coach did not recommend renewal of aid for an athlete, the coach would have to justify his decision to a university oversight committee. They promised that athletes could take their pleas to an unbiased faculty group.

The stage was set. Wade R. Stinson, athletics director of the University of Kansas, represented the NCAA Council. The Big Eight Conference wanted the one-year limit. Stinson made the motion, and a show of hands convinced the presiding officer that more than two-thirds of the delegates had approved the constitutional amendment. It took less than 90 seconds.

Coming one year after the freshman eligibility decision, this was a historic turning point and a major extension of NCAA cartel authority. We became the national agency enforcing a uniform one-year ceiling on the aid offer, regardless of the academic and economic qualifications of the recipient. Yet there were no protests of a new "federal" intrusion into the workings of college financial aid committees. No one spoke on behalf of home rule and institutional autonomy.

Thus, Proposal 39 had rendered obsolete the several procedural safeguards put in place with the original 1956 grant-in-aid legislation. The exigencies of big-time athletics—the need to win and survive—in time would also strip away the safeguards promised in the one-year grant legislation.

Formerly, faculty representatives and athletics directors would justify their squad lists and financial aid decisions to their university athletics committee, which would pass the recommendations to the university financial aid committee. In many cases, the latter group came to believe they were being used and concluded that, since the sports people were paying for the awards with generated or donated money, they should do whatever they thought best.

Pledges that one-year grants would be renewed if the athlete tried hard were sidestepped as the not-good-enough player was persuaded to transfer to "a place you can play." This advice was usually best for both parties; a thwarted coach could make next season's practice regimen difficult indeed. Thus, the one-year freshman tryout had been legalized.

After lunch, a debate began at the same 1973 convention over the NCAA's 1.600 academics rule. Opponents of the rule sent the representatives of two colleges of modest athletics achievement up to the microphones.

Bob Tierney of Queens College scored the legislation as "a violation of institutional autonomy ... self-determination and a [discrimination] against certain types of students." Robert Behrman of City College of New York was not far behind. Repeating most of Tierney's points, Behrman concluded with the novel thought that we should "enhance the image of our organization [the NCAA] by voting to abolish 1.600 once and for all."[20]

Listening to them, I could not understand how educators could condemn such a modest academic standard. The conventional wisdom that smaller colleges stand for amateurism and high academic standards, checking the professional tendencies of the big powers, isn't necessarily so. On that day, the smaller colleges had the votes to block both initiatives, but they chose to put their own interests first—their interests in recruiting and enrolling whomever they wanted and in awarding financial aid on the most liberal terms.

Alan Chapman took the floor to point out that with freshmen eligible, the opportunity to exploit the system without academic restraints at the national level could prove disastrous. To offset the comments of Tierney and Behrman, Bill Leckie of the Colorado School of Mines tried to persuade some of his small-college peers not to "retreat from academic standards."[21]

No such luck. The convention deleted the 1.600 legislation, 204-187.

Losing the 1.600 rule was one of the most painful experiences in the 22 years I had then served as executive director. It was a terrible day for college athletics. Supposedly responsible educators had voted for sports expediency.

The two Palmer House decisions in 1973 meant that prime recruits needed only to present a 2.0 high school grade point average, regardless of subject matter or test scores, to be eligible for varsity athletics and a full ride. The players' grants-in-aid for the second year would be determined on the basis of how well they played and practiced the first year.

The net verdict of the colleges' decision: the NCAA had a proper cartel role to play in limiting the financial aid rights of the athlete, but setting academic minimums for athletes was an intrusion upon institutional freedom.

For a decade afterward, the weak 2.0 requirement for high school graduates would provide recruiters an open door to solicit whomever they wanted until the NCAA adopted Proposition 48 in 1983 at the urgent behest of a committee of college presidents. Since then, that rule has been revised, but generally upheld, most recently as revised Proposition 16.

The results of our 1956 experiment with the grant-in-aid had become abundantly clear. The grant, which Pop Houston, Ralph Aigler, and I had backed as a possible cure for under-the-table payments, had become an industry-controlled contract for athletes, with academic standards to be determined by each college.

Although the convention had not supported his position on academics, the delegates at the end of the day elected Alan Chapman the NCAA's 21st president. Alan was not enamored of big-time athletics and wondered out loud whether there would be a place for institutions like his own Rice University in the altered scheme of things.

The new secretary-treasurer was Richard P. Koenig of Valpariso University, a congenial, religiously oriented former basketball player. He argued privately that the NCAA should create an "NFL subdivision" and let the biggies pursue their professional practices without the NCAA "Good Housekeeping" label.

In the many convention postmortems, Alan and I waxed philosophical and took consolation in the position that the membership had heard the arguments and voted in a democratic manner. To label all the anti-1.600 voters as NFL acolytes was clearly unfair, we thought. Dick agreed with Alan that we should begin yet another effort to change the disturbing course of things.

Today, having returned to teaching after serving as dean of the Rice University engineering school, Alan still believes the loss of the 1.600 legislation immediately after freshmen were declared eligible led to the exploitation and badly tarnished image of college athletics in the 1980s.[22] The prediction Alan made at the 1973 convention was transit perfect: recruiting did become merciless, spurred to new intensity by the growing rewards of television. The best-intentioned institutions and coaches would have to meet their competition at the level their competitors set. The tyranny of the lowest common denominator would control.

Notes

1. NCAA, Official 1990 NCAA Football Records Book, August 1990.
2. John W. Gardner, speech at inauguration of Kenneth Pitzer as Stanford University president, June 14, 1969.
3. Professor Philip B. Kurland, speech to the Chicago Bar Association, *Chicago Tribune,* January 29, 1970.
4. Philip W. Semas, *Chronicle of Higher Education,* February 15, 1971.
5. Legislative History, Military Selective Service Act of 1967, Senate Report, May 4,1967; House Report, May 18, 1967.
6. U.S. House of Representatives Report no. 267, May 18, 1967, 1350–51.
7. Ibid.
8. Data provided by Dr. Vance Grant, National Center for Education Statistics, U.S. Office of Education, April 23, 1991.
9. Information for this account was drawn from conversations with Warren S. Brown at the time and subsequently; Warren S. Brown, interview with the author, June 9, 1989.
10. *Boston Globe,* March 23, 1975.
11. Information for this account was drawn from conversations with Ronald J. Stratten at the time and subsequently; Ronald J. Stratten, interview with the author, June 12, 1990.
12. Marino H. Casem, interview with the author, August 11, 1987.
13. H. Boyd McWhorter, letter to Walter Byers, July 11, 1983.
14. Frank Howard, letter to Walter Byers, February 20, 1969.
15. Allan Bloom, *The Closing of the American Mind* (New York: Simon and Schuster, 1987), 94.
16. Joe Lastelic, *Kansas City Times,* September 12, 1967.
17. Resolutions Adopted by National Association of College Admission Counselors Delegates Assembly, Chicago, Illinois, October 11, 1969.
18. Anne B. Speirs, special memorandum to the membership of the College Entrance Examination Board, November 14, 1969.
19. Alan J. Chapman, interview with the author, May 2, 1990.
20. NCAA, NCAA Convention Proceedings, January 14, 1973.
21. Ibid.
22. Chapman, interview.

Chapter 11   Rules Are Not for Enforcing

For most of my career, I was in conflict, both publicly and privately, with coaches. When they sought more grants-in-aid, I campaigned for fewer. As they steamrollered their way to platoon football, I battled for limited substitution. When they wanted extra basketball games, I asked for a shorter season. When the conferences continued to permit basketball coaches to blackball conference game officials, I sought a national officiating standard with no blacklisting. When I backed stronger enforcement, prominent coaches ridiculed the rules and damned the NCAA police force.

Behind the publicized disputes, however, there always has been a cadre of coaches who believed in their profession and stood for honorable conduct.

Among them was Darrell Royal, a former Oklahoma quarterback who became head football coach of the University of Texas Longhorns in 1957. His teams won 30 straight games at one point during 1968–70, 6 straight Southwest Conference titles (1968–73), and 3 national championships.

Royal, a polite man who shunned pretense, was of better-than-average height and (like myself) often wore cowboy boots. I asked him once why he liked to wear them.

"I need the height," he deadpanned.

"Okay," I said, "but when six-footers like you wear them, I don't gain anything with mine."

That didn't score any points with Darrell.

In the 1970s the Longhorns began losing vital games, including those involving the University of Oklahoma. You don't survive at Texas if your teams lose to OU or Texas A&M very often.

Barry Switzer succeeded Chuck Fairbanks at Oklahoma with the 1973 season. It wasn't long before his personal and social antics, along with a winning record, began erasing memories of the gentlemanly conduct of former coach Bud Wilkinson and his years of winning. Bud coached 17 years at Oklahoma and retired with a .826 victory average, while Barry Switzer closed it out after 16 years with an .837 average.

Barry began ridiculing Darrell about his guitar strumming. Darrell was good enough on the instrument to pick with some of the great personalities in Austin, Texas's premier country music locale. Switzer implied the Texas coach was unable to excel in guitar playing and coaching at the same time, and that was why OU was winning.

Darrell, however, had another theory. He and Arkansas Coach Frank Broyles, his longtime friend and conference rival, flew to the Kansas City airport during this period to discuss with me the rampant cheating taking place in the Southwest Conference and along the Texas-Oklahoma border. Part of this was the result of the gradual dilution of Southwest Conference enforcement after Commissioner Howard Grubbs's job had been threatened during the volatile Texas A&M case. Grubbs's successor, Cliff Speegle, was a former football coach himself and understood that there are few dividends to be gained from investigating your employers.

Darrell and Frank were convinced that we office-type NCAA people did not understand the realities of the recruiting wars. "It's out of control," Darrell told me as we sat in an airport meeting room. He shook his head in reproof.

Frank, who speaks to most subjects with evangelical zeal, embellished Darrell's point at length. Darrell and Frank advocated lie-detector testing. They both said they would lead a seminar on enforcement techniques for NCAA investigators. They would tell our investigators the ins-and-outs of coach-booster relations and tricks of the trade in the hope that we might start catching violators.

I told them I would be crucified if I permitted our staff to be schooled by particular coaches. Rival coaches would accuse the

NCAA of doing the bidding of their athletics enemies. Darrell and Frank were particularly upset at our inability to prove the connection between the college coach and the booster who was paying money to a player.

"Now, Walter," Darrell said in his patient way, "you must know there isn't an alumnus in this country who's going to waste his valuable time and spend his valuable money on an athlete that a coach isn't going to use. If the booster recruits the wrong athlete and the coach doesn't play him, then the booster looks like a fool and the coach makes an enemy of a friend."

Darrell's point was clear. In the real world, a coach's impassive, low-key comment, "We *sure* would like to have that boy," is the only message necessary. If a booster or a talent scout friend arranges for additional benefits, that is a matter between the player and his new acquaintance. The coach walks away from it. He doesn't know anything about it. Darrell was only verbalizing what I knew to be true.

"Another thing I've never understood," Frank said, "is why your investigators can't walk through a dormitory parking lot at OU and write down the license plate of those new sports cars the athletes are driving. Then you could trace the ownership and financing."

He had hit a tender spot. Providing new automobiles to recruited athletes had become so rampant in the great southwest that Alan Chapman of Rice University, who was serving on the NCAA Council at the time, suggested the NCAA should revise its grant-in-aid definition of commonly accepted educational expenses to read: " . . . fifteen dollars per month for incidental expenses and *one new Trans Am sports car.*"

Our investigators had worked hard on the car problem, and we knew there were a number in the OU parking lot. They could also be found at many other schools, usually financed through banks located in the hometown or the area from which the recruit came. The banks would explain that their financing was no different from other arrangements made for area students and, in fact, the deal for the athlete probably made more sense. After all, the good player might well sign a big bonus contract with a pro team at the end of his senior year and pay off the car loan.

During one of our investigative evaluation sessions, I asked Warren Brown, our enforcement chief, "How do we know that at the end of a player's eligibility, the banker and the car dealer don't erase the debt because they are so happy with superstar's performance?"

"We don't," Warren smiled.

Art Bergstrom, then in charge of NCAA operations and personnel, laughed ruefully as he recalled his efforts to pin down the origins of more than one car driven by college All-Americans.

"Even the player who doesn't pan out as a superstar but becomes a reliable performer may well have the balance of his car note picked up by a grateful alumnus," Art remarked. "We've simply never had the personnel or tools to run down these so-called loan agreements. Bankers take the position that it's a confidential transaction and none of the NCAA's business." (Although the NCAA can threaten to penalize a university unless it persuades the bank to open its records, the problem has not been solved.)

At our airport meeting, neither Frank nor Darrell offered specific information that the NCAA could use as evidence against their competitors. In 1973, we did hit Oklahoma with a two-year probation for violations involving fraudulent transcripts, fringe benefits, improper inducements, and excess entertainment. Similar violations led to solid cases against SMU in both 1974 and 1976. None of the findings were complete enough or the penalties heavy enough to take the profit out of cheating. And Darrell suffered for it.

He later described to me how he was called on the carpet before former Texas governor Allan Shivers, who was then chairman of the university board of regents. Darrell explained to Shivers that he could not compete with some of his rivals in the conference and could not successfully recruit against OU because of the escalating illegal offers.[1]

"Why don't we match them?" Shivers said. "Let's join them."

The Longhorn coach told Shivers he simply would not play the game of fighting fire with fire. From that moment forward, Darrell

Two long-time rivals and close friends, Darrell Royal (*left*), head football coach at Texas (1957–76), and Frank Broyles, Arkansas head coach (1958–76), at Texas's Memorial Stadium in December 1976, prior to their last Arkansas-Texas football game at which they simultaneously announced their resignations as head coaches.

told me, Shivers became his enemy. Shivers, now deceased, reflected the Texas propensity for high political manipulations with the game of college football, a custom that would be carried to the ultimate by Governor William P. Clements in the SMU scandals.[2]

Darrell was forced to announce his resignation in December 1976, coincidentally at the same Texas-Arkansas game at which Frank Broyles reported his own resignation. Only clever politicking by NCAA faculty representative J. Neils Thompson, a civil engineering professor, saved the second half of Darrell's employment contract and allowed him to stay on at Texas as athletics director.

It was three months after Darrell resigned that Bob Oates, sports columnist for the *Los Angeles Times,* predicted a brave future for a whole bevy of new football coaches in the Southwest Conference, including Freddie Akers, who had taken Darrell's place at Texas. Other newcomers that Oates cited were Steve Sloan at Texas Tech,

Lou Holtz at Arkansas, Homer Rice at Rice, Grant Teaff at Baylor, and Ron Meyer, who had moved from Nevada–Las Vegas to SMU. Admittedly, they were a young, personable group.

"The Southwest Conference is thus a conference with some of the most imaginative football men now active," Oates wrote after attending an NCAA-sponsored media seminar. "Taking advantage of the NCAA's new rules—and its healthier new recruiting climate—this mostly Texas league has become a model in vitality and competitiveness for the rest of the nation."[3]

In the summer of 1976 Michael Johnson, faculty rep at the University of Houston, complained about the imaginative recruiting tactics of Texas A&M. He felt he was sitting on a powder keg. When I met with Mike, he posed a simple question: How could Texas A&M supply an athlete with a 1979 Trans Am that cost about $8,350 retail?

I said we would find out.[4]

The CEO of the bank that supplied the car loan was a strong A&M supporter, but he provided evidence that the bank had lent money to 10 Aggie students, only 2 of them athletes. This 5-to-1 ratio seemed to satisfy the NCAA Committee on Infractions as meeting the "sin test": Is the benefit "available to the student body in general"? The committee concluded it was an acceptable transaction.

I was angry. We had contributed to the arms race by inaction, and I conveyed my displeasure to Bill Hunt, who was supervising the matter, in an August 1979 memo. There apparently were no evidentiary requirements for A&M to prove that the 10 loans carried comparable terms as to interest, repayment, and principal amounts. Major sports athletes surely didn't constitute 20 percent of the student body.

Darrell had been prophetic; it was out of control. A majority of Southwest Conference members were headed for NCAA probation in the next five years, with SMU destined to earn the death penalty. The inability of the NCAA apparatus to deal with the mounting violations—the reluctance to be tough and put the burden on the university—had contributed to the firestorm.

Friendly Foes

Meanwhile, the estrangement of two friends, Wayne Duke and Charles M. Neinas, was about to become a factor in enforcing the rules of collegiate sport as well as an ominous portent for NCAA football television controls.

After 11 years as an NCAA staffer, Wayne had left in 1963 to become the Big Eight commissioner. I hired Chuck Neinas to replace him in the NCAA job, and they were close friends afterward in their professional associations.

In 1971 Bill Reed, the Big Ten Conference commissioner, died in office. It was a loss for the conference as it was for his many friends, including me. With the Big Ten job open, Chuck Neinas asked me to recommend him for it, and I agreed. Then Wayne told me he had been asked to apply for the post and wanted me to endorse his candidacy. "You've already got a good job," I told Wayne. "I'd like to help Chuck get a top position, and I've told him I would support him."

Neinas felt he was an odds-on favorite for the post. Don Canham, athletics director of the University of Michigan and a power in Big Ten politics, was committed to him. The chair of the selection committee was George H. Young, dean of the law school at the University of Wisconsin (which Chuck had attended as an undergraduate) and chairman of the NCAA Committee on Infractions. George was a particularly good friend of mine. I had written him a letter strongly backing Chuck.

The committee had three candidates to consider—Chuck, Wayne, and Jack Fuzak, NCAA faculty athletics representative from Michigan State University. They were all interviewed at the Howard Johnson Motel in Des Plaines, Illinois. When Chuck Neinas returned to the NCAA office in Kansas City, he seemed crestfallen.

"How did it go?" I asked him.

"What do you say," he replied, "when someone asks about your philosophy toward intercollegiate athletics?"

Wayne called me the next day to report: "I think I've got it." And, indeed, Bob Ray of the University of Iowa called him to confirm it a bare 24 hours after the Des Plaines interviews.

I later learned that Edwin H. Cady, a nationally recognized professor of late nineteenth-century American literature, had done much to torpedo Chuck's candidacy. Cady was the outspoken faculty athletics representative of Indiana University. During the interview, his questions as well as those of others went beyond administrative skills and the ability to put together a budget. Cady probed for the philosophical bases from which Chuck would draw strength in making decisions as conference commissioner. Chuck had seemed unprepared.

"The questions we posed were not esoteric," Cady said. "They were no different from those I posed when we interviewed coaches. Chuck's answers simply were unresponsive."[5]

Wayne had plotted his approach to the Big Ten on the basis of "experience and enthusiasm" plus knowledge of the conference, its people, and its history. When Wayne left for the Big Ten, Chuck applied for the vacated Big Eight Conference post and succeeded Wayne in November 1971.

Still, Chuck carried the scars from his loss of the more prestigious position and later told Wayne that he would show those Big Ten people.[6] Chuck's ambitions were frustrated again a decade later when, as executive director of the College Football Association, he discovered the Big Ten and Wayne Duke would not join the CFA's planned takeover of football television for all major colleges. By that time, their public civility and barroom kidding merely camouflaged a growing hostility and private resentment.

In 1971, still good friends, Duke and Neinas took on executive duties with two conferences that still believed their commissioners should enforce the rules.

The faculty reps and athletics directors of the Big Ten and Big Eight were not so naive as to believe that rules governing money and recruiting were self-enforcing. To them, the idea of "trust your neighbor" being pursued on the west coast was self-indulgent complacency. In fact, by the early 1970s there was regret within what is now the Pac-10 Conference that, scarcely a decade before, the conference universities had rid themselves of a vigorous conference commissioner, Vic Schmidt, and had put in place their "mutual trust and confidence" program.

We had caught Cal-Berkeley in major violations in 1971 in a hotly contested case in which the validity of the 1.600 academic standing of the highly skilled Isaac Curtis and Mike Brumsley was a big issue. Cal Athletics Director Paul W. Brechler had been commissioner of the Western Athletic Conference before taking on the stewardship of Cal athletics in 1968. He argued that Cal should not fight the NCAA on the issue. Vice-chancellor Bob Kerley, speaking for the university chancellor, sharply disagreed with Paul. The top managers of the university met and the vote was 6-1 (Brechler dissenting) not to bow down to the NCAA.[7] The Golden Bear Athletic Foundation filed suit in federal district court in September 1971 to force the NCAA to lift its penalty.

The conference was aghast at the Berkeley developments, realizing that under its mutual respect program it had little authority to deal with the problem. Wiles Hallock, who by then had taken over as conference commissioner, said it was the Cal-Berkeley case that turned the corner for the conference.

"We realized we didn't have any enforcement or compliance procedures," Hallock explained, "and the only power we had was to declare their games forfeit." Robley Williams, a Cal-Berkeley biochemistry professor, faculty representative, and NCAA Council member, bitterly fought the case at all levels.[8] "No nit was too small for him to pick," Wiles recalled with a smile.

I too remember the heated NCAA Council argument with Robley over NCAA investigative procedures and penalties, but Cal was not the only conference school where enthusiasm for winning was getting out of bounds.

Jack Hubbard, the president of the University of Southern California from 1970 to 1980, was a sports buff, altogether comfortable with the athletics crowd. It was not uncommon for Hubbard to be on the sidelines at USC's home football contests wearing game cleats. After one of these occasions, Dave Maggard, who had succeeded Paul Brechler as athletics director at Cal-Berkeley, told Hubbard that he was impressed with the size of USC's linemen, averaging 280-plus pounds.[9]

"Jack," Dave asked, "where in the world do you find those big boys for your line?"

"Why, David," the USC president answered solemnly, "we go into the library to look at the students studying there, and we ask the biggest ones to come out for football."

Then Hubbard and Maggard broke up in laughter—competitors but allies in the knowledge that college sports were no longer conducted for regular students.

Two decades of negligible conference enforcement led to an 8.5 upheaval on the Richter scale in 1979. Wiles Hallock and his key investigator, Michael Slive, attended a hearing at Tempe, Arizona, at which eight Arizona State football players were questioned about fake summer-school grades they had received to become eligible for that fall's football season. Rocky Mountain College in Montana had offered the summer courses in California, where the Arizona State players lived—an interstate scheme of offering extension course credits that is practiced by many fully accredited colleges in search of new money.

Mike Slive had done a fine job of preparation. All eight football players signed affidavits stating they had neither attended the extension course nor studied, yet they were given B grades vital to their eligibility.

Later that winter, Swede Johnson, vice-president of the University of New Mexico, telephoned Wiles with a tip that UCLA, Oregon, and Oregon State also might be involved. Swede was worried about his own university as well.

The evidence of academic cheating at the three additional schools was overwhelming, and soon the University of Southern California was also on the hook—but not for pushing their players through fake courses provided by *other* colleges. The USC players had enrolled for speech courses on their own campus in which little attendance was required and false grades were awarded.

USC faculty representative Jack Larsen appeared deeply

wounded by such charges during a May 1980 Pac-10 Council meeting at the Del Coronado Hotel in San Diego. He argued that since USC had uncovered its own chicanery, it should be dealt with more mildly than the other four institutions. This can be a good argument for leniency in college infractions cases. Not so this time.

Doug Hobbs of UCLA, chairman of the Pac-10 Compliance Committee, promptly responded: "On the contrary, Jack, the difference between obtaining bogus grades from a junior college and granting such grades from within your own university is akin to the difference between patronizing a house of ill repute and owning one."[10]

That put-down didn't stop USC. In August, USC President Jack Hubbard rose during a meeting of conference presidents to plead that USC should not be treated the same as the other schools. After listening patiently, his conference colleagues voted to penalize USC fully.

When Hubbard was apprised of the decision during a postmeeting social hour, the USC president sighed and philosophically remarked: "You know, we had a flimsy case, but I gave it my best shot."[11]

On August 11, 1980, the Pac-10 presidents announced that five conference members—Arizona State, Oregon, Oregon State, UCLA, and USC—were ineligible for the 1980 conference football championship and all postseason football games. In addition, football games were forfeited, Oregon was deprived of three future football grants-in-aid, and Oregon swimming and USC track were hit. The reason: "unearned [academic] credits, falsified transcripts and unwarranted intrusion" of athletics interests into the "academic processes" of the five universities.[12]

Fights within the Family

The Pac-10 could take some solace from the fact that their good friends in the Big Ten also had law-and-order problems. Shortly after Wayne Duke took Bill Reed's place in the commissioner's chair, I was responsible for starting an investigation that put Wayne into sharp conflict with Michigan State President Cliff Wharton.

I had stopped in Ann Arbor to visit my friend Don Canham at Wolverine Sports, his private sports equipment mail-order firm that had helped make him a multimillionaire. Don, the Michigan track coach, had succeeded Fritz Crisler as University of Michigan athletics director. Football Coach Bo Schembechler, whom Don had hired from Miami (Ohio) University in 1969, joined us for a chat.

It quickly became clear why he had stopped by as the talk turned to recruiting and cheating. Bo always has been a man of great energy, conviction, and persistence. He had played for Woody Hayes at Miami of Ohio, and had inherited part of Woody's explosiveness. Bo shifted into high gear. He leaned forward, pointed his finger, and charged: "They're buying players at Michigan State. They're taking good players away from us. They've got a slush fund."

As he continued, I thought back to Fritz Crisler's comments when he was condemning Michigan State's free-wheeling activities in the late 1940s.

This encounter led me to send a confidential memorandum to the enforcement section outlining the generalized allegations. An investigation began. Soon Michigan State was considering firing its athletics director, Burt Smith, as a way out. We had not yet developed the full story, but Michigan State's top management apparently felt that dumping Burt would get rid of the NCAA nemesis and satisfy Big Ten Commissioner Duke.

The investigation broke into the press during the summer months before the 1974 football season. Ohio State Coach Woody Hayes had made derogatory comments about Michigan State recruiting. The reporters kept after him as the season got under way, and writers in Michigan suggested that Hayes had turned in Michigan State to the NCAA.

Ed Weaver, the Ohio State athletics director, talked to me about the problem in January 1975 and later called me to say that, considering the hate mail and talk-show commentary from Michigan, he anticipated real problems when the Buckeyes played at Michi-

Wayne Duke (*left*), former Big Ten Conference commissioner, with Don Canham, former athletics director for the University of Michigan. The two had many disagreements during their tours of duty in the Big Ten, but they ended their careers as good friends.

gan State that fall. He wanted me to take some of the heat off Woody Hayes.

"Well, I'm bound by confidentiality on these things," I told Ed. "If things get rough near game time, maybe there is something I can do." Our information had actually sprung from three principal wells—Michigan, Ohio State, and Notre Dame.

Ed Weaver was a calm, highly experienced professional. When he telephoned me again, I sensed he was genuinely alarmed. I took him seriously and agreed to help. So I issued a press release stating that the allegations about Michigan State had come from several sources and that Woody Hayes was not the primary one.[13]

Weaver also called Burt Smith at Michigan State to arrange for extra protection around the Ohio State bench. Burt came through in spades. There were enough plainclothesmen and state police on hand to withstand an armed onslaught.

The Ohio State special teams were on the field to open the season at East Lansing in September 1975. Just before game time,

Ed Weaver thought it best to enter the dressing room and come back onto the field with Coach Hayes. Ed, who is six feet four inches tall and about 220 pounds, walked out to the field bareheaded alongside the six-foot-tall Hayes. Immediately, the boos started and quickly reached a crescendo as they came into full view of the capacity crowd. Woody stopped, looked up at his companion, and remarked: "You know, Ed, I don't think these people like you."

The boos did not fully stop until the Buckeyes shut down the Spartans' offense and took an early lead over Michigan State. The final score (21-0) made the enforcement case a moot issue with the crowd.[14] It was not a moot issue, however, in Michigan State's executive offices.

The university and President Wharton had not been particularly helpful to investigators. Wharton was leaning on Duke in an effort to neutralize the commissioner. He had appointed himself as head of the university investigating committee, which was considered a mistake by some of the more savvy East Lansing observers.

As things moved along, it appeared Burt Smith would become the sacrificial lamb. The NCAA had evidence there was outside money, probably from more than one source, but we were short on operating details. Nevertheless, the NCAA applied heavy sanctions to Michigan State in 1976 as part of a three-year probation for multiple violations including free automobile transportation, special credit accounts at a travel agency, free clothes at a local haberdashery, and cash spending money.

It was Burt's former son-in-law, Ken Erickson—a Michigan State booster—who brought the facts out. Erickson was unwilling to see Burt Smith take all the blame. He telephoned Duke in late January 1976, saying he had two check stubs from a fund that had paid the indicated amounts to Dennie Stoltz, the head football coach.[15] Now Duke had what he needed and he called Wharton.

"I began by saying, 'Cliff, I know you and I have had our differences on this, but I have some information which I think you ought to have. I think you are getting bad counsel.' Cliff was very reluctant."

Nevertheless, the two men had lunch together at the president's home, Cowles House in East Lansing. Duke showed Wharton the check stubs.[16] "These were written to Dennie Stoltz," Duke said.

Erickson had diverted various contributions designated for an established and bona fide alumni fund into a special bank account. It was from this account that checks were written to various people to benefit Michigan State athletics.

NCAA prosecutions frequently are like family fights, complicated by tangled personal relationships. By this time Jack Fuzak, who had competed with Neinas and Duke for the Big Ten commissioner's job, had been elected NCAA national president. Not only was he still the faculty representative of Michigan State, but Dennie Stoltz had coached Jack's son at Alma College. Fuzak had supported Stoltz's appointment and he was embarrassed by the scandal. He removed himself from the hearing process and did nothing whatsoever to interfere with our investigation.

This was happening at a time when the NCAA was coming under persistent attacks for what critics called "selective enforcement." After our investigation of his California State, Long Beach, basketball program, followed by a UNLV inquiry, Jerry Tarkanian insinuated that Byers and his sleuths went after the poor people of college athletics and left the rich alone. Chuck Neinas, then commissioner of the Big Eight Conference, also suggested to college associates that the NCAA favored Big Ten and Pac-10 institutions.

So much for that. Here we were in 1976, embroiled with Michigan State, whose faculty representative was the NCAA national president.

After most tough cases, investigators are plagued by continuing curiosity: Did they really dig out the whole story? Commissioner Duke was no exception. As the dismissed Coach Stoltz was about to leave East Lansing, Wayne Duke had a drink with him in a bar chosen by Stoltz.

"I said, 'Dennie, why don't you tell me what happened? If you don't, I'll tell you what happened.'" Silence. Then Wayne continued, "You were caught up in a machinery, which was set up before you ever came on the scene, and you couldn't overcome it. This was a pattern that was set up way before you by your predecessors, and you were caught up in it and you just couldn't stop it.

"And I said, 'It's all over, and it's all done. Why don't you tell me what happened?'" Duke reported Stoltz would not respond.[17]

The penalty knocked the school off NCAA television for three years—aggravating Notre Dame, which had a home-and-home football series with Michigan State and thus lost potential television appearances with the Spartans. Since television money usually is shared among teams in the same conference, the Notre Dame opposition to TV bans as an NCAA penalty is supported elsewhere in the collegiate community. Banning a conference big timer from the tube costs all other conference members thousands of dollars. They don't like it.

Duke was well on his way toward learning from real-life experience the lessons that Vic Schmidt and Howard Grubbs had tried to teach him.

Before he was hired, when the Big Ten job was up for grabs, Don Canham had supported Chuck Neinas. As a result, my friend Don never liked my friend Wayne Duke, who won the competition. Sensing the dangers, Wayne on the advice of Howard Grubbs had asked for and obtained a five-year "evergreen" contract somewhat like mine with the NCAA. The contract came up for challenge before the first automatic-renewal provision could take effect.

Ohio State and Michigan had tied 10-10 for the Big Ten championship at Ann Arbor in 1973, and Dennis Franklin, the Wolverine quarterback, was injured. The tie left unresolved the question of which of the two teams would go to the Rose Bowl. Bo Schembechler felt he had outplayed Woody Hayes. Michigan later accused Duke of implying during the decision-making process that the Michigan quarterback would not be well enough to play on New Year's Day, allegedly steering the vote toward Ohio State. The charge was proved untrue in a subsequent conference hearing.

The Michigan people nevertheless were insulted. Although the Big Ten athletics directors' vote had decided the issue in favor of Ohio State, Michigan blamed Duke for the Wolverines' exclusion from the Rose Bowl. The debate left bruised feelings, particularly after Bo engaged in shotgun criticisms that hit assorted athletics directors.

Bo pointedly challenged Elroy Hirsch, Wisconsin athletics director, for his vote against Michigan. Bo even suggested that those who voted for the Buckeyes didn't know much about football. Well, Hirsch had earned the sobriquet "Crazylegs" during a super career at Wisconsin, Michigan, and two pro teams, including nine years with the Los Angeles Rams. He didn't have to take that from a pouting football coach, no matter who that coach was. Further, Bo didn't have any varsity letters from Michigan, while Elroy, during the war years, had earned four varsity awards in four different sports at Michigan in one year.

The integrity of Hirsch and the University of Wisconsin was on the line in a major media dispute. Frank Remington, Wisconsin faculty rep and a respected law faculty member, considered it a violation of Big Ten ethical conduct standards. This was a code that Remington had written at the request of Duke and Big Ten athletics directors, who had confessed they needed conference backing to control the sniping and complaints of their coaches.[18]

The conference wanted Bo to apologize to Hirsch and the entire Big Ten Conference. Bo wouldn't do it. Most of the participants in this squabble later attended a conference outing at the Nordic Hills golf course at Itasca, Illinois, where peace negotiations took place. While others played golf, Wayne and Don sat on the patio and tried to patch things up. Having personally tried to reconcile these two friends, I knew from experience that Wayne Duke is a forgiving person and Don Canham is not.

"I said, 'Don, get Bo to apologize,'" Wayne told me later. "'We will have all this behind us, and I'll call these other people and tell them.' He [Canham] said, 'I'm not going to do it.'"[19] Not much was done to muzzle Bo, and shortly thereafter the revenge factor set in.

Big Ten faculty reps and athletics directors had wanted a commissioner who would be above athletics politics when they hired Duke in 1971. An evergreen contract was a symbol of security and the conference's faith in him. Politics were under way to change that.

Michigan President Robben Fleming, a reasonable man who restrained the strong-willed Canham and Schembechler more times than generally known, chaired the Big Ten presidents meeting at which Wayne Duke's evergreen contract was replaced by a year-to-year agreement. The results were preordained by back-home politicking before the respective presidents arrived. The decision was that the presidents felt the commissioner should be hired on the same basis as college faculty and university administrators, that is, a year at a time. Never mind that faculty members enjoy tenure and university vice-chancellors seldom are required to beard the lions of intercollegiate sports in public view.

Ironically, a short time before, the Big Ten presidents had assumed control of the hiring of the conference commissioner, taking it out of the hands of faculty representatives and athletics directors. Since the commissioner had to deal regularly with the athletics element, the thought was that he would be more comfortable knowing college presidents sat above the fray and would not be swayed by the day-to-day warfare of college athletics. Unfortunately, too many college presidents speak of integrity and athletics reform in public and play a game of Tammany Hall politics in private.

Living year to year didn't deter Wayne. In 1980 the University of Illinois hired Mike White as its football coach. White had been dismissed by Dave Maggard, athletics director at Cal-Berkeley, for cutting corners. In seven seasons at Cal White sported a 37-32 record. However, in his last four years he was 28-15-1 and was 8-3 in 1977 when Maggard bid him farewell. Dave took a lot of heat for getting rid of a winning coach and was surprised when Illinois hired him from the ranks of pro football.

The man who engineered his hiring was Neale R. Stoner, former athletics director at Cal-Fullerton, who took over in 1979 as athletics boss at Illinois. Coincidentally, Donald Shields had been president of Fullerton during Stoner's time there, and Shields moved to SMU in 1980. With that double exodus from Fullerton, each ended up in two of college sports' most notorious infractions cases.

The word from the Pac-10 to the Big Ten conference office was that university officials needed to keep their eyes on Coach White.

Duke was present at an Illinois meeting where White was introduced to the populace. Mike White was an attractive, disarming person who had a penchant for turning people, young and old, into true believers. Duke probably underestimated Mike's magnetism when he decided to warn the chiefs of the Illini.

On this occasion he saw Stanley O. Ikenberry, president of the Illinois system, and John E. Cribbett, chancellor of the Champaign-Urbana campus. He asked to talk to them about White and later was invited to lunch on the patio of Ikenberry's home. Most university system bosses do not micromanage the respective campuses, but Mr. Ikenberry had repeatedly made it clear that where Illinois athletics and Big Ten relationships were concerned, he was the head man.

Duke described that luncheon meeting. "I said to President Ikenberry: 'This is going to be very difficult for me to say to you. You have a tiger by the tail here, and his track record is not all that good. I just think you ought to be forewarned.'"

The two university officials were far from pleased.

"They were upset. 'What are you doing about Woody Hayes, Bo Schembechler, and Bob Knight?' they asked. Going in, I had thought they might appreciate my help."[20]

In talking to me later, Wayne made roughly the same bemused remark Vic Schmidt had uttered almost thirty years earlier. "I was trying to help. I thought I was supposed to try to keep things clean."

Wayne's premonition did come to pass.

Gwen Norrell, Michigan State faculty representative and member of the Big Ten Eligibility Committee at that time, recalled other factors of which Duke wasn't aware. Gwen was nationally respected for her knowledge of academic testing, analysis of transcripts, and course standards. She was a member of the NCAA Council from 1981 through 1984. Gregarious and popular, she always exhibited a refreshing candor.

She told me academic and eligibility decisions on the Illinois campus arose from strange sources. "They would tell the registrar's office what they wanted done," she said. "They would tell the admissions office what they wanted done. And those people on the academic side went along with those people over there in the athletics association [Illinois Athletics Association, the corporation that operates the schools' intercollegiate programs]. I'd never seen anything like that in my life.... If they wanted a guy there, I don't care what, whether it was a swimmer or a tennis player, they just said we want him and they got him."[21]

The record showed that some players with academic deficiencies were sent to Parkland Community College, a nearby junior college, for academic healing. The athletes came back to Illinois qualified.

In May 1980, the Big Ten ruled a University of Illinois transfer student, David Wilson, ineligible because of academic deficiencies. Wilson, a quarterback, began practice and filed suit August 19 in local court against the Big Ten, the NCAA, and the university. The Big Ten complained that a senior employee of the university athletics association had "arranged" the previous May "for an attorney to represent" Wilson. The conference felt it had been blindsided.[22]

An intense legal battle began, with Illinois's interests fully prepared. The Illini were determined to keep Wilson eligible for the 1980 season. The case started out as a debate over such things as whether playing less than one-half of the first game in junior college should count as a season, and the proper way to calculate junior college credit. The Big Ten and its attorney, Byron Gregory, had to play legal catch-up in trying to persuade Illinois courts to lift the preliminary injunction granted by the Champaign County Circuit Court permitting Wilson to play.

Late one night, as he worked in the Big Ten office, a light clicked on in Byron Gregory's mind. He realized that the middle initial of Wilson's name was incorrect on the transcript that was then in evidence.

In the course of the eligibility wrangling, Illinois had sent a staff member to California to find a better transcript. The Wilson transcript that the University of Illinois was defending was not quarterback David C. Wilson's, but that of another Wilson, David B., who had attended the same California junior college. Quarterback Wilson's GPA was calculated at 1.81, but David B.'s was figured at 2.67, and his was the transcript before the court.

Surely revelation of this sleight of hand would be enough to gain court support for the Big Ten—so Byron Gregory thought. The circuit court did dissolve the injunction on September 17. The plaintiff appealed to the Illinois appellate court, which reinstated it. The Big Ten didn't expect the state supreme court to go along, but, by a 4-3 vote, the court left the injunction intact. Wilson played out the season.

Reaction to the Big Ten "persecution" of the Illini was bitter and prolonged. Even the Illinois legislature denounced the enforcement effort.

"Illinois charged that the Big Ten was on their back and looking over their shoulder," Gwen Norrell told me, "and that the conference was out to get them no matter what they did."[23]

Meanwhile, the legal issue was back in Champaign County circuit court, and Wilson continued playing under the original preliminary injunction. He completed 43 of 69 passes against Ohio State in November for 621 yards, six touchdowns, and an NCAA record.

Coach Mike White had signed Wilson to a letter of intent in January 1980 to play immediately for the Illini. Wilson's passing skills had vindicated the coach's instincts. After the season, Illinois asked for waiver of conference rules so that Wilson would be eligible for the 1981 season.

At a Big Ten faculty representatives meeting in Minneapolis, Illinois sought to reach better terms with its conference colleagues. The Illinois officials, President Ikenberry and Illinois Chancellor John Cribbett, were immediately upset to learn that Duke had told the Big Ten faculty reps that an NCAA investigation was under way, which it was. Duke said that Ikenberry and Cribbett, during a break, accosted him angrily, believing he had prejudiced their effort to settle things. President Ikenberry says he does not recall the incident.[24]

Frank Remington, one of the strong men of both Big Ten and NCAA enforcement, became irate at the attitude of the Illinois group and the pressures they were exerting through the still-unresolved lawsuit.

"You know," he told the group, "my experience in the field of criminal law leads me to conclude it is unworkable to negotiate a sentence with a convicted criminal, and I feel the same way about negotiating a penalty with a conference institution which refuses to support the decision of the conference as to the academic eligibility of the student-athlete."[25]

Later Frank told me that that day in Minneapolis was one of the most irritating of his career, which spans more than three decades as an expert in criminal law and nine years on the NCAA Committee on Infractions, including five years as chairman.

"We [the Big Ten conference group] were in one room," he explained, "and the Illinois people in another. Emissaries went back and forth." The Illinois people were holding the threat of the continuing lawsuit over the heads of the Big Ten faculty representatives as a primary negotiating weapon.[26]

On Saturday, May 2, 1981, the conference through Commissioner Duke announced that Big Ten faculty representatives had voted unanimously to put Illinois on probation for three years and levied other sanctions. The Illini hostility against Wayne Duke hung on. The garage door of his home was splashed with the Illinois orange and blue colors, and he received threatening phone calls.

The Wilson case shook up the Big Ten Conference more than any other case. Personal relations were damaged. After the dust settled, Ikenberry, as chairman of the Big Ten's Council of Ten presidents, set out to hire a new Big Ten commissioner.

Wayne had grown tired of the fight. He mentioned during a plane trip with Neale Stoner, the Illinois athletics director, that he was considering retirement. It wasn't long before a prominent Illinois alumnus called and told him of an insurance-annuity plan that Wayne found very attractive. The commissioner was assured the conference would approve a generous arrangement.

In talking with Ikenberry, Duke sparred for time. But after living contractually year to year, Wayne realized the collegiate version of a golden parachute looked pretty good. It was time to say good-bye.

Wayne retired from the Big Ten at the age of 61 after a meeting in June 1988. The Council of Ten presidents asked him for any parting advice he might have for them.

Wayne told me that when he looked around the table, he noticed that many of them represented institutions that had fought the cases he brought to them. His eyes fell on Robben Fleming, representing Michigan at the meeting. Bob Fleming had retired as president several years earlier and had agreed to serve briefly as interim president after then president Shapiro departed and before James J. Duderstadt assumed the head chair. Wayne said: "Bob, you will remember you were the chair of the Council of Ten when I was placed on a year-to-year basis. I said then, Bob, that it was a mistake, and I say it to you again today. One thing the Big Ten needs to do is give my successor a contract and, after that, give him your support."[27]

Jim Delany, another former NCAA staffer, succeeded Wayne with a five-year contract. In the first six years, his compensation almost doubled. A former NCAA investigator, Delany understands the benefits of not investigating your employers.

Nearly three decades had passed, but the reason Vic Schmidt and Wayne Duke both departed early from their respective posts was that they tried to require their employers to live by the rules their employers had adopted.

Present-day conference commissioners emphasize compliance programs and rules seminars. They negotiate TV contracts, run conference championships, and argue for larger money grants from the NCAA. They serve as diplomats who are expected to negotiate differences with the NCAA. Promoters and diplomats have more fun than prosecutors. They leave tough enforcement matters to the NCAA. The one exception to this is the NCAA's former public relations director, Tom Hansen, in the Pac-10 Conference where he uses the well known talents of David Price, a man who has earned the respect on more than one occasion of the NCAA's best enforcement operatives.

But while it often has the will, the NCAA itself—just like a conference—has critical problems in enforcing the rules, particularly against coaches and colleges that use the nation's court system, their friends on the NCAA Council, or threats of government action to frustrate the process. Illinois, under the direction of President Ikenberry, is one example of failed presidential leadership. But one coach manipulated the system more skillfully than anyone else. In the process, he became a sort of living legend.

Notes

1. Darrell Royal, conversation with the author, March 2, 1987.
2. Information for this account was drawn in part from Lou Maysel, *Austin American-Statesman,* December 21, 1986.
3. Bob Oates, *Los Angeles Times,* March 29, 1977.
4. Walter Byers, internal file memorandum of meeting with Michael Johnson, February 2, 1976.
5. Edwin H. Cady, interview with the author, January 14, 1991.
6. Information for this account was drawn from conversations with Wayne Duke at the time and subsequently; Wayne Duke, interview with the author, September 29, 1988.
7. Information for this account was drawn from conversations with Paul W. Brechler at the time and subsequently; Paul W. Brechler, interview with the author, April 13, 1991.
8. Wiles Hallock, interviews with the author, May 30 and June 4, 1990.
9. Information for this account was drawn from conversations with David L. Maggard at the time and subsequently; David L. Maggard, interview with the author, July 30, 1990.
10. Information for this account was drawn from conversations with John R. Davis, Douglas H. Hobbs and Wiles Hallock at the time and subsequently; Hallock, interviews.
11. Ibid.
12. Pac-10 Conference, Media Release, August 11, 1980.
13. Information for this account was drawn from conversations with Ed Weaver at the time and subsequently; Ed Weaver, interviews with the author, June 18 and August 8, 1990.
14. Ibid.
15. These developments were telephoned by Wayne Duke to Walter Byers and summarized in an internal NCAA memorandum, February 4, 1976.
16. Duke, interview.
17. Ibid.
18. Frank Remington, interview with the author, July 19, 1990.
19. Duke, interview.
20. Ibid.
21. Gwen Norrell, interview with the author, July 12, 1990.

22. Information for this account was drawn from conversations with Wayne Duke, Frank Remington, and Gwen Norrell; from various newspaper articles, including Associated Press and United Press International stories appearing in the *Chicago Tribune, Chicago Sun-Times, Champaign-Urbana News-Gazette,* and the *St. Louis Post-Dispatch,* May 3–6, 1981; and from a recording of the media conference involving David C. Wilson and Stanley O. Ikenberry, May 19, 1981.

23. Norrell, interview.

24. Stanley O. Ikenberry, interview with the author, January 31, 1991.

25. Frank Remington, letter to Walter Byers, August 8, 1990.

26. Remington, interview.

27. Duke, interview.

Chapter 12

Beating the System

The farmhouse where Jesse James was born in 1842 still stands near Kearney, Missouri, 30 miles northeast of the home where I was reared. He and his brother, Frank, were folk heroes.

Jesse and Frank robbed from the rich and gave to the poor, we were told, just like Robin Hood. They were brave and chivalrous. They had fought for the South in the Civil War and were persecuted thereafter by northern lawmen, who sought revenge.

That was the tale we heard during our school days in the 1930s. Later, we were told that the James brothers rode in the war with southern guerrillas—sometimes with "Bloody Bill" Anderson, whose band reportedly once killed 25 Union prisoners. In the course of their later robberies, the James brothers reportedly shot more than a dozen men.

Still, that original romantic yarn—as told by sympathetic newspapermen and the Jameses themselves—helped keep the brothers free to rob and kill for 16 years. Jesse himself was finally shot, but not by the law. One of his own gang killed him in 1882. Then Frank was pardoned by the governor and came home to embroider the story for several generations of paying visitors at the Kearney homestead, where he died peacefully in 1915.

You might say the James boys beat the system.

A Living Legend

Jerry Tarkanian is basketball's winningest coach (24 seasons, .837 victory percentage). With his wife's loyal assistance, Jerry tells *his* own story. It goes something like this.

He was the "social worker" coach, the compassionate "Father Flannigan" of big-time athletics. He took the underdogs, poor students from the inner city, and gave them an education while building great teams.

The big basketball powers at other universities, mostly cheaters themselves, became jealous of this Long Beach–Las Vegas upstart. Since they couldn't beat him on the court, they decided to convict him off the court on trumped-up charges.

They turned to Walter Byers and the NCAA staff to get the job done. In newspaper articles, Jerry had dared speak out against the NCAA. Byers and his enforcer David Berst had long wanted a pretext for revenge. With charges filed by the anti-Tarkanian rich people of college basketball, Byers and Berst had what they needed.

The NCAA's gendarmes interviewed witnesses and lied about what they said, fabricating charges to persecute the coach. Jerry Tarkanian was denied his constitutional right to due process of law and crucified by the all-powerful NCAA. Yet Jerry triumphed over this evil and UNLV won the 1990 Final Four.

Coach Tarkanian told versions of this story for some 20 years to the media, in the courts, and before a congressional committee. A man who never turned down an interview, he knows the art of modern public relations: tell the same story enough times and people will believe it. Play to the suppressed rebellion of the American psyche.

Unlike the James boys, Coach Tarkanian did not break the law of the land—only the rules of the NCAA. But just as they beat the system of their day, Tark the Shark whipped the NCAA and the intercollegiate athletics system it represents.

None of the many NCAA attackers pulled the legal and media levers as shrewdly as Jerry Tarkanian. His court case alone cost the NCAA nearly $1 million. Though the NCAA won its Supreme Court appeal in 1989, after twelve years of legal battling, it has proved to be little more than a pyrrhic victory. The principal punishment Tarkanian has suffered so far seems to be the sleepless nights he describes to reporters.

Tarkanian became famous as an underdog martyr to the big basketball powers that he says never get punished for their sins.

Yet, during the 1970s and 1980s, 13 of those powers—Florida State, Kansas, Duke, Illinois, Minnesota, Cincinnati, Auburn, Memphis State (twice), New Mexico, Wichita State, San Diego State, Baylor, and South Carolina—suffered major NCAA penalties.

Tark was walking testimony to the modern redefinition of institutional control of athletes. He did what he wanted to do; his university did what he wanted it to do.

Three questions are pertinent to the UNLV case. Was Tark given a fair hearing? Was he guilty of violating NCAA regulations? And what does this whole experience say about the likelihood that the NCAA—or any supposed voluntary, private organization—can enforce a complex set of increasingly arbitrary rules on all of the nation's colleges?

For the answers you have to start at California State University–Long Beach, where Tarkanian was hired as basketball coach in 1968. Dr. Stephen Horn took over as president at Long Beach two years later. It was at a banquet on the *Queen Mary* in honor of his university's highly successful basketball coach that Horn first became aware something was amiss.

Horn told me he was discussing student-athlete letters-of-intent with his tablemate, Coach John Wooden of UCLA. Letters-of-intent are a form of contract signed by prospective athletes with a college to bring the recruiting process to an end. Horn said Wooden abruptly told him: "Frankly, Steve, that's one problem at Long Beach. Your coach doesn't follow the same letter-of-intent that other schools do."

Suspicions aroused, Horn not long afterward replaced Athletics Director Fred Miller with Lew Comer, then told Comer he wanted Long Beach recruits to sign a proper letter-of-intent. As Horn explained it, "Lew came back from the athletic department in a few days and said, 'They seem to have an NCAA manual down there, but it doesn't look like it's been opened.' I told him, 'Go to it, Lew.'"

In the next two years, Horn reported, 17 people in the Long Beach athletics department were dismissed. An NCAA investigation also was under way at the time.[1]

Tarkanian recalled that period in his 1988 book, *Tark,* in which he speaks of how much Long Beach residents wanted him to stay.[2]

People told him years later, he says, that "Horn was embarrassed about losing a coach the community wanted and that he felt the publicity was demeaning Long Beach State."

Stephen Horn flatly denied that. He said Tarkanian had been on a job interview in Las Vegas during a regional NCAA basketball tournament. Horn explained that the coach came to his office to report he had decided to stay at Long Beach.

"I said, 'Jerry, no, you're not. You're going to Las Vegas. That's it.' He looked me in the eye," Horn related. "He's sort of a walking innocent. He looked me in the eye and blinked and said, 'You know, Dr. Horn, I haven't violated any NCAA rules.'"[3]

A few years later, Tarkanian was still of one mind. "The NCAA has been after me for nine years," he told a *San Bernardino Sun-Telegram* reporter in 1977, "but no one has ever said what I did to deserve it. I got one guy [David Berst] mad at me six years ago, and he's still hounding me. I'm sick of it."[4] Two years later, the coach reported in a sympathetic Associated Press series that "Long Beach blew my mind; it tore my heart out.... It hurt me more because the charges were so ridiculous."[5]

"He comes on innocent," agreed Stephen Horn. "That's hogwash. If I thought he was innocent, he would still be here [at Long Beach]. I don't care whether the NCAA thinks he's guilty or not. I would have protected him if I thought he was innocent."[6]

Having done, in his view, a reasonable job of cleaning up the situation, Horn was dismayed by the NCAA investigation and the prospect of NCAA penalties. Our infractions report did note that the majority of violations had occurred before Horn took office. In January 1974, the NCAA Council described the violations—divided almost evenly between football and basketball—as being among the most serious it had ever considered.

The Council cited both Head Coach Tarkanian and certain assistant coaches for arranging free airline trips for basketball players beyond those permitted by NCAA rules. They charged the head coach himself with arranging three months of free lodging for one prospective recruit; making a cash gift to a recruit; promising another that his family would be moved from their home to Long

Beach, with a job to be arranged for his mother; and other transgressions. An assistant basketball coach was cited for arranging
fraudulent test scores for a student-athlete.

The Long Beach athletics department fell into a brief depres-
sion, which was described that month by two *Los Angeles Times*
reporters who found the place quiet except for a thumping noise
from an office. "Inside," they wrote, "an assistant sports information director is throwing darts at a board covered with a picture of
Walter Byers.... The magazine cutout of Byers is riddled with holes.
'Wanna take a shot?' he asks a visitor. 'Everyone else here has.'"[7]

By then Tarkanian had jumped to the University of Nevada–Las
Vegas, which had been under investigation by the NCAA enforcement division since November 1972. To believe Coach Tarkanian's
oft-repeated charge that our persecutions followed him from Long
Beach to UNLV, you have to believe that our clairvoyant investigators had guessed the coach's destination about a year before he
took the new job.

Located only a mile from the Las Vegas Strip, the university
had had problems with its athletics department before Jerry came.
Five athletes had been arrested in May 1973 on narcotics charges.
John Lindblom, a columnist for the *San Jose Mercury News,* wrote
that the foyer to the Las Vegas Convention Center, where the Runnin' Rebels then played, had been dubbed "bread alley" by the
basketball team. "Individuals of varying descriptions wait outside
for the players after a game and bless them with varying denomi-
nations of money," Lindblom wrote.[8]

The NCAA scrutiny of the school after Tarkanian arrived was
the continuation of an investigation already under way. As the
case progressed, we received allegations about Tarkanian's post–
Long Beach activities, and these became part of that inquiry.

The atmosphere, however, had changed. Our investigators
found that out quickly. Hale McMenamin, the 25-year FBI veteran
who joined the NCAA investigative staff in 1975, got a tip from
an FBI source that people in Las Vegas would seek to discredit our
investigators, going so far as to arrange for them to be arrested in
hotel rooms with prostitutes and planted drugs.

At a 1984 court hearing in Las Vegas, Tarkanian said the rumors of such antics were started by Tony Morocco, an assistant coach at UNLV. "It was all a joke," Coach Tarkanian added. Apparently the UNLV coaches were standing outside the gym and Morocco supposedly said NCAA investigators ought to be set up with marijuana and prostitutes. That apparently was the end of it.[9]

Joke or not, Warren Brown and his enforcement staff believed it was a possibility at the time. Organized crime *was* involved with certain Las Vegas enterprises, and the casinos and hotels were often the scene of fund-raisers for Tarkanian's basketball program and entertainment for Runnin' Rebels recruits. Whereas the rumored setup seemed far-fetched, I thought it made good sense for the NCAA investigators to be doubly alert.

Meanwhile, McMenamin was turning up important leads in the UNLV case. In October 1975, he drove outside Las Vegas to the home of Harvey J. Mumford, a Las Vegas schoolteacher and part-time UNLV faculty member. Mumford admitted Hale, and they chatted while a Monday night pro football game played on the tube.

The talk turned to David Vaughn, who two years before had dropped out of Oral Roberts University and sought to attend UNLV after a recruitment visit. Vaughn's wife explained to the press then that the player's decision had been based on factors frequently appreciated by UNLV recruits.

"He liked the guys," she said, "and he stayed in Caesar's Palace and met a lot of movie stars such as Harry Belafonte."[10]

Mumford's story was that Tarkanian had approached him to ask if Mumford would look after Vaughn and his wife when they arrived. Mumford did, though Vaughn first had to enroll in a junior college to get credits required to enter UNLV. That still didn't make the youth eligible to play for UNLV.

Mumford told McMenamin that Tarkanian then asked him to give Vaughn a grade if the youth merely signed up for Mumford's UNLV class but didn't attend. Mumford said he agreed, but he told Hale he regretted doing this and felt Tarkanian took advantage of him, as Tark knew Mumford would find it hard saying no to anything that would help the team.[11] Mumford also cosigned a note to buy furniture for the basketball player but ended up paying most of the amount himself.

These statements later would be summarized in a lengthy NCAA confidential report that became part of the U.S. Supreme Court record, one of the several court settings for the long-running Tarkanian-UNLV-NCAA legal arguments.

The Mumford assertions also factored directly into the 1977 NCAA Council charges against UNLV

That Tarkanian referred two players, Robert (Jeep) Kelley and Ricky Sobers, to Frank Denton, a Las Vegas travel agent and university booster, to provide free airline transportation beyond that permitted by NCAA rules;

That Tarkanian reimbursed a student in cash for an airline trip;

That players were given free clothing by a Mr. Slacks outlet there;

That players on grants-in-aid were given free lodging, Kelley, for instance, at the home of Mr. and Mrs. Burrell Cohen, university boosters;

That one athlete received free meals at the Las Vegas Hilton any time he desired through the arrangements of a booster, Howard Kincaid;

That another booster and part-time sports agent was paid by the university when he brought two recruiting prospects to the campus;

That Tarkanian arranged for Harvey Mumford to give the B grade to athlete David Vaughn with the understanding the athlete would not be required to do the course work; and

That with Tarkanian's encouragement Mumford cosigned a $600 note for Vaughn and eventually paid $400 dollars of it.

Also listed were infractions committed during the era of Tarkanian's predecessor, John Bayer, but those charges were only lightly contested by the university. It was the findings involving Tarkanian since his arrival at UNLV for the 1973–74 season that were bitterly challenged.

Most of all, UNLV hotly contested Coach Tarkanian's two-year suspension from coaching, a demand imposed upon UNLV by the NCAA. The Infractions Committee had invoked a "show cause" provision in NCAA rules that required UNLV to suspend Tarkanian from coaching or itself face severe penalties.

The suspension would have allowed Tarkanian to remain at Las Vegas as professor of physical education at any salary the university chose to pay. In that 1952 Kentucky case, we canceled a full year's schedule for the team, sidelining the coach along with it. In the Las Vegas case, the team could have played. Only the coach would have been sidelined. But Tarkanian argued that this action threatened his "perks," the outside income coaches receive through endorsements, TV contracts, and sports camps. These would dry up, he said, if he wasn't the head coach.

Attacking the Investigators

Jerry Tarkanian, deservedly praised for his attack-oriented coaching philosophy, followed those coaching instincts in his battle with the NCAA. He judged that the best game plan was a high-pressure, full-court press. His plan to beat the system was clear during his August 1977 hearing before the NCAA Council at the Hyatt Hotel in Knoxville, Tennessee.

There, his attorney pointed out that he had statements from our five principal witnesses denying they had revealed the facts against Tarkanian that were the basis of NCAA charges. Lawyers on UNLV's side attacked our enforcement staff, implying that David Berst had conspired with six investigators to concoct phony evidence. The suggested scenario was that different investigators had interviewed different witnesses and then, ignoring what was said, made up detailed sets of facts, names, and dates and had carefully constructed imaginary events to unjustly convict the Las Vegas coach. The UNLV-Tarkanian lawyers charged further we had denied Tarkanian his constitutional due process rights. The accused should be permitted to cross-examine his accusers.

After repeated charges by Jerry and his wife that our investigators played dirty, the Committee on Infractions devoted four-and-a-half hours exclusively to the allegations at a special hearing held at a Kansas City hotel in March 1977. The committee asked for and received all of UNLV's charges of putative improprieties. Our staff was not shown the material before the meeting. Tarkanian's attorney, Sam Lionel, asked about 75 percent of the questions; Berst and Hale McMenamin were his principal targets. Tarkanian was present but not one of the interrogators.

The five-member NCAA Infractions Committee (which spent a record 26 hours in all on the UNLV case) at that time was chaired by Arthur R. Reynolds, professor of history at the University of Northern Colorado. Others who sat with him were Charles Alan Wright, professor of law at the University of Texas at Austin; Harry L. Cross, professor of law at the University of Washington; William L. Matthews, dean of the law school at the University of Kentucky; and John W. Sawyer, professor of mathematics at Wake Forest. After considering all the evidence, the committee found "no substance" to the charges of foul play on the part of the NCAA staff. The members were unanimous.

Dean Matthews said he, for one, weighed the facts presented to the Infractions Committee and decided UNLV's evidence was not credible. "I had in previous infractions hearings determined that the information reported by staff investigators to be accurate and precise," Dean Matthews noted. He said the UNLV evidence did not meet that standard.

Art Reynolds recently told me his long experience with the enforcement staff made it impossible for him to believe that Berst and six NCAA investigators would conspire to lie to the committee. Other information before the committee corroborated the investigative reports. "The different men, the different facets of the investigation all tied together like a jigsaw puzzle," he recalled. "It squared with what other people said."

Similarly, Charles Alan Wright said it was the meshing of the investigators' testimony with substantiating facts and documents that convinced him of the violations at UNLV. The committee found validity in certain charges against the university and the coach; others were dropped. In turn, the NCAA Council heard UNLV's arguments at two meetings, the one I mentioned earlier at

Knoxville and a second at a hotel on Cape Cod, where the university pushed hard for a deal in which it would punish itself but exculpate the coach. The council supported the coach's suspension.

From that point forward, as the case moved into the courts of Nevada and eventually to the Supreme Court, the earlier Tarkanian suggestion about working something out was in essence the UNLV position. The school would accept institutional penalties if we would remove the suspension of Tarkanian.

The question remains: how did Tarkanian get those statements from witnesses denying evidence contained in earlier NCAA investigative reports? We may never know for certain, but an analysis of the circumstances underscores the fundamental difficulties faced by the NCAA's enforcement program.

As mentioned previously, federal and state investigators and prosecutors can speak with a witness in person or on the telephone and record his or her words and use them as evidence in court. FBI agents run sting operations against elected public officials. Professional investigators can interview by deception, indicating to one witness that another witness has testified to something that in fact he or she had not. Ordinary citizens in most states can do the same—but not NCAA investigators. Any athlete may hide a recorder on his person and record an assistant coach in the act of making an illegal deal. These tapes may be accepted by the NCAA, but NCAA investigators are not allowed to arrange secret recordings by others. The colleges' investigators may not attend, incognito, a meeting of collegiate sports boosters where illegal assistance to athletes may be discussed. A student sports reporter could legally do this and surreptitiously gather evidence.

The federal sting operations into white-collar crime in Chicago Board of Trade and Mercantile Exchange futures trading led to convictions in 1990–91. The exercise would have been an abject failure if investigators, posing as traders, had been forced to identify themselves to targeted brokers on the floors of those two exchanges.

In college athletics, we're talking about white-collar crime involving the young. Why promiscuously adopt rule after rule unreasonably restricting human behavior, then restrain and shackle the investigators hired to enforce them? The reason is that the colleges do not want to dig too deeply into actual practices.

NCAA investigators do have one power not available to ordinary citizens. The NCAA can offer a student-athlete immunity from loss of his college eligibility in exchange for his testimony—a technique we did *not* use in the Las Vegas case.

Whereas the NCAA can seldom offer witnesses anything but trouble for telling the truth about a violation, a powerful university, its lawyers, and its coaching staff command significant leverage. They can impose such quiet punishments on athletes as personal ostracism. Since the future of an athletes' grant-in-aid may be at stake, there is a financial consideration. Or cash may be used to secure silence or altered testimony.

The athlete is well aware of the values involved. Seasoned NCAA investigators like Bob Minnix and Hale McMenamin will tell you today that interviewing athletes about their current college when they have eligibility remaining is largely a waste of time.

A 1989 *Time* magazine article speaks of a "veil of silence" that prevents the disclosure of cheating. On this point, the article quotes Tarkanian as saying: "The code I was raised on was, 'You can do anything you want, but never squeal on anybody.'"[12]

The confidential report of the NCAA Infractions Committee reflects the repetitive efforts necessary to secure evidence of athletics violations. This report on UNLV was plaintiff's trial exhibit 25 in the case that reached the Supreme Court.[13]

Two of the witnesses who stopped talking in the UNLV case were Harvey Mumford, the Las Vegas schoolteacher, and Robert (Jeep) Kelley, an athlete recruited by UNLV. The Infractions Committee tracked Kelley's reversal through a series of telephone calls in 1976.

During that year, Jeep Kelley and his aunt, Frances Parker, a university-educated social worker, were in touch by phone with NCAA investigator David Berst as the UNLV case was being developed. On March 5, Mrs. Parker telephoned from her home in Port Chester, New York, to report that Kelley (who by that time had returned from Las Vegas to his home in Pittsburgh) had called her to say he "was frightened because he had been told by Jerry Tarkanian that the attorney general from Nevada wished to question him in Nevada because he had provided information to the NCAA."

She also said Mrs. Burrell Cohen, the Las Vegas housewife in whose home Kelley had stayed, had called her to say unidentified individuals in Las Vegas wished to talk to Mrs. Parker. Mrs. Parker said she was told Mr. Cohen would forward an airline ticket to her for travel to Las Vegas to "look over the city," an offer Mrs. Parker declined.

On the same day, the NCAA report states, Kelley himself telephoned the NCAA investigator confirming his aunt's remarks and saying he was reluctant to admit to Tarkanian that he had provided information to the NCAA. Kelley "indicated he was concerned in that he did not want himself or his family to be harmed based on his involvement in the case."

In two calls on April 2 and April 5, Mrs. Parker reported that Kelley's former high school principal and coach "were pressuring Kelley to sign a statement in Tarkanian's behalf and to travel to Las Vegas." Mrs. Parker said they had "told Kelley that if he refused to help Tarkanian it would affect the chance of Sonny Lewis [Kelley's half-brother, who was attending his former high school] to participate in collegiate basketball. "Mrs. Parker said that Kelley no longer wished to be involved in providing information to the NCAA in this case because he was receiving excessive pressure."

On April 22 Kelley telephoned the NCAA to say that he was then residing cost-free in the Cohens' Las Vegas home. He said a Pittsburgh attorney had given him a ticket to Las Vegas, where he had free use of an automobile. Kelley said Tarkanian had promised him a construction job in Las Vegas.

On May 11 Kelley called the NCAA twice, once to say that Tarkanian was en route to the Cohen home to obtain Kelley's signature on prepared statements that Kelley believed would contain false information designed to assist Tarkanian. He telephoned later to say he called his aunt and was advised not to sign the statements until she was able to review them. Kelley reported that, on this occasion, Tarkanian had offered to get him a tryout with the Los

Angeles Lakers or a job in a summer basketball league conducted by a friend of Tarkanian's.

According to the report, on May 12 Mrs. Parker telephoned and corroborated Kelley's description of events the previous evening. She also said Mrs. Lois Tarkanian had telephoned her on an earlier occasion, stating that if the "NCAA finds out anything," Tarkanian would lose his job.

Kelley telephoned again in July 1976 to advise that he had returned to Pittsburgh and in fact had signed various false statements in Las Vegas at Tarkanian's request. He said Tarkanian planned to assist him in enrolling at another college.

On November 29 Kelley telephoned an NCAA investigator from Honolulu, saying Tarkanian had arranged for him to receive a basketball scholarship at the University of Hawaii. Before leaving Las Vegas, the report said, Kelley was asked to sign additional statements he described as containing "the same lies as before." UNLV supporters gave Kelley from $600 to $700 for transportation to Hawaii and living expenses prior to the release of scholarship money, the report states.

Periodically, as the UNLV case proceeded through what seemed interminable NCAA hearings, I would ask David Berst whether the witnesses in the UNLV case were standing pat. For a while he said yes. But after the November phone call, Kelley stopped talking to us. Later he apparently did speak with the Associated Press reporter who prepared the 1979 series on the Tarkanian case. That reporter wrote: "Kelley admits talking to his aunt and Berst numerous times during this period but does not clearly explain why he was so willing to talk to the NCAA if he wasn't providing information against Tarkanian. He said his conversations with Berst were general and at the urging of his aunt whom, he said, hated Tarkanian because Kelley had flunked out of UNLV."

Tarkanian's position was that we had made up a goodly part of those telephone conversations.

Even the players most friendly to Coach Tarkanian sometimes make startling public statements bearing on the question of UNLV violations.

"Sudden Sam" Smith, who played guard for Tarkanian's Runnin' Rebels, returned home from Las Vegas in 1977 to sign with the Atlanta Hawks, emphasizing his fondness for his former coach when interviewed by the *Atlanta Constitution*.

"Players come to Vegas and get a nice apartment and $280 a month living expenses," he was quoted as saying. "People gave us nice summer jobs, $5–$6 an hour, for doing nothing. But there was nothing illegal I know of. I didn't have nothing. If we had won the NCAA championship here last March, they'd probably have had new cars waiting for us when we got back to Las Vegas."[14]

Eldridge Hudson, another of Tarkanian's former players, spoke up in a 1989 *Time* magazine article. "Once you get out on the floor, it's a job and you expect to be paid," Hudson said. "If a kid is busting his ass on the court, if somebody wants to buy him a car, let him have it. . . . Me being a star, I thought my mother deserved a Mercedes." The article stated Hudson, while in school, had a private apartment and drove a Mazda RX7. How did he afford it? "Easy," Hudson replied.[15]

After reading and listening for years to Jerry's nonstop commentary, much of it maligning the character of NCAA investigators, I was never sure that the coach himself ever directly denied the various charges. The Associated Press 1979 series quoted him on what he does when players ask for help.

"I'll say, 'You know people in this town as well as I do, keep me out of it.'" The AP reporter wrote that Tarkanian's attitude is that he either cannot or does not want to turn off the flow of illegal booster activities. "It's really uncontrollable. There are rabid people in any town."[16]

The AP reporter also showed Tarkanian an affidavit on the coach's behalf signed by a Long Beach athlete. Although the athlete had ranked in the top 10 percent of the freshman class on his ACT score, the English on the affidavit was difficult to decipher. One of the NCAA charges alleged that Tark's assistant coach at Long Beach had arranged "ringers" to take ACT exams to make athletes eligible. Confronted with the evidence of the semiliterate affidavit, the coach told the reporter that he didn't believe two of those athletes took the exams. In this, Tarkanian was admitting no guilt of his own—only commenting on the charge against a direct subordinate.

"I'm an educator," the AP reporter quoted Tarkanian as saying. "I can't mess around with that stuff. But I realize a lot of blacks back then didn't take their exams. The ACT exam was a reading test and it was anti-black."[17]

In a story that generally supported Tarkanian in 1978, the *Chicago Sun-Times* mentioned that Tarkanian's players were getting jobs in summer camps, free lodging, and free airplane transportation. "Any time you've got poor black kids in your basketball program," Tarkanian said in the article, "somebody is getting them their plane tickets. . . . Their mothers aren't going to cash welfare checks just to put them on a plane."[18] This highly advertised compassion for the poor youth, whom he lifts out of gloomy slums into the sunlight of higher education, has served the coach well. Whereas his real quarrel was with the unreasonable NCAA rules, his PR focus was to show the NCAA as an unfeeling, vindictive, totalitarian bureaucracy populated by dishonest regulators.

After Tarkanian's team won the 1990 Final Four, his wife, Lois, said UNLV's image problem results from the fact that Tarkanian wants to give kids a chance, even if most other schools don't think they deserve one. "Jerry has an affinity for those kids," she said. "His belief is that everybody deserves a chance. . . ."

Lois and Jerry Tarkanian obviously believe that. Coach Tarkanian, of course, dispensed his largess in direct proportion to the height, quickness, and acceleration of the player, not to mention an unerring eye for the basket from 15 feet. Coach Tarkanian's compassion surged like the sea, but only for the powerful leapers with quick hands.

NCAA hearings are conducted in accordance with administrative law principles, in which due process is observed but is less elaborate and rigid than that offered in criminal cases. In formal criminal proceedings, when life and liberty are at stake, the state exercises vast investigative and prosecutorial powers. In such circumstances, due process requirements are extensive and precise, and they should be. In administrative settings, the law has long acknowledged that procedural safeguards can be relaxed. Even so, Jerry Tarkanian received more due process in the NCAA proceedings than most citizens experience in their affairs.

A university fires its losing coach frequently without conscience and only occasionally with due process. But when a college cannot control a winning coach, the NCAA must step in to do the university's job. In such cases, the NCAA frequently encounters heated opposition, and the hearing procedure becomes a long-term legal dogfight with the university. So it was with UNLV.

One complication in the Nevada case was the congressional investigation of NCAA procedures during 1977–78. In the forefront were Rep. John Moss of California, chairman of the House Commerce Subcommittee on Oversight and Investigations, and Rep. James Santini, Nevada's lone member of Congress and the person who instigated the hearings. Santini's political motives were obvious, but lest there be any doubt, he told a thousand boosters at a UNLV basketball appreciation dinner that "...the NCAA ran into a buzz saw" when it came into conflict with Nevada's interests.[19]

Of the NCAA's 800 members, 74 had been through the violations process since 1970, and only 7 of those had gone public to complain about our procedures at the time of the hearings. What gave the congressional hearing an instant and apparent credibility, however, was the presence of the University of Minnesota as complainant alongside UNLV. C. Peter Magrath, president of this noted university, was still angry over penalties we had imposed against his school in a 1976 case.[20]

Magrath then had walked out on the Minnesota football field at halftime, asking the crowd for donations to fight the NCAA with a lawsuit. His antics exemplified a college president furbishing his local reputation with the sports crowd by fighting the NCAA monster, a familiar tactic used by public relations–conscious college executives.

Magrath's support for the congressional hearing hurt us, but we fought it out. Charles Alan Wright hit some good licks. Speaking on his legal specialty, he told the members of Congress that if he were representing a college or coach facing NCAA charges, he too might make charges that they had been deprived of due process rights. "I would do so particularly if my client was guilty," Wright said, "and I were trying to get him off, rather than making a real effort, as so many institutions have done, to find out what has been wrong with the athletics program and correct its mistakes.

"I would be insisting on the right to be present and to tape-record all interviews by the NCAA staff, knowing that this would inhibit many young athletes and they would not tell of violations. . . .

"I would be insisting that witnesses be live and subject to cross-examination, knowing that if there were such a requirement many witnesses would refuse to appear and meritorious charges would have to be dismissed.

"And if I lost before the [Infractions] Committee and the Council, I would be telling my local sportswriters that the procedure is one-sided, that the hearing was a farce, that the penalty was far too severe, and that my institution had been singled out and punished for doing what every other major athletic power is doing."

Wright had described the UNLV-Tarkanian strategy, an offensive game plan practiced by many educational institutions.

During my own testimony before the subcommittee, both Moss and Santini alternately condemned and ridiculed me. To them, Byers obviously was evil and incorrigible. John Underwood wrote a sympathetic story in *Sports Illustrated,* observing that I had been treated like an unrepentant gangster. Still, there were some light moments.

At one of the breaks, I entered the men's room to discover there was a pool of water on the floor near the urinals. The only other person there was Representative John Moss, busy doing what he had gone there to do. As he left, walking carefully through the pool of water, he glanced at me and said: "It appears the government can't do anything right."

"It would seem so," I replied.

We washed our hands, and he left ahead of me without another word. Despite the hearing room acrimony, Santini was the picture-book politician, a gregarious fellow with a ready smile. After a round of TV interviews in the corridor outside the hearing room, he came up to me, shaking my hand as if I were a Nevada constituent and remarking what a great pleasure it was to meet me. Savage your prey in public, but display fraternal goodwill in private.

We took heavy publicity blows from the congressional hearings, but the final results did not derogate our enforcement program and its people. Internal opponents were unable to use the hearings in order to make crippling changes in the NCAA procedures.[21] Such changes were proposed by the University of Denver faculty representative at the 1979 NCAA Convention and backed by, among others, the University of Oklahoma. They were voted down.

UNLV Coach Tarkanian continued to press. The NCAA Council heard a second UNLV appeal in August 1979 in Cape Code, where the university cited its efforts to reform and urged the council to exculpate its coach. The council terminated UNLV's probationary status but confirmed the two-year suspension of Tarkanian.

The coach took his "cause" into the local state trial court in Las Vegas, arguing that he had been deprived of due process of law. Arriving in town, we were acutely aware we were the visiting team, working against a home-court advantage.

Tarkanian's popularity was pervasive. Judges in the Las Vegas court system were elected by popular vote. Jim McLarney of Kansas City's Swanson Midgley law firm ably fought this uphill battle for the NCAA.

Tark's counselor had sued, not us, but the university that had so reluctantly suspended him under the "show cause" demand of the NCAA. UNLV proved a less-than-enthusiastic defendant, complicating our lives more than they did Tarkanian's. The university moved tardily at most every step.

We were unable to remove the case to federal court, and so we spent nearly eight years in Nevada courts, including two trials in Las Vegas. We battled the most popular man in Nevada, a basketball coach with the largest public salary in the state government, not counting his larger private basketball-related earnings. The Nevada attorney general, on behalf of a state institution, intervened in the case to help Tarkanian.

Judge Paul Goldman of Clark County District Court insinuated the local bias during a 1984 hearing, noting that "the view of Las

Vegas, Nevada, from Shawnee Mission, Kansas, seems to have affected the earlier and current proceedings in this long-standing dispute."[22] Judge Goldman had picked up Tarkanian's image of the underdog philanthropist suffering persecution by the Kansas enforcers.

During the two trials in Clark County, the district judges involved heard testimony by Tarkanian *about* the statements in which the NCAA witnesses had supposedly reversed earlier assertions. Yet the documents themselves were never introduced into evidence.

During the 1984 trial, Coach Tarkanian made countless statements to the media, both inside and outside the courtroom. I realized we were suffering nationally because of Associated Press and United Press transmissions of Tark's and sometimes UNLV's view of the world. We dispatched an NCAA public affairs man to Las Vegas to issue press releases giving the NCAA side. Judge Goldman ordered a stop to our releases.

"I have always been of the opinion that cases should be tried in a court of law, not in the media," the judge said. But no jury was involved. Nevada interests continued their commentary.

Art Reynolds, chairman of the NCAA Infractions Committee, remembers well how Judge Goldman questioned him vigorously, suggesting that Art would accept the NCAA investigators' word no matter what the facts.

"The judge said, 'What if it were eleven o'clock at night and the NCAA said it was daylight? Then you'd agree it was daylight?'" Art recalls. "I said, 'No, I'd get up and look out the window. If we were in Anchorage, Alaska, you could still have light with the midnight sun.'"[23]

It was no surprise when the judges in both cases found we had violated Coach Tarkanian's constitutional right to due process. UNLV was prohibited from obeying the NCAA demand that the coach be suspended. We pursued the case to the Nevada Supreme Court and finally to the United States Supreme Court in December 1988. The court ruled only on a narrow point: That the NCAA action in the Tarkanian case was not governmental or "state" action, and that the NCAA therefore need not answer to federal due process standards. It meant, in effect, that NCAA due process issues should be contested in state courts. It was a close call, 5-4. This led to the NCAA being faced with new state laws affecting its enforcement practices and opened the door for new state court challenges by aggrieved colleges and individuals.

Beyond that, the significance of the UNLV-Tarkanian case is not whether he broke NCAA rules. Of course he did. Anybody who studied the case knows it. We spent $1.0 million in opposing his legal challenge on the basis that respect for the law is essential to a civilized society, and that surely one coach should not have wild card privileges. We did what we had to do, and I suppose I would make the same decision today, though with far less certainty.

But the fact is that Jerry Tarkanian beat the system, winning millions of dollars and finally all the marbles, too, in his 16 appearances at the NCAA basketball tournament and 1990 Final Four victory. In 16 tournament appearances (4 at Long Beach and 12 at UNLV) his teams won 70 percent of their games.

Jerry's first contracts at UNLV were called tenured professional employment agreements. In 1980 his salary was about $43,000. In February 1983, Tarkanian signed a contract with UNLV President Goodall and Athletics Director Rothermel for an annual salary of $125,000 plus a "merit bonus consisting of 10 percent of the net proceeds" received by UNLV from appearances in the NCAA men's basketball tournament. It was a three-year, automatic rollover contract. It became a model for winning coaches' contracts for the next decade, many of them with bigger incremental incentives.

Assuming that Tarkanian's 10 percent was the minimum figure in subsequent contracts, his share of UNLV's tournament earnings from 1983 through 1990 probably exceeded $400,000. The NCAA's revised distribution formulas and UNLV's conference distribution rules make a precise estimate difficult.

Tarkanian's share—won directly from the NCAA he has battled so long—as well as all the income he derived from sports endorsements, basketball camps, and other activities, is sufficient evidence of his victory.

Certainly he was a skilled coach and a sound tactician. He did more game coaching than the casual TV viewer might suspect. He made effective adjustments in the course of battle. Originally known for their run-and-gun offense, the Rebels frequently won with devastating defensive performances.

At the same time he made the wise choice of challenging the NCAA in the media, in Congress, and the courts. It cast him in the role of a perpetual underdog, and Jerry's skill in playing David to the NCAA's Goliath kept the NCAA on the defensive.

In July 1990, the Committee on Infractions, chaired by a history professor from the University of Virginia, decided to terminate the battle and applied a modest one-year penalty barring UNLV from the 1991 NCAA basketball tournament. Jerry yelled foul! Promptly UNLV came to the Infractions Committee to present what it called "newly discovered information"—threats of a new legal action by Tarkanian and/or his players, accompanied by an expression of the coach's willingness to drop the old lawsuit if the committee would agree to a penalty acceptable to Tarkanian.

This was a procedural ploy to establish grounds for reopening the matter. NCAA policy dictates that a case will not be reopened at the request of the college unless significant "newly discovered evidence" directly related to the original findings has surfaced, or it can be shown that the Infractions Committee or council committed a prejudicial error.

The fact that the UNLV coach, his players, or both, might file a new lawsuit to permit the Runnin' Rebels to defend their national championship in 1991 did not meet either test. The NCAA Infractions Committee agreed to this quid pro quo expediency and, in a startling display of mistaken judgment, the committee sat down with the violators to negotiate a reduction of the penalty. A primary condition was that Tarkanian and UNLV would bring the old legal case to a close. This applied to the original legal challenge, which the 1988 Supreme Court decision, in effect, had sent back to Las Vegas trial court.

UNLV proposed four alternatives to the punishment already levied; the committee came back with a compromise. Nearly 13 years after the original council-imposed penalty, the committee agreed to postpone the major punishment still another year. UNLV and its coach could participate in the 1991 tournament but would be barred from the 1992 tournament.[24]

Jerry Tarkanian beat the system. He left the NCAA in distraught circumstances. The NCAA abandoned its penalty of suspending coach violators, while maintaining its awesome power over the eligibility of young athletes. It disclosed to the collegiate world its willingness to negotiate penalties. It announced at the 1991 NCAA Convention something about a critical study of its procedures. Near the end of the game, Tark's full-court press panicked the NCAA into some major errors.

If the Infractions Committee gave up the penalty of suspension in Jerry's case, how could they in good conscience apply it in the future to a modestly successful coach who decides to confess because he doesn't have adequate legal funds or alumni support to apply the Tarkanian pressure? Frank Remington, who had led the battle in 1980 against the University of Illinois when officials used a pending lawsuit as their primary negotiating weapon, believed then and believes now that violators should not negotiate their own penalty. "It should not be their choice," Frank said during the trauma of the Illinois case. In 1991, no longer a member of the NCAA Infractions Committee, he repeated that conviction relative to the Tarkanian case.

Unlike schools that work quietly within the system and accept the results, the violators at both Illinois and UNLV have shown what can be accomplished by employing experienced, outside legal counsel and appealing for justice in state courts. All of this has not gone unnoticed by entrepreneurial coaches mining talent in the recruiting fields of the nation, or by the NCAA policing the action. More and more penalties are now negotiated. The results are duly reported in the *NCAA News,* much like EPA and OSHA fines are reported and accepted as the price of getting business done.

Violations are so prevalent that they have become classified as secondary and major by the NCAA. The secondary cases have become an industry within themselves. There were 150 such cases in 1987. In 1993, there were 900, a fivefold growth.[25] Approximately 75 to 80 percent involve NCAA Division I members. Major cases have remained static, averaging about 22 per year during the same period. For comparison, in 1975, the NCAA membership approved a substantially expanded enforcement effort and in January 1977, there were 10 active cases being worked on and 17 colleges were serving penalties.[26]

Notes

1. Stephen Horn, interview with Charles Hammer, March 18, 1989.
2. Jerry Tarkanian and Terry Pluto, *Tark* (New York: McGraw -Hill, 1988).
3. Horn, interview.
4. Bob Padecky, *San Bernardino Sun Telegram*, February 8, 1977.
5. Associated Press series, in the *Washington Star*, March 6–8, 1979.
6. Horn, interview.
7. Dwight Chapin and Ted Green, *Los Angeles Times*, January 18, 1974.
8. John Lindblom, *San Jose Mercury News*, November 25, 1973.
9. Bob Palm, *Las Vegas Sun*, June 15, 1984.
10. *Los Angeles Times*, November 14, 1973.
11. From conversations by Walter Byers with Hale McMenamin; Hale McMenamin, interviews with the author, February 2 and March 3, 1990.
12. Ted Gup, *Time*, April 3, 1989.
13. NCAA, NCAA Committee on Infractions, Confidential Report no. 123 (47) to the NCAA Council, published in Document no. 87-1061 in the Supreme Court of the United States, October Term 1987.
14. Chris Cobbs, *Atlanta Constitution*, July 7, 1977.
15. *Time*, April 3, 1989.
16. Associated Press series, March 6–8, 1979.
17. Ibid.
18. John Schulian, *Chicago Sun-Times*, reprinted in *Los Angeles Times*, March 7, 1978.
19. Bill Fisher, *UNLV Yell*, April 24, 1979.
20. Max Nichols, *Minneapolis Star*, August 9, 1977.
21. Nancy Scannell, *Washington Post*, November 29, 1978.
22. Associated Press, *Kansas City Times*, June 26, 1984.
23. Arthur Reynolds, interview with Charles Hammer, April 8, 1989.
24. Supplemental Report Regarding the NCAA Show-Cause Requirement to the University of Nevada, Las Vegas, November 29, 1990.
25. Cynthia J. Gabel, interview with the author, November 8, 1994.
26. NCAA, NCAA Council Minutes, January 7–12, 1977, 24.

Chapter 13   **Not Enough
Money**

After winning on the platoon football issue in 1965, the advocates of Bigger-Is-Better scarcely paused for breath. They were on a roll. The next thing they needed was more coaches. The King of the Hill in that regard was Paul (Bear) Bryant, who symbolized the all-conquering coach who rode the crest of the phenomenal growth of college athletics.

A three-year letterman, Bryant had been the "other end" to the famed Don Hutson on Alabama's winning Rose Bowl team in 1935. The Crimson Tide had fallen on hard times in the late 1950s; the alumni wanted him to come back to his alma mater to put down those land-grant college upstarts from Auburn.

He returned in 1958 and led the Tide to six national championships, 12 Southeastern Conference (SEC) titles, 24 consecutive bowl games, and a 232-46-9 record. He also racked up his third infractions case—a minor one this time, earning him only an NCAA reprimand. During the Bear's reign at Tuscaloosa, however, Auburn suffered through three NCAA infractions cases and earned six years of probation and penalties trying to play catch-up to the 'Bama Tide.

With trusted Sam Bailey at his side, Paul took charge in the Southeastern Conference. He commanded a growing army, listing 17 football assistants.

Bear Bryant was not the only one, but he certainly was in the vanguard of coaches who believed that since football brought in the money, it should have first call on spending it. Whatever he spent on assistant coaches, new offices, grants-in-aid, and better training facilities, his competitors had to match. Many were eager to do so. For instance, in 1969 SEC football coaches importuned their presidents to increase the limit on football grants-in-aid. At that time the SEC permitted 40 new grants each year with an overall total of 125 full rides permissible each year.[1]

The major colleges had active recruiting rosters of 75 to 100 football prospects. Costs for recruiting individual players ran as high as $12,500, and it wasn't long before there were examples of an institution spending as much as $25,000 recruiting a basketball "franchise" player.

Lou McCullough, head recruiter for Woody Hayes at Ohio State and a 20-year veteran of this trench warfare, described the gourmet experience of one red-hot Ohio high school star in 1971.

"On Monday Coach John Ray of Kentucky took a prospect to lunch during the school day. That evening Coach Bo Schembechler of Michigan took the same prospect and his coach to dinner. On Wednesday Coach Bill Mallory of Miami University took the prospect and his family to dinner. On Thursday Coach Dick Bestwick of Georgia Tech had the prospect and his girlfriend to lunch, and on Thursday evening Coach John Mummey of Ohio State took the prospect to dinner. On Friday and Saturday the prospect visited a Southeastern Conference school for a 48-hour weekend, where he had his meals furnished for two days."[2]

Such excesses, as well as the coaching overpopulation, and the upsurge in grants-in-aid, were major reasons for growing sentiment within the NCAA that the costs of college athletics must be controlled. During a 1965 NCAA lobbying effort in Congress, we prepared a fact sheet listing revenues of more than 600 four-year colleges that conducted varsity football. We were unable to pin down exact profit and loss, but our best estimate was that only 65 to 75 actually were making money from football.[3]

During the 1960s, football attendance increased 44 percent. Meanwhile, national television revenues jumped 287 percent. The new money, however, was chasing the 174 percent increase in football costs. The major colleges reacted during the 1970s by raising football ticket prices by some 66 percent to $10.00 and basketball tickets rose about 110 percent to $6.50.

Even Penn State's Joe Paterno, who more than a decade earlier had ridiculed my negative stand on two-platoon football, told the

Syracuse (N.Y) *Herald-Journal* in 1974 that he now saw the need for economy. "Going back to one-platoon football would drastically cut expenses," he said. "Football coaches have got to take a lead in this.... We used to travel with 35 to 38 players. Now we take 60 to 62."[4] This was largely a public relations gesture by one of football's committed big spenders of the Bryant model.

During the mid-1970s we were in Congress again debating Title IX requirements that mandated comparable expenditures for men's and women's sports. For that purpose, we undertook a special study of 77 major Division I-A football-playing institutions for fiscal year 1976-77. Only 39, or 51 percent, reported an operating profit from their football programs.[5] Still, football coaches of the era explained away the heightened football expenditures by claiming they paid not only their own way but everybody else's, too. Football, they said, paid for the nonrevenue sports.

The accounting variables in college athletics make it difficult if not impossible to know whether a big-time sport pays for itself, much less whether it generates net receipts to finance the deficit sports. Actual cost accounting, in the sense of a hard-nosed business analysis, isn't done. In past times as today, through university-approved accounting techniques, many big-ticket items are shunted off athletics department budgets to be paid by student fees, donated booster/alumni funds, other departments of the university, or state appropriations. Capital expenditures for buildings or permanent equipment as well as the maintenance and upkeep of facilities may be in the university's overall accounts and current operating budget, with fractional accounting charges to athletics. Consider the following creative strategies:

> Indiana University, entering the decade of the 1960s, handled its football stadium costs with a student fee of $24 per semester (equivalent to $84 in 1990 dollars) to retire the 20-year bonds. These fees were not gate receipts; students paid whether or not they attended games.
>
> The University of Texas in the 1970s hit on a novel plan for enlarging its football stadium to 81,000 seats. By designing a 15-story physical education building behind it, they cut

Cartoon lampooning University of Wisconsin plan in the late 1980s to finance the athletic department's $1.0 million debt by a $10 per semester mandatory, segregated student fee.

stadium costs by $2 million and financed the building itself through endowment funds and student user fees.

At the University of Arizona and Arizona State, the cost of tuition and fees for 317 grants-in-aid, per year per school, came from the taxpayers, through state appropriations by the Arizona state legislature. This major taxpayer subsidy stiffened the competitive climate for all Pac-10 Conference members. The two relatively new Arizona members of Pac-10 received a legislated underwriting of a big cost item, while Cal-Berkeley, for example, was charging the Cal athletics department for that part of each grant-in-aid.

At the University of California, Los Angeles, Athletics Director J. D. Morgan avoided tapping Bruin athletics receipts to build its $5.5 million basketball facility, Pauley Pavilion. He obtained $2 million of tax money from the state board of regents for a "physical education teaching facility," $1 million from regent Edwin W. Pauley for whom the structure was named, another $1.4 million from a fund drive, and the balance of $1.5 million out of registration fees from students.

Even private schools such as Syracuse University in New York find a way into taxpayers' pockets to finance sports. Their stadium (which holds 50,000 for football and 33,000 for basketball) was built with $15.00 million in urban development tax money, $9.75 million from private sources, and $2.75 million from the Syracuse-based Carrier Corporation, for which the structure was named the Carrier Dome. It seemed a shrewd public relations investment for Carrier, which contributed only 10 percent of the cost.

As to off-budget expenditures, during 1985–86 the University of Oklahoma athletics department spent $3.6 million from sixteen special accounts maintained under the umbrella protection of the OU Foundation. In a detailed report, Jerry McConnell of the *Daily Oklahoman* pointed out that the $3.6 million was on top of the $5.2 million held in endowment funds on behalf of 300 athletics grants-in-aid. Withdrawals from the special accounts covered such expenses as complimentary tickets for staff, travel costs that exceeded the athletics department budget, construction, and promotions.[6]

In a strategy that became increasingly popular during the 1980s, NCAA colleges shifted part of the subsidy for players who meet poverty guidelines from athletics department budgets to the federal government's budget through Pell grants. In Division I, poverty-level players with full-ride athletics scholarships who qualified for a maximum $2,300 federal Pell grant could keep a combined $1,700 on top of their full-ride grant-in-aid. As to the $600 balance, the university athletics department customarily received a credit against its overall grant-in-aid costs. In Division I-A, contributions in 1988–89 "from alumni and others" constituted 14 percent of total revenues, according to an NCAA survey.

Do *any* major sports programs make money for their universities? Sure, but the trick is to overspend and feed the myth that even the industry's plutocrats teeter on insolvency.

When the Bryant regime concluded at Alabama, there were reserves of $16 million. Successor Ray Perkins and the new order went on a spending binge, including stadium expansion, and took on about $38 million in debt. In searching for new revenue sources, they raised donation requirements for prime season tickets, upsetting some old-time supporters. These Tide loyalists didn't believe Alabama finances should be in such bad shape.

Perhaps the best example is the biggest of the big, the University of Michigan. The Wolverines own every NCAA football attendance record, customarily averaging more than 105,000 spectators for six or seven home games, compared to the Division I-A per-game average of about 41,200.

"I have to fill that stadium out there," Bo Schembechler told me shortly before he retired. Gesturing to the beautiful Michigan facility that Fielding Yost built and Fritz Crisler enlarged, Bo said: "I'm hired to win games. We pay for everything around here." He might have added: "We also spend it as fast as we make it."

During Don Canham's successful 20-year reign as athletics director (1968–88), Michigan athletics paid its own bills but incurred more of them than anybody else, judging from the NCAA revenue and expense studies.

In 1989, Bo's last year as Michigan head football coach, the school was working under Don's last budget. Total revenues were $16.5 million, of which $9.3 million came from spectator admissions, $1.6 million from television, $1.2 million from bowl games, $809,000 from merchandise sales and concessions, $649,000 from endowment income, and the remainder from a variety of sources. (TV and bowl game receipts are based on a Big Ten Conference distribution formula, and the budget figures do not represent income from fund-raising.)

Total expenditures in 1988 were $15.8 million, including $5.5 million for team and game expenses, $4.9 million for wages and benefits, $1.8 million for physical plant, and $1.3 million for administrative costs. These figures place Michigan's excess receipts ("net profit") at about $700,000. The cost of grants-in-aid was only 19 percent of expenditures.

The Michigan revenue figures for 1989 were 581 percent more than the $2.4 million that Michigan garnered in 1968. At the same time, Michigan's expenditures increased about 605 percent over the 1968 figure of $2.2 million.[7] By comparison, from 1968 through 1988, the consumer price index rose 240 percent.

At the other end of the Division I-A spectrum, the "revenue sports" definitely do not pay for themselves. University of Toledo history professor Eugene Hollon was irritated by his university's determination, along with that of its sister institutions in the Mid-American Conference, to compete with NCAA biggies in Division I. In 1970 he wrote to me: "I think that they [the students] are absolutely correct in objecting to the policy of so many universities, which force them to buy athletic tickets which they don't want in order to support armies of mercenary athletes and right-wing autocratic coaches."[8]

Hollan's point of view, shared by many faculty members at the time, has been largely ignored in the colleges' keep-up-with-the-Joneses spending spree. Mandatory student fees earmarked for athletics have become an accepted part of the budget process.

Interestingly, it wasn't cash-poor Toledo but wealthy Michigan that led an effort to stanch hemorrhaging athletics budgets at major universities in 1975. These perceived runaway costs led to the NCAA's Economy Convention.

A Temporary Victory

The regular NCAA convention in January frequently is bypassed in favor of special NCAA conventions if big issues are at stake. So was it in August 1975, when the Economy Convention assembled at the Palmer House in Chicago. This time, I thought, good things will happen.

Robben Fleming, president of the University of Michigan, was a major force behind the 1975 gathering. He stimulated the NCAA to organize a preliminary group of faculty representatives, athletics

The University of Michigan Football Stadium

directors, and presidents who recommended ways to cut athletics expenditures.

The eventual proposals included the following: limit Division I football programs to 95 grants-in-aid at any one time, with only 25 of those to be awarded to new players each year; limit football coaching staffs to a head coach plus seven assistants and two graduate assistants; hold basketball to 15 grants overall with 5 new ones permitted each year; fix basketball coaching staffs at a head coach, one assistant, and one graduate assistant. Also on the con-

vention agenda were amendments to limit squad sizes, restrict recruiting, and ban travel uniforms. The proposed football squad limits, for example, stipulated that 60 players could dress for the home team, and the travel number was 48.

Missouri's Al Onofrio liked the proposals, saying the 25-95 limitations would even up the "depth factor," which caused the less fortunate to be overpowered in the second half by big squads from rich football schools. There were other coaches, however, who thought the limits, particularly the initial 25, would safeguard the current advantages of the dominant teams. Jack Mitchell of Kansas was one of them as was Jim Walden, formerly at Washington State and later at Iowa State. Jim criticized the restrictions as a device to prevent an ambitious coach from building a program through numbers and catching up with the traditional winners who have built-in recruiting advantages. Time has shown that Al Onofrio and Walter Byers were wrong. Jack Mitchell and Jim Walden were right.

Coaches hired to resurrect moribund programs know by heart the success story of Johnny Majors. He left Iowa State with a record of 24-30-1 to become head coach at the University of Pittsburgh in 1973. Pitt Chancellor Wes Posvar authorized 83 football grants-in-aid for John's first recruiting class, bigger than many colleges' entire varsity squads. Once they were corralled, Coach Majors carefully culled the group. The surviving nucleus in John's four years at Pitt won 33, lost 13, and tied 1. They played in three bowl games, concluding with a 27-3 victory over Georgia in the Sugar Bowl on January 1, 1977, as Majors packed his bags and headed for his alma mater, Tennessee.[9]

The goal of the NCAA economy advocates in 1975 was to save money for the colleges. We also believed that the rules would spread player talent as well, helping the aspiring programs.

We thought it was worth a special convention and the economy reforms were adopted that summer. I left the convention floor reassured that college management did have the courage to face up to the escalating demands of successful coaches.

But in the basement coffee shop of the Palmer House late that day, I encountered a pair of gloomy faces that warned me of trouble ahead. Two advocates of bigger-is-better, Boyd McWhorter, Southeastern Conference commissioner, and Hootie Ingram, at that time his chief assistant, were conversing morosely in a booth. From their frowns, they could well have been heavily leveraged margin players on the day after a stock market crash. I went over in the hope of maintaining cordial relations.

Boyd had been a leader in demanding reasonable academic performance from athletes in his conference and had been a nationally respected advocate of the NCAA's 1.600 academic legislation. But he resented the NCAA's one-member, one-vote policy, which often gave little schools an edge. Boyd and Hootie represented big schools that could spend big bucks on coaches and players.

They did not like the economy legislation. Their particular focus of outrage that day was the vote that eliminated travel uniforms. The big schools liked to outfit their athletes in uniform sports jackets and slacks when they traveled. For major league football it was a piddling expense in their view, perhaps $6,000 to $9,000 per team. The elimination by the NCAA *federales* of this positive local option was the ultimate insult.

"Isn't that the silliest thing you ever heard of?" Boyd asked me. "If the other schools can't afford it, why don't they form their own organization? Why do they feel they have to dictate to us?"

I was sympathetic to the resentment of the high dollar producers at being controlled by those with lesser programs. At the same time, athletics deficits were mounting. Was there never going to be a time when the colleges, although happy in their not-for-profit environment, would slow down the rampaging costs of big league football? Despite such gloom among the "losers," I thought that the moderates had won a key engagement.

In rapid succession, however, four legal attacks were mounted against both coaching and squad limits. The University of Alabama sued us in federal court in Birmingham to set aside the squad legislation, and two of Bear Bryant's assistant coaches sued in the same court to knock down the restrictions on the number of football coaches. Barry Switzer of Oklahoma also fought the coaching limits in another lawsuit filed in Oklahoma City. Determined to let the sports world know that basketball now was as important as football, Bob Knight of Indiana sued in state court in Indianapolis to block the basketball squad restraints.

Power coaches of the modern era were at work, condemning the cost-cutting measures as bad for the players, injurious to the coaching profession, and economically misguided. Battling Alabama football interests in Birmingham and the Big Red in Oklahoma City was disheartening enough, but we also had to convince an Indiana judge that the NCAA knew better than Coach Knight what was good for basketball. These were tough, on-the-road contests, but eventually we won them all.

Visiting Birmingham during a football weekend that fall in 1975, I encountered Alf Van Hoose, sports editor of the *Birmingham News,* during a pregame reception at a downtown hotel. He took my arm and said: "There's somebody I want you to meet."

Steering me across the room, he introduced me to a man he said was Sam C. Pointer, Jr., the federal judge handling the Alabama cases against the NCAA. The man looked like the judge. After I struggled awhile to make stilted conversation, the crowd around us broke up in great laughter, giving the hoax away. The fellow was, indeed, a look-alike, but not the judge.

After adjusting the squad numbers, Judge Pointer sustained the squad limit rules but decided against the NCAA on the coaching limits. In a successful appeal, we won the right to enforce the latter restraints.

While squad limits are not a part of today's reform agenda, the Indiana case, which had a lifespan of 17 days, deserves more than a footnote. It highlighted the traditional rationale of coaches against cost-cutting efforts: "The savings amount to little more than pocket change."

The 1975-enacted NCAA basketball squad legislation capped the traveling party at 10 players. Indiana officials testified that 1974–75 Indiana basketball receipts were $512,998, and basic expenses, $283,929. Travel costs were only $51,479.

They said the basketball team traveled by private university plane, and the 21 seats were paid for. The savings from squad cutbacks would be only $1,749 for the entire road schedule. In comparison, restroom attendants at IU home games cost $4,076 for the home season. Knight testified that trimming three players from the squad would be terrible for morale. The judge refused to grant the requested preliminary injunction, reasoning that a judge in a small Indiana town should not be deciding such questions for 700 colleges. Indiana abandoned the lawsuit.

While the NCAA won the early legal rounds, adroit coaches set out to circumvent the rulings for their long-term advantage.

On the issue of squad limits, the NCAA membership gave

ground to intensifying complaints by coaches, and, at the next opportunity, they revoked the limits, conceding that the number of players suiting up at home or traveling on the road was a local matter, best left to game contracts or conference rules. This decision has earned hardly a mention in past summaries of NCAA reform failures. It becomes of major significance, however, when considering ways to enhance competitive balance without the pages of constricting "amateur rules" that imprison today's players.

On the football side, the colleges soon had more graduate assistant coaches, part-timers, and volunteer coaches. Athletics departments hired weight coaches, who were not counted, and assistants to the athletics director, who supervised recruiting. The fact that an assistant athletics director spent 50 percent of his time on football recruiting did not make him a football staffer.

College football stayed with its expensive two-platoon system, and today there are administrative assistants for football operations and full-time video crews to videotape practice and game action. They break down the tapes to show individual player performance and deliver copies to the individuals daily for off-hours viewing. Basketball assistants of one kind or another, sitting on the bench at game time, seem to outnumber the players in uniform.

The NCAA won the court decisions, but creative coaches won the war. The numbers for football and basketball coaching and support staffs are as large as ever. And retrenchment proposals (even the modest ones of the 1991 NCAA Convention) have little effect, since administrative support staffs for the major sports are essentially beyond the reach of national legislation.

Athletes *Are* Different

Encouraged by the seemingly sweeping victory at the Palmer House convention, a band of college presidents thought the time was right to make the financial need of the recipient—instead of the player's athletic skill—the governing criterion of full-ride grants-in-aid. The NCAA leadership supported the effort. I believed it would soften the "pay-for-play" image of college sports. Reform-

Indiana University basketball coach Bob Knight with Calbert Cheaney, 1993 All-American basketball player for Indiana University. In 24 years, Knight's Hoosier teams have won three national championships.

ers reviving the "need" issue argued that such a policy would reduce costs and take college athletics one healthy step back toward the more amateur status that existed before the full-ride grant was adopted in 1956.

In January 1976, Stanley E. McCaffrey, president of the University of the Pacific, argued on the convention floor that athletes who cannot document need should not be granted room, board, and books. "The athletes are granted special privileges and thus become a group apart," McCaffrey said. "I believe it is entirely fair and possible to defend the granting of *tuition* [for athletes], just as we grant tuition for other talented majors in drama, debate, and music." Additional grant money, he argued, should be based only on financial need.[10]

Edward M. Czekaj of Penn State, speaking on behalf of 30 major NCAA Division I football schools, told the convention those schools wanted to continue the full ride for athletes. "We firmly believe in granting aid based on athletic ability and not on need," he said. "We have lived with this philosophy a long time. It is a good philosophy, and we prefer to keep it that way."

Little did I know as I heard Ed speak that those 30 schools were on their way to becoming the nucleus of the College Football Association.

The Reverend Edmund Joyce of Notre Dame told the convention that "full rides" were the only way to do it. He eloquently condemned the need basis for aid as an irresistible invitation to cheat. Everyone knew by this time that the grant-in-aid system had not reduced athletics crime; I guess Father Joyce was saying it could be a lot worse. He also said Division II and III colleges had good reason to support need as a basis for the grant since those schools had to use university funds to subsidize athletics operations.

"I can find no justification in my own mind," he told the convention, "for using operating or endowment income to bring in a good wrestler at the cost of losing a fine mathematician."

But he added that the situation in Division I football and basketball was entirely different. There, he said, parents realize "that their son's effort will generate far more revenue for the school than the cost of his grant-in-aid.

"The family is proud for the son's sake," he continued. "To reverse this practice now and force the parents to go through a distasteful and perhaps demeaning disclosure [to establish financial need], when it is the school which badly wants their son, is not going to sit well."[11]

Thousands of parents who each year assist their children in applying for scholarships, loans, or grants go through that same "distasteful and demeaning disclosure." The distinction articulated by Father Joyce amounted to a confessional. In the first instance, the college was seeking an athletically qualified high school senior whom it believed would help bring in net dollars to the college beyond the costs of its grant-in-aid program, and he or she deserved special privileges. In the latter case, it is reasonable for parents seeking so much as a loan for an academically brilliant nonathlete to reveal their innermost financial secrets, including a copy of their federal income tax returns.

Still smarting from the cutbacks adopted the previous August, the aristocracy of college football—those accustomed to winning and dominating the Top 20 polls—didn't want more changes in the ground rules. If the less affluent couldn't afford the costs, tough luck. Get out of the way. To camouflage that underlying truth, full-ride advocates underscored these arguments:

> Students in big-time revenue sports return huge benefits to their institutions in terms of money, morale, and publicity.
> The all-encompassing commitment required of student-athletes to survive in the major revenue sports should merit a full ride.
> Administration of the need formula can be manipulated.

The hotter and more divisive the debate, the clearer it became to all: Athletes were a specialized group brought to the campus for a specific purpose. The "need" advocates believed that using the need-based formula would help to legitimatize the compensation plan. Importantly, the financial aid officer of the university would administer the money. The coaches' control of full-ride grants would return to the university scholarship committee.

The final vote was close—120 to 112—but need was on the losing side. A valiant effort was mounted in 1981 to resuscitate the corpus delicti, but NCAA's Division I voted 148-101 to bury need-based financial aid for the big-time universities.

Three weeks after the 1976 convention, James B. Higgins, athletics director of Lamar University in Beaumont, Texas, wrote to me expressing satisfaction with the action taken, which he thought would make Lamar "highly competitive very shortly at *any* level." Jim, a former football coach popular with his big-time colleagues, spoke confidently about competing with the major leaguers, expressing the perennial optimism of college athletics' have-nots. He went on to say, "We were particularly relieved that the odious 'need' issue was finally defeated although most alarmed at the narrow margin. Aside from our philosophical opposition to the principle involved, we feel that much of the grant-in-aid burden can now be relieved by utilization of government programs."[12] Jim had in mind federal Pell grants and loan monies.

The highly acclaimed cost-cutting measures of the 1970s did not achieve their purpose, and the colleges soon were reaching for more dollars wherever they could find them. When the value of the federal Basic Educational Opportunity Grant (BEOG) for poverty-level students jumped from $452 per year in 1973–74 to $1,400 in 1975–76, college officials took notice. They began suggesting that coaches fill out the BEOG forms for eligible athletes.

The poverty grant would cover part of the athlete's grant-in-aid, thus enabling the college to use its own money to finance other athletes. The BEOG grants subsequently were renamed Pell grants after Sen. Claiborne Pell.

After the full ride had been inaugurated in 1956, student-athletes on athletics grants had been allowed to keep payments for participation in ROTC or National Guard training. But other federal or state payments would require, under NCAA law, a dollar-for-dollar cut in the college's athletics grant.

In 1961, federal payments under the War Orphans Educational program were excused, allowing qualified athletes to collect those sums and still receive the full athletics grant. In 1967, payments from Social Security insurance programs and non-service-connected ones from the Veteran's Death Pension program were also exempted. In 1970, payments to athletes under the GI Bill of Rights were added to the exemption list.[13]

These government programs had emotional and patriotic appeal. The Pell grants elicited a different response. At the outset, the colleges effectively took back the poverty-level athlete's entire Pell grant by holding the player's combined aid to the NCAA limit.

Then, in hotly debated, gradual steps, the colleges voted to liberalize the amount of Pell money the athlete could keep before the college reduced his or her grant-in-aid. The battle was fought out at several NCAA conventions, with debates directed to such uninteresting amendment titles as "Types of financial aid included

in limit," and "Elements of Financial Aid." The dullness and com-
plexities of the topics discouraged media coverage. The diversion
of poverty funds to athletics programs never became the public
issue it should have.

The original grant-in-aid concept of the mid-1950s had allowed for $15 per month for laundry money. The rule was ex-
panded in time to include course-related supplies. These extra
benefits were eliminated by subsequent NCAA economy actions,
and this irritated the bigger schools almost to the same degree as
the ban on travel uniforms.

Repeated efforts were mounted to reestablish a monthly cash
stipend, many arguing that it should be $50. These initiatives were
averted because the people in the know were turning to Pell grants
for extra cash for needy players. The in-house argument was that
parents of middle-class athletes could make up the loss of $15 per
month, and a share of the federal poverty grants would recompense
the needy ones. Tapping into federal poverty money for Division I
athletics programs became a common practice.

The 1982 NCAA Convention voted that eligible student-athletes in effect could keep $900, or half of the then-maximum
$1,800. It worked this way: the university financial aid officer
credited the athlete with the maximum Pell grant for which he or
she qualified. If it was $1,800, then the financial aid officer notified
the athletics department that, in accordance with NCAA rules, the
player's athletics grant-in-aid would be reduced by $900. The ath-
letics department then could use that budget money for other purposes.

Some council members argued vigorously against giving students "that much Pell money." In Division I-AA, particularly, colleges needed the extra money to cut their grant-in-aid costs.

Hootie Ingram, who then was athletics director at Florida State
University, protested to the NCAA Council that we were playing
games with the Pell funds, and trouble was sure to follow. I agreed
with Hootie and recommended a change in NCAA legislation.[14] For
a while we heard rumblings that the U.S. Office of Education and
possibly some members of congress had raised questions about
combining need-based Pell grants with full rides.

The NCAA Council felt reassured, however, after their Washington meeting in April 1988, at which Senator Claiborne Pell served as dinner speaker. Those present said he told them it was perfectly proper for Pell grant recipients to receive assistance from other sources, including athletics grants, and that did not alter their financial need status.

The NCAA membership has gradually settled its differences by raising the cap. By 1990, the maximum that could go to a Division I athlete when combining the Pell and a full ride was $1,700 on top of a full grant-in-aid. The difference of $600 (maximum Pell of $2,300 minus $1,700) could be used to reduce the college's costs. In Divisions II and III, the maximum that could go to a poverty-level athlete over the full-ride amount was $900, leaving $1,400 for the college. This confirms that Division I athletes are worth more money and that the Division II and III institutions rely to a greater extent on federal underwriting of athletics costs.

What's wrong with this practice? According to the government, nothing. A federal official summarized the government's view in 1990. "A poor youngster walks into the university with a $2,300 Pell grant entitlement. Now the athletics department has some athletics scholarship it wants to give him. Well, we would say you can't reduce the Pell grant [in conforming to the NCAA rule], so reduce that athletics scholarship. The Pell grant is fixed. It can't be touched. It's inflexible, and what is malleable is the local university's grant-in-aid."

There was and is considerable disagreement as to the equity of the federal government–NCAA accommodation. Not only are federal education funds being disproportionately allocated to college athletics, the NCAA cartel steps in and dictates who may keep what. During 1975–76, Bob Timmons, who coached world-class track athletes at the University of Kansas, assisted one of his athletes, Clifford Wiley, in a lawsuit aimed at overturning the NCAA Pell grant rule. Wiley was receiving $1,400 in Pell money plus $2,621 from a university grant-in-aid. He was ruled ineligible in the spring of 1976 because the total was over the NCAA limit. Wiley won in federal district court, gaining a preliminary injunction, but lost at the appeal level. The decision essentially was that no significant federal question was involved. (Wiley later went through law school and became a Kansas City attorney.)

Bob Timmons retired with four NCAA championships to his credit, and he feels the same today as he did when the Wiley case was filed. "It's Robin Hood in reverse," he argues. "A kid gets a Pell grant, but they [the NCAA] don't let him keep all of it. That means the rest of his money goes right back in for additional scholarships. His money goes to other grant-in-aid athletes, who could come out of families who are multimillionaires. We steal from the poor and give it to athletes who couldn't qualify for the Pell grant.

"The Pell program was designed to help an individual person in need. It's not to finance athletics departments. They think that's their money, but they took it from somebody who doesn't have any money."[15]

Bob argued that the maximum Pell grant of $2,300 per year, or $255 per month for the nine-month school term, is not a lot of money even for an athlete whose room and board, tuition, books, and fees are paid by the full-ride grant. He asserts that at many schools it is not enough to cover essential expenses, such as home-to-college travel.

"Some students *have* to go home and return to college at least once a year," Timmons says. "Wiley lived in Baltimore. He didn't have money, his parents didn't have any. How does he get home? Today you're talking about $600 to make a couple of trips like that in a year."[16]

Another Pell grant lawsuit was filed in 1979 in federal district court in Oklahoma City by Dexter Manley, an outstanding Oklahoma State University football player who later played for the Washington Redskins. Fourteen other Oklahoma State athletes joined Manley in the suit against the university, the NCAA, and the Big Eight Conference. They attacked the limits the university and the NCAA set on amounts they could receive from their Pell grants.

Later, while playing for the Redskins, Manley gained national publicity as a victim of college athletics who never learned how to read. At Oklahoma State, however, he did enjoy certain amenities.

He testified in the 1979 trial that he was driving a 1977 Mercury

Cougar, for which in 1977 he had made a $2,000 down payment; he was receiving from $200 to $300 monthly in Social Security surviving child's insurance benefits and $625 per semester from the Tenneco Oil Company, where his deceased father had worked. His full-ride athletics grant-in-aid covered tuition, fees, and room and board. In addition, he collected a Pell grant of $756 during each of his first three semesters at Oklahoma State, a total of $2,268 in federal poverty funds.

Bill Brubaker of the *Washington Post* wrote in 1987 the money was necessary to cover Manley's $174 monthly car payment and the other expenses of a college lifestyle that had led his teammates to nickname him "Hollywood."

"They called me Hollywood because I dressed nice and I had a nice car and I had a nice watch," Manley told Brubaker. "Just my personality."[17]

When his Pell allowance in effect was cut off after the third semester, Manley sued the NCAA. He and the other plaintiffs lost the Oklahoma City lawsuit on the precedent fixed during the earlier case filed by Clifford Wiley; there was no substantial federal question.

The Pell grants have become life-sustaining transfusions for many university programs. Even at Cal-Berkeley they make a difference. Cal receives enormous grants for research and has an endowment base larger than most state universities, but overall Pell money added a vital $7.7 million a year in 1989. Some 5,200 or 24 percent of Cal's students received Pell grants averaging $1,479 that year.[18]

The federal government has been dispersing $3.0 to $4.0 billion in Pell money to the nation's colleges for transmission to 2.8 to 3.3 million students. The funds are administered by each college, and the poverty-qualified student remains eligible for the Pell grant as long as he or she is making satisfactory progress toward a degree as determined by the college. In other words, if the student is doing well enough to suit the school that gets the money, that's good enough for the federal exchequer. The fact that taxpayers are subsidizing college athletes at a more favorable rate than nonathletes also is accepted by all parties.

"That's a joke, coach"

The struggle over money and power in collegiate sports seemed to escalate in tandem with college sports' ascendancy in the TV ratings. While the major-league colleges and their men's coaches were fighting over the apportionment of money and publicity, women sports leaders decided to get their share.

The battle began with passage in 1972 of Title IX of the federal Education Amendment Act, a single title that gained more publicity than the entire antidiscrimination law of which it was part. Title IX prescribed equal rights for women, including those in college athletics programs.

Almost instantly, the law brought the NCAA into conflict with the Association for Intercollegiate Athletics for Women (AIAW). The women's organization sought equal opportunity and equal treatment for women, charging that "the men" wanted to take over the women's programs as a means of stopping them from getting a fair share of the money. The AIAW finger-pointing took in the NCAA—me personally and our staff in Mission, Kansas—big-spending football coaches, and, in general, the "old boy's club" that was trying to maintain the status quo.

AIAW leaders such as Leotus Morrison of James Madison University and Chris Grant of Iowa said women should have a separate organization so women could control it. Otherwise, women's athletics would duplicate the unsavory practices found in men's programs. The men would control the budget dollars and shortchange the women. If women stayed separate, they could develop and control their own programs.

The AIAW-NCAA dispute focused on the history of women's sports. In the early years of this century, college women seldom played tough, competitive team sports. Such games as tennis and golf became acceptable, but group sports largely were confined to physical education exercise classes. There were "play-days," but won-and-lost accounting and team standings were out. Copying malestyle aggressiveness was deemed unladylike.

Increasingly in the 1920s and 1930s, some women pushed to enter more competitive sports. Opponents said that women didn't have the endurance for full-court basketball. Most high school and college rules limited players to half court. At one time players were not permitted to bounce the ball. Later, three bounces were permitted before passing—a policy designed to prevent excessive exertion. Coaches stressed the social benefits to be gained from sports.

But I knew from my sports-writing days that women could play with the best. In the mid-1940s, I was reporting sports for United Press out of Chicago and covered the "All American" championship tournament at the Tam O'Shanter Country Club in Niles, Illinois. I followed Babe Didrikson Zaharias around the course as she averaged 77 strokes for four rounds. She was a graceful but awesome competitor, capable of 280 yards-plus off the tees, but she was not pleased with her score the day I watched.

An Olympic multisport star, she and her husband, George Zaharias, drew the biggest crowds at the suburban Chicago tournament. Zaharias, a professional wrestler, seemed to go out of his way to demonstrate his support, and the fans seemed thrilled to watch a superstar woman performer.

While great female athletes were competing in the Olympic games, women were not accepted on a day-to-day basis as athletes on the college campus. Many prominent male physical educators supported the expansion of women's sports, but the local and national physical education leadership, part of a group called the American Association of Health, Physical Education, and Recreation (AAHPER, later the AAHPERD), was slow to give ground. They added dance to their other interests but did little to change their position on competitive sports. A growing number of its women members were dissatisfied and wanted to train high-skill female athletes for head-to-head competition.

Serious changes were anticipated when, in 1971, this group of women athletics administrators within the AAHPERD formed the AIAW.[19] In 1973, it began holding women's national championships for badminton, basketball, golf, gymnastics, swimming, track and field, and volleyball. The growing interest in women's sports was demonstrated by the fact that women accounted for 57 percent of the increase in intercollegiate athletics participation from 1971 to 1973.

The women were demanding equal opportunity and had the force of federal law behind them. Why should men control the money, the facilities, and the political power centers of the universities? On those campuses where men's "revenue" sports ostensibly paid their own way, the answer was: We generate the wealth; we come first.

The standing fact, however, was that women sports administrators had little influence and stood at the end of the line at budget time before Title IX. Even at Occidental College, a Division III liberal arts college with no big-time sports ambitions and no significant sports "gate," the men's basketball team used the gym for practice in the prime afternoon hours; the women scrambled to practice mornings and late at night. Women players were budgeted $4 for gas money for game trips to nearby colleges, whereas men received $25 for gas money and food. The difference, the women's coach was told, was because the men needed to eat after they played. Women wouldn't be as hungry because they didn't play as hard.

"That's a joke, coach."

Women coaches didn't laugh.

Long-smoldering female resentment ignited in the AIAW. The NCAA, with its publicized wealth and male-dominated hierarchy, was an obvious target, and Walter Byers as head of the masculine empire was the prime quarry. Women of the AIAW compared the money spent on football to that spent on all women's sports on the same campus. They said the disparity was ludicrous.

It's tough for a woman to do battle with the football coach on a Division I-A campus, but a collection of determined women at the national level—with political support and media attention— could take on the NCAA and look very good indeed.

Nowhere were the issues more vigorously contested than in the halls of Congress and within the federal bureaucracy, where the implementing regulations of Title IX were being written. The AIAW, supported by other national groups including the National Organization for Women, argued Title IX meant that 50 percent of the resources of a college devoted to intercollegiate athletics should be allocated to female sports, and women's athletics should be operated separately from men's. Their theme was equal numbers and equal dollars. If the number of athletes wasn't equal, then equal dollars should be committed anyway until the women could catch up. If this reduced the excessive costs of football, so much the better.

The men's view, as espoused by me, other NCAA officials, and our Washington legal counsel, Bill Kramer of the Squire, Sanders & Dempsey firm, was that male money sports had been built up over half a century. To decree that football and women's field hockey immediately deserved the same per capita expenditures was financial lunacy. We contended income-producing sports should be exempted.

We clearly were on the defensive and needed all the arguments we could mount. Our legal contention was that Title IX applied to overall university operations and not to individual activities (a single sport) within a given program (athletics). Then we pleaded for time, arguing, "The men and the NCAA, itself, didn't discriminate against women. Women's athletics leaders discriminated against themselves through the years by refusing to accept competitive athletics as a proper pursuit for teenage women."

One rebuttal deserved another.

"Well, fellows," the women responded, "you created the full ride, and if you want to give 95 of these freebies to football players and 15 to basketball, then we will start with 110 grants-in-aid for women, and we'll negotiate from there as to use of facilities, coaches' salaries, and travel and food dollars."

While arguing for reasonable rules writing in the nation's capital, we tried to work out a peaceful settlement with AIAW leaders. After one tense meeting at the O'Hare Airport Hotel in Chicago, John Eiler, athletics director at East Stroudsburg University, Pennsylvania, and an NCAA committee member, offered to buy ice cream cones for everyone. Most of us went to the basement level of the hotel, and some stood and some sat as we ate the ice cream. John, a veteran of campus faculty warfare, quietly explained to me, "The strategy here, Walter, is that one person simply cannot be mad at another while you're both eating ice cream cones." It was a nice touch—a good ending to a difficult day.

Despite all the meetings, the NCAA and the AIAW were on a collision course. By 1975, 331 NCAA member schools, or 46 percent of the total, were not members of the AIAW. Most of those schools, plus other NCAA colleges served by AIAW, preferred that the NCAA enter women's athletics. Women on college campuses familiar with NCAA finances calculated the NCAA would have to pay the expenses of women athletes competing in NCAA championships, as they did for the men. Some women at AIAW-NCAA member schools were concerned about the potential conflicts on campus in governing women's athletics by AIAW rules and men's athletics by NCAA rules.

A significant tilt in favor of the NCAA came on a winter day in February 1980, when two women athletics administrators, Mary Alice Hill of San Diego State and Linda Estes of the University of New Mexico, came to see me. June Davis of the University of Nebraska was scheduled to be there but had been stopped by heavy snows.

We sat in the conference room at NCAA headquarters in Mission, Kansas. I had gotten to know Linda and enjoyed bantering with her. She was a political activist, and she relished people-to-people action, whether it was New Mexico Democratic politics or college male vs. female disputes. Linda, however, used a no-nonsense approach that day. She and Mary Alice wanted women in key positions within the NCAA, and they wanted the NCAA to be the national governing body for women's athletics. Both of them were key players in the burgeoning world of women's athletics, and their decision in favor of the NCAA gave my dwindling confidence on this issue a shot of adrenaline.

One of their objections to the AIAW was the group's conduct of championship tournaments, which reflected the "all-comers" philosophy of physical educators; that is, at the end of a sports season, all the teams should come together for the national tournament regardless of won-lost records. All-comers' meets were useful as women's athletics were rapidly expanding. That approach is also admirable for defusing much of the hype and supercompetitiveness that men's athletics exhibits. The NCAA approach consistently has been that only the best teams should compete for the national title.

Right or wrong, the women represented by Estes and Hill sought high-level competition and national exposure for women's college sports. They were committed to the NCAA's philosophy—to the winner belongs the spoils. It paralleled their Olympic Games experience: Go for the Gold!

Another consideration was that the AIAW tournaments did not have the name identity of the NCAA and were not showcasing the best action and the best athletes. Women were trying to gain visibility and credibility, and they wanted for themselves the media recognition lavished on Division I men's sports.

Sensing a critical division in their ranks, the AIAW leadership stepped up their attack. Condemning the NCAA with zeal were Donna Lopiano of the University of Texas at Austin, Margot Polivy, AIAW's militant legal counsel, and others who successfully portrayed us as ruthless corporate raiders.

It seemed our best strategy would be to establish a toehold. In 1980 we moved to set up NCAA women's championships in five sports, basketball, field hockey, swimming, tennis, and volleyball—but only in Divisions II and III. The stakes weren't as high, and we had more support there. This set the stage for the major battle one year later.

The 1981 NCAA Convention was at the Fontainebleau Hotel in Miami Beach. There we proposed to establish championship tournaments for Division I and also to guarantee women designated representation on NCAA committees and in the governance structure.

It was an unusually cold January for southern Florida; the Fontainebleau had no heat for its meeting rooms or most guest rooms. Delegates wore sweaters and topcoats in the hotel. The debate, however, generated enough heat in the main ballroom on voting day so that the delegates' multiple complaints to Convention Manager Lou Spry stopped for the first time that week. Donna Lopiano, as AIAW president, spoke against the proposal, but Judith R. Holland, a former AIAW president, supported it. Holland, head of the UCLA women's program, told the *Miami Herald:* "What we're asking for is simply a choice. We are trying to allow more options for women, the same type of opportunities men have."[20]

Judy Holland (*left*), senior associate athletics director, UCLA, and Linda K. Estes, associate director of athletics, the University of New Mexico, were prominent in shaping the future of women's intercollegiate athletics by supporting its integration into the NCAA during the fractious years of the 1970s.

She was referring to the fact that men's programs had the option of competing in the NCAA and NAIA. By a margin of 69.5 percent of the voting delegates, women became a mandated part of the NCAA governing structure. By the narrowest of margins, the vote for Division I women's tournaments also passed. The NCAA had moved foursquare into the field of women's athletics—an act that soon made us the target of an AIAW antitrust lawsuit filed by Margot Polivy.

The AIAW canceled all of its championships. I couldn't understand it. Apparently the strategy was intended as proof that the all-powerful NCAA had put them out of business. Yet it seemed a terrible mistake, since the AIAW had eliminated its most valuable service for AIAW colleges. The lawsuit was going to be the last roll of the dice, with all the AIAW chips on the table.

The case was tried in federal court in Washington, D.C. I played a small role, testifying principally about NCAA finances and TV deals. The AIAW contended that the NCAA had used (1) its deep pockets to guarantee expenses for women to compete in NCAA championships, making the AIAW events less attractive, and (2) its network contacts to gain TV exposure for NCAA women's championships and to block the AIAW from a network TV contract. The first contention was true; the second was not. We won the lawsuit.

Probably more important than that was the decision of Tom Jernstedt, now NCAA chief operating officer, to hire Ruth Berkey in September 1980. A Pepperdine University product, Ruth was athletics director for Occidental College when she chose to become the women's foremost representative in a predominantly male organization. She set up the first Division I women's basketball championship and built the solid foundation that exists today for full participation of women within the organizaiton. Today the NCAA conducts 34 championships for women among the three divisions and combined events for men and women in fencing, rifle, and skiing.

The phenomenal growth in women's participation established one fact: It was the culture of the times, not their Creator, that had limited their opportunities.

The Badge of Respectability

The costs of Title IX and the entry of women into the big time should not be blamed for today's highly publicized financial problems for college sports. Two-platoon football was the culprit in the 1960s, and Title IX was held responsible in the 1980s. As we enter the 1990s, the complaints of insolvency are louder than ever. The most frequently proposed cures are a national football playoff and conference realignments to gain more TV dollars. At the heart of the problem is an addiction to lavish spending.

One might think intelligent college presidents would try to keep their institutions out of the major-league sweepstakes of college sports. On the contrary, generations of presidents have led the

Anne Donovan (*left*), 1981 All-American basketball player for Old Dominion and player of the year in 1983. Cheryl Miller, four-time All-American for the University of Southern California (1983–86). She became head women's basketball coach at USC in 1994.

charge to have their colleges compete in NCAA Division I, where the biggest and the richest dominate.

Michigan State, UCLA, and Houston became the prototypes for the state college segment of higher education that wanted to obtain major status with the elite universities of big-time sports. Bowling Green and Miami of Ohio, after extensive campaigning, were accepted as "major league" in 1961.[21] This helped their colleagues in the Mid-American Conference—Kent State, Marshall, Toledo, and Western Michigan—to win elevation in the late 1960s. There were specific allegations then, and continued concern now, that in order to meet the minimum football attendance standards of the top division, Mid-American Conference members have inflated their figures.

In the 1970s (before Division I, II, and III were created), the NCAA's "major teams" category increased from 113 to 144, a 27 percent upsurge.[22] That was just a beginning.

The Pacific Coast Athletic Association staged an all-out campaign to join the big spenders. In 1974 the PCAA, today's Big West Conference, included Fresno State, Cal State Fullerton, Long Beach State, University of the Pacific, San Diego State, and San Jose State. The six averaged 12,092 spectators per home football game.[23]

By 1976–77 the NCAA had created the three-division segregation of its members for competitive and legislative reasons. There were 144 colleges in Division I.[24] The bottom 56 had an average football attendance of 17,500 spectators. This compared with the top three teams' average attendance of 90,520 and the approximate 40,000 average of the top 88.

The passionate desire to be associated in the press with the big-name universities is best illustrated by California State University at Long Beach and its president, Steve Horn. Long Beach had slipped into NCAA Division I in 1973 when its average home attendance for football was 3,333. That year the home gate football receipts there were reported as $17,864, of which $576 came from student fees and tickets. Steve Horn remarked at the time: "It is obvious that in terms of spectator support, the program is in difficulty."

He concluded that the most direct means of resurrecting his faltering finances was to tap into other schools' income. Steve had big ideas. He decided that the 1975 Economy Convention was the place for his crusade.[25]

Horn inflamed the major sports schools when he argued that grants-in-aid for football should be cut from 105 to 75 by 1976, 70 a year later, and finally to 65 in 1978. Steve had given up on the notion of eliminating two-platoon football, but he argued the grant reduction would not require that and would save money.

"It's somewhat like reducing nuclear armaments," he said. "Unless everyone agrees to limitations on an overall plan, no one will reduce voluntarily."

He also proposed a radical income redistribution plan to apply to bowl games and TV receipts. He argued, for example, that allocating 50 percent of the net proceeds from NCAA football television to all Division I football members made sense, and then 25 percent each could go to Divisions II and III. Steve saw merit in the National Football League distribution system for talent and TV money—all in the name of equalizing competition. Steve indicated that what's good for the NFL should be good for the NCAA.

Meanwhile, the American Council on Education officially recognized the plight of college sports, something it's been doing off and on for 40 years. ACE scheduled a presidents' discussion devoted to "The Crisis in Intercollegiate Athletics." Chairing the meeting was Steve Horn. His thesis was once again that the NCAA's affluent members should share their income with the less affluent. He contended that the biggest and the not-so-big all were in the same Division I fraternity.

Steve's fight for major income sharing in NCAA Division I was opposed by the NCAA leadership, including me, and the NCAA Football Television Committee, led by Seaver Peters of Dartmouth.[26] Steve lost the engagement, but that sort of populism was enough to convince many Division I millionaires that a new national organization was needed to replace the NCAA. The College Football Association soon would issue the call to arms.

Division I football grew from 144 members in 1977 to 191 in 1987, a 33 percent increase during a decade when insolvency and impending financial ruin were the repeated complaints of most Division I colleges. These dour comments were taken seriously despite the fact that the price for better football tickets increased during the 1980s by around 70 percent, from an average $10.00 to $17.00, and basketball tickets increased about 85 percent, from approximately $6.50 to $12.00.

Budget deficits, criticism of the colleges' preoccupation with big-time athletics, reformers calling for deemphasis in major sports—all of this through the years has resulted in more and more institutions wanting to play at the major league level, regardless of how much it costs. Given the lack of an academic standard that measures an institution's quality, college after college has turned to "NCAA Division I" as a nationally recognized badge of respectability. Leading the institutional commitment to the big league? Most often, it's a university chief executive officer.

Notes

1. Associated Press report, New Orleans, Louisiana, January 1969.
2. Lou McCullough, letter to John A. Fuzak, March 16, 1971.
3. NCAA, NCAA Fact Sheet Appendix B, June 5, 1965.
4. Arnie Burdick, *Syracuse Herald-Journal,* November 20, 1974.
5. NCAA, NCAA Financial Analysis Study (based on data supplied by 77 universities for the 1976–77 college year), September 1979.
6. Jerry McConnell, *Sunday Oklahoman,* February 8, 1987.
7. Comparison of revenue and expenses statements for the Board in Control of Intercollegiate Athletics, University of Michigan, years ended June 30, 1968, and June 30, 1988.
8. W. Eugene Hollon, letter to Walter Byers, August 24, 1970.
9. Johnny Majors with Ben Byrd, *You Can Go Home Again* (Nashville, Tenn.: Ruthledge Hill Press, 1986), 127.
10. NCAA, Proceedings of the 3d Special NCAA Convention and 70th Annual Convention of the NCAA, January 14–17, 1976.
11. Ibid.
12. James B. Higgins, letter to Walter Byers, January 23, 1976.
13. NCAA, Supplements 1–4 Prepared for Special NCAA Committee on Deregulation and Rules Simplification, 1989.
14. Walter Byers, letter to Eugene F. Corrigan, February 9, 1987.
15. Bob Timmons, interview with Charles Hammer, October 8, 1989.
16. Ibid.
17. Bill Brubaker, *Washington Post,* May 10, 1987.
18. Robert Black, interview with the author, September 6, 1989.
19. AIAW, Association for Intercollegiate Athletics for Women Handbook, 1979–80.
20. Jack Falla, *NCAA: The Voice of College Sports* (Mission, Kansas: National Collegiate Athletic Association, 1981), 170.
21. Jack Waters, History of Major College Football Classification, December 29, 1976.
22. NCAA, Division I Football Membership List, August 4, 1976.
23. NCAA, List of Division I Football-Playing Members with Average Attendance Less than 17,500 for 1974–76 Seasons, August 4, 1976.

24. The NCAA membership reorganized itself into Divisions I, II, and III at the association's first special convention, Chicago, Illinois, August 6–7, 1973.
25. Stephen Horn, memorandum to presidents of NCAA member institutions, July 11, 1975.
26. Seaver Peters, memorandum to NCAA member institutions, August 1, 1975.

Chapter 14　The Pursuit of Power and Money

As the 1970s came to an end and the golden era of television growth approached its zenith, multiple warning flags appeared. They cautioned that a new athletics civil war was in the making, this one over television booty.

The three national networks had dominated the television explosion during the 1970s. Now their empire was under attack from the burgeoning cable industry. Independent stations were busy forming loose networks to acquire movies and sports programming.

Greed was gnawing at the innards of college athletics. Rich schools within the conferences increasingly rebelled at sharing their television and other revenues with less-affluent conference relatives. Blood is thicker than water, but there has been many a bloodletting among kinfolk when a substantial inheritance is divvied up.

The University of Texas at Austin—its athletics operation under less skilled management after Neils Thompson and Darrell Royal departed—wanted to keep more of its radio and TV income. If this hurt Southwest Conference first-cousins like TCU and Rice, so be it.

In the Big Eight Conference, Oklahoma threatened to bolt unless others conceded to changes in the money-sharing formula. Bob Devaney, athletics director at Nebraska and a counterbalancing force to Oklahoma in the past, went along with the OU demands. "Why tear up the conference over this?" he asked. Bob thought a difference of $60,000 to $100,000 didn't justify a knockdown fight.[1]

The University of Southern California announced it would reexamine its Pac-10 membership unless there was a dramatic change in the dollar distribution within the conference. During the tenures of Jack Hubbard and Jim Zumberge in the USC president's office, the Trojans had found it increasingly difficult to justify sending money north to such conference members as Oregon State, Washington State, and the University of Oregon. USC, secure with its huge Los Angeles population base, publicly declared its reluctance to continue playing in such remote hamlets as Corvallis, Oregon, and Pullman, Washington.

At the same time, regional syndicators were telling college sports authorities that the NCAA television plan was barring the colleges from truckloads of regional advertising dollars. These siren voices reached eager ears among those maneuvering to form the College Football Association. The founding fathers of the CFA— Chuck Neinas of the Big Eight, Rev. Edmund Joyce of Notre Dame, and Fred Davison of Georgia—first promised to advocate the interests of the big-time colleges and their football coaches vis-à-vis the NCAA in matters of operating policies. The real issues, however, were who would control football television and whether the NCAA would survive an insurgency designed to demolish the organization or at least render it obsolete. Despite protestations to the contrary, the CFA was going for the jugular, its momentum sustained by pent-up resentments.

A Declaration of War

Diverse interests came together to form the College Football Association. The University of Notre Dame, led by its de facto athletics boss, the Reverend Edmund P. (Ned) Joyce, had forcefully opposed NCAA football TV controls since their inauguration in the 1950s.

Father Joyce had been upset by a minor NCAA enforcement case against Notre Dame in 1953 and was also offended by another one in 1971.[2] The university's objection to including TV sanctions in penalties imposed upon NCAA rules violators had been restimulated by the Michigan State case of 1976–79. The NCAA penalty banned the Spartans from television and contemporaneously eliminated Notre Dame's games with Michigan State from possible national television selection or even local sold-out release in the South Bend area.

In the early 1950s Notre Dame and the University of Pennsylvania had combined to fight the NCAA's initial television controls. Notre Dame's opposition, alone or in combination with a few others, however, had not been strong enough to win then or in later years. In the late 1970s, however, Father Joyce fully recognized that a collection of some sixty or more institutions flying the CFA flag would be a formidable weapon in finally bringing the obnoxious NCAA restraints to an end.

Notre Dame was the critical, behind-the-scenes power player pushing for the new group, but plenty more big timers marched in lockstep moved by other motivations.

There was Neinas, Big Eight commissioner, still resentful that he had lost his bid for the job of Big Ten commissioner. The job had gone instead to Wayne Duke, who supported the NCAA in the developing battle.

Neinas and Georgia football Coach Vince Dooley convinced Fred Davison, president of the University of Georgia, that NCAA TV controls were keeping millions of network dollars out of the reach of big-time college football teams. Davison became the CFA's first chairman.

All of this seemed logical to such potent football coaches as Barry Switzer of Oklahoma, Bear Bryant at Alabama, Joe Paterno at Penn State, and Hootie Ingram, a veteran of the Southeastern Conference and soon to become athletics director at Florida State. They believed the NCAA, with its picky, outmoded restraints on recruiting and grants-in-aid, probably *was* fouling up football TV controls just as Chuck Neinas said.

After all, Neinas had worked for the NCAA; he had been on the NCAA TV Committee; he should know. Neinas convinced even his former employers, the Big Eight Conference, that freedom from NCAA TV controls would catapult the Big Eight into the multimillionaire class.

The forces coalesced on February 2, 1980, when the College Football Association held a press conference in Kansas City to announce the hiring of Chuck Neinas as its first executive director.[3]

Reverend Edmund P. (Ned) Joyce, the University of Notre Dame executive vice president, with James Frank, president of Lincoln University, who became NCAA president in January 1981. The CFA-NCAA dispute was in full bloom at the time this picture was taken in 1980.

Father Joyce took pains to say the CFA was not out to destroy the NCAA, nor should it be viewed "as an organization on the verge of revolting from the NCAA."

Although CFA leaders would deny, from time to time, any interest beyond football, Joyce said that if the CFA were successful in football, "it might pave the way in basketball." Neinas chimed in: "We could do for basketball what we are doing for football."

In his column, Joe McGuff, sports editor of the *Kansas City Star,* called it "the first shot in an athletic civil war."[4] Ted O'Leary, longtime Kansas City correspondent for *Sports Illustrated,* viewed the exercise with skepticism. "I just did not believe that the Reverend Joyce was telling the whole story," Ted remarked to friends.

Don Canham of Michigan had backed Neinas for the Big Ten job and was a constant critic of Wayne Duke through most of

Duke's commissionership. Don had been a behind-the-scenes force in the Big Ten, trying to persuade his conference friends to align with the CFA only as a means of reorganizing the NCAA, not destroying it. Michigan president Robben Fleming was a restraining force. He didn't like the CFA platform.

All of the back-and-forth conversation didn't blur Don's 20/20 eyesight when it came to measuring economic forces. He was surprised when I telephoned and brought him up to date on the CFA's plans to offer a competing football package during the next TV negotiations.

"Christ, this is not the time for that!" Canham told me. "That's a mistake." Don planned to call Joe Paterno and try to slow the thing down. He thought that disrupting television restraints could prove an economic disaster, particularly for the less successful schools.

At a 1980 CFA meeting in Dallas, Neinas emphasized to the group's membership that he was concerned about credibility, finances, and recruiting. Jackie Sherrill, then at the University of Pittsburgh, echoed his words. "I think we need to get our credibility back," he said.[5] SMU Coach Ron Meyer agreed: "Obviously, it was in our minds to conquer public opinion."[6] SMU was on the way to setting an all-time record in NCAA penalties, and Sherrill later resigned as head coach of Texas A&M because of highly publicized irregularities.

Chuck implied that I had conspired with two other former NCAA staffers, Wayne Duke of the Big Ten and Wiles Hallock of the Pac-10, to steer television millions into those conferences' coffers, keeping it away from the Big Eight.

Overlooked by CFA stalwarts was the fact that the seven-state Big Ten area embraced about 25 percent of the nation's population, while the Big Eight, in addition to Missouri, covered such plains states as Colorado, Kansas, Nebraska, and Oklahoma and included only 9 percent of the population. Los Angeles County, home base for USC and UCLA, sheltered more people than the four Plains states combined.

Yet CFA supporters were not to be dissuaded. Eddie Crowder, University of Colorado athletics director and an NCAA TV Committee member, once stood up before a Big Eight Conference meeting and implied that only the NCAA barred the path to discovery of a new Fort Knox. "There's megabucks out there," Crowder said.

The Big Eight was convinced. The University of Texas brought along the Southwest Conference. The Southeastern Conference believed the NCAA should be brought to its knees for other reasons, mainly the members' absorption with making rules designed to inhibit the most successful programs.

I quickly found myself fighting on the front lines of the athletics civil war predicted by sports editor McGuff. Longtime good friends were mixed up in a conflict that at times defied logic. You couldn't distinguish friends from enemies without the most up-to-date scorecard.

This was the political cauldron in which the NCAA began the intense football and basketball television negotiations in 1980. In a span of fifteen months, we worked out football television contracts with ABC, CBS, and the Turner Broadcasting System and went through a grueling basketball negotiation, finally leaving NBC for CBS. Almost overnight the colleges' attitude and the mood of the industry had changed.

With the CFA eager to establish itself and cripple the NCAA, we obviously had to produce good contracts for the colleges. These deals would profoundly influence the future course of college football and basketball, the political structure of the NCAA, and the CFA's credibility.

Complicating the whole affair for me was the fact that all the major players at the networks had changed. Roone Arledge was preoccupied with masterminding ABC News's efforts to knock CBS News out of first place; Jim Spence was now the number one man for sports but still was required to clear big decisions with an increasingly inaccessible Arledge.

Bill McPhail had departed CBS to join Ted Turner in Atlanta. All I knew about CBS Sports was the network would send more people to a meeting than the other two networks combined. Almost all of them were strangers. Bob Wussler had succeeded Bill McPhail, then came Frank Smith, Van Gordon Sauter, Neal Pilson, and Peter Lund—all in a period of 1977 to 1984.

Carl Lindemann had been removed from NBC in 1977, his former aide-de-camp, Chet Simmons, was there for two years, and then Art Watson appeared, these changes occurring in a period of four or five years. The television networks were playing musical chairs in their sports departments.

As it turned out, two veterans and a newcomer would be primarily responsible for the departure of the glamorous NCAA Final Four tournament from NBC. They were Kevin O'Malley and Carl Lindemann on one side and Art Watson on the other—CBS vs. NBC. Lindemann now was wearing CBS colors and would prove to be a key player.

NBC had held the TV rights to the Final Four since 1969, all under the Lindemann regime. His successor, Art Watson, was faced with an expiring contract, and NBC might not have the rights after 1981. He opened negotiations with complimentary remarks about the tournament followed by a threat: if NBC didn't get a new contract, the network would not carry in-season college basketball. He spread the word throughout the college community.

Art's declaration was quickly relayed from conference to conference, and many of the leagues that were supporting the CFA—the Southeastern, Southwest, Big Eight, and Atlantic Coast—thought they had found additional reasons to be upset with me and the NCAA when it seemed our tournament negotiations would adversely affect their in-season basketball deals.

Watson had been executive vice-president in charge of NBC's owned-and-operated stations for about six years before becoming head of NBC Sports in 1979. He came to the bargaining table in a small triangular meeting room at the Hyatt Regency Hotel near the Chicago airport in November 1980 sporting a tough, management-vs.-labor psychology. He brought along Geoff Mason and Don Wear, two attractive young people who could have benefitted from a longer internship.

The NCAA had a great negotiations committee that year, including Dave Gavitt of the Big East Conference; Wayne Duke of the Big Ten; Wiles Hallock of the Pac-10; and Tom Jernstedt of the NCAA staff. Jernstedt knew as much about TV and college basketball as all three of the NBC execs. Duke and Hallock were ex officio members because of other NCAA basketball and TV committee positions. The fact that these two were at the negotiating table and other conferences were not merely added fire to the CFA's expanding complaints.

Art Watson and his two young friends explained to us that television sports were on the rocks and that the decline of audiences argued against increased rights fees. They proceeded to tutor us, inexperienced as we were, in the realities of the marketplace.

In each football negotiation, Roone Arledge had bemoaned the millions of dollars ABC had lost in carrying college football under the terms of the previous contract. Here, however, Art was expanding the stratagem: the entire industry was facing potential insolvency. Tom Jernstedt and I later dubbed Watson's exercise the "NBC Doomsday Episode."[7]

In the ensuing discussions, Geoff Mason or Don Wear frequently would follow up a Watson remark by saying: "Now, what Arthur means is..." then proceeded to use unnecessary time to expand on Art's statements. This probably was a by-product of the NBC tutorial mindset that the NCAA neophytes needed a lot of educating. Whatever the reasons, Jernstedt couldn't believe that subalterns could get away with such seeming disrespect for their boss. It certainly wasn't NCAA style.

As we talked, I looked around and thought it lucky that we had reserved a small meeting room, because it appeared NBC would expect us not only to buy lunch but pay rent on the room as well.

It was clear that Art, the quintessential native New Yorker, believed Big Apple folklore that people west of the Allegheny Mountains still communicated by smoke signals. I could almost see a cartoonist's balloon above Watson's head, in which his thoughts were revealed: "We'll fake these outlanders right out of their boots!"

In any case, we were not convinced by Watson's approach; further, we did not believe NBC would live up to his threat and get out of college basketball if they did not secure a new tournament contract. The American sports scene offers few attractive sports events from late January to March 15. We soon got up and walked away from the table.

You have to realize that I became pretty serious about such

things. The Division I men's basketball tournament and its TV contract are the NCAA's crown jewels. Tournament income, for practical purposes, finances the entire organization. As I was leaving office, tournament gross receipts exceeded $70 million per year, with ticket sales accounting for around 13 percent and TV fees approximately 85 percent. For the 1993–94 fiscal year, NCAA total revenue was $182.0 million with TV rights fees, almost all related in one way or another to the basketball tournament, making up 78.0 percent.[8] The tournament generates the TV largess that now is acknowledged to be the lifeblood of the organization.

With the NBC negotiations off to a rocky start in the winter of 1980–81, Carl Lindemann saw his opportunity to take revenge for his removal by NBC management. He had accepted a consultant position with CBS. His knowledge of the tournament, gained in his years as head of NBC Sports, was of major league quality. So was his scouting report on NBC and Watson's tactics. Through the years, I have been impressed by the networks' spy operations. Each network seemed to have well-placed moles in the others' offices, and their information proved correct far more times than not.

Lindemann, working with Kevin O'Malley, longtime loyal CBS executive, plotted the strategy that enabled CBS to pick up the loose ball that Art Watson and NBC were about to fumble. Carl had a penchant for understatement. He would see me from time to time and say: "Walter, I want you to know we're serious about getting the tournament." Nothing more.

One day his casualness turned to exultation when he called me to report that "the boss," Gene Jankowsky, had given the sports division the green light to go after the tournament.

Kevin O'Malley flew into Kansas City with Van Gordon Sauter early in 1981 on an exploratory visit. Sauter, the new CBS Sports chief, was basically a news executive. When we met at the airport Marriott Hotel, Sauter remarked that he was not much of a sports fan. "I do enjoy going to an NBA game once in a while," he told me.

I glanced at Kevin. His face impassive, Kevin shook his head ever so slightly. Kevin and Carl had done their homework on everything except schooling Sauter in how to open a prenegotiation conversation with the NCAA.

Sauter's access to the top corporate offices at Black Rock, however, proved to be the key to CBS's entry into the college basketball marketplace. In his sales speech to corporate insiders, Van Sauter compared the NCAA tournament to an oldstyle political convention: The people are there! They're passionate! They're screaming! "It has lungs!" was the punch line. Lungs became the operational code word for the network sports department's project to place the CBS imprimatur on the NCAA men's championship.[9]

Despite the doomsday tactics NBC had pursued in Chicago, NBC still had a strong position under the renegotiation provisions of its contract. NBC was carrying in-season basketball games in deals with various conferences, and the network urged conference commissioners to call members of our negotiating team as we worked.

They pressured Dave Gavitt and Wiles Hallock to vote with their conferences' interests. Commissioners such as Cliff Spiegel of the Southwest Conference and Carl James of the Big Eight resented Duke and Hallock, from two rival conferences, being at the scene of the action. They felt their concerns about the NBC in-season boycott threat were being ignored by the NCAA.

We agreed within our negotiations committee that at each meeting, each committee member would report to the others on any contacts since the last meeting by the networks, conferences, and individual colleges. Big money was involved, and we needed to maintain faith in one another.

In the final round of negotiations, March 2–4, 1981, NBC changed its tactics. They belittled CBS. While still threatening not to telecast in-season college basketball games if they lost the NCAA tournament, Watson referred to CBS's laid-back sports management style and lack of basketball expertise. Art suggested that whereas CBS may be able to name all the teams in the NFL, their management team wouldn't know where to locate the schedules of the 50 best basketball teams in NCAA Division I. There was speculation by NBC negotiators about how much money it would cost the colleges if NBC did not win the contract and abandoned its telecasting of in-season games. NBC's final offer was $45 million.

We then met with the CBS team made up of Sauter, Neal Pilson (vice-president for sports contracting), Lindemann, Terry O'Neil, and O'Malley. They had brought along O'Neil, recently hired from ABC, to emphasize they had an established producer familiar with college sports on their team and ready to go. It was there we made the NCAA tournament deal with CBS for three years (1982–84) for essentially $48 million.

The NBC team occupied a suite at the end of the hall on the same floor where we were meeting with CBS. Three of us—Wayne Duke, Tom Jernstedt, and I—took the long walk to tell the NBC people they had lost the contract. The NBC executives knew what the message was as soon as they opened the door. It was the custom of the times to telephone with good news and deliver the bad news in person.

We had taken great precautions to make sure all parties would be advised before we released the news through Dave Cawood in the NCAA office in Mission, Kansas. The ever-efficient Mr. Cawood never had the chance to announce it. Within 15 minutes of the time we informed the two networks, Cawood was swamped with calls from the national media. NBC and CBS officials were quick to let their favorite media reporters know they had not forgotten them.

Carl Lindemann thus avenged his dismissal by NBC, a payback that has resulted in CBS having the Final Four since 1982. Despite losing the contract, NBC immediately changed its tune and announced it would continue televising college basketball, covering some 40 in-season games in 1982–83. Watson also saw nothing wrong in poaching on CBS's tournament preserve.

One such incident in 1983 inflamed the normally cool Neal Pilson, then president of CBS Sports, who fired off a letter to NBC's Art Watson saying he was "shocked" to learn that NBC had incorporated highlights of "our semifinal NCAA Championship Games in its Sunday afternoon Al McGuire special.... We had previously informed NBC that we would *not* grant permission for the use of such footage.... NBC knowingly and willfully violated our copyright."

Neal told Art that cameramen under the direction of an NBC

producer were present inside the University of New Mexico "Pit," the below-ground-level arena that was site of the 1983 Final Four in Albuquerque. The poachers were shooting material, Neal said, "again in violation of our rights" and contrary to NCAA instructions. Art quickly shot back, that NBC had "duly noted" Neal's objections, that the coverage had been put together under license agreement with an outside producer, and that there were freedom of speech issues here that hadn't yet been explored.[10]

Art simply believed his great in-season announcer duo of Dick Enberg and Al McGuire were more identified with college basketball than the less well known CBS crew featuring Gary Bender. Having blown the negotiations, NBC was trying to catch up by coming in the back door with subsidiary tournament programming positioned as closely as possible to game action.

Prospecting for TV Gold

Before the basketball bargaining of 1981 was finished, the last of the big football television negotiations had begun. It started quietly enough but soon built up to explosive tension.

By this time the College Football Association had made a command decision: Knock the NCAA out of football television and, in time, the CFA could replace the NCAA in all things. Their first-step strategy was to wean one of the networks away from the NCAA and into an exclusive football contract for their 63 big football schools, all of which were also members of the NCAA.

Art Watson, frustrated at losing the Final Four, publicized his willingness to give the CFA fabulous sums for a Saturday night football package. He said college football would be the biggest thing in town: prime time live on NBC. The network's executive producer, Don Ohlmeyer, promised that his innovations and ingenuity would make college football's TV value grow by $50 million to $60 million within five years. NBC also disclosed it would share legal expenses with the CFA in defending a CFA-NBC deal if the CFA-NCAA donnybrook ended up in the courts.[11]

At that time, NBC was submerged in third place, behind CBS and ABC. Their prime-time programming was in disarray. It was conventional wisdom in the industry for the third-place network to reach out for sports as the means of climbing back up the Nielsen ratings ladder. ABC started the custom, NBC followed suit, and then CBS—shocked by its precipitous decline—engineered multi-billion-dollar sports deals for major league baseball, the Olympics, and a new contract for the NCAA tournament in the belief that the tactic still works.

Nonetheless, the idea that the games of 60 of the bigger colleges, without the Big Ten and Pac-10 teams, had enough Nielsen muscle in the 1980s to survive on Saturday night for the next several years was not taken seriously by most network executives. Yet Watson's NBC offer, an announced $180 million for four years (1982–85), enabled Neinas to tell the colleges he could deliver that pot of gold.

If the NCAA basketball contract with CBS had been Carl Lindemann's revenge on NBC, this phantasmagorical offer by Watson represented NBC's revenge on the NCAA—all's fair in love, war, and TV negotiations.

Many of the CFA schools were uncertain about what to do. Chuck Neinas wasn't sure he could deliver all of his members for the deal. Nor was I sure of their loyalty to the NCAA.

The established networks, with far more buying power than the cable interests, wanted to lock up top programming. Now more than ever, it was essential for the colleges to get the best long-term deal that we could. In negotiations that started with ABC in the spring of 1981 and continued through final meetings with the Turner Broadcasting System in January 1982, we divided the football package between ABC and CBS, adding the Turner Broadcasting System for a two-year cable deal.

The ABC sessions proved particularly grueling. Roone Arledge's longtime aide, Jim Spence, was the man on the scene that year. Spence brought along a newly acquired sidekick, Charlie Lavery. The NCAA negotiations team included two members, Eddie Crowder of Colorado and Marvin Tate of Texas A&M, who were both CFA supporters at a time when the CFA was trying to undermine our negotiations by talking simultaneously with Spence as well as NBC about a CFA exclusive contract.

After unsuccessful efforts in San Francisco and Kansas City, ABC and NCAA negotiators gathered in Denver in July 1981. We had been haggling all day in a hotel meeting room near the Denver airport, had gone to supper separately, and had returned to the ABC suite on the hotel's top floor.

The NCAA wanted $131,750,000 from the network for half of the college football over-the-air (as distinct from cable) television rights in a four-year deal. We argued over the contract until nearly midnight. It was an endurance contest.

In his book, *Up Close and Personal,* Spence said I was grouchy and argumentative that night, threatening to cut it short and take a flight for home.[12] He was right.

Jim kept claiming I had made certain concessions during our earlier discussions that day and now was recanting. He went on and on with that line. I finally blew my stack, yelling at him: "You're lying, you sonofabitch, and you know it!"

Our attorney, George Gangwere, reached over to touch my arm. George had been through other negotiations with me and, at such heated moments, he would light his pipe and look as calm as if he were watching a ballerina dance her way through a Tchaikovsky number.

"Relax," George whispered. "This is just a negotiating tactic. They're not serious."

At about that time, Jim and Charlie Lavery seemed to shift gears. They said they had to call New York to see if there was any way we could make a deal. I judged the call to be a stall to wear us down. They might be calling out for pizza for all I knew.[13]

But they apparently did make a call from the bedroom of the suite to Roone in New York. It took quite awhile. They said they had trouble getting through to Arledge. Some time later Lavery rushed out of the bedroom laughing. He fell on his knees with supplicant gestures and announced: "Ah, Master, we think we can make a deal!"

We all broke up at Lavery's performance.

Jim says in his book he did not intend to lose the college football contract under any circumstance, "but it was important to me to take something—a crumb, if you will—back to New York.

I wanted to be able to tell my superiors that we got the NCAA to knock off $250,000 from the final offer."[14]

However, I would not budge from the figure we had finally set. Despite the ABC pathos, beautifully timed, the answer was no.

"There would not be one single crumb for me to take back to New York," Jim recalls. "Strike one for the cowboy from Kansas City. He had made his point. He had once again stuck it to the television hotshots from New York."

I don't know the price of crumbs in New York, but in Emmett, Kansas, you could have bought the entire Byers Ranch cow herd for $250,000. Anyhow, I thought it was a modest surcharge for the negotiating pain and suffering we had endured. The NCAA had its $131,750,000 from ABC for four years.

ABC detested yielding its exclusive position as "the college football network." As the NCAA set out to complete the deals with CBS and a cable network, ABC was determined not to be "used" in the negotiations as the top-dollar buyer while another network got a sweeter deal. In a telegram, Roone made that abundantly clear.

DEAR WALTER,
IT IS INCONCEIVABLE TO US THAT WE COULD ENTER INTO
AN AGREEMENT WITH THE NCAA AT THESE
EXTRAORDINARY LEVELS FOR A SPLIT NETWORK
FOOTBALL PACKAGE THAT IS DESIGNED FOR PARITY
WITHOUT GUARANTEES THAT WE WILL NOT BE REQUIRED
TO PAY MORE THAN ANOTHER NETWORK FOR THE SAME
PACKAGE. I CERTAINLY HOPE THAT YOU WILL NOT CAUSE
OUR 16-CONSECUTIVE-YEAR RELATIONSHIP, WHICH HAS
BEEN ONE OF THE MOST ENDURING AND MUTUALLY
SATISFYING IN THE HISTORY OF TELEVISION, TO COME TO
AN END OVER WHAT WE CONSIDER TO BE AN ABSOLUTELY
VITAL AND REASONABLE NEED ON OUR PART FOR ANY
FUTURE TWO-NETWORK RELATIONSHIP.
ROONE ARLEDGE

We finally did wrap up the details of the ABC deal, with a handshake, in Newport, Rhode Island, late in the evening of July

24, 1981, and with CBS in Providence, the next day. The cable deal with Turner Broadcasting was put together the following January. Months would pass before the contracts were signed, but we believed we had greatly expanded national network coverage of college football and put the kinds of dollars in place that would prove irresistible to the most ardent CFA supporters.

From the 1980 level of $31 million with ABC, the NCAA football package had increased more than 125 percent. The total, spanning four years with ABC and CBS and two years with Turner Broadcasting, was $281.2 million, the last and biggest of a string of television deals that stretched back more than thirty years. The contract covered all the prominent "independents" and major conferences including the Big Ten and Pac-10 games—a bigger and better inventory of games than would have been available in the CFA deal covering about 63 schools for which NBC had offered a munificent $180 million.

After those negotiations, I received a letter from Carl Lindemann, the man who along with Al Rush in 1976 had given me a refresher lesson in negotiating: "I am pleased to hear the ol' master has not lost his touch," Carl wrote.[15]

Everybody from Carl to Jim Spence has either praised me *for* or accused me *of* being a tough, get-top-dollar negotiator. That's mostly hype. The facts of the matter are relatively simple.

When a network buys a license to telecast a sports property, it justifies its judgment by promoting viewership of that event to the maximum, which, of course, increases the return from commercial sponsors. Next, the network will badger the property owner or rights seller to obtain the maximum number and length of commercials. It will also arrange for a pregame show and a postgame show, plus perhaps a review program of the previous week's action, in which it customarily controls content as well as commercials. If the network doesn't recover its costs from the primary event, it gets back costs and a nice profit through ancillary programming.

A negotiation comes down to pushing the networks to be innovative in maximizing an event's potential programming and commercial value. The marketplace works effectively, providing top dollars for the best events and run-of-the-mill prices for ordinary events.

As we renegotiated an event like the NCAA Final Four based on the increased audience figures developed by the network's own efforts, a vital factor was whether the event was strong enough to compete in prime time, when far more TV sets are normally turned on.

Networks with mediocre prime-time programming can use more individual games from the tournament than the Number One network with a hot prime-time lineup. That becomes a vital factor in the dollar column.

From 1973 to 1981, the overall network hours that NBC devoted to tournament coverage swelled from 14 hours 5 minutes, to 21 hours 34 minutes. CBS started off with 26 hours 18 minutes of coverage and, by 1990, it was televising 47 hours 12 minutes. More than 10 hours were devoted to prime-time coverage of tournament games.[16] A decade earlier, network executives would have laughed you out of their offices for suggesting that an NCAA regional tournament game could survive in prime time. A major contributing factor to the switch in attitude was and is the decline of all network TV ratings, including prime time.

To be honest, negotiating skill is an overrated part of the total exercise. Knowing the numbers and physical endurance are critical. The main point is that the event's growth in ratings, the ability of media hype to create a "happening," total hours broadcast, and number of commercials for the event dictate the dollars. The rights owner, in this case the NCAA, grudgingly but inevitably has permitted more and more commercials to interrupt the contest's flow to maximize the TV payoff. I was a part of that inexorable process, and today more commercials in the name of "revenue enhancement" are the basis of the current CBS basketball tournament contract due to expire after the 2002 tournament.

That final football deal during 1981–82 inspired the grandest overbid I had seen to that time. The Turner Broadcasting System bought the NCAA supplementary series of football games not selected for telecast by ABC or CBS. The three bidders for that deal differed incredibly in their assessment of its worth.

We opened the bids January 26, 1982, at Kansas City's Crown Center Hotel, discovering that the USA Network had offered $800,000 plus some incentives for a two-year contract. By comparison, the ESPN offer seemed quite reasonable: $5 million to broadcast 20 "left-over" games in each of two years.

The shock came when we opened the Turner Broadcasting System's envelope and found they had bid $17.7 million for 16 games per year for two years. Ted Turner must have mistakenly figured that the Getty interests, who owned ESPN, at the time, were going to mortgage their oil reserves to outbid him and win the contract.

Neither ABC nor CBS was happy with the cable contract. CBS argued that Turner cable could not exist except as an extension of the over-the-air capabilities of superstation WTBS, which was a direct competitor of the CBS station in Atlanta. While CBS wrote angry letters, ABC quietly stoked up its boilers for major legal action against Cox Broadcasting and the NCAA in Georgia state courts.

Kansas City's Swanson Midgley law firm, continuing its run of picking good lawyers for our faraway legal fights, employed a young Atlanta attorney, James J. Thomas II, and we worked furiously setting out the facts. He lost in the trial court but won a unanimous 6-0 decision in the Georgia Supreme Court.[17]

The two major networks were upset by the cable deal, but they should have found comfort in the dissatisfaction of Ted Turner and his executive officer, Bob Wussler. The impact of their huge bid wasn't fully felt until after the first season. TBS was losing big money. Then Wussler, president of WTBS and executive vice-president for Turner, campaigned strongly for contract changes to give him a greater choice of teams and games. We agreed to some modifications, but because of restraints built into the ABC and CBS contracts, it was far from all he wanted. His frustrations reached the boiling point.

In March 1983, Bob telephoned me in my office, and I listened to one of the most profane attacks by one person on another that I had experienced.

Wussler didn't use any new terms, but his varied combinations of four-letter Anglo-Saxon expletives reflected sheer mastery of the form. He ended up yelling: "You're a sick old man!"[18]

Awed by his vituperative skills, I held my tongue through it all—highly unusual for me. I finally said: "Do you have anything else to say? If not, I'm hanging up." He didn't, so I did.

I was boiling. I immediately told my secretary, Lydia Lopez Sanchez, a wonderful help to me for 14 years, that if Wussler called back, I would not talk to him.

The Wussler conversation had started at 2:27 P.M. and ended after fire and brimstone 10 minutes later. At 2:40 P.M. he called back and was told I would not talk to him. His secretary told Lydia that Bob wanted to leave the following message: "Walter, you're a wonderful person! Please call me! Bob."

I didn't, but later we carried on business as if nothing had happened.

Notes

1. Remarks confirmed in a telephone conversation with Don Bryant, assistant athletics director, University of Nebraska, April 26, 1991.
2. NCAA, NCAA Infractions Report no. 68, August 2, 1971.
3. College Football Association, media release, February 2, 1980.
4. Joe McGuff, *Kansas City Star,* February 3, 1980.
5. Media reports of CFA annual meeting, Dallas, Texas, May 30–June 1, 1980.
6. Ibid.
7. Information for this account was drawn from conversations at the time and subsequently with Thomas W. Jernstedt; Thomas W. Jernstedt, interviews with the author, October 1990.
8. NCAA, Treasurer's Report, Fiscal Year Ended August 31, 1994.
9. Leonard F. (Len) DeLuca, interview with the author, April 22, 1991.
10. Neal H. Pilson, letter to Arthur A. Watson, April 14, 1983; Arthur A. Watson, letter to Neal H. Pilson, May 5, 1983.
11. Associated Press report, *Kansas City Times,* August 19, 1981.
12. Jim Spence, *Up Close and Personal* (New York: Atheneum, 1988), 131.
13. Information for this account was drawn from conversations with George H. Gangwere at the time and subsequently; George H. Gangwere, interview with the author, August 22, 1990.
14. Spence, *Up Close,* 132.

15. Carl Lindemann, Jr., letter to Walter Byers, November 21, 1983.
16. CBS, Report to NCAA Men's Basketball Tournament Committee, July 1990.
17. Supreme Court of Georgia Opinion, *ABC v. Cox Broadcasting Corporation*, December 6, 1982.
18. Walter Byers, telephone log, March 8, 1983; Robert J. Wussler, letter to Walter Byers, March 10, 1983.

Chapter 15   Enforcing the Antitrust Laws

The huge, three-network contracts fashioned in 1981 marked the end of the NCAA football television deals. The sheer size of the packages probably assured their ultimate destruction. High stakes and big money attract all sorts of folks, including modern versions of P. T. Barnum and Captain Hook. At least they're fun; the dangerous ones are the instant experts emboldened by superficial knowledge.

All-Out Civil War

The CFA was determined to torpedo the NCAA arrangements with ABC, CBS, and TBS. Their tentative contract with Art Watson and NBC provided for $180.0 million for the four football seasons beginning in 1982. The CFA, however, had to deliver an inventory of games and committed colleges of sufficient quality or no deal. Thus, the CFA had to persuade the big timers of NCAA, minus the Big Ten and Pac-10 loyalists, to opt for the NBC deal. Chuck Neinas argued that a CFA football power could make as much as $7.7 million during the four years while its share of the larger NCAA contract would be about $6.1 million.

We tried to warn CFA members of the consequences, contending that the insurrection was motivated by a core group more interested in gaining political power than generating new millions for the colleges. We argued that the megabucks promised by the CFA messiahs would not be there.

Pulling the hardest oar in all of this was Wiles Hallock, commissioner of the Pac-10 Conference. Wiles attended CFA meetings in his role as chairman of the NCAA TV Committee. In his polite, measured way, he carefully laid out the statistics.

The NCAA hammered the point that increased audience fragmentation already had caused a decline in viewing. The great championship events—the Super Bowl, Final Four, the World Series—were as attractive as ever. But the Nielsen high of 11.3 in 1980 for all televised network sports was eroding. The four-year, 1979–82 average of 9.8, in fact, had declined to 7.9 by 1983.[1] More fragmentation through increased cable offerings, with more games available, would result in a further decline in ratings. In 1980–81, there were 15 million cable homes, a 19.8 percent penetration of the universe of TV homes. Two years later, there were 26 million cable homes.

The CFA listened politely to the NCAA speakers. Then Chuck Neinas, supported by Dan Gibbens of the University of Oklahoma, DeLoss Dodds of Texas, and other true believers from the Atlantic Coast and Southeastern conferences, allowed how cable would be the source of new wealth if only the major football colleges could free themselves of the NCAA yoke.

Joe Paterno also weighed in with his economic appraisal of why Penn State would no longer give its property rights to the NCAA. "Because the NCAA has entered into a four-year agreement that not only entails telecasting, it's also involved in cable. None of us know where cable is going. Look at the Leonard/Hearns fight. That's a 15-16-17 million dollar deal. What's a Notre Dame/Southern California game worth on a Saturday? Fifteen million? Is it worth $50 million five years from now?"[2]

At the time, advertiser-supported cable essentially meant a reallocation of advertising dollars, not an untapped gold mine of new money. Pay TV promised to generate big new bucks, but that had been little more than a pipe dream for college officials.

CFA and NCAA copy machines used up reams of paper during the summer of 1981 as the two sides sought to persuade their dual members to the righteousness of their causes. The NCAA took the position that because CFA members also were NCAA members, they were bound by all valid NCAA legislation—including the television plan.

Charles Alan Wright, chairman of the NCAA Committee on Infractions, said that willful, premeditated violations would result in prompt hearings by his committee. Wright, a constitutional scholar, was a professor on the law faculty at the University of Texas at Austin, in the heart of CFA country. Across campus, DeLoss Dodds, Texas athletics director, ignored Professor Wright and worked for the CFA and for Neinas, who had been his boss when they were both in the Big Eight Conference.

The next step was for the CFA to check its hole card. How many CFA colleges would back the Davison-Neinas leadership?

The preliminary agreement between the CFA and NBC was ratified in Atlanta, Georgia, on August 21, 1981, by a vote of 33 in favor, 20 against, and 8 abstaining or invalid.[3] A final vote was set for September 10. If at that time the CFA could produce a sufficient number of colleges to participate in the NBC schedule, the deal would be done.

The destruction of the NCAA television plan promised heavy losses to the Big Eight Conference, which, next to the Western Athletic Conference, was to suffer most from the ultimate CFA victory. But the Big Eight voted 75 percent in favor of the CFA-NBC action. That vote was partly a tribute to Chuck Neinas, Big Eight commissioner before he became head of the CFA. It also resulted from the conference's fear of anti-NCAA Oklahoma, which overrode any clear-headed evaluation of conference interests. The Oklahoma Sooners' periodic, implied threats that unnamed trustees might force OU to leave the conference had paralyzed the Big Eight majority's resolve more than once.

Final decision time was approaching. Chuck Neinas asked Paterno to urge the president of Penn State, John W. Oswald, to issue a special bulletin to his counterparts at all CFA institutions. Oswald was fully conscious of Joe's popularity with Penn State trustees and alumni. He promptly dispatched a memo on August 28 in which he mourned the anti-CFA position of the Big Ten and Pac-10 presidents. He went on to emphasize that Penn State would vote for the CFA at the critical time.[4]

Art Watson, still sore about the roughing-up he took in the basketball negotiations, reaffirmed Chuck's predictions about new

Wilford S. Bailey (*left*), NCAA president, 1987 and 1988, with Charles M. Neinas, executive director of the College Football Association. They were good friends and political allies on most intercollegiate athletics issues.

wealth for CFA football on television. Meanwhile, I still thought our firm but yet-to-be signed deals with ABC and CBS plus TBS looked pretty good. It was a madcap scene that summer with people, including me, offering to sell rights they were not sure they could deliver, and network executives offering to buy rights that might never be available.

Trying to counter the CFA moves, the NCAA scheduled a special convention in December that would deal with a major criticism by the CFA schools—the clutter of too many colleges in NCAA Division I. If we satisfied those complaints and gave the football powerhouses more control, perhaps they would reject the lure and illusions of the CFA.

The promise of a special convention slowed the CFA momentum. Under pressure from several of its members, the CFA decided to postpone its final decision to December 14—after the NCAA Special Convention in St. Louis. It was there that Division I was split into two divisions, I-A and I-AA. The top division was cut from about 180 to 105 football schools. The CFA opposed even this new configuration, contending that members of the Pacific Coast Athletic Association (now Big West) and the Mid-American Conference had no right to be in the same room with the biggies.

Barry Switzer, Oklahoma football coach, in a burst of candor had told the media in August that what was needed in college athletics was a collection of some 40 major football-playing universities.[5] This was considered a public relations boo-boo by the CFA and the president of Oklahoma went public to say Barry didn't speak for him or the CFA membership. But Barry was correctly broadcasting the views of many football coaches.

"We could set our own rules," he explained. "Maybe give the players $50 a day [he meant "a month"]. Get rid of the 95 [total NCAA overall football grant limit]. We sign 30 every year, so let's educate [provide scholarships for] the whole 120. I don't care how many coaches Missouri has. If they want 20, let them have 20.

"I suppose Ohio State could drop me [cancel their OU game] if Walter tells them to. But we'd just pick up somebody else.... If we're expelled from the NCAA it could enable us to do some things that are realistic."

The decision to shrink the NCAA's top division was long overdue. The 105-team configuration didn't satisfy the Switzer block, or meet the CFA's goal of 80 or so in the top division, but it was close enough. This December response by the NCAA, plus the good television contracts we had already negotiated, carried the day.

So many CFA members opted out of the CFA-NBC television plan that, on December 14, the organization advised NBC it could not deliver a sufficient game inventory to proceed with the arrangement. At that point, the NCAA's deals with ABC, CBS, and TBS were in place and began operating.

The December 14 referendum defeat was ignored by the CFA leaders. To hell with plebiscites! They promptly decided to attack NCAA TV controls through the courts. The CFA thus set out to enforce the federal antitrust laws. The universities of Georgia and Oklahoma were designated as plaintiffs, and Oklahoma City was selected as the playing field. A former Oklahoma City mayor was hired as the lead lawyer.

Some CFA schools questioned whether CFA money—including

their own contributions—should be used to finance the lawsuit against the NCAA and, in effect, themselves. It became a major issue in the spring of 1982, but the CFA board persisted and Chuck Neinas assured the Oklahoma City lawyer that if the CFA membership rebelled at paying legal fees, then Oklahoma and Georgia would ante up the full amount.

The case started in federal district court under a visiting judge from New Mexico, Juan Burciaga. Lead-off witnesses were two university presidents, Fred Davison of Georgia and Bill Banowsky of Oklahoma. They testified that substantial profits due from their successful football programs were being denied because the NCAA had robbed them of valuable business property rights.

I thought our case was critically damaged by Davison's testimony as president of the CFA. He made it clear that neither athletics competition nor education had much to do with these proceedings.

Davison headed the Georgia Athletic Association, a not-for-profit corporation that managed Georgia's athletics and carried $12 million in debt. As I noted in chapter 1, he told the court that football generated $5 million a year at Georgia and that the NCAA was curtailing the university's business activities. You'd never guess from Davison's words that there was any difference between football at Georgia and the citizen-owned Green Bay Packers, except for the unstated fact that the former enjoys a federal tax exemption and enforces a ceiling on player compensation.

A key question in the Oklahoma City lawsuit was whether the NCAA's motive in TV control was to limit the output of the product in order to raise prices. Our lawyers argued that the underlying purpose was to create more competitive balance among the teams through wider distribution of television appearances, money, and publicity. By preventing Notre Dame, for instance, from getting its sixth national TV appearance in a two-year period, TV controls opened up a network appearance for another college.

At one point, it was suggested the NCAA should simply distribute the money among the schools without restricting the number of appearances. That implied money alone is the competitive issue. Legal analysts, at the time and since, have contended that forced distribution of money among the schools would be as much an antitrust violation as the appearance limitations.

It seemed to me that TV appearances *did* help bolster the morale, publicity, recruiting effectiveness, and fund-raising ability of weaker teams, thus improving overall intercollegiate competition. In trying to dramatize this critical point, I thought we needed testimony from someone like Eddie Robinson, whose 52 years of coaching Grambling football (counting the 1994 season) has made him the winningest coach in football history, surpassing Bear Bryant's record. Eddie had made the Grambling football Tigers a national symbol of black pride. His teams had been selected for national network appearances as part of the NCAA program.

Eddie had an engaging manner. Since he had come up the hard way, I thought he would make a persuasive ally. When I called him to ask if he would testify, he quickly replied: "Sure, I want to do it. The plan has been great for Division I-AA institutions and particularly the black colleges." Eddie was indeed an effective witness.

Nevertheless Burciaga concluded at trial's end that NCAA TV controls did not contribute to competitive balance. He decided our evidence was not persuasive. It was a finding of fact at the trial-court level that we were never given a chance to overturn. The appeals court accepted the trial court's fact finding.

From that point forward, the NCAA was arguing pure business antitrust law, having failed to convince the trial court on a critical factual issue. We were playing catch-up. When Eddie and I would meet on subsequent occasions, the trial episode became a standing joke between us.

"You were very impressive in Oklahoma City, Eddie," I would tell him. "Your testimony convinced everybody but the judge."

"I'm sure I had him convinced," Eddie would laugh. "Something must have happened to change his mind after I left town."

The NCAA lost the court battle first in Oklahoma City, then at the Tenth Circuit Court of Appeals in Denver. We appealed to the Supreme Court.

The American Council on Education was prepared to file an amicus curiae brief with the Supreme Court. The proposed brief was well done and supported many of the NCAA arguments, but the effort was killed by ACE executive prerogative, reportedly at the behest of Davison.

When the case was heard before the Supreme Court in June 1984, the CFA got what it asked for. It was clear from the questioning that day that Justice Stevens had his mind made up, and he knew an antitrust violation when he saw one. Byron White, former University of Colorado All-American halfback, and William Rehnquist, soon to be Chief Justice, were the only justices to vote for the NCAA.[6]

The other seven justices found that the colleges, working through the NCAA to control television rights, clearly had crossed the line from not-for-profit educational activities into the business world. The NCAA's limitations on the "output" of televised games amounted to restraint of trade as well as other violations of federal antitrust statutes.

Since we lost, it was not Oklahoma-Georgia or the CFA that had to pay the legal fees. We paid $1.3 million in fees to NCAA lawyers, of which $795,124 went to the lawyers themselves, $407,193 to expert witnesses, and $50,000 for related costs. Judge Burciaga also ordered us to pay the plaintiffs' bills of $983,955. The funeral for our NCAA television plan was a dandy. It had cost us $2.24 million to bury it properly. The CFA decided not to seek treble damages.

I strongly backed the NCAA defense of the lawsuit, convinced the action was in the long-term best interests of college football. Now that the dust has settled, I believe the Supreme Court's decision was inevitable. Legal pundits have dissected its meaning in numerous treatises, but the simple message is that the commercial and monopoly activities of not-for-profit educationally related groups are not sacrosanct.

Certain comforting words about the NCAA's efforts to maintain amateurism, which I attribute to the influence of Justice White, found their way into the Supreme Court opinion, but they don't soften the underlying message.

The colleges, their student financial-aid practices, and the operations of their athletics programs are increasingly vulnerable to challenges under antitrust and tax laws. Artificial restraints on individual rights and the maximizing of commercial opportunities by the colleges for themselves and their executives are destined to trigger even more serious challenges to the educational and sports cartel.

As the lawsuit over football ground on in 1982, the CFA continued its efforts to sweep up basketball and form an organization that would replace the NCAA.

In a bulletin issued in January 1982 to the CFA Board of Directors, Neinas noted what he called "an increased interest in changing the College Football Association to the College Sports Association to enable [the CFA] to address issues related to basketball and other sports.[7]

"The major football-playing universities are opposed to financing a welfare system for intercollegiate athletics," he added. This reference to sharing the big schools' moneys through the NCAA with institutions that generate little if any NCAA income struck a responsive chord then—just as it can stir latent passions today.

The CFA strategy centered on removing the NCAA from football television and then undercutting the NCAA in basketball. Since about 75 percent of its income was generated by the Final Four tournament, the NCAA would be fatally crippled.

During the Final Four championship at New Orleans in 1982, the CFA held a meeting to discuss this concept, but in more subtle terms. Dave Gavitt of the Big East Conference, chairman of the NCAA basketball committee at that time, told his CFA friends that tampering with the NCAA basketball money machine was madness.

If hard-headed football coaches wanted to destroy the NCAA football TV program, that was their business, Dave said. But the NCAA men's basketball tournament—the event that stimulated all of college basketball—was something else. Helping to illustrate his point, more than 61,000 spectators were in the Superdome in New Orleans that weekend for North Carolina's one-point championship victory over Georgetown.

Pointing out that 1982 tournament teams would receive almost $11 million, Dave suggested CFA officials should confer with new economic advisors. Even a Notre Dame voice spoke against a repeat of the football takeover in the sport of basketball. Gene Corrigan, athletics director at South Bend, walked into the CFA meet and, in effect, told the football-dominated assembly: "Don't do it." That cooled the ardor of many.

Television has been a fickle siren for the CFA. It led to the Supreme Court and a smashing victory of sorts. But it also created the ultimate obstacle to the CFA's expansion plans in basketball by serving as the stimulus and midwife to a brand-new college sports conference. This new league grew out of discussions between Dave Gavitt, then athletics director and basketball coach at Providence College, and Jack Kaiser, athletics director at St. John's in New York City. They believed that an eastern basketball conference could generate enormous dollars from the East Coast television markets.

The plan called for a set of eastern colleges that would dominate college basketball in four of the nation's top eight markets—New York City, Philadelphia, Boston, and Washington, D.C. At a key meeting in May 1979, seven charter members formed what became the Big East Conference: St. John's, Seton Hall, Connecticut, Boston College, Georgetown, Syracuse, and Providence. They wanted Philadelphia; they added Villanova.

A PR firm recommended Big East as the preferred commercial title. The conference's mission was singular—the pursuit of wealth. Of its eight stated goals, almost all of them were about money: Originate a TV network, run a postseason tournament, be successful financially, sell and create identity, and promote the conference name for merchandising and corporate sponsor income.

Penn State did not receive an invitation. At the time, Big East planners viewed basketball there as a low-key activity that filled in the time between the bowl games and the start of spring football practice.

Rutgers, however, did receive an invitation to join the Big East. In the rapidly expanding New Jersey market across the Hudson River from New York City, it would have been an ideal fit. Rutgers also would have offset the impression that the Big East was a Catholic-dominated basketball conference.In fact, if Rutgers had agreed, the invitation to Seton Hall would not have materialized.

Both Penn State and Rutgers were committed to the Atlantic 10 Conference in basketball. If Rutgers joined the Big East, it would demean the status of Atlantic 10 basketball and Penn State. A "yes" might terminate the Rutgers–Penn State football series. Rutgers got the message and turned down the Big East, bowing to the pressure of Penn State.

The league's first schedule was in 1979–80. From a first-year budget of $175,000 to a 1988–89 budget of $11.2 million, the conference cruised in commercial overdrive behind Commissioner Dave Gavitt's unerring economic instincts.[8]

The Big East success gave CFA strategists a major problem. How could the College Football Association, which for years had objected bitterly to an NCAA Division I embracing colleges that didn't have big-time football, try to absorb into its plans for basketball nine institutions that (except for Connecticut) either didn't sponsor football or played it with unrecruited volunteers?

A CFA basketball tournament without the premier teams in Boston, New York, Philadelphia, and Washington, D.C., would be lampooned out of existence by the sophisticated eastern media.

Former basketball coach Dave Gavitt had helped to frustrate a former basketball radio announcer named Chuck Neinas. Checkmate.

Defining Greed

Old-line football coaches who believed in a strong running game contended that "if you live by the forward pass, you'll die by it." The CFA, for all of its efforts, has remained a one-dimensional organization, and its frustrations have mounted year by year.

The first move the CFA made after the dissolution of NCAA TV controls was to attempt to reestablish friendly ties with the Big Ten and Pac-10 conferences. Overtures went out to the prominent athletics directors and key football coaches in those conferences.

The message was that if they would associate with the CFA, the eighty or so major football schools together could generate millions more television dollars, fashion better recruiting rules, increase values of grants-in-aid for football players, and all in all provide inspirational new leadership to replace the stodgy, small-school-dominated NCAA. The CFA was baffled and angered when the Big Ten and Pac-10 refused to go along.

Byron Gregory, then Big Ten attorney, repeated after the Supreme Court decision what he had said before the trial. "The major football-playing institutions in the country cannot band together and perform under a new name what the courts of the land say they cannot do under the NCAA name."

The CFA discounted Byron's views, perhaps thinking he was Wayne Duke's personal mouthpiece. Charley Scott, associate academic vice-president of the University of Alabama, had been a voice of moderation in the CFA camp and a strong NCAA supporter for years. But in January 1984, he told Duke to get rid of his "holier-than-thou" attitude and join with the CFA in a new national program to generate national revenues.[9] Charley confessed he had been piqued about Big Ten attitudes for a long time, saying he first encountered Big Ten "elitist" views about athletics when he was attending Purdue in 1951.

Setting up an all-encompassing college football TV cartel without the Big Ten and Pac-10 conferences would be akin to organizing OPEC without Saudi Arabia. The CFA went its way, selling football television rights first to ABC, then to CBS. The Big Ten and Pac-10 went their way but in reverse order, selling football rights to CBS and then to ABC. In fact, ABC barely missed putting it all back together during the first post–Supreme Court negotiation.

For the football seasons of 1987–90, the CFA had dropped its asking price from $72 million to $59 million. ABC had offered $55 million for the rights. In a last-minute flash of independent judgment, Bob Iger of ABC increased that offer to $57 million without his boss's approval. It wasn't enough. CBS got the rights for an announced $60 million. The actual price was more like $64 million.

CBS was able to offer what might have been considered an overbid, except CBS relieved itself of union costs in producing the games. The deal was made by CFA's Chuck Neinas with CBS's then vice-president for program acquisition, Peter Tortorici. The CFA would be "responsible for the below line production costs in accordance with the specifications agreed upon with CBS."[10] Thus, the CFA could arrange for cameramen, lines, and technical support services with nonunion personnel, or personnel subject to different union rules, thereby keeping in its pockets the profits from production and cutting CBS's costs. The $60 million was separate from payments for those CFA services, unallocated in the interests of both parties—CBS for purposes of its union contract and CFA for tax and budget purposes. The CFA provided these subsidiary production services for 69 games according to CBS.

ABC could not get away with what CBS got away with. Charles Stanford, network counsel for ABC, explained that if a third party does production for ABC, or NBC for that matter, either one must abide by their respective union contracts.

The NCAA had explored production possibilities in connection with selling the network rights for the NCAA Final Four tournament as well as other NCAA championship events. Legal counsel George Gangwere had told us we should not do it unless we wanted to produce leftover games not used by the network buyers, which we did. He warned that the NCAA could be liable for federal business taxes based on unrelated business income if we substituted for a tax-paying commercial firm in an established line of business.

We had been subject to ongoing IRS and state tax challenges to NCAA tournament program production and profit-sharing arrangements. We had repeatedly been questioned about ancillary marketing and merchandising business connections and whether the NCAA was entitled to continued exemption from Kansas property and sales taxes as an educational institution. George recommended that we not open up another door for further tax challenges.

The theory is that a not-for-profit, tax-exempt organization shall not compete with tax-paying businesses in a market not related to their basic tax-exempt educational purposes. Be that as it may, the CFA became a TV producer as a partner with CBS. The CFA went on to close a deal with ESPN.

Meanwhile, Jim Spence's unswerving loyalty to ABC for some 25 years had come to an end. When told by Roone Arledge in January, 1986, that Dennis Swanson, a former Big Ten sports announcer, had the job, Jim left his office and didn't return. His longtime friend Chuck Howard urged him to go back, pointing out that Jim was risking a lot of contract buy-out money. Spence said, "To hell with it." Jim later confirmed that the Cap Cities/ABC management dealt with him fairly.

Roone, a Columbia University grad, had never felt that Jim Spence of Dartmouth had the savoir-faire to keep up amid New York's fast-paced social clubbism. Although Jim was a competent and loyal line officer, he was never completely free to run sports. Clearly, Arledge was concentrating on ABC News, but he insisted on retaining the final word on major sports issues during Jim's tenure. This hurt Jim's effectiveness.

As the new kid on the block, Dennis Swanson made it clear he was in charge, and if there were any Roone Arledge loyalists left in the sports department, they had better understand that. Furthermore, Swanson indicated he was his own man and did not have to clear big decisions with Arledge. The distaste between the two reached such proportions that top management told the parties to cool it. They did, and since then Dennis has made it a point to compliment Roone's remarkable record as TV sports and news executive.

However, Roone's longtime control of ABC Sports was at an end, and the temper of the times persuaded Chuck Howard he should leave. He did so with a sizeable settlement, sweetened by the value of his ABC stock, worth a lot more than when he began acquiring it.

Having gone through those many years of NCAA football's exciting partnership with television, I felt a sudden sadness mixed with considerable nostalgia. A significant changing of the guard had taken place. College football had benefitted from the visionary and enthusiastic leadership of some of the industry's best TV executives, producers and directors. Equally important were the superb play-by-play announcers associated with the game—Mel Allen, Lindsey Nelson, Curt Gowdy, Chris Schenkel, and Keith Jackson to mention a few. Television admittedly is a fickle business, but no one stayed longer or did a better job than the remarkable Keith Jackson. He's still going strong, despite Roone's lack of

Three of the major players of ABC football TV operations during the NCAA series. *From left to right:* Chuck Howard, producer, Andy Sidaris, director, and Keith Jackson, broadcaster for college football games for nearly 30 years.

support in the latter part of the 1970s and disinterest in his contract renewal in the 1980s. It took Dennis Swanson to sign Keith to a new contract in 1986. A versatile, multisports announcer, Keith will be best remembered for his devotion to college football.

Do We Have a Deal?

After missing the overall CFA contract, Swanson was invited to deal directly with the Southeastern Conference for 1987–90. Harvey Schiller, the new Southeastern Conference commissioner, wanted to make a big inaugural splash. He felt that the Southeastern Conference's identity was buried under the CFA umbrella. Just as the power schools in the NCAA plan had resented the influence of smaller schools, the most powerful conference in the CFA resented its similar submergence. It was time for the SEC to become singularly identified on TV just as the Big Ten and Pac-10 were identified in their own televised contests.[11]

Having just arrived at the SEC from the Air Force Academy where he had been faculty athletics representative, Schiller was conscious of the college sports industry perception that the SEC was inferior academically and athletically to the Big Ten. He also knew that the SEC couldn't get a new image across by being a subsidiary of the College Football Association. He went to New York to see Dennis Swanson. Dennis decided to open up his checkbook and buy SEC football rights.

The contract between ABC and the SEC followed the format of the CFA contracts, and the dollars were essentially the same as the ABC agreement with the Big Ten and Pac-10—four years for about $50 million, or $6.25 million annually per conference. The SEC offer would have enabled ABC to put together a TV lineup of games similar to the days of ABC's NCAA package.

"Harvey did an effective negotiating job," Dennis Swanson recalls. "We didn't want to go that high, but we did it to enable us to tie up the three major conferences we wanted."

A deal had been made that would shatter the cornerstone of the College Football Association. Would the Southeastern Conference now stay united? Politics and negotiations reached feverish proportions, and the major players descended on SEC headquarters in Birmingham, Alabama—ABC, CBS, College Football Association officials, and the SEC delegation.

Harvey communicated with me several times during much of this, ostensibly to ask questions and draw on my experience in TV negotiations. He was nervous as the vote approached, and I really think he just wanted an outsider to commiserate with him. Although he fretted that the whole ABC deal might go down the drain, the final vote was 9-1 to accept the ABC proposal.

SEC attorney Frank Bainbridge noted that the only two points needing settlement were a change of LSU night games to daylight hours and the renegotiation rights for the future. Bainbridge agreed with Swanson that these issues could easily be resolved.

The CFA officials were stunned. Their most important conference was defecting. They fought back desperately. Chuck Neinas and DeLoss Dodds headed a CFA man-to-man defense. Individual contacts were made throughout the SEC. Old-time loyalties and past commitments were recalled. The NCAA was again cited as the ultimate target. There was presidential lobbying by Martin Massengale of the University of Nebraska, the first non-SEC president to accept the top elective post with the CFA. President Joab Thomas of Alabama, a former CFA chairman of the board, and the top management of Florida and Tennessee began campaigning for a rescission of the Birmingham vote.

It all worked. The SEC reversed itself, walked away from ABC, and decided to stay with the CFA. From 9-1 in favor of the ABC deal, the SEC vote went to 4-6 against. The four institutions that stayed hitched to ABC were Auburn, LSU, Mississippi State, and Vanderbilt.

In the process, the SEC obtained goodly concessions from the CFA as to its separate identity and the number of games it would have on the 1987–90 CFA programs—the power conference exerting its will on the CFA, just as power schools and conferences had worked their will on the NCAA.[12]

Schiller called me to explain that, as to the ABC deal, "all we had was a handshake" anyway. Really, there was no final commitment with ABC, he said. I told Harvey that was not the story being told in the TV industry. On the phone he sounded wounded and distraught.

Harvey later accepted the top salaried position with the U.S. Olympic Committee, then renounced it and returned to the SEC commissionership. By that time there was so much hostility in the conference toward Harvey that he regained his job by a one-vote margin. Soon, Harvey reversed his course again and in mid-1989 he reaccepted the USOC position. The good colonel changed directions faster than the Air Force jets he once flew.

Dennis Swanson is a man who believes that what goes around comes around. At the time, he told Schiller that ABC felt secure that it had an enforceable legal agreement, but the network wasn't going to contest the matter in the courts.

Indeed, it did "come around." In 1990 Dennis and ABC put the

TV rights for college football back under the ABC banner—Big Ten, Pac-10, and CFA. He went one-up on Arledge by also acquiring rights to the Rose Bowl, an event Roone had long coveted. Starting in 1991, ABC once again was set to become "the network for college football," as the trio of Roone Arledge, Chuck Howard, and Jim Spence had liked to call it. But at the last moment, Notre Dame defected.

The Irish secretly made a deal with NBC, ignoring its CFA comrades-in-arms. Swanson and ABC ended up once more having bought something the seller couldn't deliver.

On January 17–18, 1990, CFA executives were negotiating a new football TV contract for 1991–95. Reverend E. William Beauchamp, faculty representative of Notre Dame, was secretary-treasurer of the CFA and a member of the negotiations committee. While the CFA was in final bartering with ABC, Notre Dame quietly was making a deal with NBC. According to Swanson, Chuck Neinas and TV consultant Mike Tragar reached agreement late in the evening of the January 18 with ABC and ESPN, subject to CFA ratification. Notre Dame games were a part of the CFA inventory purchased by ABC.

During a telephone conference the next day in which Father Beauchamp participated, the agreement was approved, and CFA called ABC to confirm the deal and report the committee was unanimous. During this same period, Richard A. Rosenthal, Notre Dame athletics director, had entered into independent negotiations with CBS and NBC.

Immediately after telephone ratification of the ABC deal and unaware of the impending Notre Dame defection, Neinas dispatched a letter of agreement dated January 19, 1990, to Steve Solomon, ABC senior vice-president for sports, confirming 28 "basic points." Big Eight Conference Commissioner Carl James reported to his bosses on February 8 that the ABC-ESPN transaction was worth $300 million for five years.

Two weeks later, in a February 22 memorandum to the CFA membership, Chuck announced that the CFA would have to renegotiate its ABC-ESPN agreement as a result of Notre Dame's defection to NBC. The switch cost the CFA roughly $35 million for the five years and was worth about the same to Notre Dame.[13] Again, Dennis Swanson "believed we had a valid legal remedy, and once again, we decided not to pursue it."

"We don't object to what Notre Dame did. Our quarrel was with the manner in which they did it. I still feel that way," Swanson told me recently.

The Reverend Beauchamp, executive vice-president of Notre Dame, followed up this performance by subsequently writing a nationally distributed article confirming that athletes are paid to play, but their present grant-in-aid compensation is sufficient. He remarked that "Twenty or thirty years after a playing career, the enduring memory for most athletes will be of the competition and camaraderie—not the cash."[14]

During the CFA lawsuit, we had commended the merits of NCAA controls by trying to explain that the big schools' lust for money, left unrestrained, would trammel the less fortunate schools. We didn't impress the court with this point, but eight years later the message registered with CFA officials.

When Notre Dame pulled out of the CFA-ABC contract, it was Vince Dooley, Georgia athletics director, who proclaimed: "I wasn't surprised by this, I was shocked. Surprise, shock, greed, and ultimate greed—that is the reaction I'm getting from people."[15]

It's a tough business. Hardened veterans of the entertainment industry have learned that colleges can play it as rough as anyone. And the CFA has learned that living on the entertainment bubble can be a precarious existence. Still alive after the SEC insurrection and the Notre Dame defection, the CFA came under federal investigation.

It started innocently enough after the Supreme Court decision when a national group of college athletics directors became distressed about the condition of college football—first, the lower TV financial returns, and second, the increased number of games being televised. They feared the long-term impact of such TV saturation on game attendance.

Leading this group was Sam Jankovich of the University of Miami, later general manager of the NFL New England Patriots. As a former athletics director in the Pac-10 Conference, Jankovich

Vince Dooley, University of Georgia football coach for 25 years (1964–88), and its current athletics director, was an avid supporter of the College Football Association and expressed outrage when Notre Dame deserted the CFA to enter into a football television contract with NBC.

believed he was the appropriate bridge between his CFA colleges and the Big Ten and Pac-10.

Sam's group of athletics directors in the late 1980s hired a lawyer in Washington, D.C., then prepared a comprehensive and well-crafted national TV plan that would bypass both the CFA and NCAA and ostensibly would meet the terms of the Supreme Court ruling.[16]

One option would be to take the plan to Judge Burciaga and see if he would indicate informally whether it met the basic concerns he had with the NCAA when he rendered his original decision. This option was abandoned, perhaps because of still-echoing sentences from the judge's memorandum opinion. "If today's victim of a price-fixing conspiracy is tomorrow's price fixer," Judge

Burciaga wrote, "the Sherman [antitrust] Act can be employed against it. Free-market competition must be restored to this industry."

The Sam Jankovich group presented the new TV plan to the U.S. Justice Department for an advisory ruling.[17] The Justice Department referred it to the Federal Trade Commission (FTC). This triggered an FTC investigation into the legality of past and *current* CFA contracts. The inquiry was broadened to include the Big Ten and Pac-10 contracts. The FTC not only suspected that what the CFA's 63 members had been doing was illegal but also raised the question of whether a combination of any two big-time conferences violates antitrust laws.

The FTC investigation started in March 1989. By early 1990, the FTC's Washington office already had four legal-length, five-drawer file cabinets filled.[18] The matter played out about the time that CFA members abandoned the CFA as their football TV control agency.

Big dollars entail high risks. When millions in TV rights fees are involved, the potential for near-term revolution is always there. We found that out as our rights fees for college football escalated during the late 1970s and early 1980s, and again when they were deflated after the Supreme Court decision. CFA apologists explained that the organization might not have attacked the NCAA football TV controls if I had not been so unbending. They said that the threat of expedited infractions penalties by Charles Alan Wright was a major irritant. These claims, valid or not, do not excuse the basic economic misjudgments.

In South Bend at the time, Gene Corrigan was more candid. The Notre Dame athletics director, simply said, "We shot ourselves in the foot."

From 1981 to 1986, college football TV ratings dropped 35 percent from an average 12.7 to 8.2. In the same period, pro football was down 15 percent and baseball 7.0 percent.[19] In 1982, Division I-A football colleges averaged a record 43,689 fans. In 1992 the average was down to 41,170.

In explaining increased college athletics department deficits to the *Dallas Morning News,* after the NCAA breakup, Fred Jacoby,

Southwest Conference commissioner, cited lower TV revenues. "It played right into the hands of the networks," he said. "They just cut their rights fees in half."

In the Big Eight Conference, birthplace of the CFA revolution, the pain was enormous. In 1984 the Big Eight received $3 million from network football TV appearances and $1.3 million from regional syndication, a total of $4.3 million. In 1987 the conference's football TV revenue was $2.8 million. In 1988 the Big Eight had two fewer network TV appearances, the lowest total since 1980. The minutes of a conference meeting that March officially acknowledged the loss had "a significant financial impact" upon the conference.[20]

Two years later the Big Eight Conference became bitter. During their March 1990 meeting, Big Eight athletics directors confronted their commissioner, Carl James, with evidence of a secret deal CFA officials had struck with the Southeastern Conference to keep the SEC in the 1991–95 CFA football TV package.

Jake Crouthamel, athletics director at Syracuse University, earlier had circulated a highly critical letter charging that the CFA's most recent negotiations involved private "deals"—Jake called them "extorted concessions"—undertaken to benefit the SEC without the knowledge of the CFA TV committee or the membership.[21]

Big Eight athletics directors had seen the Crouthamel letter, concurred with it, and said, in effect, Neinas had made under-the-table arrangements to keep the SEC with him and had shortchanged the other members. The conference concluded that Neinas should not be involved in television negotiations "because his position rests upon the successful completion of a television contract, providing too much opportunity for conflict of interests that might not serve the best interests of *all* constituents of the CFA."[22]

Big Eight Commissioner Carl James, who had been on the CFA negotiating committee, apologetically confirmed that 22 percent of the appearances in the new agreement had been guaranteed to the Southeastern Conference. The anger among the athletics directors was more than Carl had bargained for.

In the athletics civil war they started, Fred Davison, Father Joyce, and Chuck Neinas chose football television as the field on which to do major battle with the NCAA. In more ways than one it was a bad call for the CFA. Notre Dame achieved its objective, but the CFA missed a politically propitious moment to restructure control of college athletics, dazzled instead by TV glamour and the prospect of network dollars.

The organization's ambitions to rout the NCAA will never be realized. Probably a new national group should take over. The CFA, however, is in a moribund state. Its time has come and gone. Even as the CFA had worked its destructive mission against NCAA football television, a different breed of reformers were on the attack to improve the academic side of college athletics, blaming the NCAA for the colleges' academic shortcomings.

Notes

1. Five-Year Average, Regular Season and Championship Sports Series (1979–83), May 3, 1984, based on A.G. Nielsen Company's annual ratings.
2. *Philadelphia Bulletin,* August 21, 1981.
3. Associated Press report, *Kansas City Star,* August 21, 1981.
4. John Oswald, memorandum to CFA membership, August 28, 1981.
5. Quoted by Al Carter, *Daily Oklahoman,* August 22, 1981.
6. Supreme Court of the United States Syllabus, June 27, 1984.
7. Charles M. Neinas, memorandum, January 13, 1982.
8. Information for this account was drawn from conversations with David Gavitt and John J. (Jake) Crouthamel; various newspaper articles.
9. Charley Scott, letter to Wayne Duke, January 6, 1984; Wayne Duke, letter to Charley Scott, January 23, 1984.
10. Charles M. Neinas, letter to Peter Tortorici, September 22, 1986.
11. Information for this account was drawn from conversations with Harvey W. Schiller, David E. Cawood, Len DeLuca, and Dennis Swanson; Dennis Swanson, interviews with the author, August 9, 1989, and February 20, 1991; Len DeLuca, interviews with the author, April 18 and 22, 1991.
12. Ibid.
13. Information for the preceding account was drawn from Dennis Swanson, interviews with the author, February 20 and April 19, 1991; DeLuca, interviews; Charles M. Neinas, letter to Steve Solomon, January 19, 1990; Charles M. Neinas, memorandum to CFA membership, February 22, 1990; Carl James, Fax memorandum to Big Eight Conference athletics directors and faculty representatives, February 8, 1990.
14. Rev. E. William Beauchamp, *NCAA News,* June 26, 1994.
15. William F. Reed, *Sports Illustrated,* February 19, 1990.

16. Sports Marketing & Television International, Inc., Division I-A Directors Association Football Plan, Greenwich, Connecticut, September 1988; Keith Dunnavant, *Sports, Inc.,* January 9, 1989.

17. Bert W. Rein, letter to Charles F. Rule, September 6, 1988.

18. Stephen W. Riddell, meeting with Walter Byers, March 13, 1990.

19. Nielsen Television Index, College and Competing Team Sports Football Television Ratings, Division I-A Directors Association Football Plan, January 9, 1989.

20. Big Eight Conference, Minutes, December 7–8, 1988, 2694.

21. John J. (Jake) Crouthamel, letter to Charles M. Neinas, February 12, 1990.

22. Big Eight Conference, Minutes, March 8, 1990, 16.

Chapter 16

Academic Standards and Athletes

After the civil rights and Vietnam War riots of the 1960s and the defeat of the 1.600 academic standard in 1973, a decade of mediocre academic values and free-handed recruiting passed before the colleges tried once again to enact an NCAA academic floor—a minimum standard to stop the slide of member colleges toward easier admissions, suspect courses, and softer grading.

This time it came in the form of Proposition 48, developed by a committee of the American Council on Education (ACE), the college presidents' lobbying organization in Washington, D.C. They proposed at the 1983 NCAA Convention that, beginning in 1986, entering freshmen would be eligible for athletics grants and game competition only if their high school grade point average was at least 2.0 in a core curriculum *and* they had achieved a minimum 700 of the combined 1,600 points on the SAT or 15 of 36 composite points on the ACT exam.

The equation implementing the former 1.600 rule had allowed high school grades and test performance to complement each other. Proposition 48 would require freshmen student-athletes to clear both hurdles—high school grade requirement and test minimum. But if unsuccessful the first time, they could repeat the tests. The hurdle was not high; many even considered it embarrassingly low. The College Board, creator of the SAT, indicated that of a group of 1.5 million college-bound students tested in 1982, 85 percent of the men and 80 percent of the women could meet the proposed standard.

I was in the middle of the storm at the Town and Country Hotel in San Diego as the 1983 NCAA Convention battle developed over this issue. Before describing that struggle and the succeeding years of guerilla warfare that have weakened Proposition 48's original scope, let me explain why I believe academic standards on a national comparative basis are needed not only for college athletes but for all students.

Today's huge educational factories ingest some 2.3 million first-time freshmen each year and graduate a little more than 50 percent of those students in five years.[1] Too many of those graduates emerge with assorted diplomas that camouflage the soft course work behind them.

Public relations–conscious educators divert attention from these overall academic failings and concentrate on media exposés of athletics shortcomings, implying that college academic problems are confined to the sports arena. They too often blame college athletics as the villain that exploits the victims of the system, innocent athletes.

One such exaggerated story involved Brian Rahilly, a 6'10" University of Tulsa basketball player who left the school without a degree. Brian's aim had been to play in the NBA, where salaries averaged $600,000, and later to become a sports broadcaster. At the time his story was picked up by the national media, he was earning $8,000 a year with the Topeka Sizzlers of the CBA.

"We're talking career here," Brian told *Time* magazine. "I was shortchanged. There are times I feel that I was nothing more than a piece of equipment, like a football or a practice jersey that the Tulsa athletic department owned."[2] Rahilly was from a white, middle-class background. When the media story concerns a minority person from the inner city, the bashing of college athletics becomes even more righteous.

Dexter Manley of the Washington Redskins tearfully told a U.S. Senate panel on illiteracy that despite his four years at Oklahoma State University, he had neither graduated nor learned to read. Sen. Barbara Mikulski, Democrat of Maryland, then commented indignantly: "You didn't fail, sir. The system failed you."

Kevin Ross, a 6′9″ former basketball player who did not graduate, complained on national TV talk shows that he had never
learned to read in four years at Creighton University. Ross later
achieved nationwide notoriety when he dropped furniture from a
Chicago hotel room onto parked cars eight floors below. Then, in
1989, Ross filed suit for money damages in Chicago's Cook
County court, charging that Creighton knew or should have
known that he was "ill equipped and unable to successfully participate in the university's academic program" and failed to teach
him adequately.

People magazine has said Ross was the victim "of victory-
minded coaches, teachers, and school officials who prized re-
bounding over reading." Ross himself explained the hotel episode
in a press interview by saying, "I was really tired of being a victim
of society."

That is the hyped-up tale fed to the public—the poor, academically unqualified student used and victimized by his athletics department, but implicitly *not* by the faculty or the university administration.

While there are scandalous goings-on in college athletics, the
saga of the exploited "jock" drop-out is simply the smoke screen
that obscures some unpleasant truths about American higher education.

It's hard to mourn for those like Rahilly who never learned
that $600,000 jobs are not there for the taking, even for top college
graduates. Or for those few, like Manley, who may regret their
illiteracy while benefiting from a million-dollar deal with a professional team.

A more balanced view of educational exploitation is that the
college admissions office and faculty exploit the athlete by taking
on board a poorly prepared student and providing to him or her
course work of minimum quality so the athlete can meet minimum
eligibility standards. The athlete exploits the college by blaming
the college for his or her lack of learning when it is the student
who failed to respond because of limited interest. The exploitation
is mutual.

Post-High School Therapy

Kevin Ross's full story, untold by the national media, is perhaps the best example of the reality behind one side of victimization myth.[3]

Bill Norton of the *Kansas City Star* went to Ross's former junior high school, where he interviewed librarian Mary Conrad.

She remembered a ninth-grade library tour there, during which the young Ross had chatted with a group of girls instead of using the card catalog or looking at books. Conrad reminded Ross that they had come there to use the library.

"He said, 'I don't have to, I'm a basketball player,'" Conrad recalled.

Conrad and Carol Horton, Ross's remedial reading teacher, used their own money to buy books for him and help improve his reading. "He was not a student who wanted to learn," according to Horton. "That was the last thing on his mind....I think the only reason he stayed in school was because of his talent at basketball."[4]

Creighton University of Omaha had a student body with an average composite score of 23.2 of a possible 36.0 on the ACT. Ross's composite ACT score was 9. The admissions office rejected him, but the athletics department appealed. Creighton's vice-president granted an academic exception—a frequent recourse at most colleges—and Ross was offered a full-ride grant-in-aid.

When Ross's first-semester grade point came in at 1.7 on a 4.0 scale, the athletics director arranged a softer schedule, which permitted Ross to get A's in squad participation, theory of basketball, theory of track and field, and introduction to ceramics, plus C's in photography and theology. His grade point average that second semester was 3.0. All the courses were faculty sanctioned, and Creighton is fully accredited by the North Central Association. Critics condemn test scores as being biased and inaccurate, and they like to cite cases like this to show that the ACT failed its mission in not identifying a 3.0 college student.

Creighton gave Ross not only a full ride but also spent $2,000 sending Ross to a remedial reading program at the University of Missouri, Kansas City, where he often missed classes. Creighton bought him glasses to correct an eye problem, thought to cause his line skipping in reading. In doing so, the university risked an NCAA violation for providing excessive compensation. He lost the glasses and did not attend eye exercise sessions Creighton set up for him. Tutors in his junior year said he missed appointments or, when he did arrive, would be unprepared.

Much later, after Ross's appearance as an illiterate college athlete on the Phil Donahue show, the *New York Times* quoted Ross as saying of Creighton University: "They looked at basketball players as things. When our eligibility ran out, they didn't care about us."

Many coaches will argue that an athlete's lack of academic progress should not be the only measure of his or her advancement in a college environment. After all, a good coach can take a poorly prepared high school student who can reverse dunk with either hand, teach him how to dress well, be polite, and intelligently answer Billy Packer's questions on network television—all of this making the youngster a better individual and better prepared to deal with the real world.

Clifford Adelman, senior research associate in the U.S. Department of Education, examined the question from a different perspective.[5] Adelman extracted data from the National Longitudinal Study of the high school class of 1972, about 8,101 students associated with four-year colleges or universities. Of these, 134 were varsity football and basketball players, and another 93 were varsity players in other sports. Because the overall sample included all students, the total of 227 athletes is not large, but the sample is "naturalistic." "Those are the fish that were in the sea," Adelman explains. "We did not sort the fish first, letting some in and some out."

He compared the academic performance of the varsity athletes with that of several other groups involved in the study, one being performing arts students. Starting college, the football and basketball players had the lowest mean high school class rank of all the groups and displayed the lowest test scores. More of them came from families of lower socioeconomic status than any other group.

Those varsity football and basketball players who graduated took longer to do so than nonathletes, earned lower grades, and pursued less demanding courses, Adelman said. But varsity athletes, including those in the major sports, completed the bachelor's degree at only a slightly lower rate than the other groups. A far larger proportion of black varsity athletes (50 percent) earned the bachelor's degree than black nonathletes (26 percent).

This success in graduation, Adelman reasoned, occurred because varsity athletes are recruited heavily, offered scholarships, and thus enter college immediately out of high school—sooner on average than the other groups. They are also supported by a broader safety net of services—coaches' exhortations and academic advisors' hand-holding—than other students.

Adelman found that, at least in the first decade of their working lives, former varsity football and basketball players did well economically, whether or not they earned degrees. They experienced less unemployment between ages 25 and 32, earned incomes above the mean for all students who attended four-year colleges, and owned homes at a higher rate (77 percent) than any other group of students in the study. Former varsity athletes in the other sports kept pace in home ownership at 77 percent.

Adelman noted that, according to the evidence, this economic success did not arise from participation in pro sports. Next, he compared the experience of athletes with that of performing arts students. Many of these students pursued narrowly specialized degrees that, as Adelman writes, do not pretend to do more than prepare individuals for roles in the performing arts. Such jobs are scarce in the customary job market.

The performing arts aspirants tended to come from high socioeconomic brackets and do well on academic tests. Yet in the first decade after college they experienced downward economic mobility—the highest incidence of unemployment, the lowest earnings, and the second-lowest rate of home ownership among all student groups studied.

Adelman's work helps to dispel the myth of the academically "victimized" athlete. Nevertheless, I agree with the media's instinct that something is wrong with the massive, subsidized education program for college varsity players. The critical question is *who* should benefit from the "free ride" as long as this system is permitted to continue.

The majority of athletes, who are great players and reasonably good students, should be beneficiaries. But should the Brian Rahillys, Dexter Manleys, and Kevin Rosses receive the maximum grant-in-aid before bona fide remedial course work determines whether they are teachable? Should federal Pell grants top off the full-ride athletics scholarships, without regard to academic achievement? The 1995 NCAA Convention answered yes. Under pressures to increase player compensation, the convention decided that full-ride Division I grant-in-aid athletes may keep as much as $2,400 of Pell money per academic year; in Division II the cap was set at $1,500. In effect, the college cartel raised the compensation cap by permitting the players to keep more of the combined money. In 1989–90, the Pell grant caps were $1,400 in Division I and $900 in Division II.

It's possible, of course, for a highly motivated poor youngster to attend college on a Pell grant of $2,400 plus some loans and job income—possible, but difficult. The Pell grant alone may barely pay tuition at most universities. That is why, at Philadelphia's Franklin High School, only about 20 percent of all seniors customarily go on to college. The full-ride athletics grant-in-aid makes a dramatic difference, however, for Franklin seniors on the basketball team. They have gone on to college at a far higher rate—from 50 percent to 77 percent. The full-ride grant-in-aid (tuition, fees, board, room, books and course supplies) plus the new figure of $2,400 beats the Pell, loans to be paid back, and working a job.

"Our kids, if they don't get the scholarships, they don't go to college," explained Dr. Norman Spencer, Franklin principal.[6]

For many, sports is the magic carpet out of the inner city, too often unavailable to any athlete who does not focus intently on his or her sport. The bright students—good but not nationally rated in the high school football and basketball scouting polls—become the dispossessed victims.

Other victims of superathlete selection include the high school students who watch from the sidelines as this drama of opportunity is played out. Are these the lessons they should learn—that intellectual development doesn't matter compared to athletic success? That the star athlete is passed through high school into college and academic failings have no consequence? The tragedy of such a catechism approaches scandalous proportions. It may be today's reality, but it should not be the lesson we teach tomorrow.

Playing the Game

Still, winning is the aim of sports. Coaches argue that some of the spoils—at least a full-ride college scholarship—should go to the victor, the youngster who jumps the extra inch or shaves two-tenths off the hundred.

At last count, some 106 U.S. colleges are committed to major league football, and 301 are determined to play Division I basketball. These disparate colleges, with little in common, have lashed themselves and their coaches into the same straitjacket of rules. Each college then demands that its coaches win more games than its competitors.

All coaches realize that the maximum compensation package offered to the great player is rigidly controlled by the NCAA. No college is permitted to top another's money offer. The coach whose team finished last is not permitted to sign any more freshmen than the team that finished first. Last year's loser is not supposed to approve a better financial deal for a sorely needed, rifle-armed, six-foot-three-inch quarterback—but the coach better finish at least 8-3 this year or his expiring contract won't be renewed.

The coach can devise a clandestine way to sweeten the deal—a car, extra cash, an airline ticket—or he can persuade his college to bend the academic rules more than his competitors or do both. How else can he climb out of last place? This is the dilemma that prompts many schools to pursue win-at-all-costs programs, emphasizing maximum playing skills in choosing their "student-athletes."

North Carolina State succumbed to this mania. In 1985 the school publicized a freshman-class SAT average of 1,030, yet made a "special admit" of basketball star Chris Washburn, who achieved 470 (270 on the math portion, 200 [or zero] on the verbal part).[7] The special admit was approved by North Carolina State Chancellor Bruce R. Poulton. The chancellor defended Washburn's admission, then cited the player's academic achievements at Raleigh as proof of the fallacies of test scores.

"The SAT... is racially skewed," Poulton told United Press International. "Chris took a full load and passed all the courses." His four courses were history of American sport, sociology of the family, public speaking, and composition and rhetoric.[8] Poulton resigned in 1989 amid the controversy over charges about management's subservience to Coach Jim Valvano in matters of admissions and the boosting of athletes' college grades. Washburn moved on to the NBA and Valvano also departed—amply compensated by his Wolfpack admirers and ABC Sports/ESPN, where he was a TV basketball analyst.

In past scrapes involving other Wolfpack athletes, such as Charles Shackleford in basketball and Percy Moorman in football, Chancellor Poulton and his boss, William Friday, head of the North Carolina system, blamed the NCAA for low academic standards, asking why the NCAA doesn't do something about it. In other words, they argued it was the NCAA's job to reinforce the academic standards of the North Carolina system, if not at Chapel Hill then surely at Raleigh.

If the state's taxpayers are content with Poulton's special concern for high-skill athletes; if parents are not irate that their children were rejected when Washburn or Moorman was accepted; if generous boosters are enthralled with the Wolfpack's eight NCAA tournament appearances during the decade of the 1980s—why do a public-relations number on the NCAA? Because that is the way the game is played.

It's almost ritual for a college president, particularly a new arrival, to speak of the "pursuit of excellence." After making that point at faculty and alumni meetings, the president—subsequently confronted with evidence of low academic performance by the college's athletes—blames others. This perpetuates the illusion of academic integrity within college education.

Joab L. Thomas, shortly after arriving at the University of Alabama campus where he served as president for seven years, blamed the NCAA membership and "Iona and schools like that who have voted down our attempts to upgrade our academic standards."

Wise to that game, John G. Driscoll, president of Iona College in New Rochelle, New York, promptly challenged Alabama to participate in a nationally televised academic debate between members of their respective sports teams. President Driscoll wrote Joab a satirical letter in which he declared that he had exercised his presidential responsibility and had ordered the faculty, the students, and the administrators at Iona College to cease and desist "from impeding your efforts to upgrade your academic standards."[9]

Also laying it on the line in reverse was Harvey D. Berry, an assistant vice-chancellor at Raleigh, who explained the North Carolina State objective this way. "The public expects the school to be competitive," he said. "There is a beneficial aspect to it."[10]

North Carolina State has gained fame as a win-at-all-costs school in a conference, the ACC, that brags about its commitment to academic achievement. But North Carolina State was not criticized as much as its western counterpart, UNLV, although their actions seemed to run a parallel course.

Coach Jerry Tarkanian's philosophy became widely known because he talked unrelentingly to the press and wrote books on the subject. For him, winning and the players who make it possible come first; that in turn makes him a coach who does care about his charges.

Tarkanian succeeded by using players at high academic risk, including some players most other schools would not take, and he explained he was doing a service to them and to society at large. Ivy Group educators may hold UNLV in contempt as an educational institution and Tarkanian as the product of a system out of control, but the Tarkanian approach was first implemented for nonsport reasons by an Ivy Group member, Cornell University, as related in chapter 11. In fact, Tarkanian's plan appears consistent with the federal government's educational policy since the 1960s: the underprivileged should have a chance to go to college. Because many higher education officials believe colleges should search out disadvantaged young people who have "the ability to benefit" or are "teachable," even if their high school records or test scores indicate otherwise, it follows that great athletes should be pursued on the same basis. Tark probably implemented this declared policy more effectively than anyone else. Since much of the public believes the victimization stories about college athletes, Coach Tarkanian works with more force than most coaches to blunt that criticism. He fought to keep the bottom-of-the barrel academic crowd in the system. How does Tark keep them eligible?

Tark reported that he, his wife, Lois, and his chief assistant attended classes with players. He notes that at other schools the athletics departments' academic advisors perform that function.[11] Some of Tarkanian's helpers even enrolled as for-credit students in various classes with players.

The daily class process began with the help of a coaching assistant, Tim Grgurich, who became head coach at UNLV in 1994. "Tim beats on the doors about an hour before class, and he doesn't settle for the 'Yeah, yeah, I'm up' routine," Mark Warkentien, a former key assistant, explained at the time. "Tim tells the kid, 'Come out here and see me.' Only when the kid opens the door and steps outside does Tim leave.

"Then, an hour later the kid walks into class and sees me sitting there. That's a pretty strong message about how important we think academics is.... If there is a problem or if the kid needs to study, he can come to my house that night and we'll work on it."

Ann Mayo, an academic advisor, said she once sat in on a sociology class with several players new to UNLV. "I ... discovered that they had no idea what was appropriate behavior in a college classroom. They were still doing a lot of high school things—talking in the corner, dozing, all that.... The guys weren't taking notes. They had no idea how to take notes." As the class went on, she said, they developed appropriate classroom behavior.

Tarkanian's concern for his players' studies was one way of keeping them eligible for play. Two UNLV psychology professors, Dr. Joseph Raney and Dr. Terry Knapp, discovered another method that was used.

Raney and Knapp are academic researchers who completed

several group studies of athletes' academic transcripts. Among Las Vegas athletes, Knapp and Raney found "a flight from academia"— grade records thick with D's and F's and dropped courses.[12] In their first study, they obtained transcripts of 93 athletes, including all male basketball players, and found that only junior college credits obtained earlier kept many players eligible. The team's grade average in courses at UNLV was 1.96.

Although a limited number of athletes had chosen physical education as a major, that department supplied 30 percent of all UNLV credits for basketball team members, 27 percent for football, and 23 percent for baseball. "Deprived of P.E. credits," the researchers wrote, "most of the basketball players and some of the football players would likely be ineligible to play."[13]

Big-time sports programs, whether at USC, Michigan, or Notre Dame, have preferred academic "disciplines" to which they steer at-risk athletes for eligibility healing. Where serious physical education faculty members object, the academically weak athletes may be found—depending on local conditions—in communications, sociology, sports administration, criminal justice, or general studies.

As Chancellor Poulton was going overboard for Jim Valvano, Coach Tarkanian was going overboard in the South Pacific during the summer of 1986. His team went on a sixteen-day tour of the South Seas while taking a course titled "Contemporary Issues in Social Welfare," later dubbed "Palm Trees 101." For that, they earned six hours of credit—half the academic work they would need to remain eligible for the semester. When asked about the six-credit-hour course, Coach Tarkanian answered: "That course was approved by the university here. I had nothing to do with that course."[14]

In a letter to the faculty senate, Knapp protested the course, which had not been listed in any catalog and was taken only by basketball team members.

"Are we to believe that students could travel twenty thousand miles through six time zones, cross the international dateline twice, play nine basketball games, and earn six hours of academic credit—all in 16 days?" Knapp asked.[15] The professor never received a substantive answer to the question.

Nor did Raney and Knapp receive much response when they wrote to the academic vice-presidents of all members of the Big West Conference (a twelve-school league that included eight California universities as well as UNLV), suggesting a conferencewide study of athletes' transcripts similar to what they had done at UNLV. Only one of the college officials answered the letter.

UNLV is one of the rare schools where college teachers made the tenure system justify itself—allowing Raney and Knapp to conduct open research without fear of retaliation. Raney and Knapp praised the college for supporting their work—all the more credit to the UNLV administration.[16]

In fact, as a question of truth in labeling, it must be said that UNLV and the Tark are far more open than most members of the educational family, many of whom dig deeply into the at-risk talent pool and are just as creative when it comes to keeping athletes eligible.

When Proposition 48 came along in 1983, I strongly supported it. I did so, first, because it sent the right message to high school athletes, their coaches, and high school counselors. Second, although it was a low standard, those who cleared it would be better prepared to benefit from a free college education. And third, those who failed to meet it could try again after pursuing remedial work at the junior college level.

Several presidents of predominantly black colleges, whose teams were attempting to compete with the largest universities in the country, vigorously fought the proposal. Their predicament was clear.

In the past, many first-rate black athletes with good academic records had attended predominantly black schools. It was there that such great black coaches as Jake Gaither at Florida A&M, Marino Casem at Alcorn State, Eddie Robinson of Grambling, and Clarence "Big House" Gaines of Winston-Salem had made significant though largely unheralded contributions to the advancement of American black athletes.

But times had changed; by 1983 the major universities of the nation were competing aggressively for black players, and fewer were available for the so-called black colleges. The presidents of many such institutions knew they needed all the good players they could get to compete in the same NCAA Division I with such giants as Tennessee, Alabama, Ohio State, and UCLA. They did not want a common academic floor to hinder their efforts. Proposition 48, proposed for Division I, would apply to all colleges equally, the predominantly white college and the predominantly black college.

At the San Diego convention, President Joe Johnson of Grambling charged that Proposition 48 was an effort to get more whites on the big schools' teams. According to Frederick S. Humphries of Tennessee State, Proposition 48 was camouflage for NCAA racists. In essence, he charged that white bigots were trying to lighten the color of their basketball teams. Behind the oratory lay the fact that the rule also prevented Grambling and Tennessee State from giving nonqualifiers under the rule a grant-in-aid and permitting them to play as freshman.

Not all leaders of predominantly black schools echoed the charges of bias. On the convention floor after Proposition 48 was adopted, Coach Marino Casem, then at Alcorn State, asked what I thought. "I think the inflammatory speeches were a put-down of black athletes," I responded. "It's a bad message. They're arguing black athletes can't do bona fide college work. I believe they can."

Marino looked at me longer than usual, nodded, and walked away. His president at Alcorn State, Walter Washington, had not joined the negative chorus on the convention floor.

My position on Prop. 48 was also criticized by Gregory Anrig, president of the Educational Testing Service, which administers the SAT.[17] Like other test makers, Anrig expresses anxiety about using the tests to "stop" people at various levels in the educational system. This is spurious at best. Tests have been, are now, and will continue to be used to challenge, divert, or sometimes stop students at all levels, from junior high through graduate and professional schools. However delicate the test makers' feelings, those are the facts.

I agree with Gregory Anrig that the decision should not rest on test scores alone but should be combined with other factors; this was the case with the 1.600 rule, in which high school performance worked in tandem with test scores. But 1.600 was buried in 1973 and no one wanted to resurrect it. The only academic proposal on the boards in 1983 was Proposition 48, and it was a major step in the right direction.

Compromise was in the air at the San Diego convention. I feared the proposal would be critically wounded even before enactment and staff members of the ACE, which originated Prop. 48, were nervous. When the vote was finally taken, the proposal passed, supported by nearly 52 percent of the delegates. The battle was not over.

The National Association for Equal Opportunity (NAFEO), consisting of 114 predominantly black colleges and universities, contended that Proposition 48 discriminated against low-income and minority families. The group argued that the new measure "blames the victim. That is, this proposal shifts the total responsibility for academic success to the student-athlete. The proposal fails to discuss and to show the need for a moral commitment on the part of the institution to high-risk students."[18]

No concern was expressed about the victims Prop. 48 might help—academically qualified blacks, athletes and nonathletes, who never make it to college *because* of the diversion of big money grants to high-risk superathletes.

ACE President Jack Peltason and his staff returned to the nation's capital to find that NAFEO, members of the Civil Rights Commission, and others had turned up the heat. They were fearful that predominantly black colleges might resign en masse from ACE, causing an unthinkable break in the ranks of higher education's premier lobbying group.

Bob Atwell, Peltason's primary aide in athletics matters, had been regularly attacking excesses in the athletics establishment for some time. He previously had been president of Pitzer College in California and specialized in bashing the NCAA as the front for big-time college athletics.

Atwell, as Peltason's assistant, telephoned us for a meeting shortly after the San Diego convention passed Prop. 48. Ted Tow, recently retired associate NCAA executive director, and I met with

Peltason and Atwell at the Kansas City International Airport. They seemed surprised that we were not as worried as they were about the postconvention anti-48 publicity.

"It's an NCAA rule now, Jack, and we have the problem of enforcing it," I remarked. "Through the years, there have been many rules on our books which a lot of colleges haven't liked. Some I haven't liked. But we go about our business and do the job we're supposed to do."

"You must remember," Bob Atwell responded, "we [ACE] don't have any lucrative basketball tournament to hold our members together."

A valid point. Bob Atwell wanted to make certain the ACE continued to represent all colleges and, thus, present a united front for purposes of lobbying Congress and the federal bureaucracy.

After I told them that the NCAA had appropriated funds to conduct a study of the rule's possible impact, which would be available before the rule's effective date, their mood improved. That would answer the immediate attacks, both of them seemed to think. After all, everyone should "want to know the facts before any further action." We agreed the ACE and the NCAA could work closely in studying Prop. 48 but I told them that I hoped it would remain part of the NCAA rule book until a better standard came along. Left unsaid by our side was the obvious question of why ACE had not fully studied the projected impact of Prop. 48 before they submitted it.

"One other thing before leaving," Bob said. "Do you plan to campaign in Congress for an antitrust exemption?"

This was in reference to media reports that college athletics directors and other members of the intercollegiate family would seek an antitrust exemption from Congress somewhat like that enjoyed by the NFL. This would offset the Supreme Court's dismantling of NCAA TV controls, enabling the colleges to reinstate a controlled TV program without legal liability.

"No," I said to Atwell, "We have no plans to begin a push in Congress for an exemption."

He stared at me for a moment, apparently reluctant to believe me.

"You can rely on that," I told Atwell, looking to Jack at the same time.

The thought of the colleges confessing to Congress the need for an antitrust exemption to legalize some of their business practices seemed to worry the ACE leaders as much as the uproar over Proposition 48.

Test Scores vs. Game Scores

My good friend Mark Plant, tort expert at the University of Michigan and former NCAA president, was wont to remark: "I don't want the power to enact the rules, I just want the right to interpret them."

Prop. 48 was quickly interpreted to the benefit of the big timers. They were permitted to recruit players who did not have either the 2.0 minimum high school grade average in core classes or the test requirement; all they needed to obtain grants-in-aid was an *overall* grade point average of at least 2.0. The athletes could not practice or play, however, until after their freshman year. Once freshman grades established their eligibility, three years of varsity play awaited.

Major programs heavily recruited these "partial qualifiers." Some schools also continued to accept nonqualifiers, players who did not have even an overall 2.0 high school GPA. With a Pell grant and a job, the needy nonqualifier could make it through the first year with additional help from regular university channels until he or she achieved the necessary college grades. Then the athlete would be ready to play as a sophomore with a full-ride grant-in-aid and, possibly, a Pell grant as well.

At the 1989 NCAA Convention, Harvey W. Schiller, then commissioner of the Southeastern Conference, advanced Proposition 42, which closed this loophole by banning the full ride for the partial qualifier. He said many high school coaches and others were advising high school athletes to avoid a core curriculum and standard tests. Skipping the tests and achieving an overall 2.0 in high school through soft courses still qualified them for big-time athletics after one year on a college campus.

"This is an opportunity to send a message to our secondary schools that adequate preparation for prospective student-athletes is at least as important as athletic development," Schiller told the convention.

Passage of Proposition 42 by a 163-154 vote led to an outburst of anger from a few blacks and the publicized 1989 walkout at the Georgetown-Boston College basketball game by Georgetown Coach John Thompson, who denounced what he called the SAT's "proven cultural bias."

Those who had seemed so intent on plugging the loophole changed their minds in a matter of 90 days. Responding to the game walkout, NCAA officers told Coach Thompson they sympathized with his concern about the convention's approval of Prop. 42. Come to Kansas City they said, we'll talk this out. The person who urged that such a meeting be held to reconsider Prop. 42 was none other than Harvey Schiller, the man who originally advanced it on the convention floor.

The next January, at the 1990 convention, Prop. 48/42 was amended. Collaborating in lessening the rule's impact was the NCAA Presidents Commission, now the association's most publicized leadership group, and the Southeastern Conference.

There was strong opposition. Tulane University law professor Gary Roberts emphasized that only a fixed number of athletics scholarships are available, which should be distributed to qualified students.

"Proposition 42 uses SAT scores as a cutoff for distribution of scholarships," he said. "Proposition 42 opponents are using points per game as a cutoff."[19]

The 1990 NCAA Convention nevertheless softened the standard by deciding that freshmen athletes who are partial qualifiers could be recruited, receive financial aid as long as it is not an athletics department grant, and would not be counted under the NCAA football and basketball grants-in-aid limits. The partial qualifier again was defined as one who achieves 2.0 or a C average in *all* high school courses. It was a deliberate softening of the core course requirement. Such athletes could join the varsity after they passed their freshman college year.

Translated, this meant that sports-minded universities may recruit partial qualifiers and stockpile them as freshmen—but not at the expense of the athletics department. The money must come from other university funds, money that may well be drawn from the school's scholarship coffers or state and federal funds that otherwise would go to needy students who may well be better qualified academically.

The far more critical issue, however, is the academic corruption that occurs when coaches can recruit high school players who do not qualify academically. In effect, the recruiting coach tells the prospect, "Don't worry, we'll find scholarship money for you at our place, and we have a great remedial program. We'll fix you up in a year and you'll be ready to play."

Starting with the 1.600 rule, I have been committed to the proposition that if a hurdle is set in front of a motivated high school athlete and he or she knows it must be cleared to receive a full ride and play on the varsity, that high school player will clear the hurdle. The people who let that young person off the hook—who lower the academic hurdle—are guilty of a warped educational purpose.

Another debasement occurs when an individual college is allowed to measure on an ad hoc basis whether the necessary progress has been made in rehabilitating the at-risk high school graduate. Believe me, there is a course, a grade, and a degree out there for everyone.

The system cries out for a national standard of evaluation of what the college—not just the high school, but the college—has contributed to the student's intellectual advancement. Supporting local option on this issue is supporting the status quo, which is a national embarrassment.

For more than two decades, there have been attacks on the validity of testing—attacks by everyone from white professors and admissions counselors to black college presidents and such coaches as John Thompson and Temple's John Chaney. It is true that blacks and certain other minorities achieve lower average scores than whites, and this fact is often cited as the basis for charges that the tests are biased against minorities.

Why do blacks average lower scores? Poverty compounded by lackadaisical parental discipline and poor schooling is probably the most direct answer. An Educational Testing Service (ETS) study in 1988 spoke to the wealth issue by suggesting that the poverty conditions in which many black families live have played a part in lower test scores.[20] However, an earlier ETS study in 1980 was more ambiguous. After dividing students into four groups based on family income, not on race, the study found that 20 percent of students in the affluent group scored in the lowest quarter on test performance; meanwhile, nearly 33 percent of the students in the poorest group overcame their economic handicap to score in the top half.[21]

The 1988 ETS study examined the number of high school courses the seniors had taken in six academic subjects: arts and music, English, foreign language, mathematics, natural sciences, and social science/history. Seniors who took fewer than 15 high school course-years in these core subjects averaged 758 on the SAT. Those who took 20 or more averaged 1,008—a huge difference.[22] Too many high schools fail to insist upon the academic courses so vital to college entrants.

Despite these external handicaps, the hard requirements of a legitimate educational process should not be wished away. Concentration and discipline are at the heart of individual improvement, whether in academics, athletics, or career employment. Challenging students academically is at the heart of the learning process.

As to racial bias? Syndicated columnist Clarence Page noted, "If standardized tests discriminate in favor of the social standards and language of mainstream America, that is because it is that mainstream in which young jocks must swim after their playing days run out."[23]

It may be difficult to determine through academic studies the precise impact on blacks of Proposition 48/42, or what now is known as Proposition 16, as newly amended in 1995 to take effect in August 1996. The same NCAA academic standard does not stay in place for very long. In 1988, most black athletes were already meeting Prop. 48/42 standards—85 percent of those matriculating as freshmen at Division I colleges. Opponents of Prop. 48/42 had argued that 90 percent of those who did not meet the rule would be black. However, the figures for fall 1988, reported to the NCAA by 206 of the 294 NCAA Division I schools, indicate that of those who did not meet both the test requirement and the high school core course C-average, 65 of every 100 were black.

In any case, elimination of the first 100 high-risk athletes by the 48/42 rule should result in selection of 100 additional, better-qualified people for first-year grants-in-aid. Those chosen in the second round will be better students but may not be quite as good as athletes. It is likely the racial proportions will be similar.

The response of coaches Thompson and Chaney is to constantly emphasize the negative—the proportion of blacks who do not qualify. Although future numbers are speculative, a study covering football and basketball in 1988, where the impact of the propositions on blacks is heaviest, reveals the following. With Prop. 48/42 fully in effect, the NCAA freshman basketball recruits for 1988 would have been 59 percent black. Without Prop. 48/42, 62 percent would have been black.[24] That 3 percent is what the shouting is about. The youngsters in this 3 percent are the supposed game-winners that big time coaches want available *now*. The coaches are unwilling to wait a year while the players take remedial courses.

In the fall of 1994–95, as arguments were being publicized once again in support of softening NCAA academic rules, the *New York Times* neatly capsulized the issue with this editorial statement: "Proposition 48 decreased the total of black collegiate athletes in Division I schools by a little less than 600 per year. But because those who made the grade were better qualified, the number who graduated actually went up, by about 150, an increase of six percent." The *Times* urged voters at the 1995 NCAA Convention to hold the line.[25]

Instead of arguments for softening standards, the argument today should be about a phased-in increase of the current standards. I agree with such black leaders as the late tennis star Arthur Ashe that if we set the hurdle, starting in high school, the motivated black athletes of the future will clear it. Dr. Harry Edwards, former black militant, athlete, and coach, is another spokesman who is convinced that black athletes *can* compete academically as well as athletically. Edwards advises aspiring black athletes: "The chances of your becoming a Jerry Rice or a Magic Johnson are so slim as to be negligible. Black kids must learn to distribute their energies in a way that's going to make them productive, contributing citizens in an increasingly high-technology society."[26]

The problem is the academic victimology described at the beginning of this chapter. Between the colleges and their athletes, the exploitation is mutual. While the acceptance of college largess by academically deficient athletes is perfectly understandable and while blame for their academic infirmities is properly placed on a variety of factors (parental shortfall, poverty, high school indulgence), higher education still has no obligation to smooth their pathway to pro sports—if they are among the rare ones who make it.

Until they prove themselves academically, these so-called victims should not be identified as bona fide college students. They should not receive higher education's most lucrative undergraduate financial aid package plus tax payer-financed government subsidies as officially rationed by the NCAA.

The aim should be to keep these athletes identified as remedial students. Until an individual qualifies, replace him or her with the dispossessed student-athlete who wants to learn and is at least minimally prepared for college. That was the original intent of the 1.600 legislation and Proposition 48.

Set the standards and keep them in place! And rejoice that, at least for college student-athletes, we are debating academic standards. The great shame is that the same debate and like standards are not at issue for all undergraduates in a diluted "higher" education system.

Notes

1. Data provided by Dr. Vance Grant, Center for Education Statistics, U.S. Office of Education, April 23, 1991.
2. Ted Gup, *Time,* April 3, 1989.
3. Material for this account was developed from Bill Norton, *Kansas City*

Star Magazine, September 13, 1987; some quoted material was originally published in the *New York Times.*

4. Ibid.
5. Clifford Adelman, *Light and Shadows on College Athletes—College Transcripts and Labor Market History* (Washington, D.C.: Government Printing Office, December 1990).
6. Norman Spencer, interview with Charles Hammer, November 19, 1989.
7. Bill Millsaps, *Richmond Times-Dispatch,* February 10, 1985.
8. United Press International report, *Atlanta Journal,* February 11, 1985.
9. John G. Driscoll, C.F.C., letter to Joab L. Thomas, January 28, 1983.
10. George Vecsey, *New York Times,* February 18, 1985.
11. Jerry Tarkanian and Terry Pluto, *Tark—College Basketball's Winningest Coach* (New York: McGraw-Hill, 1988), 333.
12. Terry J. Knapp and Joseph F. Raney, "Looking at the Transcripts of Student-Athletes: Methods and Obstacles," *Arena Review* 11 (1987): 41–47.
13. Joseph F. Raney, Terry J. Knapp, and Mark Small, "Pass One for the Gipper: Student-Athletes and University Coursework," *Arena Review* 7 (1983): 53–60.
14. Jerry Tarkanian, interview with Charles Hammer, May 13, 1991.
15. Terry Knapp, letter to Gary Jones, September 5, 1986.
16. Terry Knapp, interview with Charles Hammer, March 6, 1989.
17. Gregory R. Anrig, Statement by Educational Testing Service, January 19, 1983.
18. National Association for Equal Opportunity, letter to the NCAA Delegate Assembly, January 4, 1983.
19. Adam Teicher, *Kansas City Times,* January 9, 1990.
20. Educational Testing Service, *Policy Notes,* March 1989.
21. Educational Testing Service, *Test Scores and Family Income,* February 1980.
22. Educational Testing Service, *Policy Notes,* March 1989.
23. Clarence Page, *Kansas City Times,* January 24, 1989.
24. NCAA Division I Survey, *NCAA News,* March 15, 1989.
25. *New York Times* editorial, reprinted in *NCAA News,* November 21, 1994.
26. *Time,* March 6, 1989.

Chapter 17   Flight from Accountability

The publicized academic plight of college athletes is small potatoes compared to the growing, nationwide discontent with the colleges themselves. Win-or-be-fired coaches did not create the present soft academic standards. That responsibility rests with an insulated industry in which college presidents, faculty members, evaluation teams, and accrediting agencies fragment accountability until the widely dispersed particles evaporate, falling on no one.

The same group of people do it all—establish courses, teach, train future teachers, determine who gets tenure, set department policy, sit on boards of the general accrediting agencies, evaluate their own performances, and appeal to Congress and state legislatures for more money.

A report by a National Institute of Education study group pointed out one obvious characteristic of the system: that hours and credits in college "do not indicate academic worth of course content." The panel stated that, in some colleges, students can earn the same number of credits "for taking a course in Family Food Management or Automobile Ownership as for taking a course in the History of the American City or Neuropsychology."[1]

"Those courses [the soft ones] are there for a purpose," President Gail J. Fullerton of San Jose State University told me shortly before leaving office. "The problem occurs when too many athletes get in one course or a given athlete takes too many of the courses."

The incongruity seems obvious. The offerings are there to attract students and tuition dollars. The courses are justified as college-level work for nonathletes, but not athletes because, I suppose, they bring with them too much public scrutiny.

Colleges are indeed ridiculed when investigative reporters expose the lax courses being offered to athletes for degree credit. Although the majority of students in most soft courses are nonathletes, college presidents skirt the main issue and call upon the NCAA to do something about athletics exploitation of academe. But the NCAA does not certify courses for degree credit. It doesn't accredit colleges so that course hours can be transferred among them or they can qualify for federal money. Why should an athletics organization be asked to clean up slipshod academic programming on the nation's campuses?

While concentrating on the presumed scholastic ills of college athletics, educators seem to ignore the illusions and shortcomings of higher education. Their priorities are in reverse order, even though many groups of experts have cited education's problems.

Among four-year college graduates questioned on literacy skills by the National Assessment of Educational Progress, for example, only 47 percent could restate the main argument of a newspaper column; 52 percent could figure out a bus schedule; and 48 percent could calculate the tip owed on a simple restaurant meal. Then there is the devastating commentary from *A Nation at Risk,* a report of the National Commission on Excellence in Education in 1983. "If an unfriendly foreign power had attempted to impose on America the mediocre educational performance that exists today, we might well have viewed it as an act of war."

A decade later the criticisms had not subsided. Milton Friedman, internationally respected economist and author, told C-Span's Brian Lamb in December of 1994 that the nation's educational apparatus "is almost a totally socialized industry and it behaves like a socialized industry, protective of its controls and rights." He harshly condemned the lack of improvement.[2]

All of this, despite the fact that the Council on Financial Aid to Education reported that private donations to higher education in the United States jumped from $715 million in 1958 to $8.7 billion in 1988. Total giving to higher education for fiscal 1993, as reported by the Council for Aid to Education, was $11.2 billion, an increase of 4.7 percent over 1992.[3] The burst of giving may be both a function of the tax laws as well as a national perception that U.S. education needs improvement; it cannot be construed as a blanket endorsement of our educational system. Yet this generosity has neither slowed the rise in college tuition costs nor discernibly improved undergraduate academic quality.

Most people, however, don't need statistics and studies to confirm the feeling that something is wrong in American education—from elementary schools to the graduate schools of colleges and universities. Lack of money is not a valid excuse. Over time, study after study shows that tuition charges and the cost of attending college outstrip the consumer price index. For nine straight years in the 1980s tuition increases topped the inflation rate.[4]

Marching in tandem with higher tuition charges are the increased dollars from federal, state, and other institutional sources. In 1989–90, total scholarship and fellowship awards by higher education institutions (not counting Pell grants) amounted to $6.7 billion, an increase of 81.3 percent in five years. Pell grant revenue was $3.4 billion in 1989–90, up 30.5 percent in four years.[5] Everybody antes up more, parents, students, donors, and taxpayers.

How wisely is it spent? Since most of these funds are disbursed by local college administrators and the primary academic standard is that recipients make *satisfactory progress* toward a degree, a loose term subject to local discretion, no one knows the answer to that question. The federal government, for example, does not set minimum standards of academic achievement before disbursing of its billions. The NCAA, however, sets such standards for the colleges when it comes to their athletes.

Deceptive Gloss

Anticipating ad hominem references to my lack of academic credentials as a former sports writer and long-term sports-oriented executive, I simply would say that for some 20 years I was the only chief operating officer of an educational organization responsible for enforcing specific academic standards upon college undergraduates at all types of colleges and universities, and administering penalties that affected the standing of the student and the college. I also was intimately involved in the formulation of several of the colleges' past and present NCAA academic rules and, finally, I was a party to financing the education of three children at seven colleges and universities, including three graduate schools.

My 30 years of debating academic issues has convinced me that one problem of American higher education is the stubborn mind-set against change held by many college educators, a pedantism based on recycled attitudes within an inbred industry. Certain standard code words are embedded in their language.

One is *diversity*. It means that the sprawling tent of American higher education should cover an incredible range of institutional types, from colleges with selective admissions and demanding course work, to schools whose curriculum consists of little more than advanced high school studies. These dissimilar institutions work together politically to assure the maximum award of state and federal dollars. Their parent lobby agency, the American Council on Education, regularly emphasizes the importance of educational diversity, a commitment to dissimilar goals, irregular standards, and unidentified results.

The second code word to watch for is *collegiality*. On the level of college presidents and faculty, it superficially means that people of goodwill and good spirit can work together to solve problems. In practice, the ethic of collegiality functions as a command: hear no evil, see no evil, and speak no evil of a fellow president or a sister institution. Collegiality requires that well-intentioned men and women should not subject one another to direct academic competition. In testing each other's students, they should not publicize the results or in other ways analyze the effectiveness of another college's instruction.

The third arcane term is *complex issue*. As used by the governing academicians, these words mean that, whatever the problem, it is difficult and needs in-depth study. Even though the measures of learning are dropping off the charts, the complex issue conventionalists respond that (1) to question teaching performance is to tamper with academic freedom; (2) the undereducated public does not understand the abstruse instructional problems involved; (3) the best approach is to appoint a committee of respected educators to review this, and (4) everybody knows that higher education needs more money.

Together, the three code words of higher education mean don't rock the boat! The system works pretty well for administrators and faculty alike. It was semantics such as these that Professor Henry Higgins may have had in mind when he flamboyantly denounced blackguards who use "language to swindle instead of to teach."

Behind the language gloss lies an urgent problem: the pervasive lack of comparative standards in higher education. Large universities have become shopping malls of education, offering something for everyone in the way of easy courses and easy degrees.[6] The smorgasbord of course offerings includes hotel management, communications 101, and driver education. It's education approved by the faculty and deans of accredited universities, and who is to protest if it's not any higher than that available at junior colleges or high schools? Educators broaden the type of courses permitted for degree credit. Students are permitted to choose more and more electives as the number of required courses shrink. Vocational courses teaching rudimentary skills or trades better learned on the job become part of degree programs.

One state university has spawned a "direct" marketing major within its business school, teaching students the junk mail and catalog business, plus skills that will help in organizing telephone boiler rooms from which callers telephone people at home to recite an advertising message. The undergraduate direct marketing degree requires 15 credit hours of such classes, titled direct marketing, market research, segmentation in markets, creating direct market promotions, copyrighting for direct marketing, and direct marketing practicum.

Another university provides instruction in fire prevention and fire outage, awarding a bachelor's degree in Fire Science. They offer hands-on training in this, which seems all to the good, I suppose. Comparably, I believe varsity athletes learn valuable social lessons of cooperation and discipline from sports competition. Later they will be better able to command respect as physical education teachers, coaches, salespeople, or leaders of industrial or municipal recreation programs. If "fire outage" is higher education, one could argue that athletes should get degree credit for practicing and playing their sports.

Not everyone wants to be a rocket scientist, mechanical engineer, computer genius, or heart surgeon. This nation also needs business people, journalists, salespeople, over-the-road drivers for 18-wheelers, and cattle herdsmen. Even so, students in "higher" education need required course work in English, history, physical science, mathematics, and economics—core courses that will be useful in any profession and, more broadly, in living a considered, conscious life. These minimums should not be waived for any excuse, and surely not so students can spend big blocks of time learning vocational tricks of the trade, which the next technical innovation may render obsolete.

Diversity is the operative code word here for the educational leadership. Administrators are reluctant to bar any subject that will fill classes, bring in tuition, and make the university grow. If academic advisors pick through the resultant smorgasbord of offerings to keep athletes eligible, athletics should not be blamed.

Challenging students' intellects and stimulating their curiosity and capacity to learn is the real higher education agenda. Placing rigorous academic subjects in their way accomplishes this.

A time barrier seems to exist between academic rote and real-life experience. This was illustrated in two recent publications. Educators defend the high cost of college education as a small investment to achieve a high-income adult life. The executive vice-president of Notre Dame noted in June, 1994, that a college education at Notre Dame is worth $100,000 and returns $400,000 of extra money in later life. He based his calculation on the Bureau of Census report that claims lifetime earnings of college graduates average $1.2 million compared to $800,000 for high school diploma holders.[7]

Considerably more current was the *Wall Street Journal* report of October 10, 1994, that traced the decline of a college degree's value. Under the headline, "Graduates Learn Diplomas Aren't Tickets to Success," the article cited U.S. Bureau of Labor statistics that reported 18.0 million college graduates will enter the labor market between 1992 and 2005, but only 14.0 million jobs requiring college experience are anticipated. Author Wendy Bounds noted that, in the years cited, more than 20 percent will settle for jobs for which they are overeducated, and the same data reported that in 1992, 20 percent of those with college bachelor's degrees earned less than the median salary for all high school graduates, $21,241.[8]

For this and many other reasons, a truth-in-labeling requirement should be imposed upon higher education's offerings and promises.

Academic Credentials

The colleges' diffused academic goals have been accepted because of an accountability vacuum. The void starts at a lofty level—in the regional accrediting agencies. These agencies organize the universitywide accreditation while the appropriate professional agencies inspect the medical, engineering, law, and other specialized schools.

Without the regional accreditors' stamp of approval, few institutions of higher learning would survive the next academic year. Academic credits would not be accepted for transfer, and federal dollars would dry up. These regional agencies safeguard undergraduate education in the United States and are the frail reed that supposedly prevents incompetent colleges from bilking the public. Yet through the years they have had such minimal impact on college academic accomplishment that their periodic visits to campuses constitute little more than a pro forma ritual aimed at requiring more Ph.D.'s on the faculty and higher per-student spending.

Like the NCAA, the regionals' duties are to impose certain agreed standards on all of their members. I marvel, however, at the vague nature of their requirements—mostly pedantic philosophizing and academic bons mots—and the subsequent nonenforcement thereof.

When the same college presidents and faculty people who control the accrediting agencies enter the halls of the NCAA, they legislate like mad and with great specificity. Athletes *shall* meet specific academic standards, *shall not* engage in outside work, *shall* consent to drug testing, *shall not* endorse products, *shall* be role models, *shall not* receive financial aid to attend summer school. But these people become fainthearted when they gather to make, or rather not make, policy for the accrediting agencies.

The six regional accrediting agencies principally measure *inputs* to education: the number of Ph.D.'s on the faculty, curricular offerings, and books in the library, plus the amount of money available from tuition, endowments, and the state legislature. They do little to measure the *output* of colleges and universities; that is, the skills and knowledge the institutions add to their graduates. They do not require testing of students leaving the schools to measure the competence of the teaching they received.

The North Central Association of Colleges and Schools, the largest of the regionals, accredits about 960 institutions in 19 states, from West Virginia to Arizona, Arkansas to North Dakota. The association has about 700 part-time evaluators, who are college faculty members. They make campus visits. In 1994–95, the staff that pushed the operation consisted of only nine profession-·als, five administrators, and eight support persons in the organization's Chicago office.

Earlier, I spoke with Jean Mather, who was assistant director of North Central's Commission on Institutions of Higher Education in 1989. She confirmed that accreditation is based on the accomplishment of a college's mission as the college itself defines it.[9]

Asked whether high school remedial work would be appropriate as a college's mission, she said that when North Central was founded in 1895, there was wide agreement as to a definition of higher education, but that agreement no longer exists. "Many community colleges offer solid courses that will transfer," she explained, "but they are also serving another population, and that's where the line gets fuzzy."

In fact, four-year, degree-granting accredited institutions also compete aggressively with community colleges (the preferred name for junior colleges) for that "other" population. They do it through low admission requirements, remedial course work, extension centers, and correspondence courses.

No surprise, then, that it's nearly impossible to find a school that is not fulfilling its self-defined mission. Dr. Patricia Thrash, North Central executive director, told me at the time that in the decade of the 1980s, only one college (bankrupt Milton College in Wisconsin) had lost its accreditation and fewer than a dozen of the 960 North Central members had been placed on probation. She said this usually occurs at private institutions whose financial difficulties have led to academic weakness.[10] So far, probation has been imposed on public institutions only when boards of trustees engage in political interference with operations of the school.

Asked whether a public university had ever been cited for weak academic programs, Mather replied: "There are such cases [of weak programs] but we work with the whole institution, not in individual programs. It's not a program review. We would be reluctant to propose so severe a sanction on the basis of one or two programs. There might be a stinging report about it."[11]

The "probation" the regional accrediting agencies deem so severe actually means only that the school promises to meet specified goals and will be subject to later scrutiny. In contrast, when the NCAA imposes athletics probation, the institution suffers tangible penalties—denial of vital recruiting tools, profitable sports television appearances, or participation in bowl games or basketball tournaments.

Although higher education has been the subject of heightened criticism, the accreditation warranty has been extended. Jean Mather confirmed that North Central's normal period of accreditation now is 10 years, but she described it as "an on-going relationship." Dr. Thrash agreed: "It's the easiest thing in the world to say that we're easy. But many institutions are on less than a 10-year cycle. All institutions send reports annually. We do monitor them."[12]

I am skeptical. An organization with a limited staff "monitoring" more than 950 colleges and universities through annual reports written by those being scrutinized? The relationship between the regionals and their members is a collegial, hand-in-glove affair. Can you imagine a respected consumer protection agency giving its highest certificate of approval for all of the cars produced by General Motors' Chevrolet division over the next 10 years based upon paperwork submitted by a committee of GM executives? Surely the performance of the nation's colleges and universities are as important as the road tests for Chevrolet cars and trucks.

James T. Rogers, executive director of the college commission of the Southern Association of Colleges and Schools, said that in the 1980s, the association had withdrawn accreditation of 2 of its nearly 800 members. Both were struggling financially and Rogers said canceling accreditation in any case is usually the final blow. "When we remove accreditation, that removes all federal funding," he commented. "Students will not go to an institution where they cannot receive government loans and other financing."[13]

The Southern Association believes that financial support is the singularly important key to an institution's worthiness and in the past five years or so it has revoked accreditation of seven institutions and denied it to two applicants. It also came down hard on the Southeastern College of the Assembly of God, Lakeland, Florida, for providing good grades to academically deficient athletes. One athlete earned 22 credit hours in a single summer.[14] More action like that, applied to big and small, would be applauded by many.

The superficial nature of the present accrediting system creates a strange irony: academic accreditation is common and easy to obtain; to gain distinction, colleges struggle to find national respectability through their NCAA sports classification that is based, in part, on such absolute, nonacademic criteria as stadium size (minimum of 30,000 permanent seats) and football attendance (minimum average of 17,000 paid admissions per home game) to qualify for Division I-A.[15]

A fixation exists in the minds of many, including college trustees and presidents, that if the university is not Division I-A in football or Division I in basketball, it is second-rate. Again and again, I was taken aback at the abject dismissal of academic traditions, as college presidents solemnly confirmed in letters and telephone calls to me that certification by the NCAA of their Division I status was critical to the future of their universities.

Driving the Kansas Turnpike in the late 1980s, I regularly passed one huge sign reading "University of Kansas, NCAA National Basketball Champions 1988," and another, "Washburn University, NAIA Basketball Champions 1987." These were their principal turnpike advertisements. The athletics stamp of success is worth publicizing.

What is particularly troubling is that the same college leaders who criticize the "weak" academic standards of the NCAA have no quarrel with the regional accrediting agencies. They obviously like the status quo: there are no enforced academic standards; local option controls.

Exit Testing

Derek Bok, former president of Harvard University, was in the forefront of the American Council on Education's drive during the 1980s to impose the test requirements of Proposition 48 on freshman athletes—an effort I applauded and admired. He also was a leader of the ACE effort to substitute a panel of ACE presidents as the control point for NCAA legislative activities. The first initiative was acted upon favorably in 1983. The second proposition, highly controversial, was defeated a year later. I could perceive no tangible gain for him or Harvard in these exercises, and I admired his tenacity in taking on the NCAA establishment on its own court in January 1984. The NCAA convention hall in Dallas, Texas, was full of some 1,100 people when he argued for a transfer of power to the ACE. He later admitted to a "challenging and somewhat intimidating" experience in arguing a tough case to such a large group of people in such a large room.

Five years later, he was good enough to talk to me about his experience. I hoped he might be sympathetic to some form of exit testing for college seniors, similar to that imposed by the colleges upon high school students, both athletes and nonathletes. But when I suggested such a testing program, not only to determine the students' own competency but also the effectiveness of their colleges' teaching, he demurred. "I don't agree with that," he said. "I think most people can tell the good schools."[16]

President Bok's answer possibly reflected the security of Harvard, the general complacency of higher education or, more likely, the winners' preference for the status quo.

The colleges routinely, year after year, measure and compare the academic worth of high schools across the nation when they judge freshman admissions, but insist upon being accountable only to themselves when it comes to measuring their own performance.

Exit testing is an idea whose time is long overdue. The strategy at the undergraduate level is not to compare exit scores among institutions. Schools whose freshmen start with poor academic credentials may indeed achieve lower average scores on exit tests. Harvard may have higher average scores. That is not the relevant issue in measuring the competency of an educational institution. What matters most is how far a school moves its students up the scale. This "value-added" indicator is critical.

Exit testing of a sort already exists, but the results are kept in-house. By that I mean the educational industry has access to the information, but college-specific results are virtually never published because it might give too much insight into the quality of education offered by various institutions. Scores are secret. This is part of the informal but enduring educational monolith.

One example of an exit test is the Law School Admissions Test (LSAT), taken by applicants for law school. Linda Whiteman, an administrator of the test organization, reports that scores are never separated according to college to reveal averages for graduates of specific institutions. The test results do leak out and lead to tacit conclusions within the educational family as to which undergraduate schools in the nation are best at preparing their students for law school. About 15 years ago, for example, the statistics of one of the midwest's premiere law schools showed Oberlin superior to Duke University for this purpose.

Admittedly, the LSAT is a test of reasoning ability taken by a select group of college graduates and should not be used as a general exit test to evaluate all graduates of a particular college. Yet the averages—if published—would help inform the public, parents, and students as to which colleges are doing the best job of preparing students for law school. This is little different than the data college registrars routinely exchange as to which high schools best prepare their students for undergraduate college work.

Another existing upper-level exit test is the state bar examination a law school graduate takes to obtain a license to practice. Steps have been taken in the state of Ohio to publicize this information. Why isn't it routinely reported elsewhere for the benefit of students and parents? Presumably because academic freedom is one thing, and freedom of information is quite another.

What if a five-year study showed that all University of Michigan law graduates passed the Ohio bar exam on the first try, but only 75 percent of Ohio State University law graduates passed? The results would require analysis, of course, since it might happen that 30 of the better Michigan graduates took the Ohio bar exam, and 275 Ohio State graduates tried it. Some academics gasp at the thought that such information would fall into the hands of an ignorant public. These comparisons happen all the time in other public endeavors; for example, when the test scores of inner-city school districts are invidiously compared to scores in affluent suburban districts. The college community's resistance to inspection should not prevent the release of meaningful facts. Education leaders can point out the complex issues we should take into consideration along with the test scores, but first let's get the information on the table.

In light of the increased public disclosure in the state of Ohio, Dean Francis Beytagh of the Ohio State Law School not long ago campaigned to persuade the Supreme Court of Ohio to give Ohio law school deans greater say in structuring the state bar examinations and, by preparing model answers, improve the subsequent grading. Dean Beytagh's position suggests that practicing attorneys who now serve the state on the bar examination board don't understand how to ask questions and grade the answers. His approach, as I analyze it, is collegial: we just want to be helpful by preparing the questions and the model answers used to judge our students' performance. It seems the real purpose is to infiltrate one of the few organizations providing outside inspection of an educational institution's performance.

Another exit exam already in place is the Graduate Record

Examination, taken by undergraduates seeking admission to graduate study. Its scores would tend to demonstrate which schools were best at preparing students for graduate work.

There is also the Academic Profile test, created by the College Board and Educational Testing Service. Nancy Beck, an ETS program director, said the Academic Profile was to be administered at the end of the sophomore year to measure achievement in general education studies, although some of the 185 colleges that gave the test in 1988 waited until the senior year. A companion to the Academic Profile is the Major Field Achievement Test, designed to measure the competence of college seniors in their majors.

It's no surprise that college-specific results of the two tests are strictly confidential. For comparison purposes, administrators of a given college will be told the composite test scores of 10 or more schools similar to their own in size and educational aims. Never are they supposed to see individual school scores except their own. Asked how ETS would react if all such scores were made public, Nancy Beck replied: "It puts too much emphasis on a single measure. The best test in the world is only a snapshot of something. Tests can be very useful along with other things."[17]

Every good coach knows that a forty-yard sprint time, bench press weight scores, vertical jump heights, and agility skills are not the final measure of a player's heart and game "smarts." But the test results are significant factors in eliminating those who, regardless of their desire, simply do not have the basic skills to compete in college athletics at the NCAA Division I level.

That also happens to be the method colleges use in applying academic test results to their own first-year prospects. The same sorting out takes place, and the colleges publish and talk freely among themselves about the average SAT or ACT scores of their *entering* classes. It is only the score of the college itself that remains top secret—the confidential statistics that disclose how well they have taught their students.

On the playing field, everything is out in the open. The university meets its traditional adversary in public competition at the stadium on Saturday afternoon before thousands of critics. Today's collegiate coaches are good at what they do because their product is scrutinized by the public each game day and, thereafter, is analyzed and reanalyzed through magnifying lenses applied by the media and booster groups.

Superior performance is the aim of college sports. The university president fires the coach who can't deliver and hires the one who can. Educating students is the aim of colleges and universities. They ask year after year for more and more money from the public to achieve that goal. In return, the colleges should not resist but, in fact, promote public measurement of their accomplishments.

Notes

1. Report of National Institute of Education Study Panel, *Chronicle of Higher Education,* October 24, 1984.
2. Milton Friedman, interview with Brian Lamb, *C-Span Booknotes,* December 28, 1994.
3. AAFRC Trust for Philanthropy, Inc., *Giving USA: Annual Report on Philanthrophy* (1994), 87.
4. College Board Survey, *Kansas City Times,* August 10, 1989.
5. U.S. Department of Education, National Center for Education Statistics, *Finance Survey,* May 1992, tables 309–10.
6. James S. Coleman, *Wall Street Journal,* May 18, 1989.
7. Rev. E. William Beauchamp, *NCAA News,* June 26, 1994.
8. Wendy Bounds, *Wall Street Journal,* October 10, 1994.
9. Jean Mather, interviews with Charles Hammer, June 27 and July 31, 1989.
10. Patricia Thrash, interview with Charles Hammer, January 18, 1990.
11. Jean Mather, interviews.
12. Patricia Thrash, interview.
13. James T. Rogers, interview with Charles Hammer, June 28, 1989.
14. Carol Luthman, interview with Charles Hammer, February 8, 1995.
15. NCAA, *1994–95 NCAA Manual,* article 20.9.6.3.
16. Derek C. Bok, interview with the author, October 12, 1988.
17. Nancy Beck, interview with Charles Hammer, June 2, 1989.

Chapter 18   The Enemy of Reform

College athletics reform movements spanning almost 90 years have been remarkably consistent. They never reformed much of anything.

For nearly 40 of those years, I was part of those visionary efforts that came to naught. We seemed to be constantly chasing the horse after it had escaped from the barn. Finally I came to realize the common factor in the many failures has been that reformers focus on the past, believing that somehow the flourishing big-time college sports industry can be returned to its original, more innocent campus surroundings, there to be maintained as a normal part of college life as our forefathers said it should be.

Attempting to achieve what in fact is an impossible dream, current reformers write more and more rules to emphasize that the athlete is just like any other student, admission policies shall not favor the best athletes, degree credit requirements shall be the same for all students, and the college is in control of varsity athletics and the athlete. These pro forma declarations of common commitment increasingly shackle the athlete with myriad proscriptions that threaten his or her grant-in-aid and eligibility, while nonathletes have come to enjoy the most campus freedom in collegiate history.

Spectators following the college "reform" game need a scorecard to keep track of the many measures that have carried the promise of change. My tally sheet shows only a few major engagements, and even in these the changes were only temporary.

I have already referred to President Angell of Michigan, who tried to limit the size of Big Ten football and to advance the academic competence of its players. He may well have been the most determined of the early reformers and the most humiliated. Unfortunately, his courageous initiatives in 1906 were negated by the regents of his own university.

In a second skirmish more than 20 years later, the Carnegie Report was publicized as a carefully documented indictment that would alter the course of college sports. After studying 130 colleges in the United States and Canada, Carnegie investigators reported that star athletes were recruited and subsidized, with deceit an integral part of the process. The *Chicago Tribune* trumpeted the report's impact in bold headlines, saying that the report "...Hits Big Ten Athletics." "Three Year Probe Indicts American College System." "Sports Policies Lead to Deceit and Chicanery."[1]

The Carnegie Report had concluded that only 28 of the 130 colleges were above reproach, and two—the University of Georgia and Oglethorpe University—had refused to cooperate. For the next 20 years, this report was a landmark reference for would-be reformers. Football enthusiasts, however, ignored it. The willy-nilly recruitment and subsidization of athletes continued without pause.

The Sanity Code of 1948 marked a heroic stand against the sports excess and cheating that the Carnegie Report had decried. The code was the first *national* endeavor to require college control of, and assert academic integrity for, intercollegiate sports. It lasted only two years, rendered impotent by football-minded colleges convinced that the game should be operated as an adjunct campus activity under special rules.

In the 40 years since the burial of the Sanity Code, the need to clean up college sports and to balance athletics with academics have been as persistent a topic among educational groups as balancing the federal budget has been in political circles. The success rates have been comparable.

Legalization of the full ride in 1956 could be classified as a reform, since it was accepted by many as a better system that would render cheating obsolete. I thought it would lead to better days, but the record shows the full ride was an act of administrative convenience for college management and a recruiting bonanza for coaches. It encouraged separation of the student-athlete from the student body, promoted self-governance for the athletics department, and sanctified an industry-wide, common pay scheme based on athletic skill. It was a change of direction, but I do not count it as a plan that caused "people to behave better," a dictionary definition of reform.

Not that we should now try to tinker with the compensation package for players. On the contrary. Given the money in today's system—most of which goes to the landowners and the supervisors—it makes little sense to think about turning back to the general principles of the Sanity Code, suggested by the NCAA Committee on Financial Aid and Amateurism in March of 1995. The retrospective focus of past and present reformers must be replaced by realistic change in the decade of the 1990s.

After the 1956 grant-in-aid decision, the next call to reform was the 1.600 rule in academics, adopted in 1965. By combining high school grades and a national SAT or ACT test score, it established an eligibility formula for any student-athlete who sought a grant-in-aid as a freshman. The test feature provided a genuine *national* measurement, one that did not depend solely on the inconsistent standards of high schools.

The 1.600 legislation aimed to refurbish the image of college athletics and was backed by a sincere belief that stronger college academic rules would prompt high school athletes to pay more attention in the classroom.

The rule endured a stormy existence, but it helped keep the athletics-academic situation from further deterioration. In revoking 1.600 at the 1973 NCAA Convention, the delegates stated in effect that imposing national academic standards was contrary to national educational policy designed to encourage recruitment of at-risk students and open college doors to all who wanted to attend.

Beneath that rationale lay a deeper level of practical reasoning. The big timers—building a national entertainment business—wanted the great players on the field, whether or not they met customary academic requirements. In the new open-door era, victory-minded coaches sensed a potential recruiting paradise.

In 1975–76, we mounted what I believe was the last serious campaign to rein in the expansive big timers. By then college athletics was a bona fide growth industry, now including basketball and headed for major league entertainment status. The summer 1975 Palmer House convention represented a daring effort by the leadership to corral the burgeoning sports colossus. Those who favored the reform package passed the necessary rules, and the momentum carried over to the 1976 winter convention. We soon discovered, however, that we were overmatched.

In the end, "need" as a grant-in-aid criterion was rejected, traveling squad limits were junked, coaching limits were circumvented, grants were restricted to one year at a time, and freshmen were ruled eligible to play varsity games. The football and basketball seasons were lengthened; special-exception games increased the in-season schedule; the postseason football market was expanded to eighteen certified games, and NCAA tournaments added more games, as did other postseason events.

In the 1980s, the colleges confirmed the wisdom of the Roman rhetorician, Juvenal, who wrote that "the love of money grows as the money itself grows."[2] More money and increased TV exposure led to enlarged stadiums, bigger field houses, and more booster donations—expansions that in turn created better teams and more money.

Money begets money, but in college athletics there never seems to be enough of it. Traditional net revenue producers in football—for instance, Notre Dame, Penn State, Michigan, and Nebraska—continually set higher expenditure levels that destroy the balance sheets of most of the other Division I-A colleges that are trying to keep up. An economic version of the Peter Principle works for the rest: all expenditures in the major sports shall be approved until our deficit reaches a level comparable to our competitors.

The cost-saving measures of the mid-1970s proved ineffective, and, during the ensuing decade, expenses surpassed revenues at the vast majority of colleges. Again, beginning in the 1990s, cost cutting was a major agenda item at college meetings. Athletes' grants-in-aid were reduced while compensation for coaches, athletics directors, and conference or NCAA officials have soared to all-time highs.

Current NCAA academic standards, subject to frequent revisions, appear to be comparable to the 1.600 legislation of 1965. Other recent internal reform initiatives are catch-up measures that also guarantee no direction-changing results. Hiring compliance officers at the college, conference, and national levels, conducting seminars on rules interpretations, and publishing graduation rates are not reforms. These efforts are aimed at encouraging "business competitors" (i.e., the member colleges) to operate more or less within the rules, and improving college athletics' public relations image.

Outside the NCAA establishment there have been repeated campaigns for change. Former athletes, lawyers, union organizers, and individual coaches have all attacked the system. Lee Corso, former head football coach at Indiana University and current football TV commentator, suggested in 1981 that when a school is placed on probation, six "scholarships" should be taken away in football and two in basketball. So long as the coach in charge when the violations occurred remains in charge, the school would not get back its scholarships. If the coach went elsewhere, the sanctions would follow him to the new school.[3] This penalty idea was dismissed as too radical and severe.

Dale Brown, head basketball coach at Louisiana State, for years has argued that varsity athletes on grants-in-aid should receive (1) a monthly allowance of $100; (2) two paid round-trips between home and college each year; (3) one paid trip for parents each year so they could watch their offspring play; (4) dental and eye services; and (5) legal representation for athletes, thus fending off unethical agents.[4]

When Dale wrote to me about such ideas, I would urge him to sell it in the Southeastern Conference first. If he couldn't get LSU and other members of the SEC to sponsor the proposal, it would be unreasonable to expect the necessary two-thirds majority of 500 or so colleges voting at the national level. Nothing happened.

More frightening to the educational establishment than any of Dale Brown's thoughts was a 1981 proposal by Allen Sack, a former Notre Dame football player and sociology professor, and Kermit Alexander, former UCLA and NFL defensive back.

Having created the Center for Athletes Rights and Education (CARE), they proposed what amounted to a players' union. They wanted collegiate superpowers to bargain with athletes over such issues as the right to tuition-free courses to complete degree requirements at any time after the athletes' eligibility expired, multiyear scholarships that do not terminate if the athlete is injured, tutoring and counseling, and the right to share revenue that the athletes generate.

There was an immediate red alert. The NCAA staff was told to get on this one right away. We asked legal counsel for a briefing about the labor rights of college students. We were assured that the National Labor Relations Board had refused to exert jurisdiction over students who are employed by private colleges they are attending. Neither would state institutions encounter problems under state laws. "We would expect states to decline to require their institutions to recognize and bargain with unions of student-athletes," was the word from our Washington, D.C., counsel.

The NCAA's policy-making council felt reassured, but Mike Scott of the Washington, D.C., Squire, Sanders & Dempsey firm at the time warned us not to be complacent. "It is unlawful in virtually every state for firemen and policemen to strike," he said, "but it happens. Similarly, most labor contracts prohibit strikes during the life of the contract, but they happen. The simple fact is that whenever a group of people band together and insist upon acting in concert, they usually have to be dealt with in some fashion or another."[5]

Dick DeVenzio, a 155-pound point guard who started three seasons for the Duke Blue Devils, graduated as a literature major and an academic All-American in 1971. After observing the increased commercialism of the 1970s, he mounted a one-man crusade in the 1980s to change the colleges financial control of the players. He sent videotapes to players, arguing: "You deserve a major share of the money—this is America where economic opportunities are supposed to be open to all." He mailed $100 checks to senior football players postdated January 3, 1994, for cashing after the 1993–94 bowl games. DeVenzio now contemplates the possibility of a delay in the start of the NCAA Final Four basketball games as players stage a temporary sit-in before tip-off.[6] Francis Canavan, NCAA executive director for public affairs, dismissed DeVenzio in the winter of 1994–95 as a publicity-seeking opportunist. Now why pick on the smaller people that way?

It seems to me the 5-foot, 10-inch Dick DeVenzio has a more appealing case than the 6-foot, 9-inch John Thompson. The successful Georgetown University coach went public in March 1987, arguing it was time for college coaches to form a union. The NCAA was considering legislation to cut coaching staffs and channel money to the colleges for coaches' endorsements involving the colleges' players and insignia. On the eve of the 1987 NCAA Final Four in New Orleans, Thompson told the media that the coaches were "tired of being the scape-goats for everything evil existing in college athletics today." The National Association of Basketball Coaches had met that March 28 with Larry Fleischer, executive director of the NBA Players Association. The issue of unionizing "is extremely important," Thompson said.[7]

DeVenzio (Duke, '70) and Thompson (Providence, '64) obviously have in mind different segments of the college sports population. It's clear which segment needs a union the most.

In any case, sit-ins, sick-outs, or union-directed strikes are not the fundamental issue at the moment. Collective bargaining will not be necessary if the artificial restraints of the NCAA are set aside. Athletes should be entitled to the freedoms that are available to other students at the university in such matters as work opportunities, the right to transfer between schools, and the right to use their name and reputation for financial gain.

Any or all of the so-called outsider ideas might have been

helpful in a comprehensive reform package. Yet, when offered, all of them encountered a united front of opposition as the educational establishment closed ranks. The collegiate family may rattle the windows with their internal disagreements, but family *is* family when it comes to defending the mutual empire.

Bulldozing the Athlete

"If you're going to survive in your job," a friend told me in the late 1970s, "you have to understand college presidents." Mark Plant, Michigan law professor, was prepping me for the increased role college presidents apparently wanted to play in reforming athletics.

"A college president presides over affairs but has limited power," Mark went on. "His is a job of persuasion. He may say that the university's course to excellence lies due north. The faculty will say we should go east. The alumni insist the course should be west. And the students want to go south. Everything continues about the same, and soon a new president arrives on campus."

The transient circumstances described in the 1970s persisted in the 1990s. The presidential lineup in Division I-A, where the biggest of the big play, reflects a free substitution principle. From 1989 to 1994, more than half of the presidents (about 58 percent) changed jobs. In a 10-year span, 1984–85 through 1994–95, only 20 presidents or about 19 percent were still presidents at the same institutions.

Presidents are not around long enough to reform the academic side, faced with tenured faculty and entrenched administrators, but it's gratifying to gain attention as reform-minded leaders at the national level, attacking the excesses of college athletics. An appealing aspect is the structure of the NCAA as a law-and-order society. Ballots are cast by certified voters, rules are enacted, and NCAA enforcement officers fan out across the country to see that all obey—athletes, parents, alumni, sports agents, coaches, friends of coaches, ad infinitum. This apparent precision appeals to some frustrated college presidents, weary of the disorder of campus politics. Others have been lured by the high publicity associated with athletics. More than a few sincerely believe athletics policy should be changed, but, after battling the entrenched establishment and NCAA inertia, they go back to more important university functions.

One might think university presidents would enter the lists of reform combat as liberators, granting the athlete many of the laissez-faire rights of today's nonathlete students. But during the many forums sponsored by the NCAA in the late 1980s, I recall only two presidents, Kenneth Keller of Minnesota and Gail Fullerton of San Jose State, who spoke to the issue of individual freedom.

During a discussion on future athletics policy, Keller suggested to the 1987 NCAA special convention delegates that too many rules were being designed to implement level playing-field theories at the expense of individual rights. He warned that higher education increasingly was being scrutinized by members of Congress. Later a senior executive of the Council on Foreign Relations in New York City, Keller still held the view that higher education is coming under "greater suspicion and examination" relative to the quality of education, contract fraud, unrelated business income activities, and the conduct of college athletics.[8]

Two years after Keller's convention remarks, Fullerton, a member of the NCAA Presidents Commission, was listening along with other presidents to a report on why NCAA deregulation was not feasible. The report by an NCAA committee stated deregulation would unbalance the competitive climate of college athletics. Gail's analysis was that whether or not the NCAA rules-making machinery achieved a level playing field, it was burying the athlete under excessive rules.

"I became somewhat exasperated," she recalls. "There seemed to be endless nitpicking. Everybody seemed so concerned that some unidentified college was going to gain an ounce of competitive advantage." She told the group, "We're so intent on leveling the playing field that we have bulldozed the athlete."[9]

Close to $1 million was expended in support of the Committee on Deregulation and Rules Simplification. The thought behind this project was that there are too many NCAA prohibitions ("No wonder we have so many violations!") and too many convoluted interpretations ("If coaches don't understand the rules, how can we expect high school athletes to understand them?").

Shortly thereafter, in an effort to develop data to support future reform ideas, the NCAA paid about $1.9 million to the American Institute for Research (AIR) of Palo Alto, California, to identify for the NCAA Presidents Commission the major ills of college athletics. These two projects moved along separate but parallel tracks, the first managed by the existing NCAA hierarchy, the second under the control of a group of presidents.

The effort to reduce regulations and simplify NCAA legalese concluded when the 1989 and 1990 NCAA conventions adopted a new NCAA Manual that was twice the size and double the weight of the old one. The college legislators took new steps to control the economics of college athletics (except in the court-banned area of television) and to safeguard the college athlete from personal financial gain. The bulky, spiral-bound manual now features a constitutional proviso that declares the NCAA mission is to protect athletes "from exploitation by professional and commercial enterprises."[10]

Here the colleges are declaring that they may financially exploit their young players and designate others (such as athletics conferences and the NCAA) to exploit them. The colleges can also grant rights to commercial firms to use the players for "commercial enhancement," a new, in-house term. An example is the Raycom Sports Network's presentation of the "Dr. Pepper Starting Lineups" to their TV viewers as the players from the two competing basketball teams individually take the floor to be introduced to the crowd.

But the NCAA constitutional restriction prevents direct dealings between the commercial, for-profit world and the athlete. This is not about amateurism. This has to do with who controls the negotiations and gets the money. The colleges strengthened their grip on the athlete at a time when other prominent "amateur" organizations have been relaxing their power over players.

The U.S. Lawn Tennis Association, the U.S. Golf Association, and the U.S. Olympic Committee were among the foremost amateur sports groups in the country as the NCAA began growing in the 1950s. Their leadership sharply criticized what they saw as the outright professionalism of the NCAA grant-in-aid after it was defined in 1956.

Approaching the decade of the 1990s, however, these groups recognized the commercial realities of the era. For example, the Olympics, bellwether of amateurism for half a century, now permits athletes to escrow big dollars and still compete for the gold. NBA greats form the nucleus of the U.S. Olympic basketball team.

The colleges, meanwhile, have expanded their control of athletes in the name of amateurism—a modern-day misnomer for economic tyranny. These regulations, like procrustean laws, require all athletes to conform. For example:

1. He or she may receive a grant-in-aid in an amount set by the NCAA, but "any other financial assistance," except from someone upon whom the athlete is naturally or legally dependent, "shall be prohibited unless specifically authorized" by the NCAA.
2. *After* college enrollment, a student-athlete may not receive compensation for teaching or coaching sports skills or techniques in his or her sport on a fee-for-lesson basis.
3. A student-athlete may not be employed to sell equipment related to the student-athlete's sport if his or her name, picture, or athletic reputation is used to advertise or promote the product, the job, or the employer.
4. Similarly, if an athlete is employed as a counselor in a privately owned summer camp, the camp brochure may identify the athlete as a staff member, but his name or picture may not be used in any other ways to directly advertise or promote the camp or, for that matter, to promote a haberdashery across the street from the campus.
5. If an athlete is employed as a counselor in a private, for-profit summer camp for young people, management may use the athlete as a part of its instructional program. The player may demonstrate his or her skills and lecture on technique, but the athlete may not be paid for the added value he or she has thus contributed to the operation.

Still, the NCAA Presidents Commission is not entirely unmindful of the athlete. Using the costly AIR survey results for support, the presidents decided to curtail sports' time demands upon the athlete "to protect and enhance" the athlete's "welfare," which is now a stated constitutional purpose of the NCAA. The commission has been campaigning for less organized practice.

Thus, three groups—the NCAA Executive Committee, the NCAA Presidents Commission, and the privately financed Knight Foundation committee of presidents—spent nearly $5 million entering the 1990s on studies, outside consultants, deregulation, and voluminous reports, all of which seem to confirm the status quo. Meanwhile, the "business of our business," as Georgia President Fred Davison described it, continues unabated.

Electronics and demographics control the direction of college athletics, not commissions and NCAA legislators. Television and its potential viewers, publicity, and fan support feed on each other. Combined, they determine the course of college football and basketball.

The major teams with winning traditions and the tie-ins by the six power conferences to the major bowl games create self-fulfilling success: more in-season TV exposure, more ticket buying at higher prices, and more donations by their supporters. The bigger the population base supporting the team, the more ticket sales for in-season and bowl games. The bigger the team following, the more TV exposure and the better the TV rating, thus increasing the team's national following. Then comes more TV money and enhanced recruiting—an endless circle of success.

Mergers and Acquisitions

Through the 1980s and into the 1990s, the most powerful conferences moved to tie up the bowl games and, once the NCAA TV plan was declared illegal, to tie up the maximum number of in-season TV appearances. An exercise of capitalistic power was under way, directed toward the concentration of wealth in fewer hands.

Most of the leading entertainment colleges were reasonably

generous before the death of the NCAA TV plan. Since that time, however, they have been less and less willing to share with their cash-poor brethren, either former allies-in-arms of the CFA or laggards in their own conferences. The rich have been busy consolidating their riches and annexing new territories.

Various college athletics conferences, setting up merger and acquisition committees in the 1990s, duplicated one more business practice of the big for-profit corporations. The goals were to develop market power in selling TV rights for football and basketball and to sew up positions in postseason football games and the NCAA basketball tournament.

The Big Ten wanted more eastern penetration and a regular TV and bowl game player; it acquired Penn State. Stanley Ikenberry, president of the University of Illinois system and a member of the NCAA Presidents Commission's reform team, was the key player in engineering that deal.

The Southeastern Conference, thinking 22 percent of the then current CFA-ABC deal would not be enough in the future, moved west of the Mississippi to annex Arkansas and then east of the Appalachians to pick up South Carolina.

This Wall Street–style dealing had discomfiting side effects. When Arkansas jumped ship from the Southwest Conference, SWC Commissioner Fred Jacoby could not understand how an old-time colleague like Southeastern Conference Commissioner Roy Kramer could be a party to conference raiding without advance consideration and consultation. They were longtime friends from their years together in the Mid-American Conference.

While Roy was offending Fred, he, too, came under fire at home for not moving fast enough. The SEC already had a team in Florida at Gainesville, but SEC athletics directors criticized Roy when Florida State went to the basketball-rich Atlantic Coast Conference. They wanted to know why it was necessary to delay recruiting Florida State in order to check out the college's position on drug testing and other such administrative details.

Bernard F. Sliger, Florida State president and another reform member of the NCAA Presidents Commission, was out in front, leading his university into the ACC. Becoming a part of the ACC basketball money machine was attraction enough, but another reason was suggested by "Scoop" Hudgins, SEC associate commissioner emeritus. He wryly observed that Florida State Head Football Coach, Bobby Bowden, then 62, wanted to finish in the top five of all-time winning coaches. At the time, he needed 29 victories to catch Bo Schembechler and 33 to pull even with Woody Hayes.

"This may have had as much influence on President Sliger and the trustees as the basketball money," Scoop said. "The ACC provides an easier football route for Coach Bowden."[11] Following the 1994 season, Coach Bowden was in fifth place in the all-time standings. He was undefeated in the ACC with 24 victories in three years.

Today, the most powerful feudal lords continue nailing down gains of the previous two decades and extending their landholdings. The conference overseers realize they must remain competitive with other ambitious lords and, if necessary, be strong enough to overpower them when the economics of the future require it. This is capitalism at work in a not-for-profit environment. Predatory business practices are pursued, cloaked by the image of higher education's respectability.

The results of conference acquisitions will be to increase the intensity of competition and heighten the need to win. Meanwhile, the NCAA Presidents Commission, on which many of these merger-minded college leaders serve, continues to discuss ways of deemphasizing the practices of big-time athletics.

One advantage of doing business as a certified not-for-profit operator is that you get to keep every additional dollar you make. Graduated federal tax tables are for other people.

Free of U.S. tax liability and apparently comfortable that federal antitrust laws will not be a factor except in football television, the major entertainment colleges have created an oligopoly in which wealth and fame remain concentrated in the hands of a few.

The bowl games graphically illustrate the point in football. During the decade of the 1970s, the most money and publicity was provided by the forty games played in the four major bowls: Rose, Orange, Sugar, and Cotton.

Just five conferences—the Big Ten, Southeastern, Big Eight, Pac-10, and Southwest—plus independents Penn State and Notre Dame—dominated these big league bowls. That group included 49 teams, but only 23 of those 49 teams occupied 78 (or 97 percent) of the 80 available bowl slots during the 1970s.[12]

By the end of the decade, the Fiesta Bowl had come of age, grossing well over $5 million per game. The gross revenues of the five major bowls grew from $35.1 million in 1980–81 to $49.4 million in 1989–90. The money remained concentrated mostly in the same hands.

At the start of the 1980s, Division I-A (the designated major league of college football) was composed of nine conferences and 25 independents, or 106 total teams. Within that group was the elite—the five conferences named above and five independents (Miami of Florida, Florida State, Penn State, Notre Dame, and Pitt), numbering 52 teams. Those 52 teams filled 96 percent of the 100 team appearances in the five major bowls during the 1980s. But of that subset, there continued to be a smaller elite: 22 teams (42 percent of the 52 or 21 percent of Division I-A) accounted for 90 percent of bowl appearances. More rules and regulations, new seasons, and different coaches, but the powerful and wealthy maintained their advantage.

For the more recent 10 years, 1984–85 through the 1993–94 bowl seasons, net income from all certified bowls (normally 18 games) was $330.20 million, of which 97 percent of the dollars flowed to 72 teams, primarily because of conference sharing formulas. Concentrating on the past five seasons and considering the current six major postseason games (the Citrus Bowl being added to the previous five), 29 teams filled the available 60 slots and 13 of those 29 accounted for 44 of the 60 appearances. The current big six games delivered 68.1 percent of the total revenue from the 18 games in 1993–94, or $60.25 million of the $88.41 million.[13]

The consolidation of wealth that took place in the 1980s accelerated at the beginning of the 1990s as the patrician conferences aggressively set out to strengthen their positions. They absorbed into their ranks those football independents (except Notre Dame) that would give them added leverage in TV and bowl game negotiations and in securing additional NCAA basketball tournament berths. At the same time, cross-conference raiding led to the demise of the historic Southwest Conference, a long-enduring, essentially Texas league that likes to recall the days of Sammy Baugh in the 1930s and five later Heisman Trophy winners, including Texas's Earl Campbell in 1977 and Houston's Andre Ware in 1989.

Sentiment has no place when it comes to beefing up the corporate bottom line in the business world of collegiate athletics. From 1991 through 1993, Arkansas skipped out of the Southwest Conference and, along with independent South Carolina, joined the Southeastern Conference; Florida State, another independent, moved into the Atlantic Coast Conference. Penn State, a powerhouse independent like Florida State, gained membership in the Big Ten. The Big East, a basketball conference originally organized by a former basketball coach, gained the momentum needed to become a football major league when Miami leapfrogged 1,100 miles north to do business with seven other mostly independents located in Virginia, Pennsylvania, New Jersey, New York, and Massachusetts. All of this put the strongest independents into major conferences, leaving Notre Dame listed with nine other Division I-A colleges as major football independents. The pillage of the ranks of the independents to strengthen the power of the major conferences can best be measured by the remaining independents' won-loss records over 10 football seasons (1984–93). In that time, Notre Dame had a .748 winning record; the other nine had a combined .413 mark. Notre Dame subsequently joined the Big East in all sports but football.

During all of this, the University of Texas was anxious to make a move, but the political powers in Austin made it clear that Texas was not to depart the Southwest Conference, leaving behind Texas A&M, or Texas Tech for that matter. The upshot was an announced transfer to the Big Eight Conference, effective in 1996, of those three Texas state schools plus Baylor to create a new Big Twelve Conference. The Western Athletic Conference, not ranked in these writings as one of the patrician elite, became the largest Division I-A conference with 16 members, adding three private institutions from the Southwest Conference, two state schools from the Big West Conference, and independent Tulsa.

Increased NCAA surveillance, more emphasis on protecting the athlete from exploitation, and presidential control of national policy—the NCAA's announced aim of the late 1980s—has led to greater concentration of wealth in the hands of six expanded conferences. The Football Watchers' Power Chart for the 1990s, reflecting the affiliation transfers of 1991–93, is reproduced as table 1 and lists three measurements. The AP poll has been the most enduring and probably the most accurate ranking mechanism for major league football through the years. The second criterion, attendance, measures the team's support and ticket income. The third criterion, qualification for one of the big six bowls, indicates a team's national attraction based on winning and TV acceptance. The Power Index is based on the number of teams each conference and the independents placed in each of these three categories in five years, 1990–94.

Within the 63 power chart colleges, there continues to be a subset of 20 to 25 teams that dominate. In the major bowls, 13 teams filled 73.3 percent of the 60 available positions in these five years. Ten of these bowl dominators were among the 13 teams that spread-eagled the Top 20 AP polls during the same period. As to the attendance leaders of college football for the first five years of this decade, the same 22 teams were in the Top 25 each of the five years, and 20 of those 22 (Notre Dame and BYU excluded) were members of the six major conferences.

At one time, Father Joyce of Notre Dame and CFA chief Chuck Neinas envisioned a football organization of about 80 major leaguers; during the mid-1980s the Sooners' Barry Switzer talked of a group of 40 or so. In fact, by that time the world of college football already had been turned into an oligopoly of about 25 big timers.

For the 1990s, the teams that have achieved the highest rank are (in alphabetical order): Alabama (SEC), Colorado (Big Twelve), Florida (SEC), Florida State (ACC), Miami (Big East), Michigan (Big Ten), Nebraska (Big Twelve), Notre Dame (Independent), Penn State (Big Ten), Tennessee (SEC), Texas A&M (Big Twelve), and Washing-

TABLE 1. Football Power Chart, 1990–94

Group	Number of Teams (N=107)	AP Top 20 Appearances (N=100)	Top 25 Attendance (N=125)	Big Six Bowl Appearances (N=60)	Total Power Index Points (N=285)
Southeastern Conference	12	14	35	10	59
Big Twelve[a]	12	24	20	13	57
Big Ten	11	15	30	8	53
Pac-10	10	13	14	9	36
Atlantic Coast Conference	9	13	10	8	31
Big East	8	9	6	6	21
Independents	1[b]	4	5	5	14
Total	63	92	120[c]	59[d]	271
Percentage of total	58.9	92.0	96.0	98.3	95.1

[a]The Big Twelve includes the current Big Eight plus Texas, Texas A&M, Texas Tech, and Baylor.
[b]At the end of the 1994 football season there were 11 independents in Division 1-A; only Notre Dame meets the criteria for listing here.
[c]Brigham Young University placed in the top 25 all five years, averaging about 18th place.
[d]The University of Louisville appeared in the 1991 Fiesta Bowl.

ton (Pac-10). Right behind these 12 are Auburn, Clemson, Georgia, Ohio State, Oklahoma, Texas, and USC. Others can be added—for example, BYU, UCLA, LSU, and Virginia—but it still comes out that some 22 colleges control the action. What hurts them hurts the rest of the 39 or so interrelated football schools. Not only year after year, but decade after decade, the mix of teams differs only slightly in measuring the collegiate hegemony that reigns supreme. Confirming the continuing advantage of the small group of entrenched elitists was the February 1995 report that 89 of the current crop of high school football All-Americans had signed with 35 colleges. Twenty-one of the 35 colleges captured 74 or 83.1 percent of the prime prospects, or 3.5 per team.[14]

The present oligopoly wants no meaningful change in the controlling rules. Their conference colleagues and other colleges they schedule go along because the money earned by the oligopolists is shared with them. That's why today's reforms—designed by the presidents of the major leaguers—reinforce current practices for the 1990s.

Basketball: The Proletariat's Game

Basketball is a game that seems to be made for and certainly is glorified by television. College management will schedule games any day or night of the week to gain TV exposure. Basketball remains relatively inexpensive, since 13 full-ride scholarships per college are permitted, compared to the new number of 85 in football. Big municipal arenas in all the major cities offer favorable contracts to the colleges. There are so many good high school players that the have-nots ardently believe they might hit it lucky and make the big time.

A frequent wisecrack during enforcement discussions in the NCAA office was that one good "buy" in basketball was enough. In truth, one superstar recruit may take the lucky school all the way. Football requires more organized planning and, possibly, multiple deals.

Another strategic advantage for basketball occurs in playing the academic game. University management may allow 4 percent of an entering first-year class of 6,000 students to be academically at-risk special admits. The athletics department then is allowed 15 percent of those 240 special admits, or 36 academic exceptions. Men's athletics likely will get at least 24, and basketball looks very good indeed when it ask for only two "specials," no matter how deeply the coach dips into the academic barrel for those two.

All this would seem to make basketball the perfect avenue for college athletics' underprivileged schools to win publicity on TV and in the national rating polls during the relatively slow sports months of late January, February, and early March. If things go well, the big publicity payoff will come with a trip to the NCAA championship in the latter part of March. This accounts for the unrelenting migration of colleges into NCAA Division I—a sore point for many of the football big timers and the old-time basketball powers. With a chance to gain a guaranteed spot for their champions in the NCAA tournament, conferences have proliferated across the country, coming up with all sorts of names—such as Big South, Colonial, Metro Atlantic, Mid-Continent, Patriot, and Trans America.

Tipping off the 1994–95 season, 33 conferences with 295 teams plus 6 independents—a total of 301 teams—started off in pursuit of basketball's Holy Grail.[15] This is a haphazard, indiscriminate mixture of colleges with only one thing in common: a basketball team. You might compare it to a Kentucky Derby field of Shetland ponies, American quarter horses, and English-Arabian thoroughbreds. Perhaps it's no surprise then that NCAA equality rules, augmented by the leveling influences that are unique to basketball, still fail to keep the playing floor level.

Controlling the action are the six power conferences of the 1990s (shown in table 1) and about 7 to 10 other colleges—Louisville, UNLV, Notre Dame, possibly another independent, and an occasional one or two teams from the Western Athletic Conference or one or two of the newly organized basketball groups. This basketball mix numbers about 70 colleges, but approximately 28 of the 70 colleges dominate.

In 1993–94, all teams in Division I averaged about 5,300 spectators per game according to the NCAA, but there were only 58 that averaged more than 8,000. Forty-three colleges of the 58 or 74.1 percent belong to the six power conferences, and these conferences' teams averaged about 10,540. There were 33 Division I basketball conferences that year and the lower 15 averaged 2,060 per conference team.[16]

During the decade of the 1980s, 26 different teams from the then 7 major conferences plus Louisville accounted for 95 percent of the teams in the celebrated Final Four of college basketball. The tally for the most recent decade (1985–94) confirms this continuing domination. The rank order for the past 10 years based on the number of teams that earned one of the Final Four's 40 available slots shows 10 from the Atlantic Coast Conference; 6 from the Big East; 6 from the Big Ten; 5 from the Southeastern; 5 from the Big Twelve; 3 appearances by UNLV; 2 from the Pac-10; total: 37; the three remaining slots went to Louisville, Memphis State, and Cincinnati.

In college football the oligopoly is composed of about 25 teams or so. They master a domain of 106 teams. Considering that the major league of college basketball now includes some 300 colleges, the basketball elite are proportionately fewer and have the same tight grip on their sport.

Pleading hard times and a desperate need for money is standard disinformation pumped out by the biggest colleges. The super rich have money. It is that great majority of colleges that seek to catch up and associate with the most affluent that have negative balances at the end of the year.

Illustrating the paradox, the most recent publicity campaign for a national football playoff is based on the argument that college athletics verges on bankruptcy. It has been suggested that the NFL, by extending its season, has endangered some of the marginal bowl games. Proponents say a college gridiron playoff is needed, something like the NCAA basketball tournament, to pump up what is perceived to be decreasing interest in college football and the bowl games, as measured by attendance and television ratings.

Dick Schultz, before he was persuaded to resign as NCAA executive director in May 1993, had fixed the inauguration of an

NCAA Division I-A football championship as one of his main goals, and he worked hard at it. There was substantial agreement among the football big timers that something should be done.

The number of NCAA college football teams, from 1984 to 1993, had increased by 11.8 percent to 560, but total NCAA football attendance had slumped to a five-year low of 34.9 million.

From 1984 to 1993, per game attendance had declined by 12.8 percent to 12,074. In Division I-A, with essentially the same number of teams (105 in 1984 and 106 in 1993), per game attendance slipped 3.1 percent to 41,281.

Attendance figures were merely a preface to the sad story of college football television ratings. The A. C. Nielsen TV audience statistics showed 12.5 rating points for in-season college football in 1969–83; 6.4 for 1984–93, and 6.1 during 1989–93. The combined ratings for the prestigious New Year's Day bowl games, covering a similar sequence of years (1975–94), had plunged from 92.1 to 69.8. Meanwhile, the NCAA basketball tournament championship game, from 1973 to 1994, had climbed from 20.5 to 21.6 on the Nielsen scorecard. The message was clear: playoffs are more exciting than waiting for the AP and USA Today/CNN pollsters to name the national champion.

When the hallowed Rose Bowl, January 1, 1994, posted a 11.3 Nielsen rating, mirroring the slumping ratings of the bowls generally, even Big Ten and Pac-10 money managers, long opposed to playoff overtures, began to take notice. The Pasadena extravaganza, the "grandaddy of them all" as NBC proudly proclaimed for years, achieved Nielsen ratings of more than 30.0 on 13 occasions from 1955 to 1984, and was only below 25.0 in 4 of those 30 years. With one Nielsen point worth 942,000 TV households in 1994, a few points mean big money, up or down, at contract time.[17]

That same January 1, 1994, the prime time so-called national title matchup of Florida State and Nebraska in the Orange Bowl achieved only a 17.8 rating. The message came through in living color: football's one-shot title game achieved 17.8 compared to the 1990–94 average of 21.2 for the NCAA roundball championship and 42.4 for the NFL Super Bowl in those years.[18]

Serious minds have worked on a football playoff plan, including TV network executives, conference commissioners, college presidents, and the NCAA staff. The net conclusion is:

1. The calendar between the end of the college season and the NFL playoff schedule can accommodate an 8-team tournament, but not a 16-team bracket.
2. The four quarterfinal games should be on New Year's afternoon and evening.
3. TV rights should bring in more than $125 million and ticket sales $28 million.
4. After operating expenses, allocations to constituent groups, and the loss of $38.5 million now derived from the six major bowl games, there should be at least $80.0 million new dollars.

It sounded good. The NCAA basketball tournament TV rights for eight years from 1995 to 2002 (anticipating 63 tournament games a year) attracted $1.725 billion from CBS in December 1994.[19] The football tournament TV rights could be around $1 billion for eight years, once the bidding is completed. This would be based on an eight-team playoff and seven games per year.

All of this was considered by an NCAA study group, but the project stalled. Insiders send out mixed explanations as to why. Division III small-college presidents were adamant against it. Extending the season was opposed by most presidents. Existing bowl game managements bitterly objected. The bowl game coalition movement was the commissioners' answer to determining a football champion and that was good enough. Maybe so.

But in my view, the real answer to "Why not?" may be found in more pragmatic circumstances. The big league conferences are not going to permit these new football dollars to be run through an NCAA Executive Committee that will skim millions for NCAA projects and Division I-AA, II, and III colleges. More important, many of the athletes interviewed about the plan thought that some of the money should go to the athletes who played in the playoffs. There was a red alert! That would mean sharing NCAA basketball tournament revenue with players. Veteran administrators recalled the player union idea described earlier. A few may have recalled

Gail Fullerton's trenchant comment about bulldozing the athlete. Or, the NCAA public affairs department many have warned about giving new life to the 10-year campaign of a former Duke point guard, Dick DeVenzio.

The football playoff scheme has forced a refocusing by the believers that more money for the overseers is good money for a good cause. Without Dick Schultz as NCAA chief executive to carry the banner, it has been concluded that a waiting game is the best game.

I firmly believe in the incentives of capitalism, the freedom of private initiative, the human will to compete, and a system wherein the more capable people receive higher rewards. I think the public affection for college athletics is exciting and I see nothing wrong with the colleges and coaches working the marketplace for all the money they can corral. If the tax code says no taxes are due, so be it. But is it necessary to pretend that these dollar-driven business practices and major league entertainment contracts are separate and unrelated to the contracts the colleges have with the players? The college negotiators quickly abandon the terminology of the business world when they get back on campus. There, the talk is about "games for kids." You'll find coaches and athletics directors frequently refer to what's good or bad for the "kids."

Thus, while accepting the highest possible commercialization of their "extracurricular" sports activities, the colleges even to this day steadfastly:

1. deny for tax purposes that they are engaged in a dollar-generating business enterprise;
2. endorse private initiative on the part of their coaches and merchandisers, but not their athletes;
3. agree that coaches and staff members should receive bonuses for winning, making sure NCAA rules deny such rewards to athletes;
4. enlarge athletics department support staffs, but vote that grants-in-aid for athletes be reduced, and
5. emphasize that job security for coaches is important and routinely pay off contracts when they are fired, but insist that

Bill Cosby, former Temple University track athlete, received the NCAA's highest award at its 1982 convention at which time the colleges honored Lynette Woodard, four-time University of Kansas All-American basketball player (1978–81).

threatened ineligibility for the athlete shall be the main NCAA enforcement tool.

Until these attitudes and policies are dramatically altered, college athletics cannot rid itself of the charges of hypocrisy and exploitation that weigh so heavily on its reputation.

Damn the Rules. Full Speed Ahead!

College athletics suffers from schizophrenia, and the NCAA rules prescription represents inadequate psychiatric treatment. The contradiction was seldom better demonstrated than in the long love-hate relationship with Coach Paul (Bear) Bryant of Kentucky, Texas A&M, and Alabama.

The NCAA's split personality was on stage for the glamour-packed 27th Annual NCAA Honors Luncheon, January 11, 1982, at the Hyatt Regency Hotel in Houston, Texas.

Walter Cronkite was master of ceremonies. Bill Cosby, a Temple track athlete in his college days, was to receive the NCAA's highest award; Jack Kemp, a former Occidental College quarterback, was among the Silver Anniversary honorees; and Lynette Woodard, a four-time, first-team women's All-American, was a standout among the current day athletes being honored. I was seated at the head table with Paul. We had designed a unique, special trophy for presentation to him, the winningest coach in college football history.

The first investigative reports I handled in my career had related Paul's infractions at Kentucky. He was involved again in a major infractions case at Texas A&M and he had sued us in the bitter dispute over coaching limits. He had supported his friend Joe Paterno and the CFA in its attack on NCAA football television controls.

Yet the entire NCAA college athletics community, 1,400 strong, was saluting the former Alabama end from Fordyce, Arkansas, as the greatest football coach in the history of the game. Paul's 323 victories had surpassed Pop Warner's 319 and Amos Alonzo Stagg's 314. Paul was a head coach for 38 years; Knute Rockne, the legendary Notre Dame coach, served only 13 years.

I too respected Paul's ability to get the job done. I remember how he had taken his first Texas A&M squad to the hills and, after intense instruction in mountain climbing, came back with a small nucleus that still wanted to play. And play they did.

Paul broke the rules. He never really apologized, but, like many old-line coaches, he wouldn't blow smoke at you when he got down to discussing cases in private.

Sitting between Paul and me that day was the Reverend Joyce, executive vice-president of Notre Dame and another respected friend-enemy.

We were all in good humor. I reminded Paul of the confrontation long ago in our Kansas City office, when Ab Kirwan wouldn't budge on the Texas A&M violations charges. How Paul, after being

The 1983 NCAA convention honors Paul "Bear" Bryant as Fred Russell, Nashville, Tennessee, newspaper executive, makes the presentation and Walter Cronkite of CBS, master of ceremonies, applauds.

told alumni couldn't give good players money, had sighed, and said, "Well, I don't have anything to argue about." How he had just put on his hat and walked out.

All three of us laughed about it.

Paul wasn't feeling well that day, and during the reception, Sam Bailey, his longtime aide and confidant, had stayed close to watch over him. The coach with the most victories in college football was dead in a year. We sent a contribution to Paul's favorite charity, the Big Oak Ranch for Neglected and Homeless Boys at Glencoe, Alabama.

Paul had played the game to win. Damn the rules, full speed ahead! And the NCAA honored him for the results.

Notes

1. *Chicago Tribune,* October 24, 1929.
2. Juvenal, in George Seldes, *The Great Quotations* (New York: Pocket Books, 1967), 666.
3. Lee Corso, letter to Walter Byers, August 21, 1981.
4. Dale Brown, letter to NCAA Representatives, September 29, 1983.
5. Michael Scott, letter to Thomas C. Hansen, October 2, 1981.
6. Dick DeVenzio, interview with the author, January 10, 1995; and Devenzio supporting material.
7. Mark Asher, *Washington Post,* March 28, 1987.
8. Kenneth H. Keller, interview with the author, February 28, 1991.
9. Gail J. Fullerton, interview with the author, October 25, 1990.
10. NCAA, *1994–95 NCAA Manual,* article 2.8, 4; see also article 2.11, 4.
11. Elmore (Scoop) Hudgins, interviews with the author, November 5 and 26, 1990.
12. NCAA, Official NCAA Football Records Book, August 1990.
13. NCAA, Postseason Football Game Reports to NCAA Special Events Committee, April 9, 1990, and Official Football Records Book, July 1994.
14. *SuperPrep* magazine offense and defense football All-American listing, as published in the *Chicago Tribune* and *Kansas City Star,* February 2 and 5, 1995.
15. NCAA, Official Basketball Records Book, November 1994.
16. Ibid.
17. NCAA, Report of Research Group to NCAA Special Committee on Division I-A Football Championships, April 1994.
18. Ibid.
19. NCAA, news release, December 6, 1994.

Chapter 19   On the Record

The innermost nature of collegiate athletics—the secret of its popularity—is the enthusiasm of youth. Their emotional commitment to their sport and their teammates brings countless thrills to the fans. Generation after generation, they have replenished the popularity of intercollegiate sports through their energy and desire to test themselves against one another. "Just give me a chance, coach, I can do it," is the young athlete's credo.

Eager to make a college team and test their skills at a higher competitive level, these young people suddenly are transferred from the uncomplicated environment of high school athletics into the sophisticated world of college sports through an intense recruiting process. Encyclopedic regulations will govern their lives, on and off campus, for the next four to six years, starting with the first recruiting contact while they are high school students. The youngsters have no choice in the matter. You can't play in college unless you pledge allegiance to the rules, they are told. Then they are warned that the NCAA can rule them permanently ineligible at all 900-plus NCAA colleges for violations of marginal substance.

The rules to which the young athlete must subscribe work for the economic benefit of the colleges and coaches. If their gluttony is to be curbed and the players justly treated, dramatic changes in the rules are required. The due process procedures of NCAA enforcement, recently challenged in a number of states, are a focal point of resentment. The mistaken assumption persists that if the due process standards can be made fair for all, then all will be fair. But they are not the problem. Oppressive NCAA laws are. Revised due process procedures in the interest of fairness do not alter the unfairness of the rules.

The marketplace of ideas has been saturated with reform proposals and legislative initiatives originated by competing groups of college presidents, faculty critics, former athletes, state legislators, sports reporters, fans, ad infinitum. Given the reform failures of the past and the diffused focus of current reform claims, the mixed efforts will change little.

The present generation of college presidents who pursue a vague reform agenda appear to be world-weary cynics, content to respond to critics by prescribing topical remedies of no lasting significance. A decade has passed since college presidents made a command decision to exert their influence on public opinion and take control of the NCAA legislative process. They first claimed victory, pointing to the accomplishments of the 1990 and 1991 NCAA conventions.

This particular exercise proved that candor (in defining the problem) and forthrightness (in dealing with it) are scarce commodities in the chancelleries of higher education. In those two legislative outings, the NCAA cut the basketball schedule by three games, but added two of the three back at the next convention; required one day of player freedom each week from organized sports practice, but permitted midweek football games, with basketball games to be scheduled for any day or night of the week; reduced the number of grants-in-aid available to athletes, but permitted all other expenditures to run wild, including salaries and the number of staff positions. Capping the money to players is an act of reform; free flow of added revenues to everyone else is dynamic capitalism at work.

In addition to the skyrocketing rise in coaches' salaries, administrative salaries have been taking off, all at a time the NCAA was cutting football grants-in-aid in Division I-A from 95 per year to 85 by 1994–95. Division I-A conference commissioners in 1990–91 averaged $133,000 in salary, with perks such as no-cost new automobiles, free memberships at private clubs, low-cost and no-interest house loans, and annuity pension contributions. The top commissioner drew $170,000 in salary, and the low was around $95,000 that year. Salary information is shared annually throughout the college sports industry. Word soon circulated that the NCAA executive director's salary and compensation package for 1992–93 was $461,202, as codified on IRS Form 990, more than twice that of the next highest paid NCAA employee and far exceeding major conference executives.[1] One year later, the top salaried I-A commissioner, Jim Delany of the Big Ten Conference, was receiving a base salary of $230,000, a generous retirement contribution, a $15,000 housing supplement, a $250,000 life insurance policy, a free automobile, and athletics and private social club memberships.[2] Roy Kramer of the Southeastern Conference was a close second and the rest were not all that far behind. Free spouse travel to several events was included.

In three-and-one-half years, from Harvey Schiller's arrival as Southeastern Conference commissioner in 1986 to Roy Kramer's appointment in 1990, the SEC staff jumped from 13 to 20—up 54 percent. From 1987 to 1994–95, NCAA full-time salaried staff increased from 127 to 229—up 80 percent. At major I-A universities, athletics department staffs increased by 30 percent or more between the late 1980s and early 1990s. Ced Dempsey was at Arizona and Rick Bay was athletics director at Minnesota at the time. They attributed the costly growth to "bureaucratic overlay" rather than increased sports opportunities for students. Pete Carril, Princeton basketball coach, noted in 1991 that film exchange "coaches" had been added to the staff armaments race.[3]

In 1994, the highly publicized buyout of the last three years of Rollie Massimino's basketball contract at UNLV, at a reported cost of $1.8 million, brought further condemnation of UNLV's peculiar behavior from those who look with scorn at the Las Vegas glitter and glitz approach to college basketball. Ignored at the same time was the $1.0 million plus package that keeps Coach Mike Krzyzewski at Duke.

For the fiscal year ended June 30, 1992, Oklahoma Sooner sports expenditures totaled $20.6 million. Of that amount, 38 percent ($7.5 million) went for salaries, wages, and benefits while only 9.0 percent ($1.9 million) was spent on athletes' financial aid. OU support groups raised $3.6 million that same year for the benefit of the athletics department.

One of the richest of the Big Eight teams has been Nebraska. The Tom Osborne football money machine generated $9.7 million for the fiscal year ended June 30, 1991, or 69.2 percent of the total intercollegiate athletics income of $13.98 million for that year. Financial aid to athletes ($2.4 million) accounted for only 15.0 percent of expenditures while staff salaries, wages, and benefits amounted to $6.0 million or 38.5 percent. One of the well-to-do-elite, the Cornhuskers netted $3.8 million from football operations prior to donations from outside groups.

All of this goes on while college leaders justify their high-dollar mergers and acquisitions as being necessary to deal with college athletics' purported financial crisis. The most publicized solutions now are to cut grants-in-aid for the athletes and create a national football championship for the colleges. While working the marketplace for more income, the major colleges whack away at a relatively small part of their budget—cutting the number of grants available to athletes while maintaining a tight lid on the amount they may receive. The evidence indicates that the numerical limits on grants-in-aid, particularly in football, work to the advantage of the rich and handicap the efforts of the middle class and poor teams to improve their lot. Maybe that's the true reason behind the 85 football grant limit.

The "reforms" of the late 1980s and early 1990s, I believe, on balance have been minor league changes in the operations of a major league industry so that the entrenched oligopoly with its entrenched beneficiaries can proceed as planned. I'm for increased pay and increased employment, but the scam occurs when educators gravely cut sports and increasingly regulate athletes in an expansive marketplace environment where other members of the college family are prospering. The publicized financial crisis is essentially a financial dislocation. Such a record makes it clear to me that the colleges have neither the inclination nor the will to change. That is why the question of how to bring about change is almost as critical as the proposed transformation itself.

Early in my time, I vigorously resisted outside intrusion into collegiate sports. The onrushing, economically magnified events of the 1980s, coupled with the continued disregard for young athletes' rights, created a necessity for change. The presidential reform movement took hold in the mid-1980s and squandered an oppor-

Walter Byers, upon his retirement, expresses to the NCAA convention in January 1988, his appreciation to the membership for permitting him to serve as executive director for 36 years

tunity to transform the industry. Significant change will not come from that source.

In fact, the rewards of success have become so huge that the beneficiaries—the colleges and their staffs—simply will not deny themselves even part of current or future spoils. I can still see those unsmiling faces of the NCAA Council members in 1984 as they waited for me to defend my suggestion that collegiate players should share in the money. It was as if I had desecrated my sacred vows.

I believe the record now clearly shows the major hope for reform lies *outside* the collegiate structure. What the colleges will not do voluntarily should be done for them.

That approach worked once before with an errant sports organization, the Amateur Athletic Union (AAU), which for most of the 1900s controlled many American sports because it controlled U.S. athletes' eligibility for the Olympic Games and other international competitions. The AAU abandoned its oppressive practices only after a decade-long battle waged mainly by the NCAA. The U.S. Congress in 1978 settled the matter by enacting federal legislation limiting the power of such organizations.

Today, history has been turned upside down. The liberator of the past has become today's oppressor. The NCAA has succeeded its former antagonist with rules as restrictive as those against which it formerly struggled. The colleges do not demand an "NCAA card" to compare with the "AAU card" once required before an athlete could enter an AAU-approved event, but the NCAA does require the annual signing of a far more comprehensive amateur declaration before grant-in-aid money is released and game togs are issued.

Like the AAU, the NCAA professes a noble purpose: "We are protecting our players' amateurism." Despite dramatically different commercial conditions, the NCAA today is as self-righteous as the old AAU and will prove more formidable than its old adversary.

The major league colleges and the NCAA are taking in staggering sums of money compared to the emaciated income of the former AAU. The NCAA alone had a $190.1 million budget for the 1994–95 fiscal year, up 9.3 percent from the previous year, and annually ends up with a multi-million-dollar surplus.[4] It commands a formidable state and national lobby, and it can call on one of the nation's most potent political forces for help, the multiple educational associations and institutions operating under the umbrella of the American Council on Education. They comprise higher education's lobbying presence at One Dupont Circle in Washington, D.C. College presidents active in NCAA affairs during the 1994–95 period engineered an NCAA commitment to open its own official governmental lobby staff in the nation's capital. Three full-time NCAA employees are to take up residence at One Dupont Circle.

Against such an array of power stands the young athlete, unorganized and a part of the system for only four to six years before
he or she moves on to be replaced by another 18- or 19-year-old.

A historical basis for federal remedies, however, has been management's exploitation of the isolated and unorganized. The structure of the colleges' control of their players and the demand that
management's pronouncements be accepted as the final word are
irresistible targets for redress and correction. Those who control
the marketplace are the same as those who define the terms and,
thus, preordain the results.

The cant and tautology of the collegiate managers routinely
proclaim that only amateurs may play college sports. The definitions of an amateur and all interpretations thereof shall be determined by the colleges through their common contract with the
NCAA. Any player who accepts money not deemed permissible by
the NCAA shall lose his or her amateur standing. The only permissible or clean money shall be that collected by the colleges and
rationed to the players under a prescribed formula set forth in the
colleges' mutual, NCAA-enforced contract. Sports dollars not subject to the colleges' laundering process are considered dirty money
if the money finds its way to a player. The athlete's amateur standing and eligibility will be ruined. For all others in the campus
hierarchy, the dollars are rewards for dedicated service. The managers' deference to their own definitions makes certain that fees
for endorsements and television appearances, payments for newspaper columns and public speeches, and, most certainly, the use
of free dealer automobiles shall constitute "dirty money" where
players are concerned but legitimate income for those who define
the rules and interpret them.

At the 89th NCAA Convention in January 1995, suggestions
that the compensation rules for players be changed prompted a
defensive circling of the wagons reminiscent of the colleges' remarkable unity in the late 1950s and early 1960s. In that earlier
time, some state commissions and courts ruled that the grant-in-
aid constituted an employment contract. Colleges that deplored the
relatively new grant system and those that embraced it as a step

toward honesty joined together at the time to oppose such a notion and quickly agreed that the grant-in-aid contract terms should be rewritten, although the net result would remain the same.

The theme of the 1995 NCAA annual meeting was the welfare of student-athletes. At the outset, however, the NCAA leadership unanimously agreed it would be heresy to permit athletes to have equal access to the marketplace, say, for example, like coaches. Labeling such ideas as "pay," the outgoing NCAA president, Joseph N. Crowley, president of the University of Nevada, Reno, said the day the colleges pay their players would be the day that his university would abolish college sports. The head of the NCAA Presidents Commission, Judith E. N. Albino, president of the University of Colorado, said such a bizarre action would force the colleges to change dramatically the way they do business. "It would fundamentally change what we are about...and put us into a business unrelated to education," she said.[5]

The highest paid conference commissioner must have thought the Albino-Crowley commentary was fine as philosophical grist for the NCAA press conference, which was held January 7, but he didn't want it to stop there. Jim Delany of the Big Ten Conference told the Associated Press January 8 that if the players "want a living wage...let them go to the NBA." Commissioner Delany, having received a one-year 11.5 percent salary boost to $256,500 for 1994–95, with his pension and life insurance benefits enjoying a similar incremental increase, failed to specify how many college seniors each year would find a living in the NBA. He further suggested to the AP a similar escape valve for undercompensated college football players, but was short on how many regular jobs would become available each year in the NFL and Canadian league for those college players, seniors and underclassmen, who felt a need for a "living wage." Might a college player enter into negotiations through an agent to determine the value of a likely pro contract before deciding between a college grant-in-aid and the pro offer? No way! That would be a violation of NCAA rules.

Jim, a former NCAA enforcement department investigator, is a leading player among the big league commissioners. The major conference chief executives, having distanced themselves from enforcement problems, are thoroughly dedicated to increasing their conferences' revenues. A side effect of these entrepreneurial efforts is that if your conference has overall higher revenue than the next conference, the commissioner of No. 1 should receive more money. Apparently that's why, at least for the moment, Jim Delany of the Big Ten is running No. 1 to Commissioner Roy Kramer's No. 2 compensation package as provided by the Southeastern Conference. Gene Corrigan, of the Atlantic Coast Conference, another expansion-minded executive, was in third place.[6]

At that January 7, 1995, press conference in San Diego, President Albino was considerably more focused than Commissioner Delany. Her comments came straight from the NCAA legal counsel's textbook; the amateur rules and myriad supporting eligibility rules are necessary to maintain the "essential character" of college sports and, for competitive reasons, there must be a common, national contract among the colleges. If NCAA general counsel Jack Kitchin had been asked, he would have added that such agreements are not violations of the Sherman Antitrust Act and are defensible under the commerce and contract clauses of the federal constitution. Maybe so, but what about Justice Oliver Wendell Holmes' comment that "freedom of contract begins where equality of bargaining power begins."[7]

The defensive responses in 1995 about "pay," however, distort the issue. The colleges are *already* paying their athletes. The grant-in-aid established that by setting up a more generous stipend than what is available to other similar, but nonvarsity, students. The uniform stipend is awarded without regard to the financial need or the academic attainment of the recipient. The present debate, in such forums as the NCAA's own newspaper, has to do with whether the pay scale and salary cap are sufficient. College leaders argue that a free education is sufficient pay for a varsity athlete, even though it is subject to being terminated or renewed annually, based on what the coaching staff decides.

Simply put, I advocate that the colleges *stop* their present national uniform pay-for-play policies and evenhandedly treat athletes like other students. Award them financial aid on the same terms and conditions, through the same processes, and by the same financial aid authority, as established for all other undergraduates. The athlete may access the marketplace just as other students exploit their own special talents, whether they are musicians playing gigs on the weekends, journalism students working piecemeal for newspapers, or announcers for the college radio station filing reports for CNN radio.

My proposals follow.

Free the Athletes

Congress should enact and the president should sign a comprehensive College Athletes' Bill of Rights. This is *not* a suggestion for new government controls; on the contrary, it is an argument that the federal government should require deregulation of a monopoly business operated by not-for-profit institutions contracting together to achieve maximum financial returns. The Justice Department has chosen not to act. The Congress should.

Such a guarantee of rights and freedoms would go far in treating the twin curses of exploitation and hypocrisy that have bedeviled college athletics in direct proportion to its intensified commercialization.

The bill of rights would preempt the state-by-state legislative actions which irritate the NCAA and the colleges, but from which they feel immune. Such state efforts, most of them related to due process issues at the moment, are pushed by legislators who sense something is out of kilter in big-time sports at their state universities. NCAA headquarters and the regional conference commissioners have dismissed these state outbursts as sporadic guerrilla warfare. True, the NCAA to date has won over those states that have tried to intrude into its affairs. It argues that the colleges and the NCAA are engaged in interstate commerce and, thus, the federal constitution is applicable to its affairs in the interest of uniform national rules; the NCAA contends state-by-state action would destroy that uniformity.

An athletes' bill of rights would guarantee that players need not sign away freedoms available to other students solely because they engage in college athletics. The bill would strike down unreasonable prohibitions ostensibly designed to equalize competition but which, in fact, effectively curtail the athletes' freedom.

The present awesome reach of these NCAA laws can only be understood by recognizing the "worst-case" mentality of today's college legislators and NCAA rules interpreters. In their eyes, if more freedom is given to the people (e.g., athletes or alumni), some unidentified college will gain a *recruiting advantage* (pre-enroll-ment enticement of a future player) or a *competitive advantage* (special beneficial treatment of an enrolled player). These open-ended terms now are interpreted by committees with almost unlim-ited imaginations as to the unbalancing evils that lurk on every big-time sports campus.

Throughout my tenure, realists believed far more in rules to maintain parity *during* recruiting than in the illusory concept that, after athletes arrive on campus, everyone shall be treated the same at all Division I colleges. Frank Remington, former chairman of the Committee on Infractions, recently confirmed that, within the col-legiate family as well as outside, there remains considerably more support for NCAA enforcement action in the former area than in the latter.[8] I believe deregulation is in order at both points.

Tom Osborne, Nebraska's head football coach since 1973, has despaired many times about the NCAA's picayune rules interpreta-tions. Shortly before I left the NCAA, he complained of the decision that athletes unable to go home for Thanksgiving could not be entertained by Cornhuskers boosters. The NCAA ruled, in effect, that a bountiful buffet in the home of a well-to-do Nebraskan would be a competitive advantage, in that players at Nebraska would be happier than, say, those at Iowa, who might have to eat Thanksgiving dinner at McDonald's. Another explanation for that decision was that if such were permitted, Coach Osborne would use it as a sales pitch during the next recruiting season. Why not let generosity to college players happen wherever people want to be generous?

The bill of rights should deal with five issues of freedom and welfare.

1. *Repeal the rule that establishes the NCAA as national arbiter*

of the term, value, and conditions of an athlete's "scholarship" and as controller of the athlete's outside income during his or her collegiate tenure. Whereas the NCAA defends its policies in the name of amateurism and level playing fields, they actually are a device to divert the money elsewhere.

Collegiate amateurism is a not a moral issue; it is an economic camouflage for monopoly practice. Some 58 years ago in his book *Farewell to Sport,* Paul Gallico, a celebrated sportswriter who became a noted novelist, wrote, "The thing that is so inexplicable is that there is nothing actually wrong with what the colleges are doing to promote good football teams for themselves except their stubborn and dishonest insistence that they are still playing the game under the old standards.... The old standards no longer exist and for that matter are probably no longer useful or valid. But by refusing to admit this, the colleges have managed to get themselves involved in a dirty and subversive business."[9]

In the 1950s, many of us set out to challenge Gallico's view of our world through new NCAA rules with strong enforcement. Our efforts, sincere though they might have been, were overrun by the pervasive influence of big money, national publicity, and entertainment excitement.

Today, observers of the sports scene echo the long-ago Gallico commentary. The *Wall Street Journal,* recognizing the business aspects of college sports, gives much attention to its competitive and commercial dealings, especially through columnist Fred Klein. In 1985, Klein noted that the real problem "is that colleges are violating their educational and parental missions in their lust for sports cash and glory... and athletes' rights need to be protected."[10]

One sold-out home football game at the University of Tennessee's magnificent Neyland Stadium can generate more than $2 million of income. The players, if they call home after the game using an athletics department credit card, are in violation of NCAA rules. The local service station operator cannot give the star linebacker a free tank of gas after he stops the Alabama Crimson Tide's late rally, but the athletics director, key helpers, and the head coach and assistants can telephone football compadres across the land

and then drive away from the game in new automobiles provided free by local dealers.

Despite its reliance on the competitive-equity defense when it comes to controlling players, the NCAA does not prohibit the colleges' open bidding for winning coaches. After eight years at Kansas State, his alma mater, basketball coach Lon Kruger was getting $82,000 in base annual salary and a total package worth $200,000 per year. Florida, determined to get its program back on track, signed Kruger to a five-year contract that—depending on incentives, shoe endorsements, and basketball camp income—could be worth $1.7 million. Kruger started work with the 1990–91 season.

Taking a cue from the Jerry Tarkanian contract model, Kruger's agreement provided for a bonus of one month's salary if he led the Gators to the NCAA tournament, another one-and-a-half month's salary if he reached the Final Four, and $30,000 in cash if the Gators played in the championship game. If 80 percent of his players graduate, Kruger would receive an additional 10 percent of his annual wage. These terms have been improved in succeeding years.[11] For the players, however, there is no money either for winning the tournament or for graduating, although they are the ones playing and going to class.

Kansas State could not match the Florida package. The NCAA level-playing-field rules do not apply here. The season following Kruger's departure Kansas State had a 13-15 record, the first time the Wildcats had finished under .500 since 1983–84. The next three seasons in the Big Eight, after 1990–91, K-State had a 16-26 conference record, or .381. The 'Gators played in the 1994 NCAA Final Four with Kruger at the controls.

Millionaire boosters are free to help their college acquire a coach. They can contribute to a foundation as a means of channeling financial benefits to him (as in the case of Lute Olson at Arizona); help underwrite new offices for the head coach, sky boxes in a refurbished stadium, and enlarged training facilities that impress young recruits and attract them to the college. All of this is legal under NCAA rules, although it tilts the playing field and gives the rich and consistent college winner a continuing advantage.

When there is the possibility that the money will go to the

student-athlete, however, the NCAA becomes adamant: There shall be uniform compensation for the players in the form of one-year contracts. No outside money!

The Athletes' Bill of Rights should repeal the one-year limit on grants and scholarships because it is simply an artificial ceiling held in place for the purposes of shuffling player personnel and allocating money elsewhere. There should be no national law restricting the term of the financial aid awarded by individual colleges to individual students.

In the 1950s, amateur ruling bodies such as the state high school groups, the NCAA, AAU, and U.S. Olympic Committee spoke of cradle-to-grave amateurism for *all* sports. Gradually, most sports governing organizations—the U.S. Olympic Committee being the most obvious—abandoned their moralistic stand on amateurism. The NCAA seems to be an island, defending its exclusive view for the benefit of its clients, the member colleges.

Beyond removing the artificial salary cap set by grants-in-aid, colleges or their benefactors should be free to provide financial assistance to athletes to attend summer school or pursue education in the years after the athlete's eligibility has expired. If a student-athlete is needy, if he or she combines athletic skill with academic excellence, a college should be free to offer that student more. Surely academic excellence combined with athletic brilliance is worth more than the amounts routinely handed out today to academically deficient players. The colleges have specific policies about the administration of financial assistance to their students. They should be followed without the national dictates of the NCAA.

NCAA Executive Director Richard D. Schultz, after meetings with the NCAA Presidents Commission and the Knight Foundation presidential study group, cut through the flotsam of the amateurism argument in June 1990, when he told a meeting at the college athletics directors annual convention, "There are a lot of legal problems with giving an outright stipend [to an athlete]. You immediately establish an employer/employee relationship, which creates other kinds of liabilities such as workmen's compensation. It would probably also make all athletics income vulnerable to income tax, and then everybody would have a problem if they had to start paying income tax on money such as television revenue."[12] Dick's comments were those of a practical practitioner. The federal tax code has indeed replaced amateurism as the rationale for the current rule book.

I don't believe the IRS code will prove any more acceptable as an argument for the status quo than the recommendation that dissatisfied athletes can seek a living wage in the NBA or NFL. The point is that in today's commercialized marketplace, the NCAA has no right to dictate a standard grant-in-aid with a salary cap and then embargo the players' income for their entire varsity careers. The college should award financial assistance to athletes on the same bases and through the same agency that makes financial aid decisions for all students. The need formula utilized in determining financial aid packages takes into account job income and other sources of support for the student. There are penalties for false reporting. For the particularly bright student, there are high dollar scholarships. The university should apply its formula to the athlete in the same manner as other students.

2. *End the NCAA ban that prevents players from holding a job during the school year.* The reasoning behind this one is that an athlete at Alabama might not earn as much working in a Tuscaloosa men's clothing store as a USC player could earn as an apprentice stagehand in a Hollywood studio. Such job income supposedly would further unbalance Division I, giving a recruiting advantage to teams where better job opportunities exist. A thin argument indeed, since a case can be made for clean air and safe driving in Tuscaloosa compared to smog and life-threatening, pedal-to-the-metal drives on the Hollywood Freeway. Every community has its own pluses and minuses.

The no-job rule also is defended on the amateur theory. There might be pay for no work or the pay might be higher than the going rate for a nonathlete doing similar work. What difference does most of that make? Employment and tax records are available. If a business pays for slovenly work, it will do more harm to the business than to college athletics. The reverse is that the athlete may benefit far more from on-the-job experience than from an extra hour of pumping iron in the college weight room.

As to the rationale that an athlete doesn't have time to work eight hours on a weekend handling inventory at the local K-Mart or selling haberdashery, the coach can easily reduce practice demands and mandatory film viewing. College sports are not supposed to be year-round activities.

Shaun Jordan, the Texas Longhorns' 1991 NCAA champion sprint swimmer, who once won five events in one meet, battled the NCAA over this general issue beginning when he was a freshman. It was then that he, along with a friend, printed 150 T-shirts with the motto, "Don't Mess With Texas Swimming." They sold out the batch in one day and decided to make a business of custom T-shirts—a business that apparently is now operating in several states. The NCAA blocked Shaun's active role in this; he went undercover and became a silent partner.[13]

Whether or not athletes should work during the playing season is a judgment they should make after consultation with their academic advisors, but without the "federal government" of college athletics preempting the right of individual choice.

3. *Require repeal of the transfer rule, which unreasonably binds athletes to their current colleges.* This restriction once had an academic purpose. When freshmen were required to wait one year before competing in varsity sports, it was argued that transfer students also needed a one-year adjustment period free from the pressures of varsity competition. The rule, however, has become a player control measure in the hands of the coach, a sort of option clause.

If the one-year college residence requirement for transfer players is limited to a transfer during the athlete's playing season, that protects the team. Any other transfer restrictions are unnecessary coercion.

The athlete, at most, has only a one-year financial deal. At the end of that year, the college can tell the player good-bye without penalty. Why should he or she not be equally free to bid the college farewell? Then consider the coach, who has a multiyear contract yet jumps ship without *any* residence penalty. Shortly before his Michigan basketball team played in the 1989 NCAA tournament, Bill Frieder had already made a deal for a new job at Arizona State.

Michigan told him to leave immediately. As Frieder's Wolverines won it all under his former assistant, Steve Fisher, Bill was busy in California recruiting for his new employer.

NCAA rules even block players from receiving financial aid at colleges to which the player transfers, as Lawrence Funderburke learned. Funderburke is a high-skill, 6'8" basketball player who ended up at Ohio State in his home town of Columbus. Lawrence first enrolled at Indiana University in the fall of 1989. Coach Bob Knight subsequently banned him from the team during the player's freshman year.

The player enrolled at a junior college, planning to transfer later to another NCAA college. He had the University of Louisville in mind. Knight used NCAA rules to block the deal. Knight was clear: no release for him to go to Louisville, although somewhere else might be okay. Apparently, the Louisville program was out because it was too successful.

Funderburke returned to Indiana as a regular student in the fall of 1990 without a grant-in-aid, intending to serve enough time to clear up his transfer status. He had a Pell grant along with a student loan, but he was not out for basketball. Knight, even with no grant-in-aid to protect, still controlled Lawrence.

Bret Bearup, a Louisville lawyer and former college basketball player, tried to help Funderburke. He understood Funderburke was confused by the rulings, and he quickly found out why. "If Funderburke is not receiving a grant-in-aid and is not out for basketball, why does Knight have any authority here?" Bearup inquired of the NCAA. "He hasn't played basketball for a year."

Bearup said he never received a clear explanation. Talking to me about it later, he asked, "You were there when the transfer legislation was adopted. Was one of the purposes to stop a college from tampering with a player in whom another college has invested a grant-in-aid?"

"Not completely, but that's a fair summary of the present purpose," I replied.

"Well, there's no grant-in-aid involved now. More important why doesn't the rule and penalty run against the tampering college?" he asked. "Why hold a young athlete hostage and deal with him as personal chattel? The NCAA rules are vulnerable because they lack respect for individual rights. The organization is destined to be balkanized."[14]

Bearup was predicting that NCAA rules would be attacked in state courts by legislators and civil rights activists. This has happened, but the NCAA has so far successfully defended itself by citing the commerce and contract terms of the U.S. Constitution. Thus, the NCAA enforcement of its rules, so the argument goes, must be consistent and they would become inconsistent and essentially inoperative under a patchwork of different state court decisions. Since the NCAA has chosen commerce and contract law as its weapons of defense, it will have to live with the consequences in arguing Sherman Act antitrust issues on other fronts.

The NCAA at present is busy fighting a major class action suit against its rule that limits restricted-earnings coaches in Division I to $12,000 per year plus $4,000 from summer camps. These plaintiffs are following the trail broken by the Supreme Court decision striking down the NCAA television plan. The coaches' lead attorney, Dennis Cross of Kansas City, argues first that the NCAA coaches rule is naked price fixing and a per se Section 1 violation of the Sherman Act. The court may choose to apply the rule of reason test, as was done by the Oklahoma City court in the television case. Even so, the NCAA will have to show some pro competitive benefits from the coaches' limits, and those benefits appear theoretical at best.

In my judgment, the one-year waiting period for transfer athletes is even more vulnerable. I realize that at present different legal arguments pertain here, but skipping that debate for the moment, the simple point is that valid local academic reasons stated by the receiving institution should govern the transfer status of students, athlete or not, without national player control influences.

4. *Force the NCAA to allow players to consult agents in making sports career choices.* Today, in the eyes of the NCAA, even reviewing a professional sport money offer and contract terms with a lawyer who is not an identified sports agent renders the player ineligible at all NCAA colleges. There may be an exception here if

the lawyer qualifies as a long-time counselor to the family of the athlete. This is true at a time when big-time coaches use agents in dealing with their colleges.

Ced Dempsey, athletics director at the University of Arizona at the time, hired Lute Olson from the University of Iowa as head basketball coach at Arizona in 1984. When the University of Kentucky job opened up with Eddie Sutton's forced departure, Lute Olson interviewed, figuring this would be a good bargaining chip in negotiating a new contract at Arizona. Olson and Ced Dempsey were good friends and men of comparable temperament. Ced was flabbergasted to find he could not deal directly with his coach but would have to deal with Lute Olson's agent in working out a new contract.

Ken Hatfield left the Air Force Academy to become head football coach at Arkansas in 1984. He was grateful for the chance to return to his alma mater (class of 1965), and Athletics Director Frank Broyles, the university president, and key trustees and alumni knew they had the right man for the long haul. Hatfield had played for Broyles in the 1960s, presumably creating an enduring kind of loyalty.

Soon Broyles found himself renegotiating his coach's contract with an agent. The big issue was whether, if Hatfield were fired, the university would pay him all monies he would lose, including the customary side deals that coaches have. Arkansas's position was that, in the event of dismissal, the university would not be responsible for anything except the salary they were paying Ken. The agent told Broyles that if this happened, the university would be sued over these issues. Hatfield would not sign the contract. "Ken felt he could go to court if we ever fired him and sue us and win all these perks, and that was the stalemate never resolved the last two-and-a-half years he was here," Frank told me.[15] Ken opened the 1990 football season as head coach at Clemson.

This is a by-product of big-time entertainment, reading like a Hollywood scenario in which the studio negotiates with the agent to keep its star performer on the payroll. However, the young players who make it all possible are banned from seeking out the best financial deals for themselves.

Braxton Lee Banks, a fifth-year football player at Notre Dame, had in hand a full ride grant-in-aid in 1990 valued around $16,000 according to Notre Dame. Eligible for the NFL draft, he wanted to find out what a pro football team might offer. He put his name in the NFL player pool. He consulted a lawyer. The NCAA ruled him ineligible. Notre Dame declined to appeal his case to the NCAA. Since an athlete does not have individual NCAA appeal rights, this blocked possible relief for him. A federal district court declined to intervene. The Supreme Court declined to hear the plaintiff's appeal. Banks ended up without a grant-in-aid or a pro contract.

5. *State legislatures should amend state workmen's compensation laws to require that major colleges and universities provide coverage for varsity athletes and other students engaged in auxiliary enterprises.* Paradoxically, NCAA rules adopted by the colleges prohibit all member colleges from providing athletes long-term insurance but permit athletes to borrow money to pay for such insurance. The NCAA, as an organization, is going to begin paying for some insurance of this nature, but the colleges, themselves, cannot and will not do so because of the haunting prospect that to do so would create an employee-employer relationship.

Enact a Competitive Opportunity Plan

There will be those who will argue that an athletes' bill of rights will wildly unbalance the system and destroy college athletics. This is the customary response of all monopolists. The point is that the self-defined equality of the present system, bought mainly at the expense of players, is much like that portrayed in George Orwell's *Animal Farm:* some are clearly more equal than others—and here the most equal of all are indeed small in number.

By enacting a Competitive Opportunity Plan, the NCAA could provide effective ways for college losers to try to catch up with winners—other than by under-the-table money or academic hocus-pocus. At present, the acceptable catch-up strategies are costly and reminiscent of margin speculators in the stock market borrowing more money to shore up their deteriorating positions.

Iowa State University of the Big Eight Conference, facing increased competition from the invasion of four Texas football power teams as new conference members, hired a new coach in the winter of 1994–95. Iowa State had enjoyed only three winning seasons in 16 years. The university president assured his new coach, Dan McCarney, that $8 million would be spent on new football offices, meeting rooms, locker rooms, and weight rooms. Better practice facilities and a new playing surface also would be forthcoming and, possibly, a loosening of academic standards would follow.[16] Kansas State University, relatively content in winning about 50 percent of its football games over the past five years, reacted to the tougher competitive climate by earmarking $850,000 to an "athletic academic learning center." A Board of Regents executive explained, "it's something...all big-time athletic departments are going to do. It's kind of a recruiting device."[17]

A coercive aspect of the power conferences' dynastic rules, reinforced by NCAA regulations, is that no college may be a member of such a conference unless it sponsors *both* major league I-A football and Division I basketball. As the Iowa State Cyclones allocated some $9 million to persuade Coach McCarney to take the job, their athletics director, Gene Smith, said several nonmajor sports may be eliminated because "we'll have major problems if we don't turn football around." This demonstrates the imprisoning effect of monopoly rules. Tomorrow's corporate thinkers in the conference's executive suite could easily consider another rearrangement of the Big 12, spinning off those that can't average at least 35,000 paid admissions for league home football games. Similar situations exist in the other major conferences.

Under the dogmatic NCAA rules, the underdogs are given little room for improvement. A Competitive Opportunity Plan is in order, and the principles of such a plan would be the following.

1. Permit weaker programs to offer more paid visits to their campuses by prospective athletes, the additional number and length of time for this exception to be subject to periodic review and adjustment.

2. Accord the have-not colleges relief from the numbers limitations imposed on sport-by-sport financial aid awards and on squad sizes for official practice sessions. These exceptions would be limited in duration and reevaluated periodically.

3. Impose limits on the number of players receiving practice gear, the size of traveling squads, and the squad size for home games.

Squad limits and freedom to transfer are critical to the entire exercise, since they would deter the stockpiling of superior players by the most successful teams.

Current grant-in-aid-limits do not stop stockpiling, much of which takes place outside of those limits. Furthermore, squad limits are easy to police. If the dominant conference teams do not want to give the weak members of their own conference, or the lower two-thirds of Division I-A, a reasonable chance to catch up, then the biggies should reorganize themselves into a national conference of 30 to 50 dominant teams and stop holding athletes hostage under NCAA rules by using the questionable legal defense of promoting equity in competition for 900-plus colleges when such equity doesn't exist even in Division I or I-A.[18]

With squad limits in place and the transfer rule modified, I do not believe teams could monopolize the great athletes at the rate they do today. Outstanding players want to play, and they will go where that opportunity exists. They can weigh the merits of a one-year grant-in-aid against a four-year guarantee, the advantages of the southern California lifestyle to that of Tuscaloosa, whether being the number three quarterback at Michigan is better than starting at Wake Forest, or whether academic support services at North Carolina move their athletes further up the learning ladder than a recruiting rival that offers a better-paying job.

These new approaches would cost the college athletics department considerably less per player. Job income and hometown support become legal and are available. In the handling of college scholarships and grants awards, follow one simple rule. For student-athletes, the financial aid officer and the university financial aid committee shall follow the same rules and policies that apply to all other undergraduate students. These policies and the decisions implementing them should be on the record and available for appropriate inspection. If the athlete has job income or hometown financial help, the player declares the amount of that assistance the same as any other student. The college then takes that into consideration in determining the amount of university scholarship or grant money to be awarded.

Practice and game squad limits and free substitution are compatible for the sport of football. Professional teams and leagues have been nurtured by and profited from practice and squad limits. As to smaller varsity squads in college football, this may require greater coaching ingenuity to prepare players to handle more than one one-way position. Considering today's staff salaries, no one should complain about working overtime.

My aim here is not to downplay intercollegiate athletics. I simply want to see the market work honestly, with fairness to all participants, including the players. Coaches routinely condemn squad limits, for both home and away games, as un-American, demoralizing, and unfair to the players. I wish they would speak out with comparable fervor against the uniform NCAA compensation cap. In any event, I would hope they abandon their fairness-to-the-players argument in this instance since that type of prevent defense has holes in it.

A friend reacted to these competitive balancing proposals by asking, "Who in the world is ever going to get the power college teams to agree to anything like this?"

"They won't," I responded, "but once the courts or the Athletes' Bill of Rights, or both, strike down the present 'level field' playing rules that imprison today's athletes, the colleges will be forced to new measures. I believe many of the colleges' present player control measures are vulnerable under existing federal laws."

Break Up Trusts, Combinations, and Monopolies

As I worked on this book, I reread the works of several sportswriters, more than a few of whom I know. There is a litany of criticism throughout many of their columns, most of it centered on the charge of hypocrisy.

When I started out as a sportswriter, I considered Paul Gallico to be a celebrity, because he had risen above the rest of us ink-stained wretches to become a novelist. Looking again at his *Farewell to Sport,* I came across this prescient sentence. "It does not take much of an imagination to picture an athletic governing body as a monopolistic organization operating an air-tight racket of supplying cheap athletic labor."[19]

Gallico was referring mainly to the AAU of that era, but the ensuing half century has verified his instinct that protecting young people from commercial evils is a transparent excuse for monopoly operations that benefit others. The colleges do take part in trusts (i.e., groups in which control of the members is vested in a single entity), combinations (an association of firms for a commercial purpose), and monopoly practices (exclusive control of a commodity or service).

Prosecutors and the courts, with the support of the public, should use antitrust laws to break up the collegiate cartel—not just in athletics but possibly in other aspects of collegiate life as well.

"A few rules are essential..."

In 1975, a Supreme Court decision in the case of *Goldfarb v. Virginia State Bar* set in motion a train of legal reasoning that has not yet run its course. Goldfarb had advertised his services as an attorney under a fee schedule that undercut the minimum fees promulgated by the Virginia State Bar. The court ruled that the bar organization, despite its status as a not-for-profit professional group, was engaging in price fixing in violation of the Sherman antitrust laws.

Before Goldfarb, the Virginia State Bar and the NCAA both had been among the many not-for-profit educational or professional and philanthropic organizations considered exempt from the federal antitrust laws. In short, *Goldfarb* said that lawyers are competing in the marketplace and a not-for-profit association may not shield them from antitrust law.

In 1976, two Alabama assistant coaches of Bear Bryant attacked NCAA limits on the number of coaches. Instead of honoring the NCAA claim to flat antitrust exemption, the Fifth Circuit Court of Appeals in New Orleans elected to examine the issues under the "rule of reason." The court found that our limits on the number of coaches were reasonable because they were consistent with NCAA objectives in fostering athletics competition by curtailing monopolistic practices of big schools and because they were an attempt to reorient athletics programs as part of the educational system.

We won the case. It was hailed as a victory, but the subtext carried an important message. The Fifth Circuit had taken *Goldfarb* another step, saying the NCAA was no longer automatically exempt. The colleges would have to justify combined national activity suggesting monopolistic practice through case-by-case analysis under the rule of reason.

George Gangwere, the NCAA's general counsel at the time, promptly warned us of the chink in the NCAA's armor. "You can no longer expect the court to dismiss an antitrust contention without some of the careful analysis customarily applied to similar acts of business or commercial organizations."

Within six years, the Supreme Court in 1984 struck down the NCAA television plan, ruling that the NCAA with its TV controls had entered the business world and violated the antitrust laws. There was reassuring commentary in the court's opinion about the goals of amateurism, but the escalating commercialization of college athletics and the insatiable appetite of college legislators for more rules presaged future problems.

In a 1988 case, the NCAA argued in the Fifth Circuit Court of Appeals that its eligibility rules "are not subject to antitrust laws because, unlike the television restrictions [in the Supreme Court case], the eligibility rules have purely or primarily noncommercial objectives."

The Fifth Circuit cited the Supreme Court's comment that the NCAA markets competition, and "horizontal restraints on competition are essential if the product is to be available at all." It added that "in some sporting enterprises, a few rules are essential to survival." In other words, to make competition possible, member teams may act in concert to form leagues and enact common rules.

The Fifth Circuit warned, however, that the rule-of-reason analysis will apply on a case-by-case basis regardless of the stated intent of the NCAA. The judges said the "essential inquiry under the rule-of-reason analysis is whether the challenged restraint enhances competition."

Jack Kitchin, present general counsel of the NCAA, argues that the NCAA can legally adopt rules to enhance competition and "to preserve the character quality of the 'product' by defining it as a college-based, academically orientated activity." He states that this makes it a different product than the professional one.

Although presented somewhat differently, this NCAA argument is not dissimilar to what we advanced during the CFA challenge to NCAA TV controls.[20] The questions essentially remain the same: do these many rules have a noncommercial purpose? Do they serve competition? Are they necessary to define a product so it can be available? The colleges argue the multiplicity of rules are requisite to giving Ohio University or Eastern Michigan a chance to beat Notre Dame in football, or the University of Missouri at Kansas City a chance to make the Final Four in basketball.

The 512-page *1994–95 NCAA Manual* contains more than the "few rules" mentioned by the Fifth Circuit. I contend most of the restraints are *not* there to enhance competition between and among the colleges of NCAA Division I (and certainly not between and among the colleges in the three divisions). The rules, based on a turn-of-the-century theory of amateurism, enforce a modern economic order. Today's educational reformers seem increasingly content to engage in a pedantic tautology. Players may not receive money, except what we give them, because they must remain amateurs to be eligible under our rules. They are amateurs if our rules say they are. Thus, they may only receive what our rules permit.

Paraphrasing a point made by Arthur Kempton in his 1991 essay, "Native Sons," which appeared in the *New York Review of Books,* the college player cannot sell his own feet (the coach does that) nor can he sell his own name (the college will do that).[21] This is the plantation mentality resurrected and blessed by today's campus executives.

The collusive aspects of U.S. higher education are not limited to athletics. The U.S. Justice Department investigated the practice of financial aid "reviews" by the Ivy colleges and others, refusing to accept a 1991 settlement offer by the schools.[22]

In 1989, a Wesleyan student, Roger Kingsepp, filed a suit against the school, saying that Wesleyan and 11 other private institutions had "engaged in a conspiracy to fix or artificially inflate the price of tuition and financial aid." This issue led to broader legal confrontation between the Justice Department and more than 20 colleges. The Justice Department considered the matter to be a case of collusion against the consumer and reasoned this was one explanation why the average tuition at private four-year universities increased fivefold while the consumer price index rose threefold between 1971–72 and 1989–90.

Subsequently, the Justice Department launched a study of what had become known as the financial-aid overlap group, which embraced 23 prominent colleges in the East, including the Ivies. Justice believed the colleges regularly discussed among themselves financial aid offers to the same individual students—the relative mix of scholarship money, loan funds, and job income required to pay the student's expenses.[23] The colleges eventually reached a settlement with Justice by promising not to share specific information regarding the financial need of student applicants or the financial aid packages being offered to the students. The settlement details were sealed as confidential, but the colleges did not concede any liability or that they had violated antitrust laws.

A meeting among business competitors to harmonize their bids on a contract is usually called a conspiracy. More than 900 members agreeing by contract through the NCAA to issue common contracts to young people recruited to play on various sports teams seems to fit that niche.

The many rules of the colleges, although officially defended on the basis of "competitive equity," should be challenged on grounds of "human equity" and individual freedom. Since full-time college faculty members are free to receive substantial consultation fees from outside interests or participate in business enterprises, surely they can rally in support of their students being freed from university rules that not only cap scholarship money but limit the private initiative of students in marketing themselves—whether it's their own feet or their own T-shirts.

Since the same college people who harvest the returns set the rules, issue the interpretations, rule on athletes' eligibility, and decide how the annual profits should be divided, I believe state and federal challenges to these artificial restraints will be necessary. Those in control believe they stand above and are immune to such threats. Higher education's defense essentially is that the colleges improve the life quality of their students and how they do it is their business.

Require a Report Card in Academics

Academic standards for athletes will improve little until colleges establish respectable, published standards for themselves and for all students. College deans, faculty members, and presidents are disinclined to use accrediting agencies to raise the academic performance level of the colleges and universities the agencies review, but they believe in specific, national standards legislated through the NCAA for athletes.

Minimal as they may be, the NCAA standards stand as testimony to the need for a national definition of what should be expected of a high school student by a "higher education" institution. In offering remedial courses and general education opportunities, college educators bemoan the failures of their secondary school colleagues. On the other end, there are devastating criticisms of the low level of academic achievement by many college graduates. The latest confirmation comes from the Harvard Business School faculty, which has taken steps to require incoming students to master basic writing and math skills before they begin their quest for a master's degree. If remedial work is necessary it is to be completed before the student enters the degree program.[24]

The undergraduate educational establishment needs to provide American parents, donors, and taxpayers with an annual "value-added" report card showing the degree of academic improvement of their students after two years of college as well as an exit evaluation at time of graduation exercises. The four-year colleges accept billions of tax dollars annually through federally financed programs. The colleges should be required by Congress to provide annual assessments of the progress of their federally assisted students.

The principle is simple: teachers grade students on how well they learn. The nation deserves to know how well the faculties teach. The colleges, for obvious reasons, prefer the current conditions, citing academic freedom arguments and "we know best" theories. But if the public is to accept the higher education label, it seems fair to ask "higher than what?" and to learn to what degree the student's academic capacity has been increased beyond his or her high school accomplishments.

The report card the colleges owe the nation is not one of those massive, conglomerate statistical overviews that the Department of Education regularly releases, but an annual individual college measurement for the record.

The first standard should be entrance statistics similar to the SAT or ACT test scores already required by most colleges but organized to work in tandem with mid-college, and exit tests. Much more important than the absolute scores would be the difference between the entrance, mid-college, and exit figures, revealing how far the college has moved its entering first-year students forward at the two-year and senior levels.

This would have intrinsic diagnostic value, and while individual scores would remain confidential, the public should see the high, low, average, and median records of appropriately grouped segments of the same student population.

As a part of the state's and federal government's requirement of reports about the "value-added" learning financed by its billions, the regional accrediting agencies for higher education, such as the North Central and Southern associations, should be required to implement minimum standards. The imprimatur of these agencies is needed before taxpayers' money is released. The agencies should analyze weak programs within a university, in addition to their overall, campuswide review, and their reports should be made public. The 10-year period of their approval should be shortened to 5 years.

Higher education leaders have stressed the value of diversity for as long as I have worked among them. It is appropriate, and overdue, to define that diversity and to appraise the value of the respective course offerings with respect to achieving the stated course goals and advancing the academic goals of the students. Mid-college and exit test results would be a part of that evaluation by the accrediting agencies. These evaluations should be publicized just as the athletics classifications and probationary actions of the NCAA are on the public record.

Publicly Report Collegiate Finances

When no taxes are paid by an industry that generates annual income of around $230 million from 18 sanctioned football bowl games and one basketball tournament, Americans paying higher gasoline taxes, increased property taxes, and 6.5 percent sales taxes have a legitimate query: why?

To clear up the mystique of college athletics financing, I suggest a federal Financial Disclosure requirement that would generate annual reports by each adjunct college business enterprise generating more than $1 million a year from all sources including product sales, television and radio revenue, donations, student fees, faculty and student ticket purchases, and allocations from the college's general education funds.

These enterprises are considered educational, tax-exempt functions although the colleges aggressively compete with tax-paying businesses in a number of commercial areas.

The colleges develop new patented products, market diet control information and health newsletters to the public at large, operate "bookstores" that offer a variety of items in competition with taxpaying commercial stores, supervise the sale of national TV and radio rights, and play bowl games for Mobil, Federal Express, and Thrifty Car Rental. Higher education is into commerce.

There is nothing wrong with not-for-profit, tax-exempt groups conducting sideline business enterprises, and the Internal Revenue Service poses the first test as to whether they should pay taxes on their profits. The court is the determiner of disputes between federal taxing authorities and the colleges.

For years, but without much success, the St. Louis office of the Internal Revenue Service has sought to tax the NCAA's commercial income. The NCAA has become increasingly concerned about its tax exemption. In 1992–93, for example, $133.6 million (77.6 percent) of its $172.0 million income came from television, confirming the NCAA as a negotiating agency for its big-time members in the television business world.

The IRS Dallas office long believed that bowl game income is subject to business taxes, not to mention in-season radio rights and game program income. More recently, Jerry Tarkanian was fighting an IRS deficiency notice claiming he owes $121,525 plus penalties for failing to report as taxable income the approximately $35,000 worth of game tickets he received annually from UNLV between 1987 and 1991 (he received 223 tickets per game).[25]

The NCAA and football bowl game authorities have responded to IRS inquiries by noting that the colleges are tax exempt, and "we are only performing a valuable service for them." After all, the "excess receipts" or year-end "surplus" (i.e., profits) go back to the colleges. Arguing for their own organizational tax exemption, the NCAA in essence contends that "We are only the sum of our parts."

Drawing the line on the commercial proclivities of the colleges rests with state and federal tax authorities, but the necessity of full disclosure of college athletics income, expenditures, and the use of tax-exempt funds is an essential part of any effort to put the facts on the record.

Today, college athletics leaders contend they are facing a financial crisis. The repetition of this refrain is hypnotic; too many listeners are lulled into acceptance. One who is not, and who has become increasingly skeptical, is Bill Rhoden, a veteran *New York Times* sports columnist. Bill has interviewed me about the validity of the colleges' plea of poverty as a reason for cutting the number of varsity sports. His calculator works as well as anybody else's in counting spectator admissions and the number of TV commercials. "It's frustrating trying to get a fix on how much the colleges exactly spend on their sports programs and the sources of all the money," Bill remarked. "It's like following the trail of the Wizard of Oz. I suspect that the colleges are so lavish in their spending that they're embarrassed and would rather not have people know all of the facts and the full story."[26] The root of the problem is irresponsible spending, Rhoden believes.

Pleas of poverty are not a good enough excuse for either cutting sports or refusing to deal fairly with the players. After fighting off the IRS on the tax issue for some 15 years, and I was a part of that fight, the colleges should tell the public how the money is collected, the sources, how it is spent, and where it ends up.

Obligatory federal reporting on a detailed form, subject to federal audit, would put the facts on the record. If the IRS, the courts, and the Congress remain content that taxes should not be applied to the diversified sources of income of big-time sports, after considering the intense commercial world in which it lives, so be it. The important result would be to open the records to public view and to a comparative analysis by state legislators, faculties, and donors of what colleges spend on sports, within the same state, the same conferences, and the same NCAA divisions.

Freedom *Is* the Issue

Too much time and effort have been spent by college reformers during recent years tilting at windmills. Some of those who want to alter or transform intercollegiate athletics are well intentioned. Most are determined to protect their own advantage in any reshuffling that may take place.

The colleges now are caught up in a conundrum of their own making. The presidential reform groups do not want to change the rules that unfairly control the players and the monopoly trusts and combinations that regulate the money. When confronted with violations of the rules, the colleges frequently resort to blaming the NCAA, which is controlled by them, for violating their due process standards. Legislators have jumped hardest on this issue in states where their flagship sports universities have been severely penalized by the NCAA, such as in Nevada, Illinois, and Florida. Applying the due process standards of criminal courtroom proceedings to the NCAA would eliminate its effectiveness. At the same time, many colleges do not want stronger NCAA enforcement. The growing sentiment is to set up an accreditation or compliance/certification process by which the NCAA would serve a function more like the regional academic accrediting agencies.

As president of the University of Illinois, Stanley O. Ikenberry argued for a program of compliance, visitations, and corrections—not confrontation—as the way to reform. After being in charge of Illinois's no-holds-barred dispute with the Big Ten Conference in the David Wilson case, he concluded the "confrontation" business was bad for everybody. "Do you actually believe that the generalized approach of accreditation can control the high volatility and the search for rewards in college athletics?" I asked.

"I think it will," he said.[27]

What has happened in the years since the 1985 NCAA Integrity Convention, when there was a ringing endorsement of strong enforcement and the subsequent promise of less regulation? The rules expand. The crime rate continues. Penalties are negotiated. At the same time, the system's benefits keep flowing to the same beneficiaries. The most depressing aspect is the continuing disregard for the rights and individual interests of young athletes. Here, the NCAA colleges regularly endorsed generalized statements about "student-athlete welfare" but rejected proposals for student-athlete freedom.

College sports *should* become a prime target for deregulation at a historic moment when the American people, in the larger society, expressed in clear terms in the fall of 1994 that they want less federal regulation of their own lives and they want the freedom to use their talents for their own personal advancement.

The first intercollegiate competition in the United States was conceived and organized by students in the mid-1840s. By the turn of the century, eastern colleges were competing in some 19 sports.[28] This all came about through student initiative and effort. The students set in place the underlying structure for college sports. Today, professional coaches, professional managers and money-minded presidents have total control. It is time to give back to the students who play sports the freedoms they deserve. At a minimum, they are entitled to freedoms enjoyed by their fellow students.

Notes

1. NCAA, IRS Form 990, Form 990-T, EIN 44–0567264,FYE August 31, 1993.
2. Collegiate Commissioners Association, 1993–94 Salary Survey; Eugene F. Corrigan, Atlantic Coast Conference, Greensboro, North Carolina, Association president.
3. Jack Etkin, *Kansas City Star,* March 10, 1991.
4. NCAA, Report to the NCAA Executive Committee, December 4–5, 1994.
5. Associated Press report, San Diego, California, January 9, 1995.
6. Collegiate Commissioners Association, 1994–95 Salary Survey.
7. Oliver Wendell Holmes, Jr., in George Seldes, *The Great Quotations* (New York: Pocket Books, 1967), 229.
8. Frank Remington, conversations with the author, August 8, 1990.
9. Paul Gallico, *Farewell to Sport* (Freeport, N.Y.: Books for Libraries Press, 1937), 215.
10. Fred Klein, *Wall Street Journal,* October 16, 1985.
11. Associated Press report, *Kansas City Star,* May 2, 1990; Lon Kruger, telephone conversaton with the author, April 15, 1991.
12. Richard D. Schultz, *NCAA News,* June 13, 1990.
13. *Kansas City Star,* April 1, 1991.
14. Bret Bearup, interviews with the author, February 12 and March 12, 1991.
15. Frank Broyles, interview with the author, March 1, 1990.
16. Associated Press report, *Kansas City Star,* November 24, 1994.
17. Associated Press report, *Kansas City Star,* December 15, 1994.
18. NCAA, The Principle of Competitive Equity, Article 2.9, NCAA Constitution, *1994-95 NCAA Manual,* 4.
19. Gallico, *Farewell to Sport,* 118–19.
20. See James F. Ponsoldt, "The Unreasonableness of Coerced Cooperation: A Comment upon the NCAA Decision's Rejection of the Chicago (Law) School,"*Antitrust Bulletin,* Winter 1986, 1003–9.
21. Arthur Kempton,"Native Sons," *New York Review of Books,* April 11, 1991.

22. Gary Putka and Paul M. Barrett, *Wall Street Journal,* March 21, 1991; Gary Putka, *Wall Street Journal,* May 2, 1989.
23. Ibid.
24. Steve Stecklow, *Wall Street Journal,* December 2, 1994.
25. Commerce Clearing House, *Tax Court Reports,* November 9, 1994.
26. Bill Rhoden, interview with the author, February 2, 1995.
27. Stanley O. Ikenberry, interview with the author, January 31, 1991.
28. Ronald A. Smith, *Sports and Freedom* (New York: Oxford University Press, 1988), 119.

Index

Schenkel, Chris, 286
Scherick, Edgar J., 85–87
Schiller, Harvey W., 287–89, 313, 314, 367
Schmidt, Victor O., 111–16, 123, 177, 184, 187, 191
Schooling Herbert, 138, 139
Schultz, Richard D., 357, 360, 378, 379
Scott, Charley, 284
Scott, Michael, 342
Seaborg, Glenn, 116
Seton Hall University, 282
Shapiro, Harold T., 191
Shaughnessy, Clark, 98
Sherrill, Jackie, 121, 257
Shields, L. Donald, 21–24, 27, 28, 32, 33, 186
Shivers, Gov. Allan, 172–73
Simmons, Chet, 86, 87, 259
Singletary, Otis A., 101
Sliger, Bernard F., 349
Slive, Michael, 178
Sloan, Steve, 173
Smith, Burt, 180–82
Smith, Dean, 125
Smith, Eugene D., 385
Smith, Frank, 258
Smith, "Sudden Sam," 208
Smith, Wilfrid, 89–90
Solomon, Steve, 290
South Carolina, University of, 197, 349, 352
Southeastern Conference, 17, 58, 68, 105, 154, 158, 219, 220, 228, 255, 258, 259, 274, 287–89, 294, 313, 349–52, 357, 367, 373
Southern California, University of, 81, 93, 113–15, 138, 177–79, 253, 254, 257, 355
Southern Conference, 68
Southern Methodist University, 2, 17–35, 73, 117, 119, 172, 173, 257
"death penalty," 18
1985 NCAA Council meeting, 24
United Methodist Bishops' Committee, 24, 26, 30
Southern University, 157

Southwest Conference, 12, 18, 25, 28, 68, 118, 120, 122, 169, 170, 173, 174, 253, 257–59, 262, 291, 294, 349, 351–53
Spartan Foundation, 43
Speegle, Cliff, 170, 262
Spence, Jim, 86, 258, 262, 265–68, 285, 286, 290
Spencer, Norman, 303
Spry, Louis J., 245
Stagg, Amos Alonzo, 45, 81, 362
Stanford, Charles, 285
Stanford University, 150, 160
Stanley, David, 31
Stern, Bill, 133
Stewart, James H. (Jimmie), 118
Stewart, Robert H., III, 26
Stinson, Wade R., 164
St. John's University (New York), 282
Stoltz, Dennie, 182–84
Stoner, Neale R., 186, 190
Stopperich, Sean, 24, 27, 30
Stratten, Ronald J., 129, 155, 156
Streit, Judge Saul S., 56
Student-athlete definition, 69
Students for a Democratic Society, 149
Sugar Bowl, 98, 350
Sutton, Eddie, 383
Swanson, Dennis, 285–91
Switzer, Barry, 8, 170, 229, 255, 277, 353
Syracuse University, 105, 106, 223, 282, 294

Tarkanian, Jerry, 1, 2, 6, 7, 9, 130, 183, 195–202, 204–11, 213, 214, 216, 306–9, 377
Tarkanian, Lois, 7, 207, 209, 307
Tate, Marvin, 265
Tatum, Jim, 119
Teaff, Grant, 174
Temple University, 315
Tennessee, University of, Knoxville, 228, 289, 353, 376
Tennessee State University, 310
Texas, University of, Austin, 18, 28, 76, 117, 119, 122, 169, 172, 173, 221,

Photo Credits